Bottle Creek

A Pensacola Culture Site in South Alabama

EDITED BY IAN W. BROWN

FOREWORD BY DAVID S. BROSE

With contributions by
Penelope B. Drooker
Richard S. Fuller
Paul D. Jackson
Hunter B. Johnso
David W. Morga
Irvy R. Quitmye
Christopher B. Rod
C. Margaret Scar
Diane E. Silvia

A Dan Josselyn Memorial Publication

THE UNIVERSITY OF ALABAMA PRESS

Tuscaloosa and London

Manufactured in the United States of America

Typeface: Baur Bodoni
∞
The paper on which this book is printed meets the minimum requirements of American National Standard for Information Science–Permanence of Paper for Printed Library Materials, ANSI Z39.48-1984.

Library of Congress Cataloging-in-Publication Data

Bottle Creek : a Pensacola culture site in South Alabama / edited by Ian W. Brown ; foreword by David S. Brose ; with contributions by Penelope B. Drooker . . . [et al.].
p. cm.

"A Dan Josselyn memorial publication."

Includes bibliographical references and index.
ISBN 0-8173-1219-6 (alk. paper) — ISBN 0-8173-1220-X (pbk. : alk. paper)
1. Bottle Creek Site (Ala.) 2. Mississippian culture—Alabama—Mound Island. 3. Mississippian pottery—Alabama—Mound Island. 4. Excavations (Archaeology)—Alabama—Mound Island. 5. Mound Island (Ala.)—Antiquities. I. Brown, Ian W. II. Drooker, Penelope B.

E78.A28B67 2003
976.1'21—dc21

2002009189

British Library Cataloguing-in-Publication Data available

Bottle Creek

To Douglas D. Anderson
A very special teacher

Contents

Figures

Tables

Foreword

> It ain't what I don't know that gets me in trouble. What gets me in trouble is what I know that just ain't so.
>
> Will Rogers

I found it difficult to resist the editor's invitation to write a foreword to this volume. It was not merely because I was one of the two discussants to the SEAC symposium at which the original field reports were presented, and it was certainly not because, with uncharacteristic exaggeration, the editor opined I might be the oldest archaeologist yet alive to have visited the Bottle Creek site ("see Bottle Creek and die"). It is because over the last two decades I have grown increasingly aware of the key that knowledge about this site may hold for understanding the end of Mississippian hegemonies along the central Gulf Coast and I have communicated that belief widely.

My awareness grew slowly. First exposed to southeastern archaeology in the 1970s, my views matured with work at the Fort Walton Cayson and Yon sites in west Florida (Brose et al. 1976). Although carefully initiated into the revealed truths of west Florida archaeology (especially Willey's monumental work [Willey and Woodbury 1942; Willey 1949]), it became increasingly apparent to me that published descriptions of Fort Walton–Pensacola culture were inapplicable to what we were excavating on the banks of the Apalachicola River (Brose and Percy 1978). We were finding a distinctly home-grown Mississippian Fort Walton society centuries before shell temper or Pensacola motifs appeared in Alabama north of Mobile Bay.

In interpreting the significance of these Apalachicola River sites as a responsible colleague, thesis chair (e.g., White 1982; Scarry 1984), or survey director, I constantly was forced to return to thinking about this Pensacola side of the traditional equation for late prehistory on Florida's westernmost coast and I learned about Bottle Creek.

Guided by N. Read Stowe, Ned Jenkins, Rusty Weisman, and I first saw the Bottle Creek site and its ritual guardian spiders on Mound Island while conducting a survey of the seaward end of the Tombigbee Waterway in 1979 (Brose 1991; Brose et al. 1983). A year earlier, Jim Knight had reviewed a paper on Fort Walton that George Percy and I had prepared for a volume on Mississippian settlement patterns (Brose and Percy 1978). Perhaps because he was still thinking of the Fort Walton–Pensacola definition that Willey had proposed, Knight (1980) commented on our failure to discuss the Bottle Creek site. While Knight was correct, it would have been difficult for any but N. Read Stowe or Rick Fuller to have said much new about Bottle Creek in 1977 when our paper was written. Indeed, had we tried to discuss Pensacola at the time it might have been as much beyond our talent as it then appeared beyond the scope of our assignment: I was convinced (and George Percy joined me in saying) that Pensacola was no component of Fort Walton, but was a veneer, overlain on western Fort Walton coastal sites in Florida. And all of the evidence garnered up to 1981 and all of the work over the decades since has strengthened that characterization of peripheral and non-conformable relationships between the once-conjoined Fort Walton and Pensacola complexes (see also Brose 1984; 1985). It is not too much to say that in the technology-rich and stratigraphically sophisticated half century since Willey's work, there is little excuse for perpetuating his initially limited glimpse into chronology and society. Worse, there is absolutely no justification for confecting Willey's limited data with fallacious historical models born of geo-aphasia and innumeracy (see Brose 1985; Marrinan and White 1998).

It is certainly true (Brose 2002) that without the Bureau of American Ethnology and scholars such as Gordon Willey southeastern archaeology would be unrecognizable. Yet one can hardly escape the belief that the Bottle Creek site and the misnamed Pensacola culture would have fared better if Willey had more closely followed C. B. Moore (Brose and White 1999) and begun his monumental stratigraphic-building survey in Mobile Bay rather than Perdido Bay. But it was to that historical accident and to an over-reliance on ceramics from uncontrolled surface collections and extremely limited test excavations (detailed in notes to a subsequently published paper [Brose 1985]) that led to a hyphenated Pensacola–Fort Walton culture. It has long been clear that southeastern archaeology needed to cut the spurious umbilical cord by which Willey had tied what he assumed to be a largely protohistoric Fort Walton to an equally misnamed Pensacola culture (Brose and Percy 1978; Brose 1984; 1985; Knight 1980). So if Pensacola is not some mysterious component of Fort Walton culture, what is it? This study of the Bottle Creek site offers the first clear answers to that question.

Long ignored amidst the twisting tidewater channels and fetid vegetation of the Mobile-Tensaw Delta, the Bottle Creek site seems an antipodal version of Machu Picchu. Opening this volume, one might hope for a comprehensive picture of the society that built and occupied this large site as North America was wrenched into history. In many ways this impeccable study, created and edited by Ian Brown, reveals why no broad reconstruction of a Pensacola culture is yet possible with any level of intellectual honesty. That is only one of the triumphs of this volume, for more than half a century ago southeastern archaeologists had been lulled into believing they already had the kind of interpretation of Pensacola culture they deemed indispensable for understanding archaeology as anthropology (i.e., Willey and Phillips 1958).

Now, with diligence and intelligent commitment, Ian Brown, his colleagues and their students here finally document some of the basic characteristics of the Bottle Creek site and, thus in many ways, aspects of Pensacola as a separate and very unusual economic, ideational, and social system. They have moved us to a first, necessarily simple model of how Bottle Creek and the central Pensacola culture might fit into its regional natural and cultural environments.

This series of papers is tied together by the ceramic analysis of Rick Fuller, one of those whose knowledge of Pensacola has both great scope and depth. He has defined a series of tightly timed ceramic sets that put sequence and dates to the culture's history. Fuller sees Pensacola ceramic industry derived from Moundville, but perhaps his most interesting conclusion (to me) is that the flourishing of Pensacola—and its period of greatest connection with Fort Walton—occurred after the fourteenth-century decline of the interior Mississippian centers. The detailed stratigraphic analysis of David Morgan provides the prehistoric site managers' work plans and gives us the structural skeleton on which to hang Fuller's Pensacola ceramic chronology.

Cross-cutting Fuller's detailed and long needed (and used) ceramic set analyses, Hunter Johnson has developed a series of culturally sensitive vessel assemblages and linked them to differing site areas and levels associated with mounds A and C. Through the long growth of the site, vessel finish and composition as well as (always rare) decorative motifs distinguish and correlate with evidence of often striking functional and/or social differences by locations whose geomorphological complexity also differs. Of especial interest from an eastern perspective is Morgan's interpretation of the post–A.D. 1250 Mound B lower construction stages where watertight clay lined walls were pulled and the former post holes covered by different sand layers—the same sequence as identified in the A.D. 1150 expansion of the plaza precinct walls at the Fort Walton Cayson site (Brose et al. 1976). Morgan has shown that this activity at Bottle Creek was repeated three or more times, usually accompanied by deposits of the burnt remains of special foods, as the mound grew in size.

Irvy Quitmyer and Margy Scarry's several seasons' work with a fine screen forcefully presents the lesson that recovery methods do, indeed, matter very much. Samples from a late fourteenth-century construction of Mound A (important, but perhaps not yet the apogee of Pensacola culture) reveal intensive but short episodes of exploiting all of the diverse protein resources of the local estuarine environment. Contemporary and later samples from Mound C represent less diverse and less rich faunal collecting, suggesting a lower caste pantry not yet dignified as Lower Alabama Cuisine. The dietary studies demonstrate that Bottle Creek occupants did not grow or process maize on the site, although they were thoroughly articulated with maize farmers and their ceremonial herbal purgatives. As do others, these studies reveal that the different precincts and mounds on Mound Island were used for a series of changing socioeconomic functions, some more akin to Moundville's Mississippian elites and others merely quotidian domestic activities. But it's not really clear to me that the site was not usually abandoned or that there were ever any non-elite or non-ceremonial events using Mound Island in prehistory. One can imagine the location as one staffed by a small cadre of "gamekeepers" responsible for providing occasional elaborate feasts for visiting ceremonious persons with their traveling retainers. At any rate, Jim Knight and Sherée Adams first suggested an econometric model for the Mobile-Tensaw Delta in 1981 and Brown's task will still be to find those mundane bottomland or upland or coastal sites from which the sustenance and occupants for Bottle Creek came.

Chris Rodning's very careful and precise historical and archaeological work at the canal on Mound Island clearly shows that this waterway, whether natural or not, was a key element in the site's functionality and was a factor in the mental geography of the site builders. His reprise of water transport again illustrates that Pensacola is an estuarine and coastal culture despite the ceramic similarities it has with riverine Mississippian sites inland. This point is reinforced by Penelope Drooker's insights on the saltpan fabric textures suggesting a possible functional origin for the site distinct from similar stations associated with major Mississippian centers further north—and the lower Tombigbee River valley is replete with the evidence of late prehistoric non-Moundvillian salt extraction (Brose et al. 1983).

Earlier and less sophisticated ethnohistory pictured the Mobile-Tensaw Delta as home of the last true *Mauvila* or *Mobilian* culture. Yet critical review shows eastern migrants to the area at least as early as A.D. 1700. The Bottle Creek site is something else. It is clear from these studies that the site was first occupied as a smaller, nearly undifferentiated Mississippian location some time around A.D. 1100–1250, a period of major Moundvillian and Coosan hegemony in the river valleys that feed the Mobile Delta from the north. It is also a period of major maturation for Plaquemine societies to the east and the equally pedigreed and soon to be largely transfigured Roods/Fort Walton societies in the Chattahoochee and Apalachicola river valleys to the west. As those societies disaggregated or relocated and/or recombined in the period after A.D. 1250, the Bottle Creek site grew, becoming the incubation chamber for a host of design motifs which have come to characterize the Pensacola culture, post A.D. 1450 aspects of which have been recognized from Bay St. Louis to Cedar Key.

I once tagged Pensacola as a society which, like early mammals finding a niche among the ponderous steps of the latest dinosaurs, grew strong and spread widely in the aftermath of the decline of more traditional Mississippian polities but only for a brief time. That was certainly an oversimplified view, now clearly needing rethinking: One must wonder not only when Bottle Creek was built, but when Pensacola developed—which may be separate questions. And one must also wonder whether the growth of Bottle Creek and the spread and development of its Pensacola design repertoire really represents the maturing of a self-identified culture. Unlike Fuller, I do expect that sites along Mobile Bay below Mound Island will eventually provide the evidence of local populations that participated in the origin and early growth of the Bottle Creek site, although the ceramics they used on Mound Island derived from and probably were ritually representative of Moundville itself. And, in a slightly different position than that advocated by Brown in his summary chapter, whatever its middle Mississippian origins, I doubt the expansion of Pensacola ceramic sets could have occurred prior to that post-1450 interior Mississippian pattern of disaggregated social capital which appears to characterize their response to economic and demographic instability.

Years ago, John Walthall and Ned Jenkins (1976) concocted the productive term "Gulf Formational" to describe that period when across the Gulf Coast cultural changes coincided to create new and dynamic modes of expression. Surely this study shows us the need for a bookend "Gulf Dissolutional" to describe the cultural dynamics during that period when late prehistoric sociocultural, military, and economic worlds across the Gulf Coast began to founder under the buffeting of climate change, European colonization, and ever less altruistic neighbors. And the historic end of this site's use is every bit as intriguing as its origins.

The problems of using early historic accounts to flesh out the thin archaeological record are certainly amplified when critical historiography is applied to their authors' purposes and frames of reference (Galloway 1993; Brose 2001). Overcoming this difficulty, Diane Silvia gives us a wonderful picture of marginalized native life in the early years of French occupation of the region. It is a long-needed corrective to the interpretative data drawn from heavily acculturated aboriginal groups in Florida or the Mississippi Valley (or in the Great Lakes whence and whither the French sojourned annually [Walthall and Emerson 1992; Brose 1983]).

It is worth remembering that southeastern archaeology began in south

Alabama and it was directed to the late Renaissance antiquarian desire to join New World archaeological and ethnographic objects with the arts of the ancient world (Brose 2002). As Ian Brown reminds us, in 1702 Bienville with an Indian guide visited an island in the Mobile-Tensaw Delta. Perhaps it was one of the mounds of the Bottle Creek site and perhaps not. What is certain is that this quasi-archaeological expedition was designed to augment the Parisian Cabinet of the learned King of France with statues taken from a pagan shrine. And behind that sacrilegious eighteenth-century Mobile Indian who led Bienville to secure the sacred tribal or family gods from Mound Island (perhaps) one must wonder whether there yet were priests who served them and if so was their service akin to that of the last faithful acolytes of an old, dying religion or were those priests like Caesar's Celtic Druids, re-purposing Stonehenge for their own contemporary needs?

I elsewhere (Brose 2002) bewailed the confusion caused by taxonomically minded museums, which defined core cultural complexes in terms of earlier named sites later seen to be ephemeral or marginal. In that same essay I noted how geocentric pride in naming often created spurious cultural structures with historical and spatial parameters based on the carelessly named artifact types claimed to be their products—even specific languages have been assigned to complexes built up from such prehistoric artifact attributes without much intervening social information. Naturally, once such archaeological structures have begun talking it seems eminently reasonable to think of them in terms of biological analogues, replete with vital processes such as growth, homeostasis, death and progeny, and evolutionary parameters (Brose 2002).

That has not been a problem with these studies, but at the risk of usurping the editor's prerogative, I would offer a few thoughts to hold in mind while reading this study and while contemplating the next steps needed in this region: Ceramics are not a culture; not even a National Historic Landmark is a culture. We may not yet see clearly Pensacola's economic or political connections with Fort Walton groups to the east, but then, we know little about late Fort Walton societies of the Red Hills region and only through hubris do we attribute those tentative concepts to significantly earlier and more westerly Fort Walton societies whose emergence into history is still unwritten (Scarry 1984; *contra* Brose 1984; 1985; Marrinan and White 1998).

The kinds of information we now have for Pensacola seem different in most respects than what we have for Fort Walton, and by meticulously constructing for us the first good chronological, stratigraphic, environmental, and material cultural structure of the Bottle Creek site, the scholars here writing move us from our comfortable belief that we understand Pensacola to a realization of what must yet be done to fill the remaining gaps in our knowledge. While we do not know nearly enough about this system, we do know that in many respects it was unlike any traditional riparian Mississippian society and perhaps it was unlike any prehistoric American Indian society north of the Huastecan coast. Indeed, based on this project we are able to sense just how interesting Mississippian societies may have become in the waning days of pre-Columbian North America.

David S. Brose

Preface

This volume grew out of a symposium that was presented at the 51st Annual Meeting of the Southeastern Archaeological Conference in Knoxville, Tennessee, in 1995. The seeds for this symposium were sown in 1932 when David L. DeJarnette of the Alabama Museum of Natural History began a project at the Bottle Creek site (1Ba2), deep in the heart of the Mobile-Tensaw Delta. The principal purpose of his investigations was to determine the relationship between the Mississippian culture represented at Moundville as compared to that represented at Bottle Creek. In the ensuing years, the Mississippian variant along this portion of the Gulf Coast became known as the Pensacola culture. Its exact relationship with Moundville is far from understood, and remains an issue today. I hope this book takes us one step closer to comprehending the dynamic interaction between these cultures, which were once linked by a river system, with Moundville in the north and Bottle Creek in the south.

A BOTTLE CREEK GUIDEBOOK: ADVICE FOR A FIELD DIRECTOR

You launch your boat at Mt. Vernon Landing. Make sure you have plenty of life preservers, a paddle, and an extra tank of gas. An extra motor wouldn't hurt either, as you never know. Check to make sure you have your poncho, as you do know. Instruct crew on importance of safety as you head out into the Mobile. When fog doesn't lift, proceed gingerly into the channel. Avoid barge by steering sharply to the right. Provide another lecture on safety and await atmospheric clearing.

Arrange man on bow to serve as sentry in crossing the river. Turn left into Tensaw River. Skies will immediately clear. Cruise at medium speed down this gently meandering river. Spot egrets, ospreys, and other forms of wildlife, but take care. If water is high, watch out for floating debris. If low, look for sawyers—required reading, *Life on the Mississippi.* Mark Twain is more than an author.

Continue on Tensaw River, avoiding Middle River to your right. Less than a mile turn right at Bottle Creek, aptly named. There's a bottleneck at the headwaters, so if the water is low, steer well to the right (starboard, west, whatever, just do it). Proceed at rapid clip; everyone else does. There is not much traffic at this time of day, but look out for logs hanging from helicopters. Stop at high bank to the right and tie up to poison ivy vine–wrapped tree. Tie loosely as tidal waters sink boats, or so I've been told. Form a human chain and empty boat of equipment. Store boat accessories beneath palmettos. First check underside of palmettos for hornets' nests.

Dole out daily jobs and responsibilities, as there may never be another chance. Rearrange backpack and don deerfly headgear. Have a crew member take the lead (advisable to choose a different person each day). Keep one hand free to slap face as you approach trail. Trail is recognizable as a thin stream, bordered by slightly higher land on either side. Watch out for water moccasins on slightly higher land. They will see you, so not to worry. Note scuffmarks made by alligator tails on the ground and bear claw marks high on trees. Refrain from obvious curiosity and stay on trail.

About a half mile into your walk stop abruptly at a mountain. This is Mound A. Note that you are standing on pottery, shell, and other debris. Apply more bug spray and listen to owl call your name. Walk back a bit and admire smaller mounds that you had already passed. You are now standing on the Bottle Creek site, one of the most important archaeological sites in the Southeast. For a thousand years others have made the same trek, but without all your conveniences. Be respectful, enjoy your work, and carry a big stick, not necessarily with the crew in mind.

Ian W. Brown

Acknowledgments

In the Preface of Brown and Fuller (1993a) I described my first visit to the Bottle Creek site. Having spent most of the day lost in the swamp, it might seem somewhat curious why I would have ever considered returning to the site to lead a project. The logistics of running a dig at Bottle Creek is something just shy of a nightmare, and yet it has been worth it. The site continues to beckon because of its size, grandeur, and significance in the culture history of the Coastal Plain in Mississippian times. This Pensacola culture site, undoubtedly the sociopolitical center, if not the religious center, for much of southwest Alabama, is and continues to be a site worthy of attention.

The Gulf Coast Survey of the Alabama Museum of Natural History began what has become known as the Bottle Creek Project in the summer of 1991. For a little over one month, between July 2 and August 7, Rick Fuller and I excavated two 1 × 2 m test units in Mound L. My nephew, Trevor Hughes, was our only permanent crew member, although we also had a lot of off-and-on volunteers (noticeably very off come back-filling time!). The 1993 field season at the Bottle Creek Project was conducted between May 17 and August 1, while the 1994 season occurred between May 16 and August 1. This work was supported by grants from the National Endowment for the Humanities (RO-22516–92), the Alabama Historical Commission, and the Baldwin County Historic Development Commission. Financial assistance was also received from the Office of Sponsored Programs at the University of Alabama and from Joseph Meaher of Mount Vernon in Mobile County. Richard S. Fuller was my prime assistant in the investigation of the Bottle Creek site. Our permanent crew consisted of Diane Silvia (93–94), David Morgan (93–94), Hunter Johnson (93–94), Kitty Roberts (93), Tony Boudreaux (93), Chris Rodning (93), Clay Gentry (93), Cary Ellis (93), Robyn Astin (94), Clete Rooney (94), Dale Jarvis (94), Kim Rutherford (94), and James Reid (94). Diane Silvia employed a number of students from the University of South Alabama as part of a field school. Participants during the two years included Ann Bryan, Denise Craig, Lee Ann Cunningham, Chris Gougen, Cheryl Halstead, Debbie Lawrence, Jared Mitchem, and Julie Robinson.

Over the course of the three seasons numerous people assisted in the excavations to varying degrees. Douglas W. Haywick, of the University of South Alabama Geology and Geography Department, did a study of sediment samples from the Mound A excavations, for which I am very grateful. Other colleagues who got their hands dirty at Bottle Creek included Jim Knight, Tim Mooney, John O'Hear, Irvy Quitmyer, Margie Scarry, George Shorter, Marvin Smith, Vin Steponaitis, Read Stowe, Greg Waselkov, and Nancy White. The following individuals devoted at least a day of their time (some many more) to the excavations: Bill Armstead, Jody Badillo, Edmond Boudreaux, Warren Carruth, Kevin Dodd, Charlie Ebert III, Phyllis Ellis, Brad Franks, Wendell Gorum, Larry Halstead, Catherine Henderson, Trevor Hughes, Ray Keene, Wade McLein, Cathy and Jeff Meyer, Elizabeth Mitchell, Eric Mueller, Mary and Kai Rodning, Cynthia Satterfield, David Smithweck, James Stokes, and Andrew Veech.

And then there was the mariner aid. Several people came to our rescue with the loan of boat equipment. Needless to say, without this help we would not have been able to accomplish our goals. Kevin Dodd and Donnie Brunson both loaned us their private boats. John (Buddy) Hastie, Tom Tomlinson, David A. (Tony) White, and Mitch White made Scott Paper Company boats available on more occasions than I would like to admit. Gregory Waselkov of the University of South Alabama loaned us a motor from the Center for Archaeological Studies, which I promptly sank. John O'Hear loaned us both a boat and motor from the Cobb Institute at Mississippi State University, which we managed to keep afloat. Boats, motors, and a multitude of adventures on the river are described in far greater detail in *Bottle Creek Reflections* (Brown n.d.).

Taking care of our Mt. Vernon home life were Berry and Glenna Cannon, our landlord and landlady. Our field headquarters at 1345 Military Road was absolutely wonderful. I'm not sure that I've ever occupied such a perfectly adapted building that suited all our purposes. Mary Amelia Halliday, a cousin of Berry's who lives in Mt. Vernon, satisfied our culinary needs for the two seasons. At the end of the 1993 season we presented her with an apron labeled "The Queen of Strawberry Shortcake," and that she was. Our neighbors across the street, Mr. and Mrs. James Greene, spoiled our crew in other ways. Not until the end of the first season did I figure out just why the crew members looked forward to staying home for "lab day." A trip to the Bee Hive Restaurant with the Greenes is something that the crew anticipated with great relish.

A number of people deserve special recognition. It's hard to pinpoint specific things that they did; they were just always there. Included in this category are: Nancy Lambert-Brown, who did most of the graphics; James Reid, whose sketches have provided a very realistic feel to the site, far better than photographs; Douglas Jones, Executive Director of the Alabama Museum of Natural History; Jim Parker, Coordinator of Archaeological and Military Properties for the Alabama Historical Commission; Charles and Wyline Ebert, friends of the first order; and Davida Hastie, Grande Dame of Baldwin County. The University of Alabama Press has believed in this project from the beginning. Anders Thompson was a conscientious and helpful copyeditor. Cameron Wesson and Gregory Waselkov reviewed the original manuscript for the Press and offered numerous extremely helpful suggestions, for which I am most grateful. Greg has continued to be a major help in permitting the use of his contour map of Bottle Creek.

Finally, I would be remiss not to mention a major stimulus for getting this volume over and done with. A couple of years ago, Dr. Charles B. Rodning, Professor and Vice-Chairman in the Department of Surgery at the University of South Alabama (and father of Chris), took me to the side at a Southeastern Archaeological Conference and reminded me that Bottle Creek's 300th anniversary was right around the corner. On March 4, 1702, the site was "discovered" by Jean-Baptiste Le Moyne de Bienville, brother of Pierre Le Moyne d'Iberville, and a future governor of the French colony of Louisiana. He, too, had quite a memorable trip to the site, one that resulted in perhaps the first substantial archaeological collection made in the Southeast. I wonder if he had Chigger-rid with him?

Ian W. Brown

Bottle Creek

1 / Introduction to the Bottle Creek Site

Ian W. Brown

The Bottle Creek site (1Ba2) is located in the Mobile-Tensaw Delta, Baldwin County, Alabama. This multi-mound Pensacola culture site was erected on the northern end of Mound Island, sandwiched between Middle River and Bottle Creek. David L. DeJarnette of the Alabama Museum of Natural History conducted preliminary investigations in 1932 and this museum has continued its interest in the site in the 1990s through the work of the Gulf Coast Survey.[1] Major excavations were undertaken in 1993–94 under the title "The Bottle Creek Project." Although I was the principal investigator for the project, this has been a team effort through and through. All of the people included as authors in this book have been deeply involved in the Bottle Creek Project right from the very beginning. This volume is a culmination of their work.

Based on the number of mounds and their size and extent, Bottle Creek is the largest Mississippian site in the region. It is situated on Mound Island, a large, generally swampy tract in the heart of the Mobile-Tensaw Delta (Figures 1.1–1.2). The site has at least 18 mounds plus various associated non-mound habitation areas and midden deposits (Figure 1.3). The linear distance between Mound O on the east and Mound R on the west is approximately one kilometer. The main mound complex consists of a central plaza outlined by mounds A, B, L, M, and N. A is the principal mound, and is quite an impressive edifice. It is a flat-topped, pyramidal mound, approximately 14 m tall. Mound B is a long, linear mound of rather un-

1. The Gulf Coast Survey is an archaeological program of the Alabama Museum of Natural History. It is under my direction as Professor of Anthropology and Curator of Gulf Coast Archaeology. The GCS occupies four offices on the fourth floor of the Mary Harmon Bryant Hall at the University of Alabama and a lab on the third floor. Its research focuses on the prehistory and history of the northern Gulf Coastal Plain of the southeastern United States. My students and I currently are conducting field projects in Alabama, Mississippi, and Louisiana.

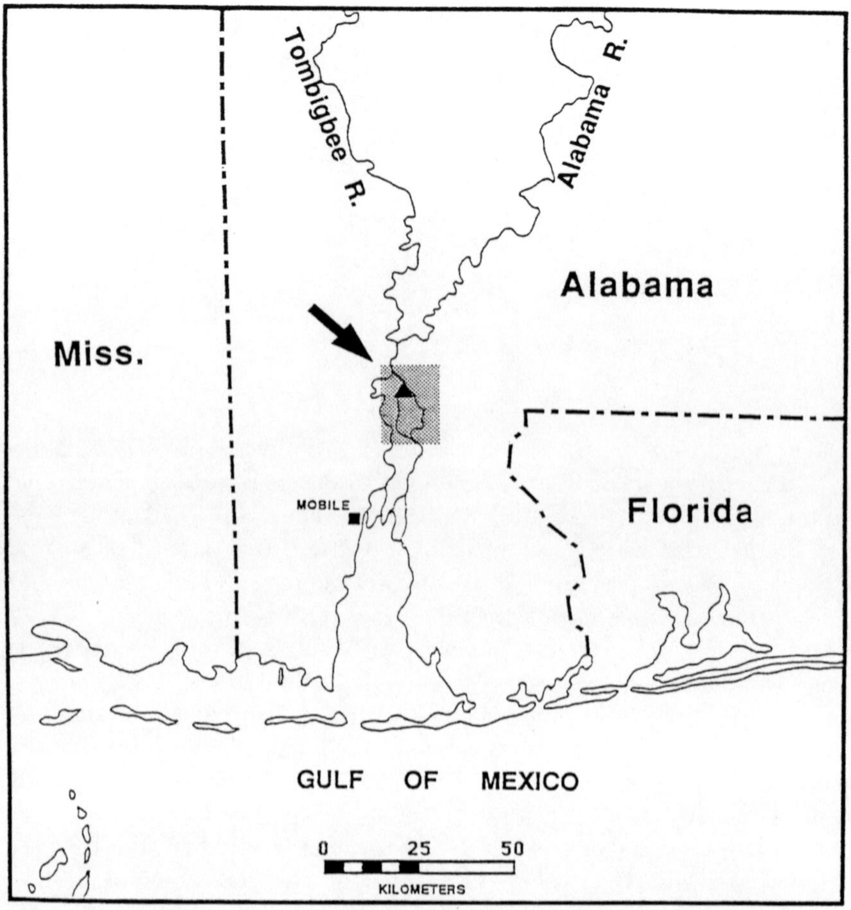

1.1. Location of the Bottle Creek site in the Mobile-Tensaw Delta, Alabama (from the *Mound Island Project*, by Fuller and Brown, copyright 1998 by the Alabama Museum of Natural History, used by permission).

usual shape, in that it may have been terraced prehistorically (Figure 1.4). It certainly is so now as the northern half of the mound has a broad platform extending in the direction of Mound A. Around the northern periphery of the site is a line of house mounds. These grew slowly through time by the accumulation of midden.

Bottle Creek was occupied primarily between A.D. 1250 and 1550 during what is referred to as the Pensacola culture (Figure 1.5). It probably served as the principal center for the region during these three centuries, in terms of politics, religion and trade. There is some evidence of earlier occupation, and Indians continued to occupy the site well into the eighteenth century.

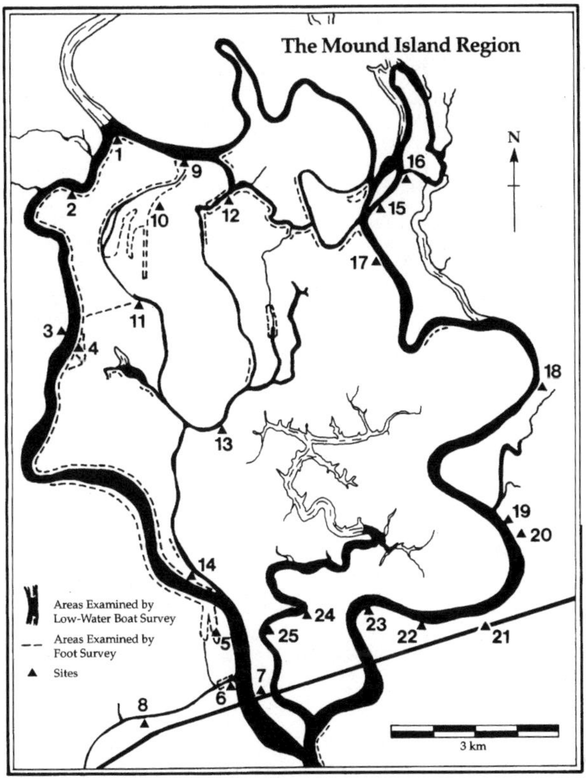

Key to Sites in the Mound Island Region:

1 Middle-Tensaw Point (1Ba272)
2 Low Water (1Ba443)
3 Middle River (1Mb107)
4 Whip-O-Will (1Ba274)
5 Carpenter (1Mb179)
6 Little Lizard Creek (1Ba195)
7 (1Ba402)
8 (1Ba431)
9 Tensaw River (1Ba271)
10 Bottle Creek (1Ba2)
11 Dominic Creek (1Ba263)
12 Bayou Jessamine (1Ba264)
13 River Cane (1Ba247)
14 (1Ba246)
15 Larry Island Branch (1Ba269)
16 Briar Lake Slough (1Ba270)
17 Fisher Island South (1Ba273)
18 Farmar's Bluff (1Ba275)
19 (1Ba212)
20 Live Oak Landing (1Ba438)
21 (1Ba253)
22 (1Ba214)
23 Squirrel Bayou (1Ba262)
24 Mifflin Lake #1 (1Ba499)
25 Mifflin Lake #2 (1Ba500)

I.2. The Mound Island region, with Bottle Creek as site no. 10 (from the *Mound Island Project*, by Fuller and Brown, copyright 1998 by the Alabama Museum of Natural History, used by permission).

The site also experienced considerable settlement and use in the nineteenth and twentieth centuries.

THE BOTTLE CREEK SITE AND PENSACOLA CULTURE

> These investigations and accounts of the Bottle Creek site indicate that this ceremonial center, in size and magnitude of construction, ranks second only to the great center at Moundville and represents one of the major protohistoric sites in Alabama and the Southeast.
>
> Walthall 1980:269

The principal occupation at Bottle Creek was by people of the Pensacola culture (A.D. 1250–1700). Pensacola culture is an archaeological variant of the widespread Mississippian tradition. It is identified by a shell-tempered

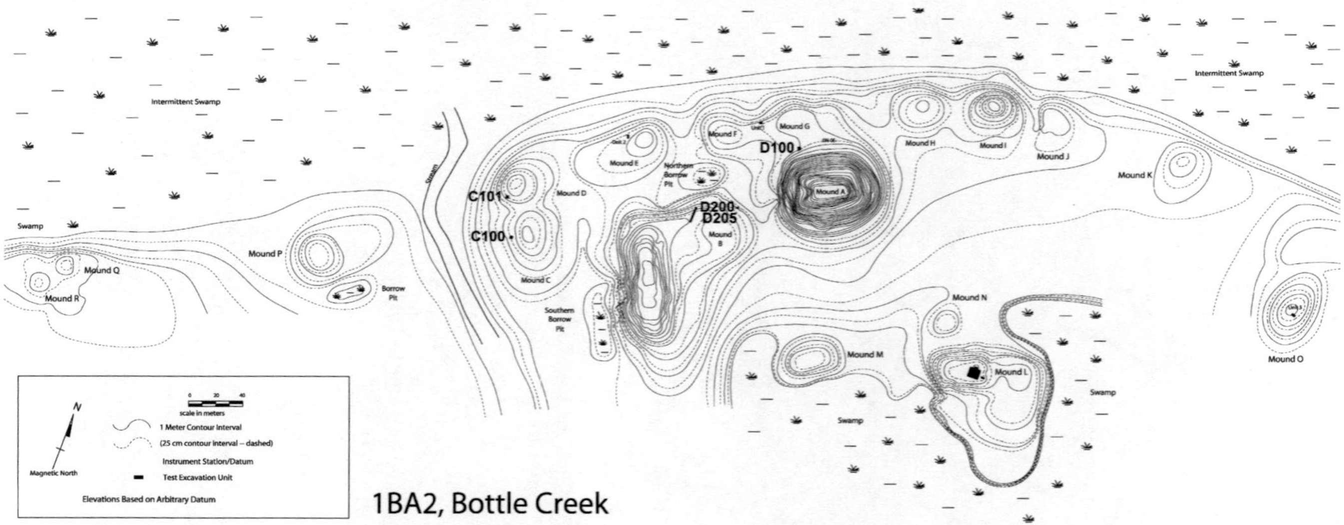

1.3. Contour map of the Bottle Creek site (courtesy of Gregory A. Waselkov, Center for Archaeological Studies, University of South Alabama, used by permission).

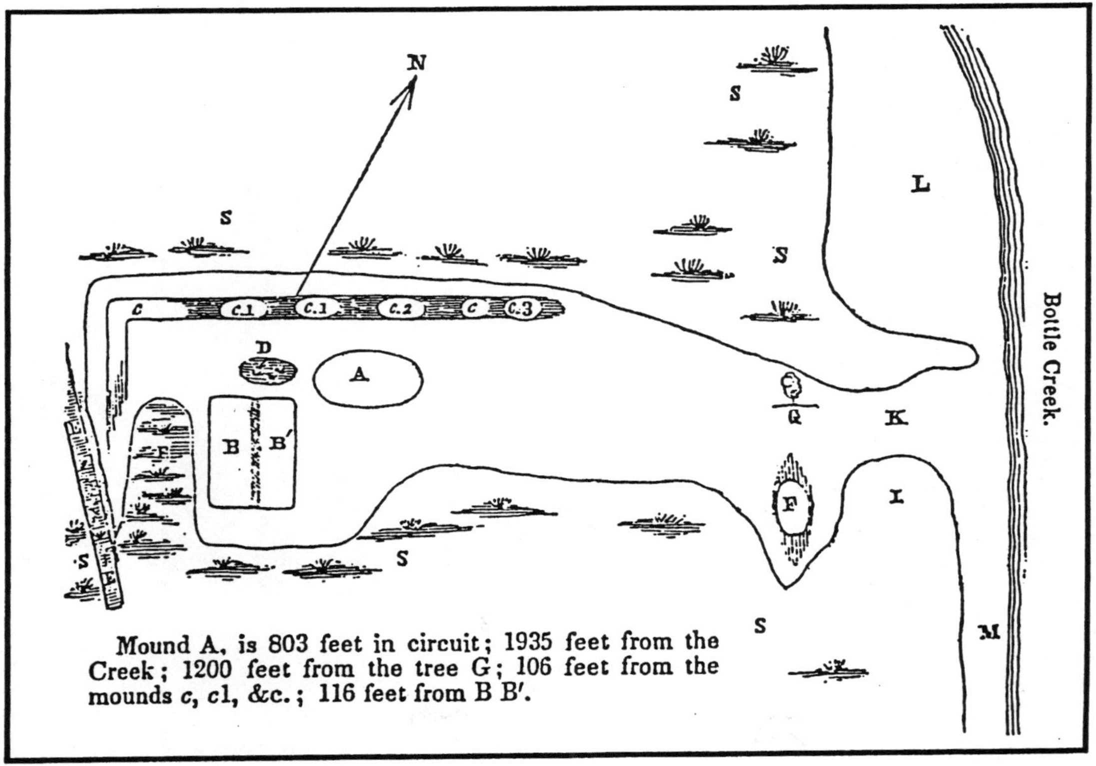

1.4. An early map of the Bottle Creek site by A. Bigelow (1853).

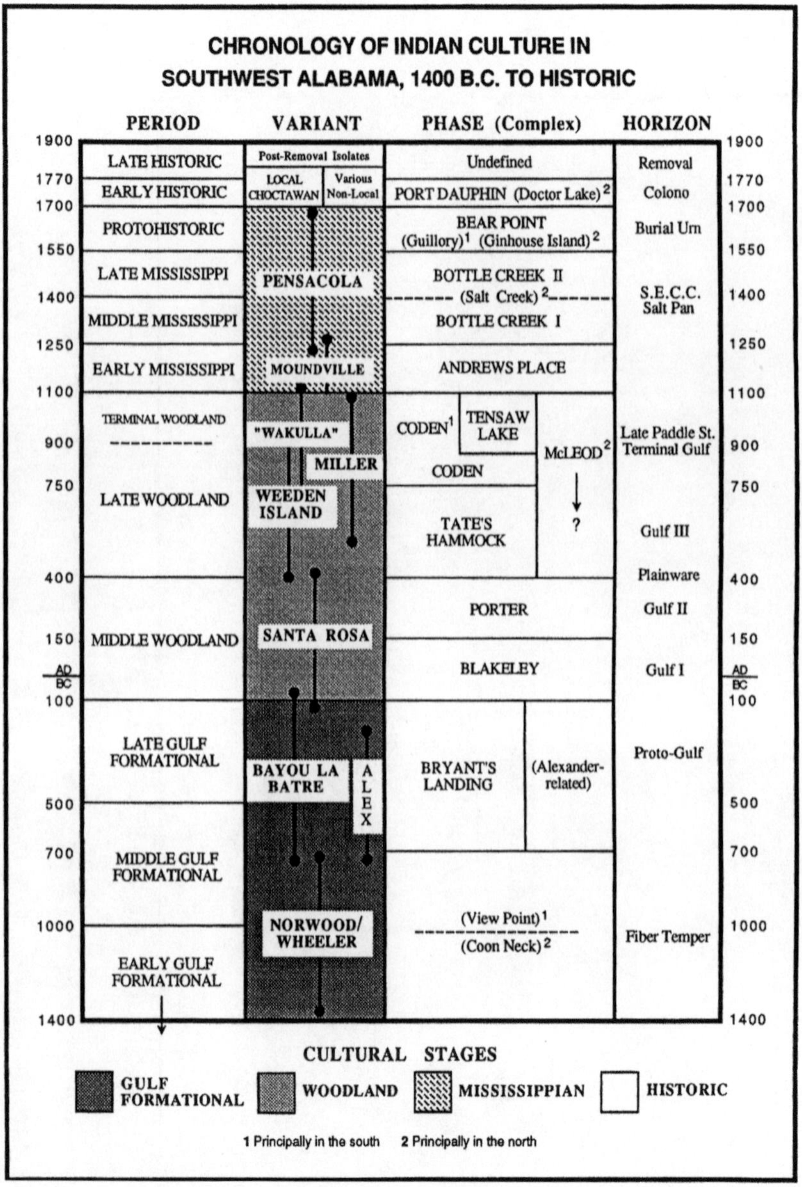

1.5. Chronology of Indian culture in southwest Alabama, 1400 B.C. to Historic (from the *Mound Island Project*, by Fuller and Brown, copyright 1998 by the Alabama Museum of Natural History, used by permission).

pottery complex and by its geographic association with the north-central coast of the Gulf of Mexico. The Pensacola culture existed at a time of increasing sociopolitical complexity, in keeping with interior Mississippian developments: "During this period a series of simple chiefdoms developed that were centered around the bay systems of the coast. One or more single-mound settlements were usually present around each bay system with outlying settlements clustered in the vicinity. While very few of the platform mounds have been investigated, they appear to have served to elevate public buildings. Mound burials are scarce. In this culture area, cemeteries were more often used for burial of both elite and commoners" (Bense 1994:234).

Pensacola culture exhibits many Mississippian characteristics, with closest parallels to the Moundville culture located to the north in the Black Warrior River valley. Pensacola culture stretches along the coast from Choctawhatchee Bay in western Florida, across the Mobile Basin and Mississippi Sound region to southeastern Louisiana. Although it is distributed extensively on the coast, its heartland is the Mobile Basin of southwest Alabama, which includes Mobile Bay, the Mobile-Tensaw Delta, and the southern portions of the Tombigbee and Alabama river valleys. The influences of Pensacola culture were felt well up the Alabama River to the vicinity of Selma. Probable trade sherds have even turned up at the juncture of the Coosa and Tallapoosa rivers. Recent archaeological research at the Bottle Creek site has shown that Pensacola culture is not totally an indigenous development. Early on, the region experienced strong contacts with Moundville populations. Evidence also suggests interactions with people of the Plaquemine culture in the Lower Mississippi Valley (Blitz and Mann 2000:59–62, 99–105; Brose 1984:182–185; Brose et al. 1983:154–156, 219; Chase 1998:89–90; Curren 1992:92–174; Davis 1981; 1984b:222–224; Fuller 1998:25–32; Fuller and Silvia 1984:3–5; Fuller and Stowe 1982; Giardino 1985:96–133; Greenwell 1984:149–153; Jenkins and Paglione 1982:14–15; Kniffen 1936; Knight 1977:147–148; 1984:199–204; Lankford et al. 1976; Mikell 1992; Milanich 1994:380–387; Morgan 2001; Neuman 1990:281–283; Phillips 1970:951–953; Rushing 1976; Stowe 1985; 1989; Stowe et al. 1981).

As the type-site for the Pensacola culture, Bottle Creek is the key to understanding the history and culture of the Mobile-Tensaw Delta in late prehistoric/protohistoric times. Because of Bottle Creek's physical isolation, little is known about the history and culture of its occupants, despite the fact that it has been in the historical literature for three centuries. Based on the number of mounds, their size, and their extent, Bottle Creek is the largest Mississippian mound center on the northern Gulf Coastal Plain. Although Bottle Creek has been recognized as an important archaeological site for well over a century, national recognition did not occur until March 10, 1995, when it became a National Historic Landmark.

There is only one other Indian site in the State of Alabama that has attained this status—Moundville—so the selection of Bottle Creek is a notable honor (Bigelow 1853; Bense 1994:234–238; Brose et al. 1983; Brown 1993; Brown and Fuller 1991; 1993a; Ensor 1993:26–27; Fuller 1998:26–28; Fuller and Brown 1993a; 1994; 1995a; 1995b; 1996–1999; 1998:54–105; Fuller and Stowe 1982; Holmes 1963; Jones and DeJarnette 1933; Knight 1984; May 1976; Moore 1905b:294–295; Pyle-Spring 1989; Rushing 1976; Silvia 2000; Stowe 1985; 1989; Trickey 1958; Trickey and Holmes 1971; Walthall 1980:267; Waselkov and Silvia Mueller 1991; Zschomler and Brown 1996:8).

The Bottle Creek site seems to have been the principal focal point for interaction in the Mobile-Tensaw Delta during Mississippian times. At the time of its occupation this site was located at a cultural crossroads. Being situated near the intersection of major east-west trails and north-south water routes (Higginbotham 1991:60; Rodning 1994; Chapter 11; Tanner 1989:12–13), it was in a unique position to affect the course of history in southern Alabama and points east, west, and north. It is most probable that the people who lived at Bottle Creek had intermittent and/or long-term contacts, either direct or indirect, with other people along the coast. There are a number of Pensacola culture mound sites along coastal waters that are believed to have been centers for small-scale chiefdoms with a two-tiered settlement hierarchy (Blitz and Mann 2000:104), but there is no other site like Bottle Creek along the coastal plain. It is in a class by itself. Whether or not these other chiefdoms were connected with Bottle Creek in some manner is not yet known. In terms of the number of mounds and their sizes, Bottle Creek is comparable with a number of Mississippian sites in the interior, including Moundville in Alabama (Knight 1996; Knight and Steponaitis 1998; Moore 1905a; 1907; Peebles 1978; Steponaitis 1983), Etowah in Georgia (Larson 1971; Moorehead 1932); and Lake George in Mississippi (Phillips 1970, 1:278–304; Williams and Brain 1983).

By the time the French appeared in the Mobile-Tensaw Delta at the end of the seventeenth century, Bottle Creek appeared to be abandoned, but it was a place still revered by historic groups in the region (Higginbotham 1991:70; Knight 1984:206; McWilliams 1981:168–169). Enough archaeological work now has been done at the site to indicate that there continued to be a substantial Native American occupation at Bottle Creek in the sixteenth through the early eighteenth centuries, but it is not yet certain who these people were. It is probable that they were the descendants of the earlier inhabitants of Bottle Creek, but whether they were Mobilians, the people with whom de Soto's army had such a tragic encounter in 1540, is unclear. The first post–de Soto reference to the Mobilians is Bishop Díaz Vara Calderón's description of the native province of "Mobila . . . on the western frontier [of Florida], on an island near the harbor of Spiritu

Santo." There is some question as to whether this island is Dauphin Island or Mound Island, but the latter, with its prime site of Bottle Creek, is certainly much closer to the eighteenth-century Mobilian villages than it is to Dauphin Island (Waselkov and Gums 2000:7; Knight 1976:109; Lankford et al. 1976; Wenhold 1936:10).

Certainly one of the more intriguing features of the Bottle Creek site is its physiographic setting. Rather than being situated on a terrace overlooking a major drainage, as are most Mississippian mound centers, Bottle Creek occupies a natural levee that is less than 3 m in elevation in a large, perennially inundated swamp (Figure 1.6). Until recently, no secondary mound sites or even very large outlying villages were known that could be tied to the principal mound center.[2] One reason for the unusual setting may be political and/or economic; its location in the heart of a major delta near the juncture of two major river valleys places Bottle Creek in the geographical center of the northern Gulf Coast.

It has been known for years that the Gulf Coast was a major thoroughfare in prehistoric times. Scholars have recognized cultural similarities along the northern Gulf Coast for quite some time (Caldwell 1958:52–59; Davis 1984a:ix; Ford 1951:66–67; Goggin 1949:34–39; Holmes 1903:104–107; Sears 1954; 1977; Willey 1949:553–570). But there were also important connections with the interior by rivers that flow south to the coast. The Mobile River system was the prime connector. Taken together, the Mobile, Alabama, Tombigbee, Black Warrior, Coosa, and Tallapoosa rivers drain a major portion of the Southeast, and their combined waters empty into the Mobile-Tensaw Delta.

The Mobile Basin has been recognized as a cultural fulcrum for the entire northern Gulf Coast (Blitz and Mann 2000:104–105). In coastal Alabama areas east of the basin there is clear evidence for contacts with Florida populations (Holmes 1903:104–107; Knight 1984:200–201; Moore 1905b; Sears 1977:176–177; Willey 1949:463–466). The interaction west of this enormous estuary, as seen in the material record, was with Lower Mississippi Valley people (Davis 1984b:222–223; Fuller and Stowe 1982:48; Kniffen 1936:413–414; Lewis 1988:117; McIntire 1958:pl.13; Phillips 1970, 2:951–953). It is clear that both prehistorically and historically the Mobile Basin was a cultural melting pot.

Today the Bottle Creek site is covered by bottomland forest, portions of which are accompanied by dense undergrowth. The latter areas are attributable to twentieth-century logging activities and to tree-falls resulting

2. In 1998 scientists identified a small, three-mound secondary center, the Crossroads Mounds site, on an upland terrace about 20 km southeast of Bottle Creek, in the vicinity of Lower Halls Landing, Baldwin County. Although this site is thought to be of the Pensacola culture, it has not yet been investigated.

1.6. Swamp in the vicinity of Mound L (GCS/94/P1/13).

from Hurricane Frederic in 1979. A relatively open forest canopy, however, characterizes much of the central portion of the site. The fact that the site is somewhat isolated, located in a large swamp, and often difficult to reconnoiter has contributed to its overall integrity.

PREVIOUS INVESTIGATIONS AND THE BOTTLE CREEK PROJECT

The most complete and detailed discussion of past work at Bottle Creek is Stowe and Fuller's (1993) essay, "The Bottle Creek Mounds—History of Archaeological Research Prior to 1990." This article is contained in *Bottle Creek Research: Working Papers on the Bottle Creek Site (1Ba2), Baldwin County, Alabama*, a volume edited by Richard S. Fuller and myself (Brown and Fuller 1993a). The purpose of that volume was to whet the appetite of students of Alabama prehistory in a major research project that was just beginning at the University of Alabama. The Bottle Creek Project, as it came to be known, has had as its central purpose the understanding of the Bottle Creek site and how it figured in the origins, development, and lifeways of Pensacola culture. This has remained a central purpose of our research in the last decade and is the overarching theme of the present volume. It should be stressed that this book builds upon the *Working Pa-*

pers volume. It adds to it rather than replacing it, although new research has certainly resulted in significant revisions. The Stowe and Fuller (1993) article is critical to understanding investigations at Bottle Creek prior to the past decade, and it is fundamental reading to anyone interested in this site. It begins with Jean-Baptiste Le Moyne de Bienville's visit to the site in 1702, at which time he walked away with five pottery "images" (see Chapter 12) from the "Isle aux Statues" (Delisle 1718) and ends in 1990, a year before the Bottle Creek Project began.

In the summer of 1990 Gregory Waselkov of the University of South Alabama made a contour map of the Bottle Creek site. This project, which was part of a National Science Foundation EPSCOR grant, also involved the excavation of three 1 × 2 m test units in various parts of the site (Mound E, between Mound F and Mound G, and Mound M). At this same time Read Stowe, also of the University of South Alabama, excavated a test in Mound O. These tests provided useful stratigraphic information as well as important data concerning the material culture and subsistence practices of the prehistoric inhabitants of Bottle Creek (Waselkov and Silvia Mueller 1991). The contour map that resulted from Waselkov's research was published in the *Working Papers* volume (Waselkov 1993), as was the first study of plant foods at the site, at which time we learned just how important corn was in the diet of the Bottle Creek people (Gremillion 1993). With a grant from the Alabama Historical Commission, Waselkov (1997) returned to Bottle Creek in 1996–1997 and added mounds P, Q, and R to the contour map. This map is what we still use today (Figure 1.3).

In 1991 the Gulf Coast Survey (GCS) archaeological program of the Alabama Museum of Natural History conducted investigations at Bottle Creek (Brown and Fuller 1991; 1993b; Fuller and Brown 1992a, 1992b). The Research Grants Committee of the University of Alabama funded this work. It set the stage for the Bottle Creek Project, research sponsored by the National Endowment for the Humanities, the Alabama Historical Commission, the Baldwin County Historic Development Commission and the University of Alabama in 1993–1994. As stated, the Bottle Creek Project has had as its principal goals understanding of the culture history of the site and the changing lifeways of its inhabitants. In the fall of 1994 the Gulf Coast Survey expanded its investigations by surveying Mound Island and the surrounding area between Middle River and the Tensaw River. It was at this time that the three additional mounds noted above (P–R) were first recorded (Fuller and Brown 1998:102–103).

There were three goals for the research undertaken by the Gulf Coast Survey in the summer of 1991. First, in order to tie together past research with present endeavors, all of the Bottle Creek collections stored at the University of Alabama were reanalyzed. This research, which entailed the reclassification of several thousand potsherds from DeJarnette's 1932 excavations and from two large surface collections made at the site in the 1970s, was published as a chapter (Fuller and Brown 1993a) in the *Working Papers* volume. Basically, this article both updated and revised an earlier study made by Fuller and Stowe (1982). Fuller and Brown presented type/variety definitions in this chapter, as well as numerous illustrations of potsherds from Bottle Creek. This study and a section of further classificatory revisions in Fuller and Brown (1998:31–37) provide the pottery-dating foundation on which the present volume stands. This is another reason why the interested student of Bottle Creek should have all three volumes (i.e., Brown and Fuller 1993a, Fuller and Brown 1998, and the present volume) in his or her library. This is not simply a plug for more sales; rather, it is recognition of limitations. Each volume in what has become the "Bottle Creek Saga" builds upon what has come before. The past is not discarded, but is enriched.

The other two goals for the 1991 research related to actual fieldwork—one involved survey and the other excavation. Because no one had ever made a systematic surface collection at Bottle Creek, Fuller and I felt that such a survey was in order. We surface collected all of the mounds at the site as well as the areas between and around the mounds (Figure 1.7). This initial survey was expanded in 1993 and 1994 and eventually published in Fuller and Brown (1998:54–105). The survey not only provided information on what areas would be productive for testing, in order to retrieve culture-historical data, but it also revealed which areas were relatively untouched by pothunting activities[3] and would, therefore, be important in yielding settlement and subsistence data.

We opened two test units in Mound L in 1991. Excavations continued to subsoil in one of the units, a depth of 2.5 m below the present ground surface. Fuller and I published a brief report on this work in the *Working Papers* volume (Brown and Fuller 1993b). These tests were not only significant in revealing culture-historical information, but they produced extremely valuable data relating to mound construction and various social activities. The bulk of the mound is believed to date to the Bottle Creek I and II phases (A.D. 1250–1550). In its early stages it experienced activities that involved the manufacture and/or use of microliths, a subject dealt with by Paul Jackson in this volume (Chapter 9). We observed a wall

3. Despite the isolation of Bottle Creek, or perhaps because of it, looting has been a problem over the years. One major phase occurred in the 1970s, which helped bring important recognition to the site's importance (Lankford et al. 1976). It was at this time that N. Read Stowe, of the University of South Alabama, helped get Bottle Creek listed on the National Register (Knight 1977:149–150). Pothunting still occurs to some extent, but the Alabama Historical Commission has recently taken important measures to protect the site.

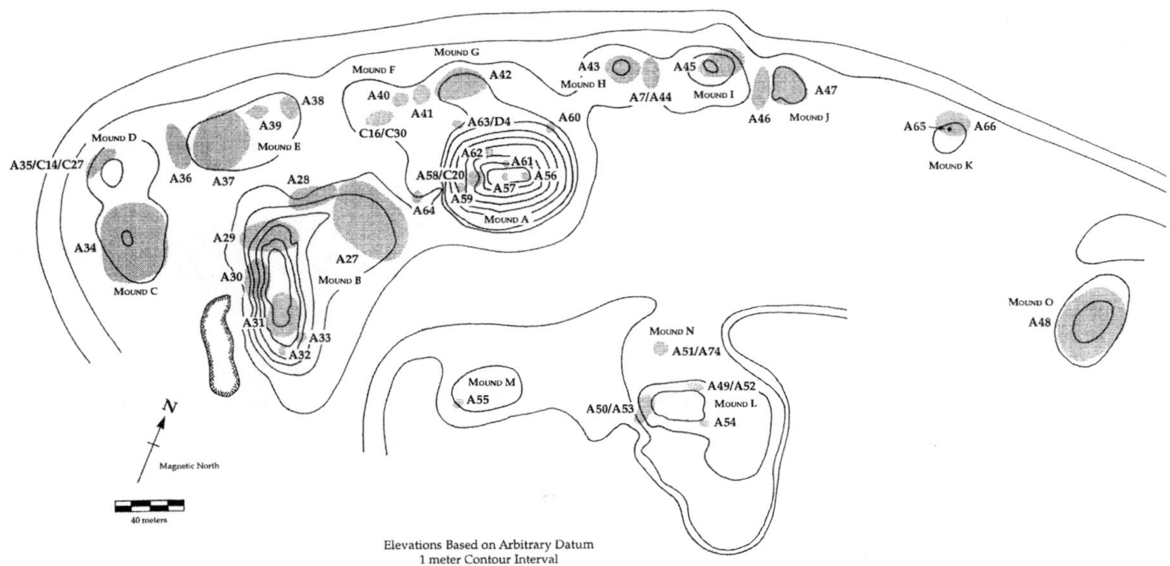

1.7. Surface collection areas at Bottle Creek (from the *Mound Island Project*, by Fuller and Brown, copyright 1998 by the Alabama Museum of Natural History, used by permission).

trench structure low in the mound and a series of thin burned layers, some of which were actually hearths. The builders eventually applied two clay caps to Mound L. In the top 50 cm of one of the two excavation units, above the final clay cap, the 1991 investigations revealed at least two structures made of single set posts.

With new funding in hand, the Gulf Coast Survey was able to continue excavations at Bottle Creek in 1993–1994. One of the goals of this stage of the research was to open up a series of test excavations in several mounds in order to explore rich middens. We hoped to secure firm chronological information and subsistence data that would aid in reconstructing both the culture history and the diet of the Bottle Creek inhabitants. In addition to examining middens in some of the surrounding house mounds (C–K), we also wanted to test a midden in the central part of the site (mounds A, B, L, M and N), which presumably would represent the trash of the elite. It was reasonable to assume that the occupants of Mound A were the principal nobility at the site, so we expected that their trash would be different from that which was produced by the residents of the house mounds. The latter people may have been retainers for the principal elite, or they may have been second-order nobility themselves. Whatever the case, it seemed plausible that the artifacts obtained in the two contexts might be different, and that the foods consumed might vary. Margie Scarry, Irvy Quitmyer, and Hunter Johnson address these issues in the present book in chapters 5, 7, and 8. In 1993 we examined two of the house mounds (C and D) and in 1994 we excavated a rich midden at the base of Mound A.

Another focus of our research was Mound L. As stated above, our work on the test units in 1991 revealed that the inhabitants of the site had erected at least two buildings on the tops of Mound L in its late stage. Although we were only able to observe a small part of these structures, it was clear that they dated to protohistoric/historic times (Brown and Fuller 1993b). As these were the first aboriginal houses to be isolated in the whole of the Mobile-Tensaw Delta at this time, it was a fundamental part of our research to expose these structures. Diane Silvia started the excavation of a 6 × 8 m block in 1993 and completed the isolation of these structures in the 1994 season, providing data that eventually contributed to her doctoral dissertation (Silvia 2000:255–300).

A final goal was to explore the construction of the central portion of the site. We had already discovered from the 1991 tests in Mound L that there was a great deal of earth movement at Bottle Creek, beyond mound construction. Not only had the visible portions of Mound L been built, but also much of the platform that supports and surrounds it was also artificial. Prior to excavation, we had assumed that this platform was natural, as it was so immense. We knew, however, that the large, lobe-shaped terrace, which comes off the northeast end of Mound B, had to have been artificial. In order to understand how it was constructed and what purposes it might have served, a 12 m long trench was excavated in the north edge of the Mound B Terrace in 1994. The chapters that follow present the results of our investigations and address the various concerns outlined above.

CURRENT PAPERS

Each paper in the present volume represents work undertaken by well-established or up-and-coming scholars who have one thing in common—they braved the trip to Bottle Creek and lived to tell about it. Only Penelope Drooker has thus far not made the pilgrimage, but not through any lack of desire on her part. Very few people can say they have been to this very isolated site, and fewer still have worked there. All of the studies presented herein represent important attempts to understand the changing lifeways of the people who actually dared to live there.

In Chapter 2, Richard S. Fuller considers the origin and evolution of Pensacola culture, including the nature and extent of influences from Moundville. He starts his study by describing the Gulf Coast Survey's work on mounds C and D. Fuller also offers a detailed description of the excavations in Mound A (Figure 1.8), complete with radiocarbon dates and artifact associations for the various well-defined midden layers. Although three 2 m square tests distributed over three mounds certainly should not be considered the final word on a site such as Bottle Creek, it should be pointed out that the pottery sample is fairly decent. The Mound C test unit alone produced more pottery (23,190 sherds, to be exact) than all excavated sites in the Mobile Bay area combined! And that's just Mound C. The sherd counts in the mounds A and D units are pretty impressive, too.[4]

For Mound A, the principal mound at the site, Fuller shows that there was a significant accumulation of midden long before there was any observable mound construction. There was also quite a lot of flooding in those early years. The first recognizable construction stage at Mound A dates to the Bottle Creek I phase (A.D. 1250–1400). The bulk of the mound was built during the Bottle Creek II phase (A.D. 1400–1550), but some use of the mound's summit occurred afterward. Fuller shows that there was significant occupation on Mound A's summit during both the Bear Point and Port Dauphin phases. In short, the principal mound at the Bottle

4. Unfortunately, because of space limitations, the artifact counts for the various units, levels, and features are not provided in this volume. As they made up more than 400 pages of the original manuscript, their presence drew the wrath of reviewers. For anyone interested in having these data, they are available from the Gulf Coast Survey at the Alabama Museum of Natural History.

1.8. The Mound A excavation unit (D100), as viewed from the north (drawing by James Reid, 1994).

Creek site was still functioning in the early eighteenth century. The ethnic identity of these inhabitants is still unknown as it is most difficult to make the pottery speak to us.

For his investigation, Fuller adopts a form of ceramic analysis involving sets that was developed by Jeffrey P. Brain in the Lower Mississippi Valley. Fuller discusses the set concept and then adapts it to the Bottle Creek data. He introduces the term "sequential sets" as a means to show and highlight continuities in local pottery traditions. He also uses the concept of "style sets" to show decorative parallels that are not necessarily tied to specific ware attributes. Having either formulated or adopted such concepts, Fuller then arranges the style sets in sequences and establishes five series, including the Weeden Island series, the Lower Mississippi Valley series, the Moundville series, the Pensacola series, and the Gulf Historic series. He describes in detail each of the sets that are included in the various series, and shows just how they fit within the various defined phases.

By virtue of his analysis, Fuller moves far beyond pottery type/variety definitions. In showing that there is a clear and well-defined structure to what may otherwise seem a chaotic array of materials, Fuller brings order to what has always seemed to me to be a very complex, mind-boggling ceramic nightmare. And mind you, this is said by someone who has spent most of his academic life sorting Lower Mississippi Valley pottery (Brown 1998)! It has long been known that the coastal zone of Alabama and Mississippi is a virtual melting pot of pottery. This mixture presumably reflects different peoples (Blitz and Mann 2000:100–101; Brown 1988; Davis 1981, 1984b). Fuller shows that there is indeed a complex blend of pottery, but he also demonstrates that the mélange is far more structured than most people realize, and that it can be understood. An example of how he shows this is his handling of the gross categories, coarse wares and fine wares. First, he groups together all of the various coarse wares and examines how they are distributed over levels and zones, and then he does the same for the fine wares. For both, Fuller demonstrates that there is a logical, regular pattern in the Mound A test unit that is repeated almost exactly in Mound C.

Having convinced us that there is order in all of this, Fuller then goes on to use this information to create a provisional chronology for the Bottle Creek site. It is this chronology that forms the temporal foundation for all of the other studies in this volume. At the risk of telling too much (too late for that) and getting too far ahead of the story, I cannot resist but say that Fuller feels there are indeed strong influences from Moundville at Bottle Creek that appear abruptly, starting at about A.D. 1100. There are influences from the Lower Mississippi Valley at about this time, too, and together they had an important influence on the rise and development of Pensacola culture.

In Chapter 3, David Morgan provides a detailed construction sequence for the Mound B terrace. It has long been recognized that Mound B has a very unusual shape (Figure 1.3). The reason we decided to investigate this mound in the first place was to figure out why it was so distinct from the other earthworks at Bottle Creek. Morgan offers a fine summary of the history of this mound in his analysis of the 12 m trench that sliced through its side (Figure 1.9). The mound began its life with a thick deposit of clay that was laid down sometime during the Bottle Creek I or II phases (A.D. 1200–1550). It is abundantly clear that post-filled wall trenches were critical to the construction process. These wall trenches may have served multiple purposes. The initial alignment first and foremost provided an outline for the shape of the mound. With that accomplished, the same posts served as an excellent retaining wall for the clay that was heaped up along its edges. The latter function is verified by the repetitive use of multiple post-filled wall trenches in the same basic positions as the mound increased in height. Morgan detected at least three stages of mound construction using post alignments in the raising of Mound B. This same technique had been seen in the 1991 excavations that we conducted in Mound L (Brown and Fuller 1993b).

Morgan also reports on the existence of two thin layers of midden that were deposited as the Mound B terrace stages were added (Figure 1.10). He argues that these layers are evidence for ritual events that commemorated the completion of construction activities. Morgan isolated two parallel wall trenches on top of the Mound B terrace, which he believes may relate to two independent, contemporary structures whose purposes are, as yet, unknown. These structures, which date no earlier than the Bottle Creek II phase (A.D. 1400–1550), certainly merit further examination.

Finally, Morgan looks at the modifications of the Mound B terrace over the last century and a half. He compares Bigelow's original drawing of Mound B (Figure 1.4) to the current contour map (Figure 1.3) and considers why there should be such discrepancies. Our trench clearly hit upon a sharp corner of the mound, and yet this is not the current corner. At present the mound terrace still continues to the east, then sweeps south in a gentle curve. Morgan examines some of the reasons for why this is so. He tends to believe that the easterly expansion is a ramp, but whether it was added prehistorically or during nineteenth-century farming activities is still not clear; all the more reason why further work is desirable in this critical part of the site.

Chapter 4, by Diane Silvia, focuses on the intensive work performed on Mound L over three seasons. After briefly reviewing the preliminary results of the short 1991 season (Brown and Fuller 1993b), Silvia concentrates on the 6 × 8 m block that was placed over a large portion of the mound's summit (Figure 1.11). She encountered a dense concentration of

1.9. Trench excavations in the Mound B terrace, as seen from the borrow pit to the north (drawing by James Reid, 1994).

1.10. David Morgan examining the midden layers in the south wall of trench unit D201 in the Mound B terrace. Dale Jarvis, to the right, is recording soil descriptions (GCS/94/P8/1).

daub in the process of excavating this block. The daub was especially thick in the southern portion, where a well-defined wall trench was exposed. This was probably the base for a thick wattle and daub wall that burned and collapsed. Silvia believes that this particular structure, which relates to the latest recorded use of the mound, dates to the middle of the eighteenth century.

Silvia then presents a summary of the artifacts found in the 1993–1994 seasons. Most are a mix of protohistoric/historic aboriginal and European materials. Despite the heavy use of this mound well into the eighteenth century, there are surprisingly few objects of European manufacture in evidence. I am especially amazed at the discovery of only four glass beads. Silvia completes her study with a detailed examination of the structures, making a valiant attempt to tease patterns out of the 689 features that were detected. Some of the patterns stand out more clearly than others.

The next two chapters deal with research conducted by C. Margaret

1.11. The Mound L block excavation, as seen from the northeast (drawing by James Reid, 1994).

Scarry on the subject of plant foods. Chapter 5 focuses on the Bottle Creek site itself. Scarry first discusses the methods involved in her analysis and then provides details on the findings. Her results confirm Gremillion's (1993) conclusion that corn agriculture was critical to the lives of the Bottle Creek inhabitants. But Scarry builds upon Gremillion's work by demonstrating that corn kernels are far more common than cupules at the site. She argues that corn was removed from the cob in off-mound locations, and perhaps even at off-site locations. Her work supports the notion that the occupants of Bottle Creek received their corn as tribute.

Scarry detected seeds from five indigenous plants in the various excavations, including chenopod, knotweed, sunflower, maygrass, and little barley. All of these plants are known cultigens elsewhere in the Eastern Woodlands, but unfortunately it is still not clear for Bottle Creek whether the seeds in question were recovered from wild or domesticated strands. Nuts are rare in the Bottle Creek plant samples, but acorn and hickory do occur to some extent. Especially interesting is the appearance of wild rice and yaupon seeds (*Ilex vomitoria*) at the site. Scarry discusses what their presence might imply socially.

Scarry's research shows quite clearly that the people of Bottle Creek were as reliant on corn agriculture as were Mississippians in the interior river valleys. This is a topic that she explores in depth in Chapter 6, where she compares the plant remains at Bottle Creek and Moundville. We know so much more about Moundville than we do about Bottle Creek, because Scarry and her colleagues have devoted much of their careers to understanding the foodways of Moundville and its polity (Scarry 1986, 1998; Schoeninger and Schurr 1998; Welch 1991; 1998). Through Scarry's own work, and that of Gremillion (1993), there is now a significant database for Bottle Creek from which to make comparisons. Suffice to say that there are important parallels and differences between the two sites that may have sociopolitical ramifications.

One thing that the Mississippian tradition in the Black Warrior manifests that so far is lacking in the Mobile-Tensaw Delta is comparable botanical information from farmstead sites. In the case of Mississippian in the Black Warrior River valley, Scarry is able to show that there are significant differences between Moundville and its associated farmsteads in terms of the relative frequency and distribution of corn and nuts. These differences are thought to be the result of Moundville's occupants having been provisioned by the surrounding farms. She believes this was the case at Bottle Creek too, but unfortunately only half the equation exists in this region. We know what occurs at the center, but we lack the farmstead data. With its century of research, Moundville does have a distinct advantage over Bottle Creek, but this is less an excuse than a sign of frustration.

There is much archaeological work that still needs to be done in the Mobile-Tensaw Delta.

The main difference between Bottle Creek and Moundville, in terms of plant foods, is the very low ratio of nut remains to corn. Although this discrepancy could be related to cultural preferences, Scarry believes it is probably more closely related to a reduction in the use of the Bottle Creek site during the fall. Seasonal abandonment is an argument made by Knight (1984:209–215; Knight and Adams 1981:41–42) many years ago, when there was very little data from which to draw. Another difference between Bottle Creek and Moundville is the much greater emphasis on fishing and foraging among the former people, no doubt a reaction to the natural bounty of the Mobile-Tensaw Delta (Curren 1978; Knight 1987). One thing seems certain: the occupants of Bottle Creek did very little primary processing of plant foods. That processing, Scarry believes, was done at the surrounding farmsteads. Proof is lacking, but the seeds have now been planted for future fieldwork. Scarry ends Chapter 6 with a comparison of ritual/symbolic plants at Moundville and Bottle Creek, focusing on yaupon and the development and spread of the black drink.

The essay by Irvy Quitmyer (Chapter 7) is the first thorough study of faunal remains from Bottle Creek and, as a result, it sets the stage for future research in the region. Although Quitmyer deals with only three column samples from two test units, what he does with these samples is intriguing. One of the samples that he analyzes comes from the middle of the Mound C unit (C100). The other two are from Mound A (D100), with one from the pre-mound A levels and the other from the upper Mound A deposits after mound construction started. Quitmyer starts his presentation with a discussion of just why it is so critical that fine mesh screens (1/8 in and 1/16 in) be used in faunal analysis. Most of the food remains that he analyzed, especially fishes, would have been discarded in the backdirt had the mesh size only been 1/4 in. His detailed discussion of the methods employed is critical reading for anyone interested in how zooarchaeological research is conducted.

After dealing with procedures, Quitmyer offers a detailed study of the faunal samples. As with the botanical remains, we are fortunate that bone preservation is excellent at Bottle Creek. In the Mound C sample alone there are 34 species of animals and 266 minimum numbers of individuals (MNI). In addition to offering species lists for each of the samples, which also includes MNI and percentage of meat calculations, Quitmyer offers a series of histograms that provide visual displays of the relationships between the samples. He shows that there was a very heavy reliance on aquatic resources at Bottle Creek overall, especially brackish water mollusks and fishes. He even breaks down the aquatic species into brackish and freshwater in his investigation of what habitats were exploited most. Quitmyer demonstrates that there is a marked difference between the size and age of modern rangia clams (*Rangia cuneata*) compared with those used by the inhabitants of Bottle Creek, with the latter being much smaller and younger than those that exist at present. These findings reveal that the inhabitants of Bottle Creek put considerable pressure on their environment as a result of their extended occupation of the region.

Quitmyer ends his essay with a discussion of the many ways in which the different faunal species could have been harvested in and around Bottle Creek. Although he does not detect obvious status differences in the faunal assemblages between elite and commoners, it is interesting to note that there is more of a tendency for fishes and mammals, especially white-tailed deer, to have been eaten by the people who deposited the food remains in the Mound A unit, once mound building began.

In Chapter 8 Hunter Johnson examines pottery vessel shapes with function in mind. He is especially interested in whether or not differences can be detected in ceramic assemblages from locations that were presumably more elite than others. Applying Fuller's stratigraphic analysis of the two test units excavated in mounds A and C as a foundation (Chapter 2), Johnson examines how pottery shape frequencies and percentages change over time in these specific locations on the Bottle Creek site. He is able to show quite effectively that the pottery used in the pre-mound levels of Mound A Unit D100 is very similar to the total assemblage of Unit C100 in Mound C, with the emphasis being on food preparation functions. But once mound building began to occur in the particular location where D100 was situated, vessels that are typically thought to be more associated with serving functions became more common. Johnson's conclusions complement the findings of both Scarry (Chapter 5) and Quitmyer (Chapter 6) for these two locations. Although these two test units represent very small windows into the site, it is gratifying to learn that the various scholars are detecting similar images on the other side of the glass.

Paul Jackson examines the Bottle Creek microlithic industry in Chapter 9. Despite the fact that stone objects are relatively rare at this mound complex, there is a surprisingly healthy representation of microliths made out of Coastal Plain agate. Jackson begins his study with some background information on several other Mississippian mound centers in the Eastern Woodlands that have yielded microliths. Then he provides a detailed description of the collection from Bottle Creek. His research deals only with the material retrieved from the 1991 excavations in Mound L. Although microliths have indeed been found elsewhere on the site, thus far they have only appeared in quantity in the lower levels of Mound L. There they have been found in association with a wall trench and various features. The microdrill form is an especially common tool type in this assemblage.

It is important to note that Jackson's study is purely formal, as he did not do any wear analysis. Jackson discusses the possibility that microliths were used for working shell or mica, but these are assumptions largely based on comparative studies. Further analysis is needed to determine the actual functions of these objects at Bottle Creek. A concentration of microliths in the initial stages of a specific mound is intriguing, as it would seem to argue for some form of specialized activities at the site. Unfortunately, there is little that can be said on this matter, as we have so little excavated data from other mounds in the central area of the site. We know virtually nothing about Mound M, for example, which structurally is quite similar to Mound L.

Penelope Drooker looks at the evidence for fabrics at Bottle Creek in Chapter 10. Most of the materials she analyzed were the result of textiles having been impressed into pottery "saltpans" or daub. Drooker first defines the different weaves identified in her research. Most specimens exhibit twill weave impressions, which is typical of basketry or matting. Simple interlaced matting seems to be the most probable material used, as it would have been very efficient in forming vessels made in earthen molds. It is important to note that twill weave mats could only have been used in shallow pits, as the material is not flexible enough to line deep pits effectively. Consequently, the resulting vessels would have to be shallow, with gradually sloping sides. Through microscopic analyses of the elements, Drooker reveals that the fabrics used to make such vessels were usually old worn-out mats. The vessels that bear these impressions have come to be known as Salt Creek Cane Impressed. Weft-faced fabrics (yarns) also appear as impressions. They probably started their lives as blankets, mats, or large bags before they were used to line molds for the production of saltpans. Kimmswick Fabric Impressed is the type name for pottery bearing weft-faced impressions.

After describing the collection, Drooker then examines the distribution of the various weaves on the Bottle Creek site. Her study of the Mound C excavations matches what Fuller found using pottery type-variety analysis. Kimmswick Fabric Impressed is common in the lower levels during the Andrews Place phase (A.D. 1000–1250), but is largely replaced by Salt Creek Cane Impressed during the succeeding Bottle Creek I and II phases (A.D. 1250–1550). Drooker then puts Bottle Creek into regional perspective by looking at the distribution of different weaves in the Eastern Woodlands. She includes information on comparable material from historic and ethnographic sources, in addition to collections from other sites. Her study is a fine example of how pottery can be used to help reconstruct the soft and pliable materials of life that seldom survive long enough to become a part of the archaeological record.

The paper by Christopher Rodning (Chapter 11) deals with water travel and its significance to the native people of the Southeast. His focus is on perennially wet environments, such as the deltaic landscape surrounding the Bottle Creek mounds. Rodning starts off with a review of the ethnohistorical and archaeological evidence for water travel in the Southeast. His discussion of the manufacture of dugouts sets the stage for what follows. The evidence for prehistoric canal construction in the Southeast is quite good. The Calusa region of southwest Florida, in particular, was witness to major canal construction aboriginally. Rodning tells us about the 4 km long Pine Island Canal at the mouth of Charlotte Harbor, as well as the canal at Naples Bay, with its 2 m tall embankments. He also discusses some possibilities in northwest Florida, like Walker's Canal near Choctawhatchee Bay, and there is even a possible canal near Fort Morgan in Mobile Bay.

After showing us that canal construction was a rare but valid phenomenon in the prehistoric Southeast, Rodning addresses Bottle Creek. Although Bigelow (1853) was a firm believer in its artificial nature (Figure 1.4), there has always been a question as to whether the "Bottle Creek Canal" might be part of a relict channel of one of the myriad nearby streams. We now know that the body of water that runs between mounds C and P (Figure 1.3) is a natural channel (Fuller and Brown 1998:134), but that does not resolve the issue. Rodning makes a good case for the channel having been modified, especially the portion that runs by the site. Considering that an enormous amount of earth would have been necessary to construct the mounds at Bottle Creek, it is reasonable to presume that at least a portion of this body of water was the result of such activities. Rodning ends his essay with a discussion of just how important water travel must have been in the lives of Bottle Creek's occupants. One thing is absolutely certain—without boats Bottle Creek never would have been.

The final section by myself (Chapter 12) serves as a concluding (but not conclusive) essay on Bottle Creek and its position in the Mississippian world. I start off with a consideration of some of the things that I believe are the highlights of what has been learned about Bottle Creek as a result of the current project. Then I look at the role of this site in somewhat grander terms by addressing a number of topics relating to why Bottle Creek came into being in the first place, how it was used, and why its meaning and value may have changed over time. This last section is speculative, to be sure, but I hope that some of my deliberations make sense. By our combined research, I do feel that we have made a giant leap forward in understanding this wonderful and most complex site, but I will let the reader be the judge.

2 / Out of the Moundville Shadow

The Origin and Evolution of Pensacola Culture

Richard S. Fuller

INTRODUCTION

Since being severed from Fort Walton, Pensacola culture has gained some independence as a coastal Mississippian variant. From the beginning, geographical continuities and general similarities in ceramic styles suggested a relationship to Moundville culture. But just how "Moundvillian" is Pensacola? Recent research at the Bottle Creek site indicates a rather sudden Mississippian appearance in southwestern Alabama in the twelfth or thirteenth century A.D. A northerly origin is suggested by pottery reminiscent of late Moundville I or early Moundville II phase types. Later components show a steady evolution away from this Moundvillian base, resulting in a distinctive regional ceramic complex and settlement pattern by the sixteenth century.

The nativity of Pensacola as an archaeological construct took place in the 1940s, when it began life as a pottery series defined by Gordon Willey (Willey 1949; Willey and Woodbury 1942). Its youth was spent largely in familial bondage to other, better known cultures, either as a hyphenated twin to Fort Walton or as a coastal stepchild of Moundville. During the 1950s and 1960s, Bruce Trickey (1958), Steve Wimberly (1960), and others attempted to forge a separate identity for Pensacola as a coastal variant of Mississippian culture. These surgeries failed to take, however, and most people continued to regard Pensacola as a hyphen-dependent poor relative of Fort Walton and Moundville. The principal problem was the lack of reliable genealogical documentation in the form of published data from archaeological excavations.

Pensacola underwent a small degree of adolescent maturation in the 1970s and 1980s, as research in southwestern Alabama by David L. DeJarnette, Vernon J. Knight, Ned Jenkins, David Brose, and others helped to establish a few lines of its cultural pedigree (Brose et al. 1983; DeJarnette 1976; Knight 1984; Sears 1977). Since then, I have updated the

Pensacola pottery typology originated by Willey (1949:353–495) and Wimberly (1960:57–190) (Fuller 1996; 1998; Fuller and Brown 1993a; Fuller and Stowe 1982). Although this recent effort has been based partly on surface collections, it is helping to delineate a more accurate Pensacola genealogy. Still, if we want to learn the true story of Pensacola culture, we must look to its heart—Bottle Creek.

From 1991 to 1994, the Gulf Coast Survey of the Alabama Museum of Natural History conducted several seasons of fieldwork at Bottle Creek. We surface collected every mound, as well as the areas between the mounds. In addition to yielding intrasite surface pattern information, this initial collecting project suggested which parts of the site might be productive for excavation. In 1991 we tested Mound L, a small platform in the southern part of the site. In 1993 and 1994 we conducted more extensive excavations on this mound (Chapter 4). My discussion focuses on mounds A, C, and D.

MOUNDS C AND D

In 1993 we excavated two 2 m square test units in mounds C and D, a closely spaced pair of small mounds located in the western part of the site (Figure 1.3). A series of soil probe tests encountered dense shell midden deposits on the mounds' western slopes. Because we wanted to recover subsistence remains as well as artifacts, we placed our excavations in these locations (Figure 2.1). Both excavations revealed deep, nearly continuous middens over two meters in depth (Figures 2.2–2.3).

In addition to the rich middens in mounds C and D, our excavations revealed evidence of a palisade wall bordering this part of the site. We also encountered the remains of probable house structures. All of these architectural features appeared to date early in the site's history (Appendix B). For Mound C, they were covered by later midden containing large quantities of well-preserved bone and shell plus a variety of plant remains, including maize. The nearly continuous midden deposits extended from the base of a superficial plow zone to the top of the early wall trench, making it difficult to sort out discrete strata for analysis. We did encounter one very dark and exceptionally rich layer of sheet midden, Feature 3, about halfway between the surface and the wall trench. This feature is a large, compact midden stain, about 10 cm thick. It was first detected at the base of Level G at 8.66 m. Feature 3 allowed us to subdivide the thick accretion deposit into smaller zones for analysis.

In the field, our initial impression of the pottery from Mound C suggested that Bottle Creek's earliest Mississippian occupants had close ties to Moundville. Some of the sherds from this early component also resembled pottery of contemporary cultures in the Lower Mississippi Valley. I have termed this initial Mississippian occupation of the region the Andrews Place phase (Figure 1.5). Sherds from the later levels indicated a progres-

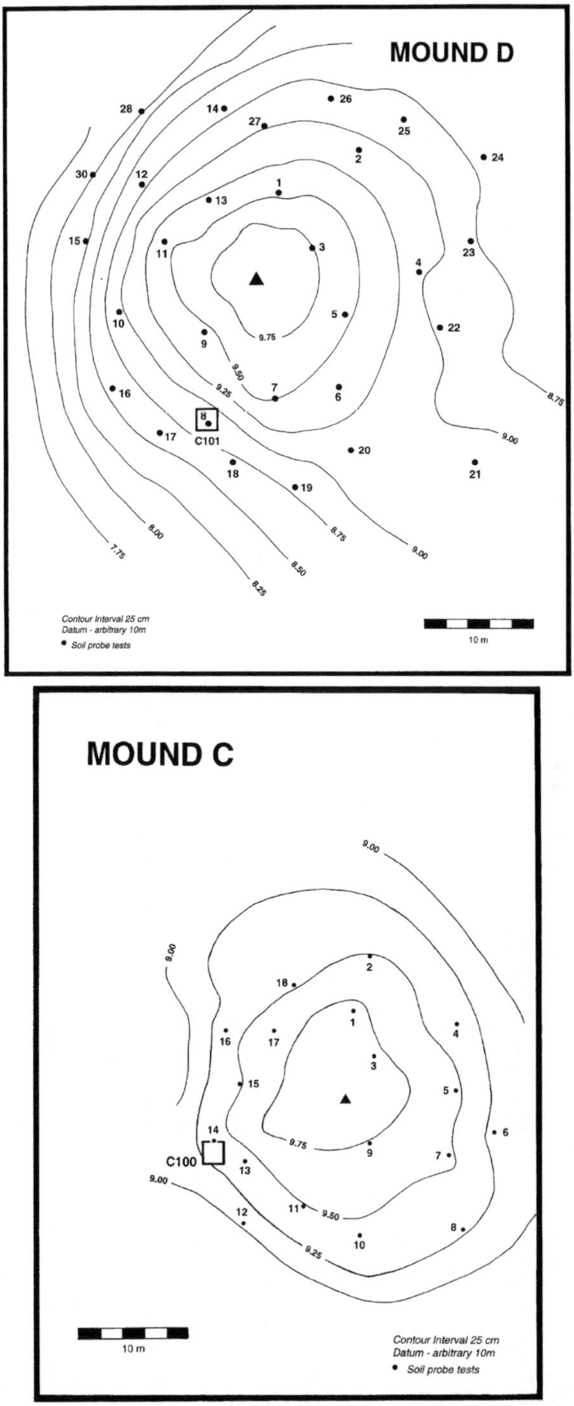

2.1. Contour maps of mounds C and D, showing the locations of soil probe tests and excavation units C100 and C101.

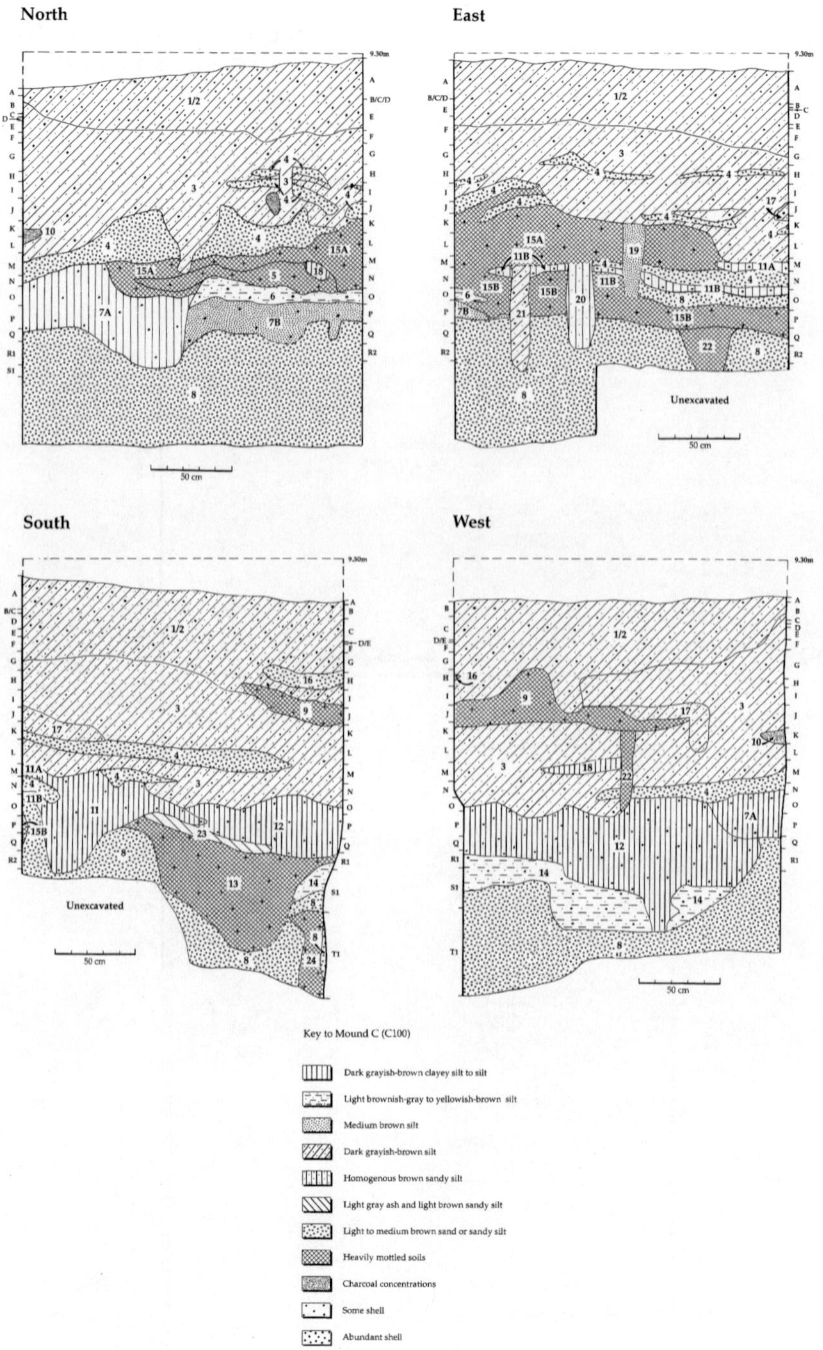

2.2. Section drawings of test unit C100, Mound C.

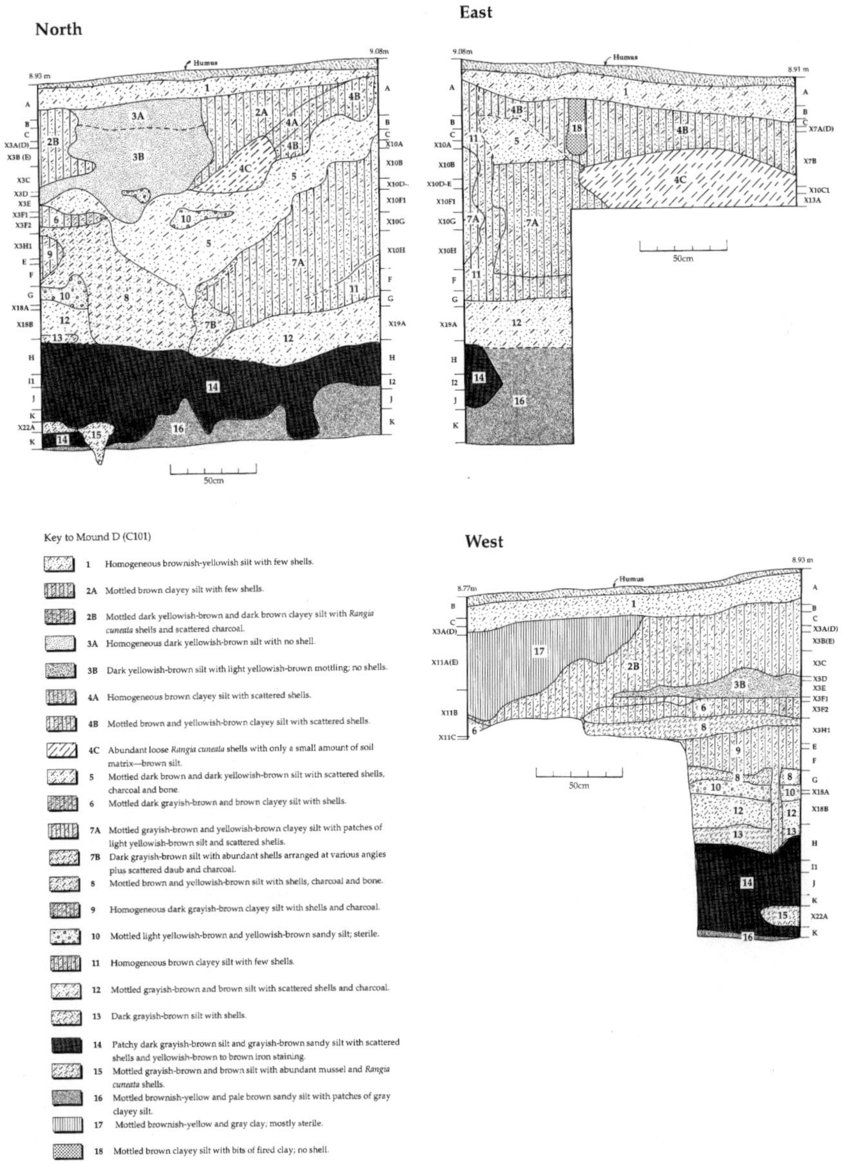

2.3. Section drawings of test unit C101, Mound D.

sive stylistic evolution toward a local Pensacola ceramic complex, as characterized by the Bottle Creek I and Bottle Creek II phases. Finally, later Bear Point phase and Port Dauphin phase wares dominated the uppermost zone, which had been disturbed by plowing and/or erosion.

Although the pottery from Mound C seemed to show excellent diachronic frequency changes in decorative styles and rim modes from top to bottom, the continuous, accretion nature of the deposits made stratigraphic interpretations difficult. We still needed collections from features or discrete cultural strata to isolate the perceived ceramic trends through time. We found the answer at Mound A, the largest mound at the site.

MOUND A

In the summer of 1994 we conducted a series of soil probe tests around the base of Mound A. These tests revealed intact and apparently stratified midden deposits on the northern edge of the mound. We then staked out a 2 m square unit at this location (Figure 1.3). The excavation reached a depth of about 2.1 m before groundwater flooding forced us to stop digging. It revealed a straightforward series of construction zones and midden strata associated with Mound A as well as a series of premound deposits (Figure 2.4).

At the top of the excavation was a superficial layer of humus and slopewash. The pottery assemblage indicated a Port Dauphin phase component that probably dates to the late seventeenth century or early eighteenth century. We have found Port Dauphin phase materials in the upper levels of excavations at various locations at Bottle Creek, but without additional work on the top of Mound A, we do not know whether or not these late materials in the test unit at its base represent a significant occupation of the big mound. A midden deposit was present in the northern, downslope end of the unit, starting only 3–5 cm below the surface (Table 2.1). Because it was near the surface, its upper portion was disturbed. The few Port Dauphin phase sherds that we found in this zone probably were intrusive from above.

We encountered a deeper, apparently undisturbed portion of this same midden at the northern end of the unit and removed it separately (upper midden). It featured abundant *Rangia cuneata* clam shells in a matrix of organic silty soil. Types and varieties of the Bottle Creek II phase (A.D. 1400–1550) and the Bear Point phase (A.D. 1550–1700) dominated the pottery from the deeper, undisturbed portion of this midden stratum. Either it represented a mixture of materials from two different occupations or it was a single transitional component. Considering the well-defined and apparently pristine nature of this part of the midden, the latter explanation

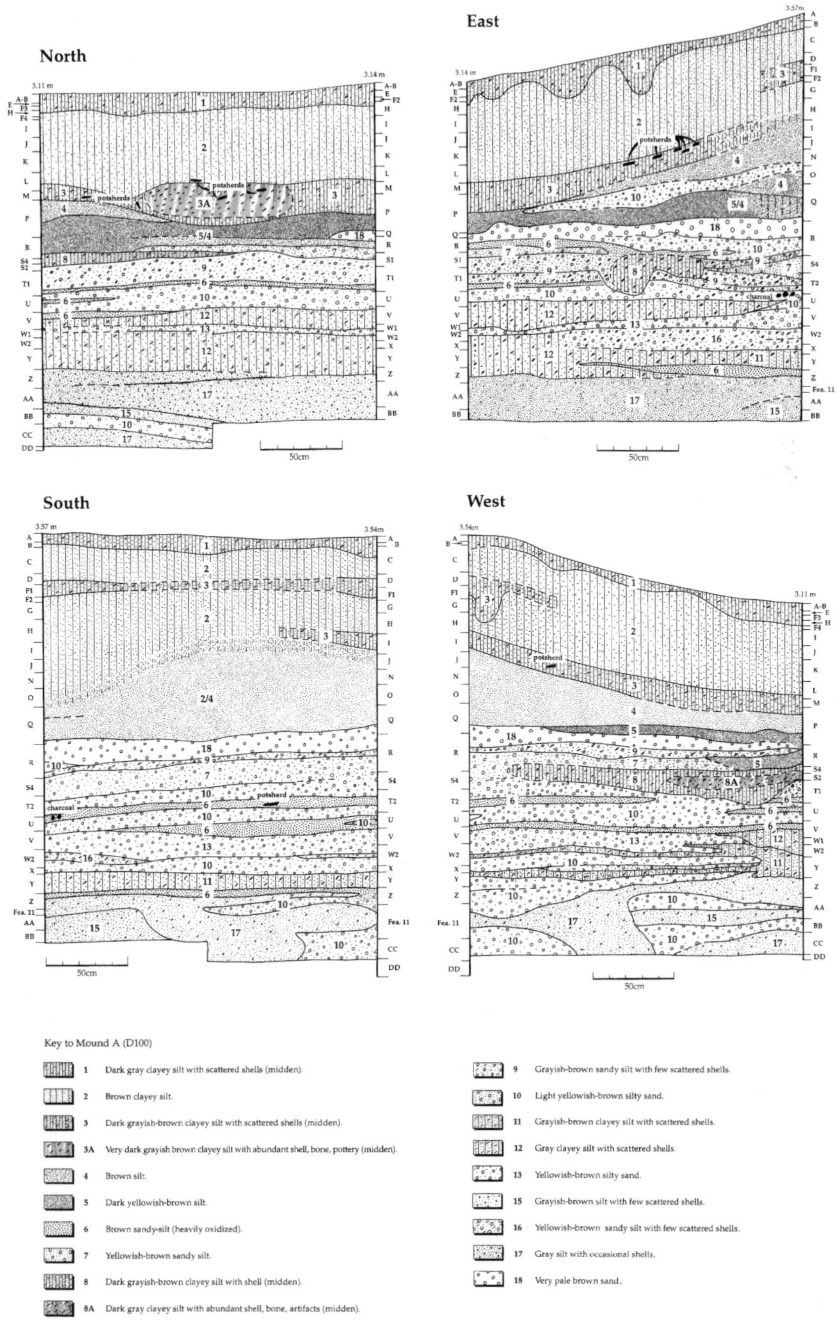

2.4. Section drawings of test unit D100, Mound A.

Table 2.1. Summary of Mound A middens, as represented in test unit D100 (Brown and Fuller 1999:Table 1)

Analysis Unit	Cultural Designation Based on Artifacts	Interesting Artifacts	Radiocarbon Dates (C13 Adjusted)	Soil Zones	Excavation Levels	Flotation Samples
Last Midden	Modern (20th century) and Port Dauphin Phase (A.D. 1650-1720s)			1	D100A D100B D100C D100D D100E	
Upper Midden	Very Early Bear Point Phase (Early to mid16th century)	Large Pensacola Inc., *var. Bear Point* Sherd with Stylized Skull Motif (Early Variant)		Upper 3	D100F3 D100F4	
Middle Midden	Early Bear Point Phase or Bottle Creek II Phase (15th or early-16th century)			Middle 3 (East, South, and West walls)	D100F1 D100F2	
Lower Midden	Early Bottle Creek II Phase (Late 14th or early 15th century)	Large Mound Place Inc. *var. Waltons Camp* Bowl and "Prayer Bowl"	A.D. 1370+/-60 (A.D. 1390+/-60)	Lower 3 and 3A	D100M D100M1 D100X3 D100EE	9
Pre-Mound Midden	Bottle Creek I Phase (A.D. 1250-1350/1400)	Mica, Cut Conch Shell Fragment, Embossed Copper	A.D. 1280+/-60 (A.D. 1320+/-60)	8 and 8A	D100S2 D100FF	10
Pre-Mound Deposits	Bottle Creek I Phase (A.D. 1250-1350/1400) Early Mississippian Andrews Place Phase (A.D. 1100-1250) Late Woodland Coden and/or Tate's Hammock Phases (A.D. 500-1100)			9, 11, 12, 15, and 17	D100W1	

seemed more likely. Further evidence of a transitional component was provided by a large pottery sherd that we found at the interface between the slope midden and an underlying construction zone. It is from the rim of a bowl decorated with an incised skull motif. Stylistically, the design is transitional between the highly abstract skulls often depicted on Bear Point phase vessels and the more naturalistic skulls that sometimes occur on Bottle Creek II phase bowls. Because the design was somewhat abstract and because skulls are more common for Bear Point phase vessels than for Bottle Creek II phase ones, I finally classified the sherd as Pensacola Incised, *var. Bear Point.* However, as I consider it an early version of that variety, the overlying midden dates to the early part of the Bear Point phase.

Below this latest slope midden was a non-midden zone consisting of brown to tan silty soil. Sherds were fairly abundant within this zone. However, rather than lying parallel to the slope, like the sherds in the overlying and underlying midden strata, they were oriented in all directions. Furthermore, the assemblage included types, varieties, and rim modes diagnostic of periods ranging from Late Woodland (Tate's Hammock or Coden phase) through late Bottle Creek II phase. I concluded the deposit represented a mound construction zone dating to the Bottle Creek II phase or early Bear Point phase. The earlier pottery was anachronistic, having been brought in with borrowed fill.

We uncovered another primary midden at the base of this late construction zone. The midden layer, including its shells and sherds, angled upslope and obviously was associated with the mound. In addition to the abundant shells and numerous animal and fish bones, it yielded a pottery assemblage dominated by Bottle Creek I and Bottle Creek II phase varieties. A number of attributes, including some rim shapes, are transitional between Bottle Creek I and Bottle Creek II modes. Charcoal from this slope midden yielded a radiocarbon date of A.D. 1370±60, C13-adjusted to 1390±60 (Appendix B). This date corresponds very well with the estimated time for the end of the Bottle Creek I phase and the beginning of the Bottle Creek II phase.

Immediately below this midden stratum we encountered a wedge-shaped zone of brown clayey silt that contained few artifacts. The composition and shape of this zone indicated it was a mound construction stage. In cross-section, it was truncated downslope by the juncture of the overlying midden with a sandy deposit. Within the excavation, this underlying sandy layer stratum was horizontal. Therefore, the overlying fill may represent the earliest building stage for Mound A, although earlier mound stages in the interior of the mound may be located beyond our excavation. This initial mound zone yielded a small assemblage of pottery dating to the Bottle Creek I phase and earlier.

Below this early construction stage we encountered a sequence of natural and cultural deposits that were oriented horizontally and thus appeared to predate the mound. They formed a series of alternating yellowish sand layers and grayish silt layers (Figure 2.5). The latter contained scattered rangia shells and sparse numbers of artifacts. Unlike the materials in the later slope middens, which tended to be oriented parallel to the slope, the few shells and sherds in these deeper strata were oriented haphazardly. The grayish silt layers also contained water-sorted patches of beige and yellowish sands. These characteristics suggested the cultural materials had been redeposited through erosion, perhaps from a nearby midden. The interleaving sandy layers indicated periodic flooding. They exhibited micro-layering, with coarse sands occurring near the bottom and finer sands toward the top. I believe each sand layer and its overlying silty deposit represents a major flooding episode. The scattered shells, bones, and artifacts were the result of the flood's impact on a nearby midden. The very small collection of sherds featured Andrews Place phase and Bottle Creek I phase markers.[1]

We encountered a small primary deposit within this premound sequence. A linear midden extended diagonally from the northwest corner to the center of the east wall. It contained dense concentrations of shells with bones and sherds in a matrix of dark gray clayey silt. It had a sharply defined edge to the northeast and tapered off more gradually to the southwest. This latter area, with its sparsely scattered shells and sherds, resembled the grayish bands described above. To the south, it merged unevenly with yellowish sand, indicating rushing water had washed out the edge. Although small, the pottery assemblage from this feature formed a tight Bottle Creek I phase assemblage. We obtained a radiocarbon date of A.D. 1280±60 (C13–adjusted to 1320±60) for this premound midden (Appendix B). This date falls well within the estimated time range for the Bottle Creek I phase.

The alternating sand/silt sequence continued below this early midden. The gray silty layers, with their scattered shells and artifacts, continued to produce assemblages of pottery dating to as early as the Tate's Hammock phase and as late as the Bottle Creek I phase. This chronological diversity lent support to our impression that these were secondary deposits that had eroded from a nearby midden.

Due to rushing groundwater, we ended the excavation about 2.1 m below the northern edge of the unit. The sand and silt layers continued to the bottom. Late Woodland and early shell-tempered sherds continued to be scattered among the sparse shells in the grayish silt layers. A number of markers, including early Plaquemine types, several Moundville Engraved sherds, and Kimmswick Fabric Impressed, indicate the deepest premound deposits date to the Bottle Creek I or Andrews Place phase. They also contained sand-tempered and grog-tempered sherds dating to

1. Douglas W. Haywick (1995) conducted an analysis of 11 sediment samples from the west wall of D100. His general conclusions were that the sediments represented in these samples were either water-lain (actual river deposits) or that they were partially sorted by running water. In the latter process, soil would have been dumped adjacent to a running stream, with the sediments having been partially reworked after they were deposited. Haywick actually favored the latter interpretation because it accounted for the small, abraded bits of pottery observed in most of the sediment samples. Because these pottery fragments were about the same grain size as the quartz sand that constituted most of the samples, significant sediment sorting had to have occurred. Apparently, rapidly flowing water passed through the site at regular intervals for the duration of the occupation represented by the D100 test. Such a situation would be expected from a site that flooded regularly (Brown 1995:7).

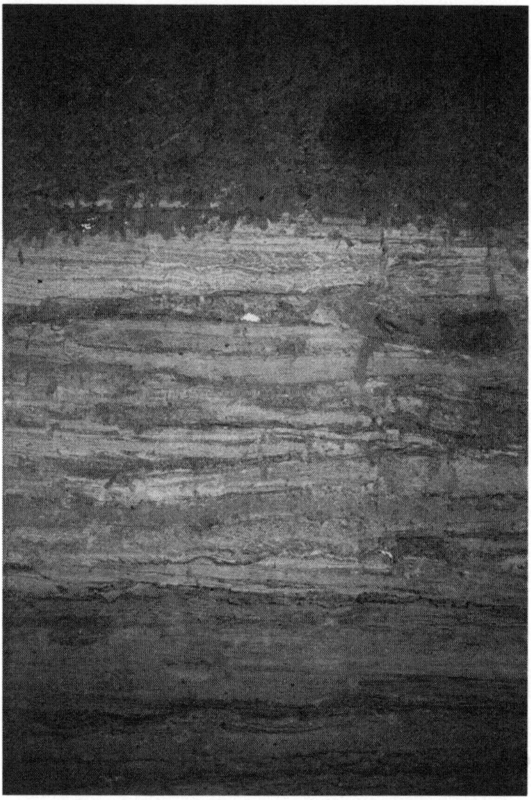

2.5. Close-up of the middle of the west wall, test unit D100, showing the thick band of alternating sand and silt layers (GCS/94/P7/4).

the Late Woodland period. The presence of Larto Red and the low frequency of Wakulla Check Stamped suggest this early assemblage relates to the Tate's Hammock phase (A.D. 500–800) rather than the later Coden phase. We obtained a radiocarbon date of A.D. 880±80 (C13-adjusted to A.D. 920±80) on charcoal from a small shell concentration near the base of the excavation. The determination probably represents an "average" date; that is, a mixing of carbon from two periods of occupation.

In summary, our excavations in mounds A and C produced a good sequence of pottery assemblages that represent much of the culture history of the Bottle Creek site. In addition to the chronological phases, the diverse decorative styles can be grouped into several distinctive series that may be keys to the origin and development of Pensacola culture. Each of these series comprises smaller constellations of decorative attributes that I have defined as style sets.

THE CERAMIC SET CONCEPT

Jeffrey P. Brain introduced the concept of the ceramic set to Southeastern archaeology in the reports on the excavations at the Winterville and Lake George sites in Mississippi (Brain 1989:80–89; Williams and Brain 1983:313–324). In those works, Brain defined the ceramic set as "a collection of ceramics that pertain to the postulated culture of a particular spatial-temporal locus and that share certain formal, nondecorative . . . modes" (Williams and Brain 1983:89). Sets were said to function as "integrative synthetic culture-historical units—neither strictly descriptive nor strictly interpretive" (Williams and Brain 1983:314). As conceived by Brain, a ceramic set consists of a group of varieties, usually of more than one type, that share a number of attributes of temper, paste, finish, and, secondarily, surface decoration or texturing. The unifying ware attributes correspond to a plainware variety (for example, *Reed*, *Addis*, or *Yazoo*) that lends its name to the set and that represents that set's membership in a regional ware tradition. Shared decorative attributes, collectively referred to as "decorative intent," indicate a particular set's relationship to a larger style tradition. Vessel shape is not a primary consideration when defining sets. However, varieties within a set may share some common shape attributes, indicating a limited number of vessel forms.

Members of a pottery set typically occur together in the same archaeological contexts where, conceivably, they could have been produced by a single group of potters during a relatively short period of time. Within the framework of a type-variety-mode classification, such sets can serve as important analytical tools for identifying archaeological components. They can be used to address a variety of topics ranging from regional integrative concerns to site-specific, primarily culture-historical questions (cf. Bitgood 1989; Brain 1988; Williams and Brain 1983).

Contemporary sets that are separated from one another by ware attributes but that exhibit related decorative attributes are termed parallel sets (Williams and Brain 1983:89–90). Parallel sets can cross-cut type when varieties of those types are distinguished by ware characteristics, but this is uncommon within a typology based largely on surface treatments. Two or more parallel sets can co-occur in the same archaeological context. However, the number of parallel sets that might be expected in a restricted provenience, such as a single house floor, necessarily will be small. This is because different sets tend to represent different functions or even different pottery traditions.

Some contemporary sets that co-occur in archaeological components do not exhibit parallel decorative attributes. These sets may represent different functional classes; as such they often are associated with different vessel forms and ware attributes as well as decoration. For many late prehistoric components in the southeastern United States, nonparallel contemporary sets tend to be related to the fineware/coarseware duality that characterizes most Mississippian assemblages. In these cases, the principal distinguishing characteristics are coarse shell versus fine shell tempering, unburnished surfaces versus burnished surfaces, and handled jars versus bottles, beakers, bowls, and plates. Examples at Winterville and Lake George are the various Yazoo sets versus the Holly Bluff and Greenville sets.

I propose that noncontemporary sets, which reflect developmental changes in shared decorative attributes, be termed "sequential sets." The presence of sequential sets at a site or at a localized cluster of sites indicates a strong local pottery tradition. When the same series of sequential sets occurs repeatedly throughout a contiguous region, a strong regional tradition is indicated. Examples of the latter in the Yazoo Basin are the Valley Park, Vicksburg, and Addis sets. Although the set definitions in that region are keyed to ware attributes, these sequential sets exhibit strong continuities in decorative styles. Similar sets occur in the same sequence throughout a large portion of the Lower Mississippi Valley, reflecting the widespread homogeneity of the Coles Creek pottery tradition. Two or more subsets may be differentiated within a set based on distinctive subclasses of decorative attributes (Williams and Brain 1983:89–90). Subsets can be entirely or partially contemporary or they can be chronologically sequential.

STYLE SETS AND STYLE SERIES AT BOTTLE CREEK

By increasing the relative importance of decorative attributes within the general ware classes, I isolated several potentially diagnostic pottery sets applicable to the collections from Bottle Creek (Figures 2.6 and 2.7). These groups can be termed "style sets." Style sets should prove to be more useful within the context of a typology that stresses attributes of decoration rather than ware for separating varieties. In addition to identifying components, phases, and cultures, they can have great utility for interpreting the roles of style traditions and horizons in material culture change. They are especially well suited to analyses of stylistically complex assemblages from regions like the Mobile-Tensaw Delta that are situated in borderland zones of overlapping style traditions.

I segregated style sets for Bottle Creek based on distinctive clusters of decorative traits. Because they are keyed to decoration, these sets are not tied to variety-specific ware attributes and therefore are not designated by plainware variety names. Rather, they are grouped and identified so as to reflect postulated relationships to regional style traditions, style horizons, and cultures. Within a series, culturally related sets that are neither

Principal Pottery Series at the Bottle Creek Site
ca. A.D. 750 to A.D. 1750

Weeden Island Series	Lower Miss. Valley Series	Moundville Series	Pensacola Series	Gulf Historic Series
Weeden Island A Set	Coles Creek A Set	Saltpan 1 Subset	Saltpan 2 Subset	Gulf Historic Set
Carrabelle Incised	Alligator Incised	Kimmswick Fabric Imp.	Salt Creek Cane Imp.	Barataria Incised
Carrabelle Punctated	Avoyelles Punctated	Moundville A Set	Pensacola A1 Subset	Chicot Red
Keith Incised	Coles Creek Incised	Carthage Incised	D'Olive Incised	Fatherland Incised
St. Petersburg Incised	Evansville Punctated	Mound Place Incised	*var. D'Olive*	Owens Punctated
Tucker Ridge Pinched	Harrison Bayou Incised	*var. Akron*	*var. Dominic*	*var. Muir*
Weeden Island Incised	Hollyknowe Pinched	Moundville Engraved	*var. Mary Ann*	Port Dauphin Incised
Weeden Island Punctated	Mazique Incised	Moundville B Set	*var. Shell Banks*	
Weeden Island B Set	Coles Creek B Set	Moundville Incised	Mound Place Incised	
Alachua Cob Marked	Larto Red	*var. Carrollton*	*var. Bon Secour*	
Furrs Cord Marked*	Mulberry Cr. Cord Marked*	*var. Moundville*	*var. McMillan*	
Wakulla Check Stamped	Pontchartrain Check St.	*var. Snows Bend*	*var. Waltons Camp*	
	Plaquemine A Set		Pensacola Incised	
	Anna Incised		*var. Gasque*	
	Carter Engraved		*var. Holmes*	
	Coleman Incised		*var. Jessamine*	
	L'eau Noire Incised		*var. Louis Lake*	
	Plaquemine B Set		Pensacola A2 Subset	
	Plaquemine Brushed		D'Olive Incised	
	Plaquemine C Set		*var. Arnica*	
	Leland Incised		Pensacola Incised	
	Maddox Engraved		*var. Bear Point*	
	Miss. Valley Coarseware Set		*var. Pensacola*	
	Barton Incised		*var. Perdido Bay*	
	Grace Brushed		*var. Rutherford*	
	Old Town Red		Pensacola B1 Subset	
	Owens Punctated (early)		Middle River Incised	
	Parkin Punctated		Moundville Incised	
	Pouncey Pinched		*var. Bottle Creek*	
	Winterville Incised		Pensacola B2 Subset	
			Moundville Incised	
			var. Douglas	

*Cord marking represents early subsets within the Coles Creek B and Weeden Island B sets. Red filmed types (Larto and Weeden Island Red) probably belong with these subsets as well.

2.6. Principal pottery series at the Bottle Creek site, ca. A.D. 750–1750.

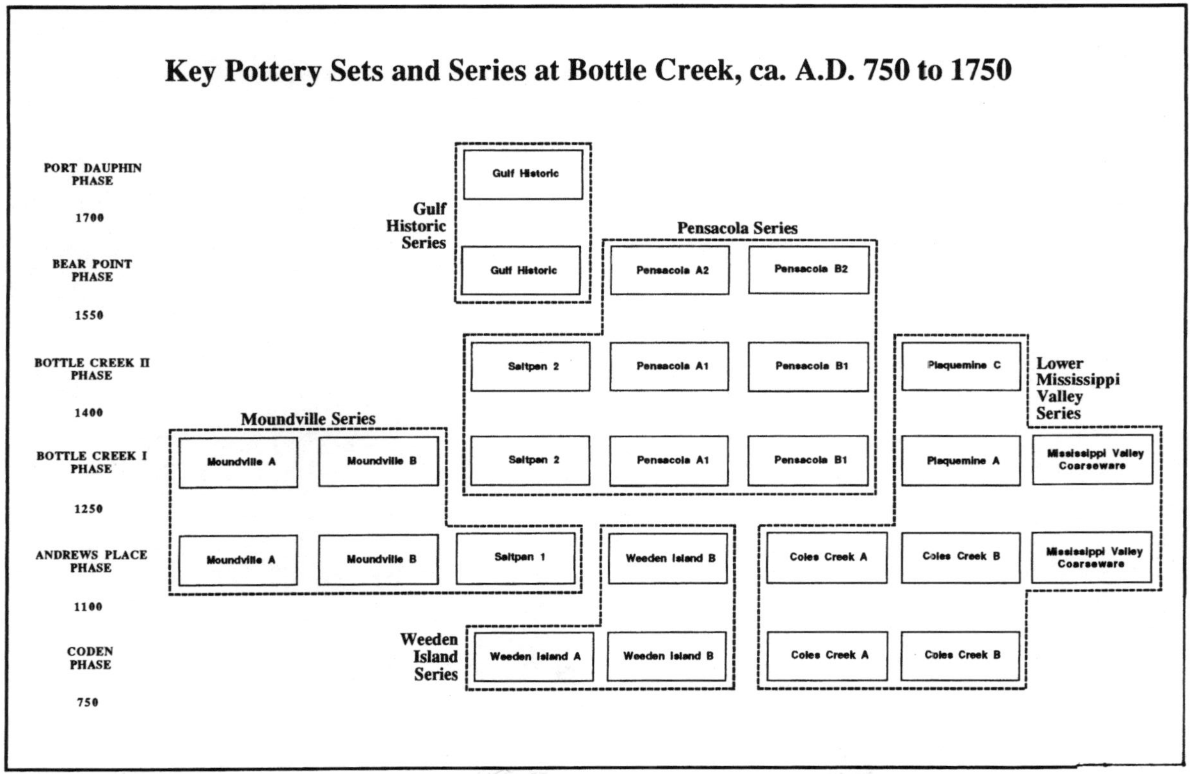

2.7. Key pottery sets and series at the Bottle Creek site, ca. A.D. 750–1750.

parallel nor sequential are designated by letters (Weeden Island A and Weeden Island B, for example). Sequential or parallel subsets are given numbers (Saltpan 1, Saltpan 2; Pensacola A1, Pensacola A2).

Weeden Island A Set

The Weeden Island A set is characterized by rectilinear arrangements of incisions, punctations, or pinching on well-made vessels that are tempered with sand. Bowls and jars with well-finished rims are typical of this set. As it is presently defined, the Weeden Island A set spans much of the Late Woodland period. I have not defined sequential subsets within this set because of the current lack of variety-level resolution within the types. However, a related subset features the complex and largely curvilinear decorations represented by the types Weeden Island Incised and Weeden Island Punctated. This subset was not present in the Mound A collection and was poorly represented in Mound C. I believe this paucity is due to the generally small numbers of Late Woodland period sherds recovered from the excavations. We have found Weeden Island Incised and Weeden Island Punctated sherds in small numbers at other sites in this part of the Mobile-Tensaw Delta (Fuller and Brown 1998:Table 72).

Weeden Island B Set

The Weeden Island B set comprises the sand-tempered, surface-textured pottery in Late Woodland period components at Bottle Creek. Although cob marking and cord marking are included, check stamping dominates this set, especially late in the period. Weeden Island Red, which also features an overall surface treatment, probably should be included as well. Because cord marking and red filming appear to be more common earlier in the Late Woodland period, the Weeden Island B set may be divided into two chronological subsets in the future.

Coles Creek A Set

The Coles Creek A set represents stylistic influences from the Lower Mississippi Valley during the Late Woodland and Early Mississippi periods. Many of its members are grog-tempered counterparts to the sand-tempered ceramics of the Weeden Island A set. In fact, Coles Creek A and Weeden Island A can be considered parallel sets. The overriding stylistic attribute for both is a design on the upper part of the vessel exterior featuring linear arrangements of incisions, punctations, or pinching. The Coles Creek A set almost certainly comprises two or more sequential subsets. I have not subdivided it here due to a problem with sorting the latest varieties of the constituent types (*Hardy*, *Manchac*, etc.) from the earlier varieties as they occur in the Mobile area. In that area, the late varieties tend to occur on Baytown Plain ware rather than the Addis Plain that distinguishes them in the Natchez Bluffs and Lower Yazoo Basin. Variations in secondary attributes, such as wet-paste incision and less careful decoration, are apparent for some of the later varieties at Bottle Creek. So far, however, I have found it difficult to sort them consistently based solely on these traits.

Coles Creek B Set

The Coles Creek B set is characterized by grog-tempered pottery featuring overall surface treatments such as check stamping, cord marking, and red filming. As with the Weeden Island B set, cord marking (Mulberry Creek Cord Marked) and red painting (Larto Red) are more at home in the Tate's Hammock phase, with check stamping becoming more common in the later Coden phase. The latter tends to be similar to *Pacaniere*, a well-made, Wakulla-like variety of Pontchartrain Check Stamped that was recognized originally at the Morgan site on the Louisiana coast (Fuller and Fuller 1987).

Plaquemine A Set

The Plaquemine A set is a local stylistic counterpart to Brain's Greenville set in the Lower Yazoo region. As in that area, Carter Engraved and L'Eau Noire Incised in the Mobile-Tensaw Delta form a special pottery complex with implications of far-ranging contacts. At Bottle Creek, they occur on shell-tempered ware as well as grog-tempered ware. For these specimens, the ware clearly is Bell Plain rather than Addis Plain. The same probably is true for Anna Incised from the site. Some of the sherds I have classified as D'Olive Engraved sherds may be shell-tempered Anna Incised and therefore belong to this set. However, D'Olive Engraved survives at Bottle Creek well after the other members of the Plaquemine A set have disappeared, eventually evolving into the Pensacola type D'Olive Incised. The situation is complicated further by the occurrence of interior engraved pottery at the Moundville site. When I initially defined style sets for the Bottle Creek collections, I included interior engraved specimens with the Moundville A set. However, many of them could be included with the Plaquemine A set just as easily. Because of this uncertainty, I took a more conservative approach and excluded D'Olive Engraved from my sets/series analyses. The vertical distributions of interior decorated ceramics from mounds A and C do show a strong trend. D'Olive Engraved (or interior Moundville Engraved, or whatever one wishes to call it) was most popular with the earlier Mississippian potters at Bottle Creek, declining in favor of D'Olive Incised in later phases (Figure 2.8).

Plaquemine B Set

The Plaquemine B set comprises a single type, Plaquemine Brushed. Although it occurs only rarely in earlier Mississippian components at Bottle Creek, the overall surface texturing of this type is so different from the decorations of the Plaquemine A set that I have separated it out here. It is the Plaquemine equivalent to the earlier Coles Creek B set. Exactly how it fits in the sequence is not known, so the set is not included in Figure 2.7. I suspect that it relates to the Bottle Creek I phase (A.D. 1250–1400).

Plaquemine C Set

The Plaquemine C set is characterized by sweeping curvilinear motifs composed of broad, trailed incisions. The principal constituents are Leland Incised and Maddox Engraved, both of which occur in small numbers at Bottle Creek. As with the Plaquemine A set, the associated ware usually is Bell Plain. Because there can be some sorting difficulties between these types and Carthage Incised and Pensacola Incised, this late Plaquemine-related set probably has been underrepresented somewhat in the Bottle Creek analysis. Even so, it is apparent that Lower Mississippi Valley influences on Bottle Creek potters continued, though those influences steadily weakened, from the Coden phase to the Bottle Creek II phase.

Mississippi Valley Coarseware Set

The Mississippi Valley Coarseware set features vessels bearing the wet-paste decorations of the types Barton Incised, Grace Brushed, Owens Punctated, Parkin Punctated, Pouncey Pinched, and Winterville Incised. Although these types occur only in small numbers at Bottle Creek, they represent an important complex associated with the site's earliest Mississippian residents. In the Mound A test excavation, the Mississippi Valley Coarseware set was confined to the deepest premound deposits, along with the Moundville A and Plaquemine A sets.

Moundville A Set

The Moundville A set is a key element of the Moundville-related pottery complex at Bottle Creek. It represents the fineware half of the classic fineware/coarseware Mississippian ceramic duad as it is manifested in Moundville culture. The principal decorated types are Carthage Incised,

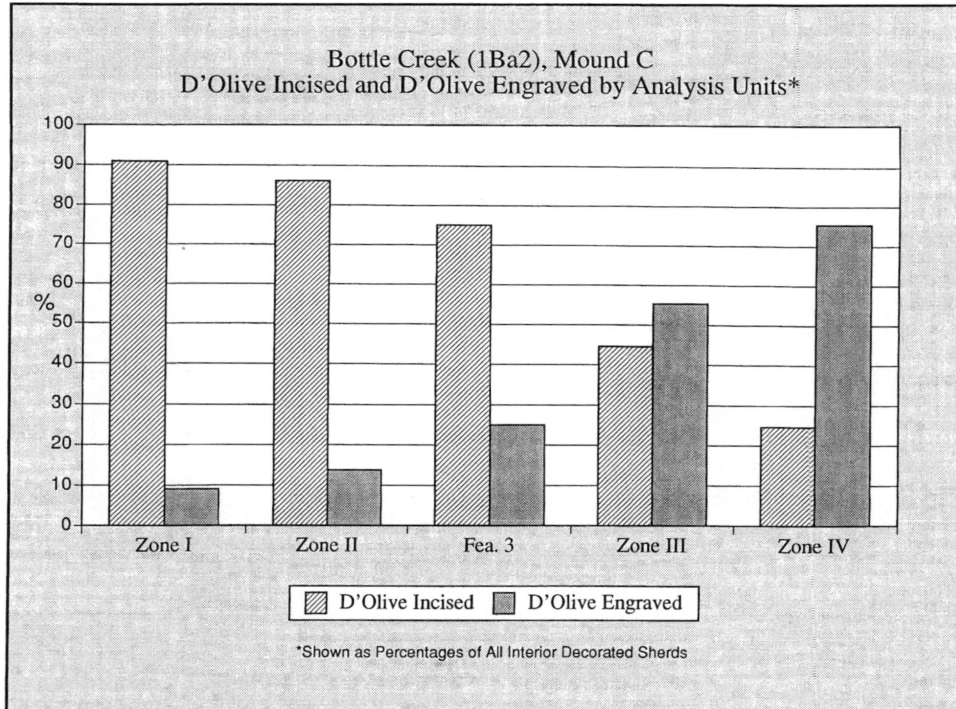

2.8. D'Olive Incised and D'Olive Engraved in the Mound C excavations, arranged by analysis units, with deeper deposits to the right.

Mound Place Incised, *var. Akron,* and Moundville Engraved. Ware attributes feature fine shell tempering. At Bottle Creek, some specimens occur on ware that might be classified as Bell Plain, *var. Hale.* However, many more exhibit local attributes that are not compatible with *var. Hale* as it is defined in the Moundville area. Black filming is an important secondary surface treatment, although it is not as common in southwestern Alabama as it is to the north. Accompanying vessel shapes are bowls, beakers, and bottles. Some of the interior engraved plate fragments that I have classified as D'Olive Engraved may belong with this set.

Moundville B Set

The Moundville B set is the coarseware parallel to Moundville A. The two are contemporary nonparallel sets within the Moundville series. The Moundville B set comprises Moundville Incised, *vars. Carrollton, Moundville,* and *Snows Bend.* At Bottle Creek, these varieties occasionally are associated with a ware resembling Mississippi Plain, *var. Warrior* in the Moundville culture area. However, most specimens occur on a local ware that I have defined as Mississippi Plain, *var. Devils Bend.* Apparently, the residents of Bottle Creek were importing few of these utilitarian jars.

It is significant that the great majority of *Moundville* sherds in the Mobile area feature short rays embellishing the arches rather than the long rays that are typical of Moundville I phase pots to the north. Furthermore, *Snows Bend* is much more common in the Mobile area than in the Moundville area. The punctate-bordered arch, which characterizes both *var. Bottle Creek* and *var. Snows Bend* (with their grog-tempered cognates to the west and sand/grit-tempered equivalents to the east), almost can be said to be a hallmark of Gulf Coast Mississippian culture. Thus, it was with some reluctance that I included *Snows Bend* with the Moundville B set. In future studies, this variety may be shifted to the Pensacola B1 subset where it will join Moundville Incised, *var. Bottle Creek* and Middle River Incised. Both of these are good markers of Pensacola culture.

Saltpan 1 Subset

The Saltpan 1 subset comprises the type Kimmswick Fabric Impressed (Chapter 10). My analyses of the pottery from mounds A and C clearly showed that fabric impressed utility vessels of the kind often referred to as saltpans are associated most strongly with the earliest Mississippian residents of Bottle Creek. The heavy utility pan of choice for later Pensacola peoples was the mat impressed type Salt Creek Cane Impressed. Farther north, Kimmswick Fabric Impressed, *var. Langston* dominates the heavy utility pan complexes at Moundville sites, as well as at Mississippian sites in the Tennessee Valley. By contrast, mat impressed pans are rare in those areas.

Saltpan 2 Subset

The Saltpan 2 subset, which contains the single type Salt Creek Cane Impressed, is partly or entirely sequential to the Saltpan 1 subset. For southwestern Alabama, it is one of the better markers of Pensacola culture. The salt springs in southern Clarke County feature dense concentrations of broken Salt Creek Cane Impressed vessels, undoubtedly representing discarded saltpans. Their presence at many other sites located well south of the salines suggests the heavy, basin-shaped vessels served other functions in addition to making salt. Postulated uses include dough pans, hearth liners, or Dutch ovens. The last possibility is intriguing. A number of Salt Creek Cane Impressed rim sherds from Bottle Creek have thickened lips with very wide, very flat, horizontal top surfaces. If vessels with such rims were inverted over similar vessels, the result might be a very serviceable Dutch oven.

Pensacola A1 Subset

The Pensacola A1 set, although manifesting some stylistic ties to Moundville, is a true component of Gulf Coast Mississippian culture. It subsumes the earlier varieties of D'Olive Incised, Pensacola Incised, and Mound Place Incised (except *var. Akron*). The stylistic attributes that separate the Pensacola A1 set from the Moundville A set include the following: the absence of trailed incision; minimal use of black filming; the absence of engraving except as cross-hatched or hatched fillers within incised zones; a greater frequency of interior incising; and a predominance of the horizontal hand-eye motif over all other SECC (Southeastern Ceremonial Complex) designs. In addition to these decorative attributes, a number of distinctively Pensacola vessel shapes, rim modes, and rim effigy styles are associated with this set. The typical vessel forms are bowls, plates, and wide-mouth bottles.

Pensacola B1 Subset

The Pensacola B1 subset is a coarseware contemporary of the Pensacola A1 subset. It comprises two classes of utilitarian jar: Middle River Incised and Moundville Incised, *var. Bottle Creek*. The latter is extremely common in prehistoric Pensacola components. Typically, it forms the largest single decorated category in Pensacola assemblages, especially those dating to the Bottle Creek II phase. As noted in my discussion of the Moundville B set, I have some doubts about including *Snows Bend* with that set rather than the Pensacola B1 subset. Analysis of the mounds A and C pottery collections suggests *Snows Bend* is present in the Andrews Place, Bottle Creek I, and Bottle Creek II phases. However, its popularity seems to peak during the Bottle Creek I phase, later than *Moundville* and earlier than *Bottle Creek.*

Pensacola A2 Subset

The Pensacola A2 subset is sequential to Pensacola A1. It represents the final and most distinctive expression of the Pensacola decorative style. The set includes the latest varieties of D'Olive Incised and Pensacola Incised, varieties that are excellent markers of the protohistoric Bear Point phase. The bowls, wide-mouth bottles, plates, and beakers of the Pensacola A1 subset continue in this subset, but a new vessel form has been added: the collared subglobular jar. In addition, rim effigies have all but disappeared by this time.

Pensacola B2 Subset

The Pensacola B2 subset is the coarseware partner of the Pensacola A2 subset and is sequential to Pensacola B1. It comprises a single class of decorated coarseware jar, Moundville Incised, *var. Douglas.* This protohistoric variety is the final manifestation of the venerable line of arch-decorated jars that began in the Moundville region five to six centuries earlier. By the Protohistoric period, the incisions have become sloppy and the placement of punctations more haphazard. Curiously enough, all variations of the arch decoration either continued or were revived with *var. Douglas*, including unembellished, short rays, single rows of punctations, and double rows of punctations. A new treatment consisted of clusters of punctations above the junctures of the arches.

Gulf Historic Set

The Gulf Historic set is the local expression of the Gulf Historic tradition (Fuller 1998:32–38). Shortly after the start of the French colonial era, simple bowls with simple rims increasingly dominated pottery complexes in the southern Lower Mississippi Valley and along the north-central Gulf Coast. Most of these featured a well-consolidated paste, very fine tempering, and smooth surfaces. Many were decorated by sweeping curvilinear designs composed of parallel-line incisions. Typical motifs include scrolls, meanders, and triskeles. By the first quarter of the eighteenth century, numerous Native American pottery assemblages in the Natchez region, the southern Mississippi Delta, the extreme Lower Yazoo Basin, the Mississippi Gulf Coast, and southwestern Alabama featured such bowls. At the same time, the jars, plates, bottles, and beakers of the Late Mississippi and Protohistoric periods waned in popularity, perhaps due to the availability of European metal and ceramic substitutes. Additional attributes of this Early Historic period pottery tradition include red filming and "colono" features, such as European-styles handles and ring bases.

In the Mobile area, the principal marker for Gulf Historic tradition is the parallel-line decorated type Port Dauphin Incised, which is tempered with very fine shell. Other, less common types with similar decorations are Fatherland Incised (fine-grog- or mixed-grog-tempered) and Barataria Incised (fine-sand-tempered). Late varieties of Chicot Red and Owens Punctated are additional minor markers of the Gulf Historic tradition in the area. When analyzing the pottery collections for mounds A and C at Bottle Creek, I grouped all of these into a single Gulf Historic style set.

THE ANALYSIS

After classifying all of the pottery from the Mound A and Mound C test excavations, I tabulated them by chronological phases and keyed them to the excavation levels and analysis units (Tables 2.2–2.5). I also examined the distributions of key rim modes (Tables 2.6 and 2.7), while Hunter Johnson analyzed the vessel shape classes (Chapter 8). To investigate the roles of the various local and non-local pottery traditions in the ceramic history of the Bottle Creek site, I combined the sets into several broad style series. The Weeden Island series includes the Weeden A and B sets; the Lower Mississippi Valley series comprises the Coles Creek A and B sets, the Plaquemine A–C sets, and the Mississippi Valley Coarseware set; the Moundville series contains the Moundville A and B sets and the Saltpan 1 subset; the Pensacola series encompasses the Pensacola A1, A2, B1, and B2 subsets and the Saltpan 2 subset; and the Gulf Historic series includes the single Gulf Historic set. Note that there is no Fort Walton series or set. This is because Fort Walton pottery is so scarce at Bottle Creek that it is virtually invisible statistically. This fact alone is strong evidence that the umbilical hyphen which for so long linked Pensacola and Fort Walton was never an accurate reflection of their true relationship. Despite sharing a limited number of shape and decoration attributes late in their histories, the two were largely independent coastal variants of Mississippian culture.

After severing Pensacola from its former Siamese twin once and for all, the next task was to assess its more familial relationship to Moundville culture. I analyzed the coarseware and fineware classes separately, plotting the distributions of the various style sets and style series by stratigraphic zones. This analysis was relatively easy for Mound A, which contained dis-

Table 2.2. Mound A, test unit (D100): decorated "Fineware" pottery sets and subsets by zone

	Zone I	Zone II	Zone III	Zone IV	Zone V	Zone VI	Zone VII	Zone VIII	Total
Gulf Historic									
Barataria Incised		2							2
Fatherland Incised		1	1						2
Port Dauphin Incised	13	6	6						25
Subtotal	13	9	7						29
Pensacola A2									
Penscola Incised									
var. Bear Point	1	5							6
var. Pensacola		1							1
var. Perdido Bay		2							2
var. Rutherford		1							1
Subtotal	1	9							10
Pensacola A1									
D'Olive Incised									
var. Dominic			7		2		3	3	15
var. Mary Ann			3						3
Mound Place Incised									
var. Bon Secour		1	3						4
var. McMillan		3	12	2	1			1	19
var. Waltons Camp		7	33	8	1	1		1	51
Pensacola Incised									
var. Gasque		3	13	8					24
var. Holmes			10						10
var. Jessamine			7	7	7		5		26
Subtotal		14	88	25	11	1	8	5	152
Moundville A									
Carthage Incised		2	5					1	8
Mound Place Incised									
var. Akron					1				1
Moundville Engraved			20	1	3	1	7	12	44
Subtotal		2	25	1	4	1	7	13	53
Plaquemine C									
Leland Incised			2					1	3
Maddox Engraved		2	3						5
Subtotal		2	5					1	8
Plaquemine A									
Anna Incised					3			2	5
Carter Engraved			11		3			4	18
L'Eau Noire Incised								1	1
Subtotal			11		6			7	24

crete cultural strata (Tables 2.2 and 2.3). Zone I was the superficial soil that overlay Zone II, the uppermost slope midden. Zone III was the underlying construction stage. Zone IV corresponded to the earlier slope midden. Zone V was the earliest construction stage. Zone VI included the latest series of premound secondary midden deposits and interleaving flood strata. Zone VII was the premound primary midden. Zone VIII comprised the deepest series of secondary midden deposits and flood layers.

The clearest trends were evident for the primary midden deposits of Zones II, IV, and VII. Not surprisingly, Zones III, V, and VI, representing either borrowed fill or redeposited midden, showed no consistent trend except that each contained elements of earlier series. Therefore, I have excluded them from the graphs in Figures 2.9 and 2.10. Because Zones I

(Table 2.2 continued)

	Zone I	Zone II	Zone III	Zone IV	Zone V	Zone VI	Zone VII	Zone VIII	Total
Coles Creek A									
Alligator Incised			1						1
Avoyelles Punctated	1								1
Coles Creek Incised			1		1			4	6
Evansville Punctated								1	1
Harrison Bayou Incised								1	1
Mazique Incised			2	1	1				4
Subtotal	1		4	1	2			6	14
Coles Creek B									
Larto Red								2	2
Subtotal								2	2
Weeden Island A									
Carrabelle Incised					1				1
Carrabelle Punctated								2	2
St. Petersburg Incised								1	1
Subtotal					1			3	4
Weeden Island B									
Alachua Cob Marked								1	1
Furrs Cord Marked					1				1
Wakulla Check Stamped					1				1
Subtotal					2			1	3
Total	15	34	142	27	26	2	15	38	299

Note: Primary Analysis Units are Zones I, II, IV, VII, and VIII.
Zone I (Levels A–E): Humus/Slopewash
Zone II (Levels F1–F4): Slope Midden
Zone III (Levels G–L): Mound Loading
Zone IV (Levels M–M1): Slope Midden
Zone V (Levels N–P): Mound Loading
Zone VI (Levels Q–S1): Flooding
Zone VII (Level S2): Submound Midden
Zone VIII (Levels S4–GG): Submound Midden/Flooding

and VIII represent the latest and earliest deposits, respectively, I included them in the analyses. Although they also show the effects of their less-than-pristine contexts, the trends noted for the primary midden zones continue in each.

As expected, the Gulf Historic series shows a dramatic peak in the uppermost zone. The nearly perfect distributions of the Pensacola series are impressive for both the coarsewares and the finewares. The latter, which comprise the Pensacola A1 and A2 subsets, form a classic popularity curve. Also impressive is the seemingly abrupt appearance of the Moundville series in the deepest levels and its gradual waning in the succeeding zones. The Weeden Island, Coles Creek, and early Plaquemine types clearly were associated with the deepest premound levels.

The frequency distributions for Mound A seemed almost too good to be true. Therefore, I decided to check them against the larger pottery collection from Mound C, even though it lacked the discrete stratigraphic zones of Mound A (Tables 2.4 and 2.5; Figures 2.11 and 2.12). First, I combined

Table 2.3. Mound A, test unit (D100): decorated "Coarseware" pottery sets and subsets by zone

	Zone I	Zone II	Zone III	Zone IV	Zone V	Zone VI	Zone VII	Zone VIII	Total
Pensacola B2									
Moundville Incised									
var. Douglas		4							4
Subtotal		4							4
Pensacola B1									
Middle River Incised		1	5		2		2		10
Moundville Incised									
var. Bottle Creek		4	24	9	8	3	15	6	69
Subtotal		5	29	9	10	3	17	6	79
Moundville B									
Moundville Incised									
var. Carrollton			2			1			3
var. Moundville				1		1		6	8
var. Snows Bend			4	1	3		4		12
Subtotal			6	2	3	2	4	6	23
Mississippi Valley Coarseware									
Barton Incised								2	2
Grace Brushed			1					1	2
Old Town Red			1						1
Owens Punctated						1			1
Pouncey Pinched						1			1
Winterville Incised					1				1
Subtotal			2		1	2		3	8
Saltpan 2									
Salt Creek Cane Impressed		2	8	4	3	1	9	6	33
Subtotal		2	8	4	3	1	9	6	33
Saltpan 1									
Kimmswick Fabric Impressed			1					3	4
Subtotal			1					3	4
Total		11	46	15	17	8	30	24	151

Note: Primary Analysis Units are Zones I, II, IV, VII, and VIII.
Zone I (Levels A–E): Humus/Slopewash
Zone II (Levels F1–F4): Slope Midden
Zone III (Levels G–L): Mound Loading
Zone IV (Levels M–M1): Slope Midden
Zone V (Levels N–P): Mound Loading
Zone VI (Levels Q–S1): Flooding
Zone VII (Level S2): Submound Midden
Zone VIII (Levels S4–GG): Submound Midden/Flooding

the excavated levels into larger analysis units as follows: Zone I, from the surface to the top of the undisturbed shell midden deposits; Zone II, from the top of the undisturbed midden to the top of Feature 3, the dark layer of extremely rich midden; Zone III, from the base of Feature 3 to the top of Feature 17, the large wall trench; and Zone IV, the midden deposits next to the wall trench and continuing to the bottom of the unit.

These Mound C zones produced frequency distributions of the style series that virtually duplicate those for Mound A. Again, the steady replacement of Moundville styles by Pensacola styles is obvious for both the finewares and the coarsewares. The full-blown introduction of the Moundville series and the smooth, unimodal distribution of the Pensacola finewares are repeated. Also repeated are the early clustering of the Weeden

Table 2.4. Mound C, test unit (C100): decorated "Fineware" pottery sets and subsets by level

	Zone 1			Zone II				Zone III					Zone IV					
	A	B	C–D	E	F	G	H	I	J	K	L	M	N	O	P	Q–R	S–T	Total
Gulf Historic																		
Barataria Incised	1																	1
Chicot Red	4	3	1															8
Owens Punctated																		
var. Muir	2																	2
Port Dauphin Incised	55	37	4	1														97
Subtotal	62	40	5	1														108
Pensacola A2																		
Penscola Incised																		
var. Bear Point	1	1		1														3
var. Pensacola	4	1																5
Subtotal	5	2		1														8
Pensacola A1																		
D'Olive Incised																		
var. D'Olive			1					7	2									10
var. Dominic	2	2			1	2	2	10	4	7	3	1	1		1	1		37
var. Mary Ann	3	1	1		4	13	3			2	8		1	3	5	1	1	46
var. Shell Banks								1						1				2
Mound Place Incised																		
var. Bon Secour				1														1
var. McMillan	4	3			7	23	2	8	2	1								50
var. Waltons Camp		2	1	7	9	8	1	13	13	7	4		3		4			72
Pensacola Incised																		
var. Gasque	6	8	6	12	2	1												35
var. Holmes		2	1	2	5	4	1	10	1	1								27
var. Jessamine	1			8	7	23	9	26	6	1	3							84
var. Louis Lake			1	1														2
Subtotal	16	18	11	31	35	74	18	75	28	19	18	1	5	4	10	2	1	366
Moundville A																		
Carthage Incised							1	1			2	6	1	3		2	7	23
Mound Place Incised																		
var. Akron					1				1			2	7					11
Moundville Engraved	1			2	13	11	2	22	35	16	16	5	6	9	6	5		149
Subtotal	1			2	14	11	3	23	36	16	18	13	14	12	6	7	7	183
Plaquemine C																		
Leland Incised					8	3										1		12
Subtotal					8	3										1		12
Plaquemine A																		
Carter Engraved						2										2		4
Coleman Incised														1				1
L'Eau Noire Incised	2				1				1			1	11	1	5			22
Subtotal	2				1	2			1			1	11	2	5	2		27
Plaquemine B																		
Plaquemine Brushed														1				1
Subtotal														1				1
Coles Creek A																		
Avoyelles Punctated														2				2
Coles Creek Incised										2						1	1	4
Mazique Incised	2						1											3
Subtotal	2						1			2				2		1	1	9
Weeden Island A																		
Carrabelle Punctated														1	1		3	5
Keith Incised																1		1
St. Petersburg Incised																	1	1
Weeden Island Incised																	3	3
Subtotal														1	1	1	7	10
Weeden Island B																		
Wakulla Check Stamped																	1	1
Subtotal																	1	1
Total	88	60	16	35	58	90	22	98	65	37	36	15	30	22	22	14	17	725

Table 2.5. Mound C, test unit (C100): decorated "Coarseware" pottery sets and subsets by level

	Zone 1			Zone II				Zone III					Zone IV					
	A	B	C–D	E	F	G	H	I	J	K	L	M	N	O	P	Q–R	S–T	Total
Pensacola B2																		
Moundville Incised																		
var. Douglas	7	7	2															16
Subtotal	7	7	2															16
Pensacola B1																		
Middle River Incised					2	2	3	15	8	14	7	1	8	2			1	63
Moundville Incised																		
var. Bottle Creek	13	4	6	21	23	38	11	19	17	7	12	7	8	3			4	193
Subtotal	13	4	6	21	25	40	14	34	25	21	19	8	16	5			5	256
Moundville B																		
Moundville Incised																		
var. Carrollton				4	2	8			1					2	1			18
var. Moundville						1		4	9	9	7	13	18	27	7	8	13	116
var. Snows Bend	4		1	9	4	9	4	10	12	18	11	11	11	3	9	3	7	126
Subtotal	4		1	13	6	18	4	14	22	27	18	24	29	32	17	11	20	260
Mississippi Valley Coarseware																		
Barton Incised								3						1				4
Old Town Red			1	1														2
Owens Punctated (early)				1					1	1	1				1			5
Parkin Punctated		1									6	1						8
Subtotal		1	1	2				3	1	1	7	1		1	1			19
Saltpan 2																		
Salt Creek Cane Impressed	1	1	4	5	18	20	2	3	12	6	4	1	9	1		1	1	89
Subtotal	1	1	4	5	18	20	2	3	12	6	4	1	9	1		1	1	89
Saltpan 1																		
Kimmswick Fabric Impressed					1						3	6	5	6	5	3	8	37
Subtotal					1						3	6	5	6	5	3	8	37
Total	25	13	14	41	50	78	20	54	60	55	51	40	59	45	23	15	34	677

Table 2.6. Mound A, test unit (D100): key rim modes by level and zone

Levels	D	F1	F2	F3	F4	G	H	I	J	K	L	M	M1	N	O	P	S2	T2	U	V	Y	Total
Rim Modes																						
"Bear Point"	2		1		1																	4
"Beckum"									1		1				1				1		1	5
"D'Olive"	1		1	2	1		3		2	1	1	4	1			1						18
"Dominic"		1						3	3		3	1		1			2	1	1	1		17
"Douglas"		1																				1
"Gasque"		6		1	5	2	2	6	1	3	4	4	1			1						36
"Jessamine"		1		1		1	4			2	4	2			1							16
Scalloped							1															1
Total	3	9	2	4	7	3	10	9	7	6	13	11	2	1	2	2	2	1	2	1	1	98

Zones	I	II	III	IV	V	VI	VII	VIII	Total
Rim Modes									
"Bear Point"	2	2							4
"Beckum"			2		1			2	5
"D'Olive"	1	4	7	5	1				18
"Dominic"		1	9	1	1		2	3	17
"Douglas"		1							1
"Gasque"		12	18	5	1				36
"Jessamine"		2	11	2	1				16
Scalloped			1						1
Total	3	22	48	13	5		2	5	98

Note: Primary Analysis Units are Zones I, II, IV, VII, and VIII.
Zone I (Levels A–E): Humus/Slopewash
Zone II (Levels F1–F4): Slope Midden
Zone III (Levels G–L): Mound Loading
Zone IV (Levels M–M1 and EE): Slope Midden
Zone V (Levels N–P): Mound Loading
Zone VI (Levels Q–S1): Submound Flooding
Zone VII (Level S2 and FF): Submound Midden
Zone VIII (Levels S4–GG): Submound Midden/Flooding

Table 2.7. Mound C, test unit (C100): key rim modes by level, zone, and feature

Levels	A	B	C	D	E	F	G	H	I	J	K	L	M	N	O	P	Q	R	S	Total
Rim Modes																				
"D'Olive"	2	8	2	1	9	10	1		1											34
"Dominic"	3	1	1			5	3	2	15	3	13	8	2	6	3	4	1	1	3	74
"Gasque"	10	12	4		21	13	2	2	1											65
"Jessamine"	1	1			1	6	18	3	7	3	1									41
"Port Dauphin"	1	4																		5
Scalloped																4			1	5
Eared																1		1	1	3
Total	17	26	7	1	31	34	24	7	24	6	14	8	2	6	3	9	1	2	5	227

Features	1	3	6	7	17	Total
Rim Modes						
"D'Olive"		3				3
"Dominic"	1	3	1	1	2	8
"Gasque"	1	5				6
"Jessamine"		11				11
Scalloped					4	4
Total	2	22	1	1	6	32

Zones	I	II	III	IV	Total
Rim Modes					
"D'Olive"	13	20	1		34
(%)	25.5	20.8	1.9		15
"Dominic"	5	10	41	18	74
(%)	9.8	10.4	75.9	69.2	32.6
"Gasque"	26	38	1		65
(%)	51	39.6	1.9		28.6
"Jessamine"	2	28	11		41
(%)	3.9	29.2	20.3		18
"Port Dauphin"	5				5
(%)	9.8				2.2
Scalloped				5	5
(%)				19.2	2.2
Eared				3	3
(%)				11.5	1.3
Total	51	96	54	26	227

Note: Zone Descriptions.
Zone I (Levels A–D): From surface to top of midden (humus, plowzone, slopewash)
Zone II (Levels E–H): Midden, to top of Feature 3 (dense sheet midden deposit)
Zone III (Levels I–M): Midden, from base of Feature 3 to top of Feature 17 (wall trench)
Zone IV (Levels N–S): Midden adjacent to wall trench, to base of cultural deposits

Island series and the late peak of the Gulf Historic series. Like Mound A, the Lower Mississippi Valley wares in Mound C show a bimodal distribution. Despite the different depositional natures of the analysis zones for mounds A and C, the frequency distributions of the key style series for each mesh in near seriational perfection. Initially I feared that the symmetrical frequency curves resulting from the Mound C analysis might be partly artificial, possibly due to my combining arbitrary and natural levels into zones. As an additional check, I analyzed Feature 3, the discrete sheet midden deposit that separates Zones II and III (see above). As can be seen in Figure 2.13, the frequencies of the fineware series in Feature 3 formed a precise fit within the overall sequence.

SUMMARY AND CONCLUSIONS

Analysis of the ceramic style sets and series from the test excavations in mounds A and C at Bottle Creek has identified some roots and branches of the Pensacola family tree (Figure 2.14). The deepest levels produced a few Late Woodland period sherds of the Coles Creek A and B and Weeden

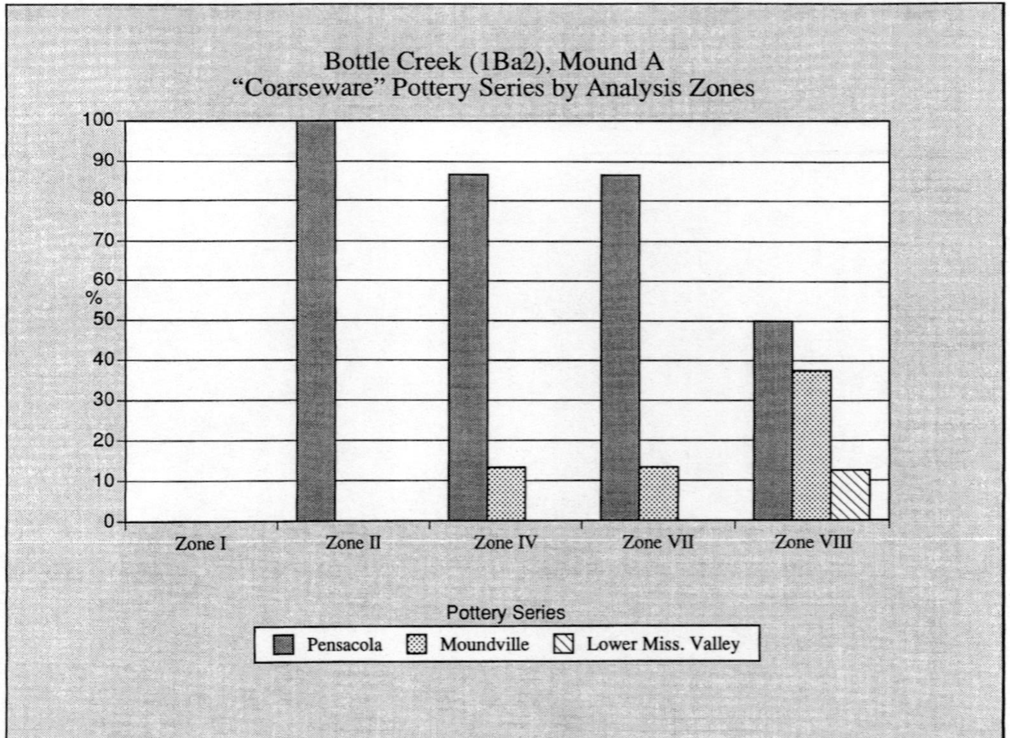

2.9. "Coarseware" pottery series in the Mound A excavations, arranged by analysis zones.

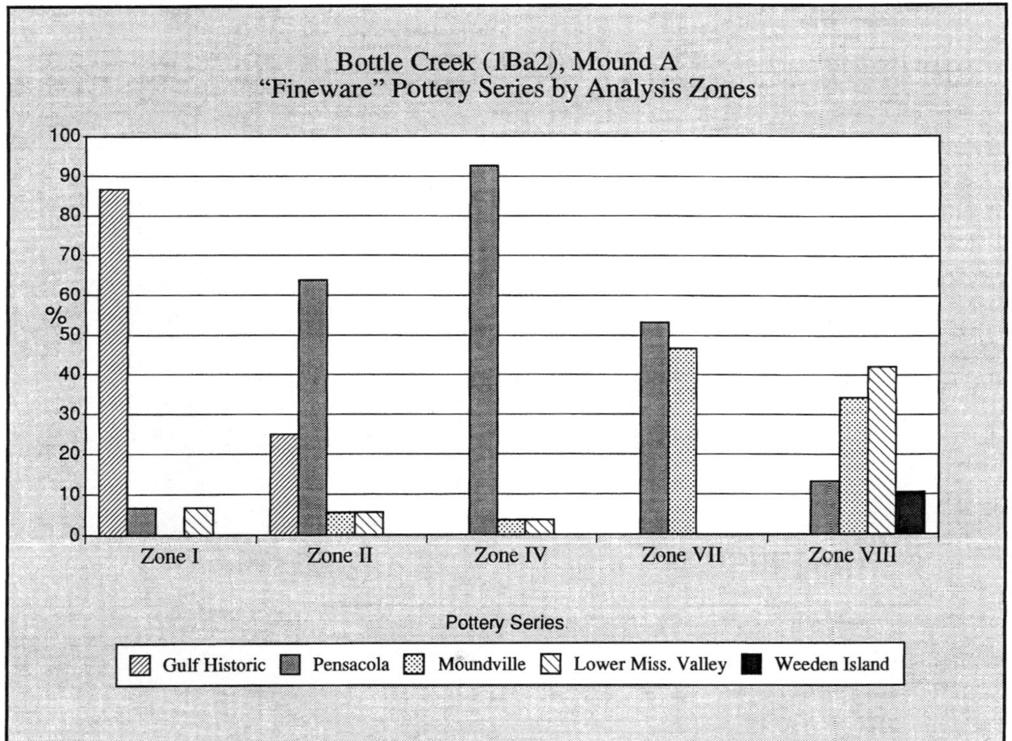

2.10. “Fineware” pottery series in the Mound A excavations, arranged by analysis zones.

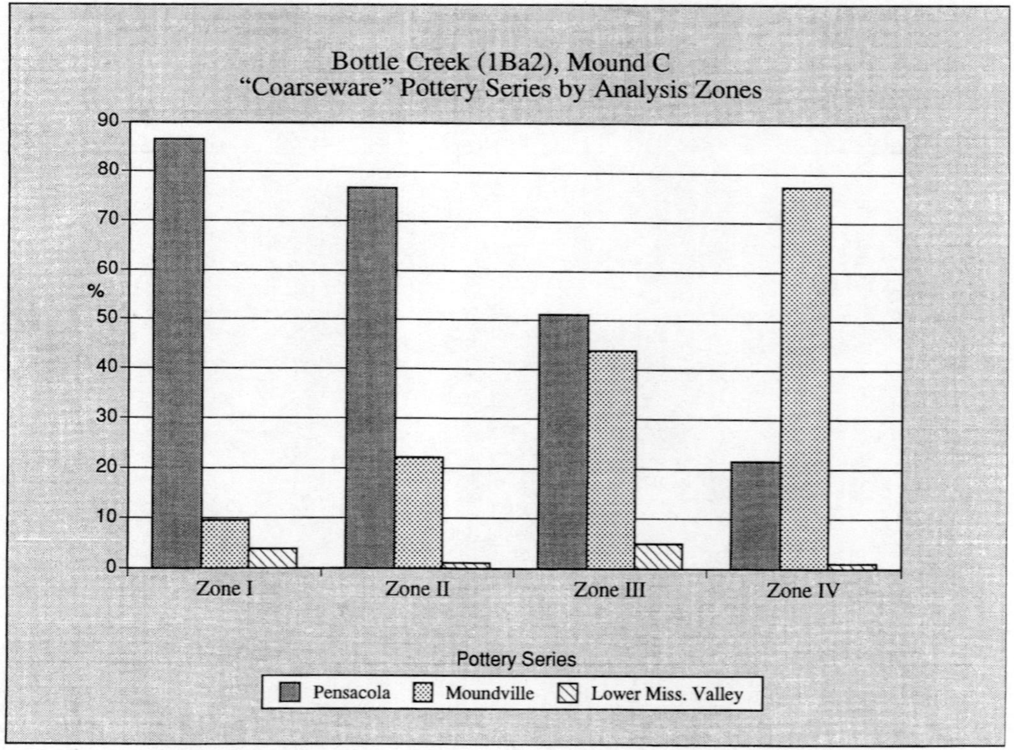

2.11. "Coarseware" pottery series in the Mound C excavations, arranged by analysis zones.

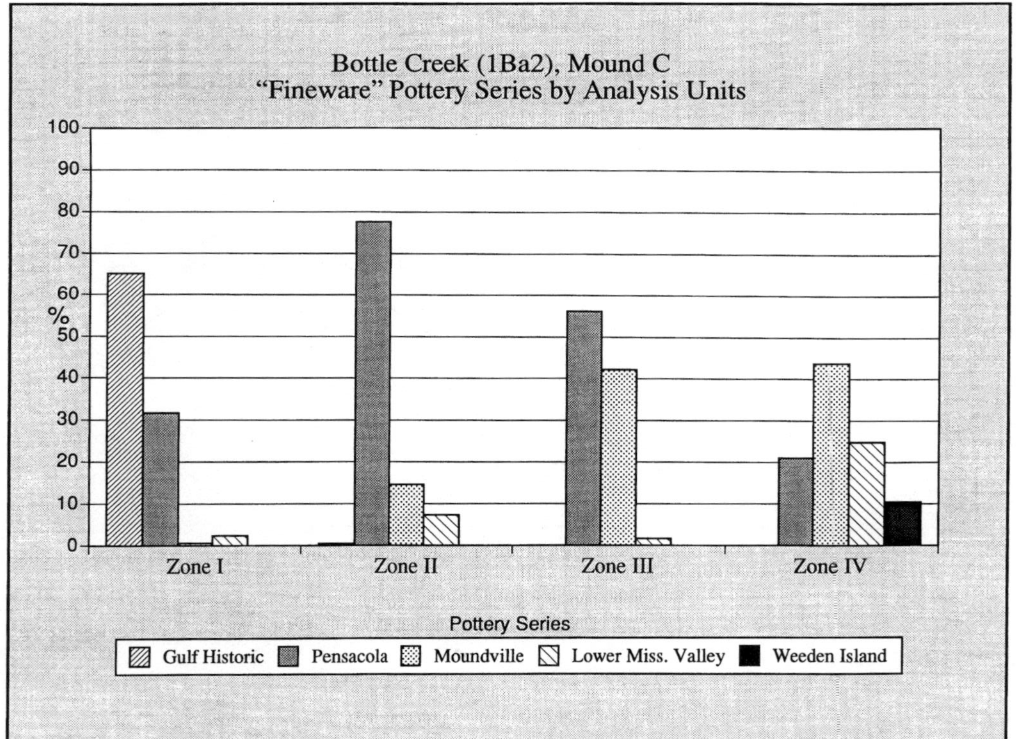

2.12. "Fineware" pottery series in the Mound C excavations, arranged by analysis zones.

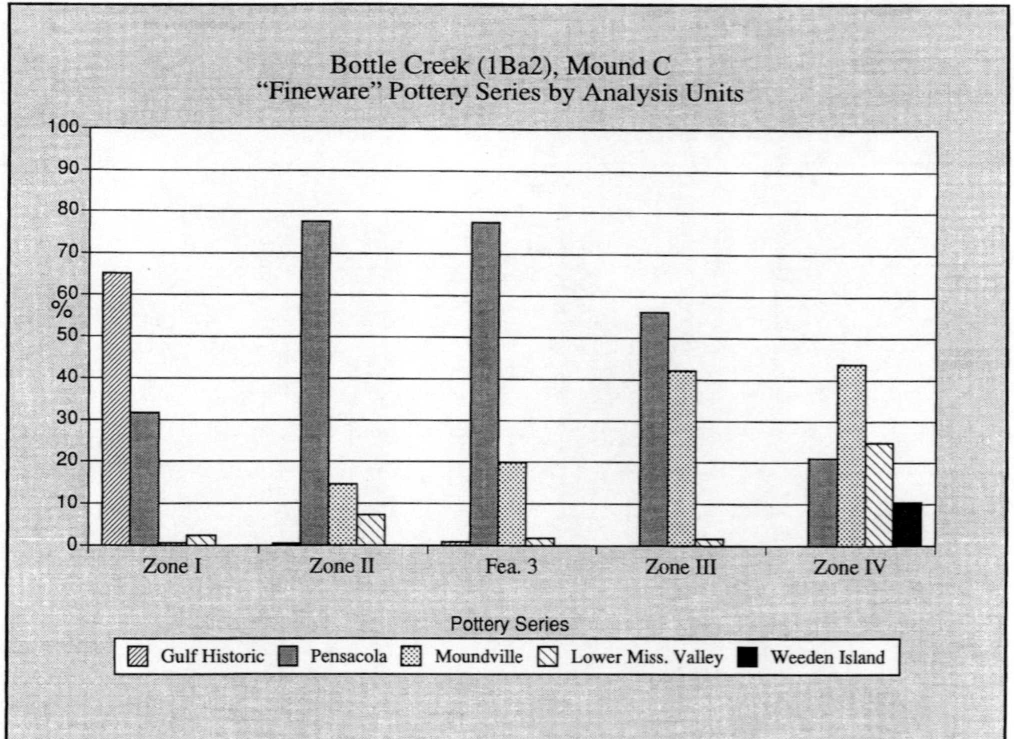

2.13. "Fineware" pottery series in the Mound C excavations, arranged by analysis zones (including Feature 3).

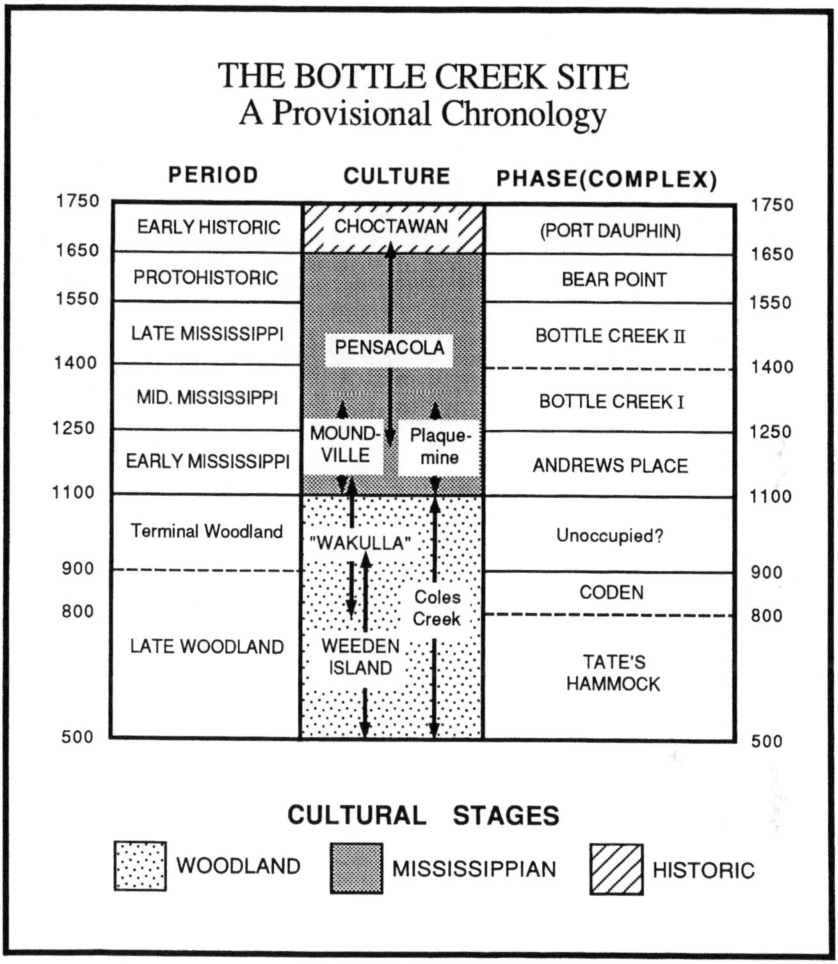

2.14. The Bottle Creek site, a provisional chronology.

Island A and B sets. These sherds indicate a probable Tate's Hammock phase component dating about A.D. 400–750. Without a larger sample, I cannot be sure if a slightly later Coden phase component (ca. A.D. 750–1100) is present as well. What is certain is that the distinctive grit-tempered ceramics of the terminal Woodland period Tensaw Lake phase (ca. A.D. 800–1100) were not represented in the excavations; neither have they been found in any of the other excavations or surface collections at the site (Brown and Fuller 1993b; Fuller and Brown 1993a; 1998; Silvia 2000; Stowe and Fuller 1993). This apparent absence is intriguing, considering that Tensaw Lake phase components are extremely common in the surrounding delta (Fuller and Brown 1998:Table 74).

The initial Mississippian component is of the Moundville-related Andrews Place phase (A.D. 1100–1250). Pottery styles and relative dating indicate this phase is contemporary with the late Moundville I and early Moundville II phases to the north. The analysis suggests a rather sudden appearance of Moundville styles, possibly a result of classic site-unit intrusion. To date, no transitional or "emergent" pottery complex, such as would indicate an in-place Woodland to Mississippian transition, has been identified at Bottle Creek or anywhere in the region. I suspect that these initial Mississippian inhabitants probably did some mound building, although that was not evident for the Mound A excavation and was ambiguous at best for Mound C. Our test excavations in mounds C and D showed that these people erected a large palisade wall. As recent arrivals, perhaps the newcomers needed a barrier to separate themselves physically from the resident population. It may be significant in this regard that the Tensaw Lake phase is absent at Bottle Creek, while it is so prevalent in the surrounding region.

Either through unconscious stylistic drift or through a conscious effort to establish a regional identity, the Mississippian potters at Bottle Creek gradually developed local styles that ultimately became recognizable as Pensacola. If there is such a thing as an emergent Pensacola pottery complex, it is manifested in what I call the Bottle Creek I phase. Although still reflecting strong Moundville influences, the pottery of the Bottle Creek I phase clearly shows the emergence of a separate stylistic identity. Some degree of that identity was due to influences from the Lower Mississippi Valley. In addition to actual grog- and mixed-grog-tempered types, Bottle Creek potters adapted some Plaquemine ceramic styles and vessel shapes to their local shell-tempered wares; this is especially evident in the prevalence of interior-decorated plates. My analysis suggests that part of the early Pensacola pottery style, as it is represented by the Bottle Creek I phase, represents a syncretic blend of Moundville and Plaquemine traits.

Throughout the Middle Mississippi period, Pensacola pottery decorations reflected ever weakening ties to Moundville. It was only very late, during the Late Mississippi Bottle Creek II phase and especially during the protohistoric Bear Point phase, that Pensacola vessel shapes and decorations showed a strong divergence from their Moundville counterparts. Toward the end of its existence, Pensacola culture had its greatest influence on the pottery complexes of its coastal neighbors to the east and west. This influence is most evident in the decorations and shapes of protohistoric Fort Walton vessels from the western Florida panhandle (cf. Lazarus and Hawkins 1976). By the sixteenth century, following the decline of the great Mississippian mound centers of the interior Southeast, a true coastal ceramic tradition had emerged, short-lived though it was.

3 / A Proposed Construction Sequence of the Mound B Terrace at Bottle Creek

David W. Morgan

INTRODUCTION

Mound B is the second tallest and second largest earthwork at the Bottle Creek site (Figure 1.3). Several general observations have led to the hypothesis that Mound B served a special role in the religious and social lives of people in Pensacola society. First, the builders of the mound positioned it strategically to form the western border of a large plaza (Brown 1994:1–4; Waselkov 1993:32, Fig. 1). Second, Mound B is markedly larger than the accretionary mounds that form an arc around the northern half of the plaza. Third, surface collections indicate that the abundant utilitarian pottery sherds found elsewhere at the site are scarce at Mound B (Brown and Fuller 1993b:166; Fuller and Brown 1998:66–72, Tables 23–28).

Mound B also is noteworthy because it is one of the most unusually shaped of all the mounds at Bottle Creek. Mound B consists of a main platform that is about 3.5 m high. This platform slopes downward to the east and southeast, and it climbs sharply on the western side to form a terrace, the apex of which stands at about 7.7 m. Because of the decline to the east and southeast, the north and northeast sections of the platform have the appearance of an embankment or ramp.

Because of the mound's distinctive attributes and potential importance for understanding Bottle Creek, it was targeted for investigations during 1991, 1993, and 1994. In 1991 and in 1994, Ian W. Brown and Richard S. Fuller collected pottery from the surface of the mound (Brown and Fuller 1993b:151; Fuller and Brown 1998:62–67). Mississippian pottery types dominated their collection. Based on the 1991 collection, Brown and Fuller assumed that the earthwork was used, if not built, during the Bottle Creek phase (A.D. 1250–1550). In 1993, we systematically retrieved soil cores an inch in diameter across the surface of the mound in order to ascertain a basic idea of upper mound stratigraphy. The northern portion of the mound seemed to have been disturbed the least, but it was uncertain how much and which portions of the mound were constructed prehistorically, since the platform's distinctive northeastern embankment and southeastern declination were suspected to have been the result of modifications during the nineteenth and twentieth centuries (Waselkov 1993:31). Excavations at the mound in 1994 were intended to resolve some of these questions by assessing the age of the mound and its method of construction.

METHODS

In June and July of 1994, we excavated a 1 × 12 m trench into the northern slope of Mound B (Figure 3.1). The trench was oriented with its long axis toward magnetic north, and it was situated in an area where the soil cores suggested the presence of relatively undisturbed strata. We divided the trench into six analytical units. Each was 1 × 2 m in size, and, from north to south, they were designated D200 through D205. We excavated each of these units by natural levels and screened all soil through 6.4 mm (.25 in) hardware cloth.

Excavations began first in the four southernmost units, D202–D205, as these lay on top of the mound platform. We encountered wall trenches, postholes, and postmolds as soon as we began excavations in D205. These features lay just below the humus layer, and they extended into units D202 through D204. These post features and wall trenches likely represent two Mississippian structures, as I will discuss further below. Given the rarity of such structures along the central Gulf Coast and their potential importance for future research, we halted excavation in these units with the intention of returning to them at some future date. Research for the remainder of the field season focused on units D200 and D201, located on the slope of the mound platform. We excavated D200 and D201 to the depth of the water table, about 2.45 m below the platform's surface.

THE DEVELOPMENTAL HISTORY OF MOUND B

Mound B is composed of a clay base and a clay cap, with intervening strata of silt and sand. The base stratum of clay served to define the ultimate shape of the mound, since the layers of silt and sand later deposited on top of the clay conformed to its general shape. Furthermore, it appears that the inhabitants of the site built a series of retaining walls to help define the form of the clay base and to hold overlying strata in place during construction. The upper stratum of clay placed over the sand and silt layers marked the final mound construction episode. After its completion, the Bottle Creek residents dug wall trenches into this clay cap for at least two late prehistoric or early historic structures. People also used the mound during the late nineteenth and/or early twentieth centuries. During this

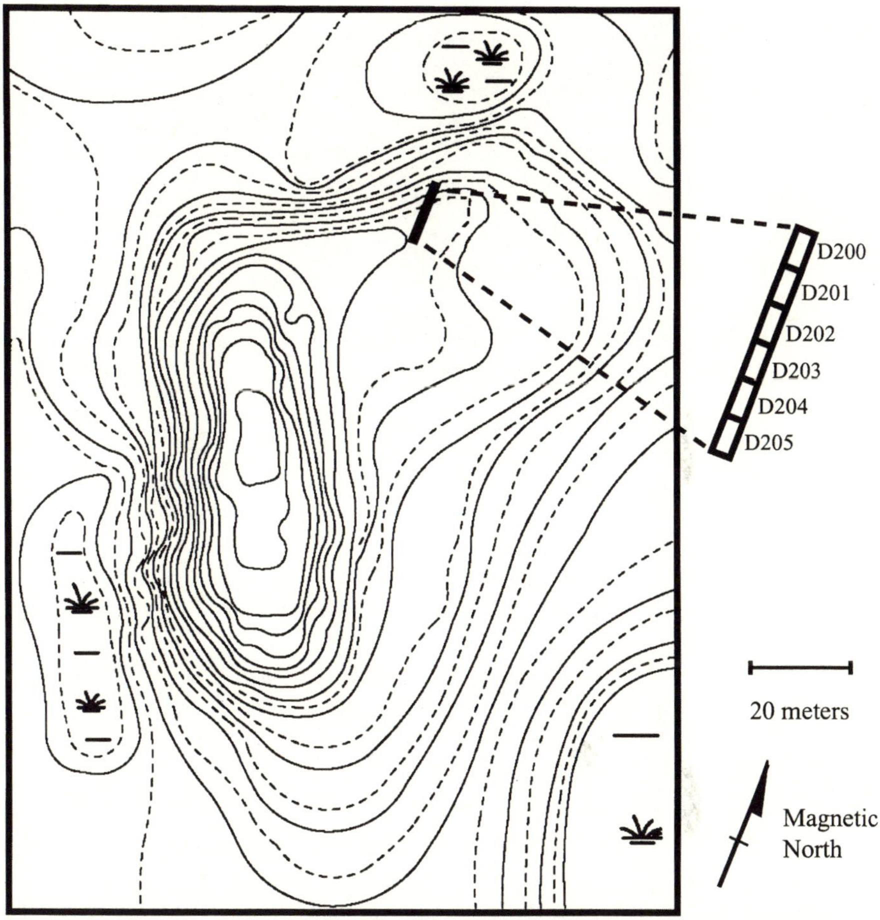

3.1. Location of the 1 × 12 m trench excavated into Mound B in 1994 (adapted from Waselkov [1993], revised in 2002; courtesy Gregory A. Waselkov, Center for Archaeological Studies, the University of South Alabama).

time they placed buildings along the mound platform and also dug at least one privy into the mound on its northern side.

Mound Construction Sequence

Mound construction in the area of units D200 and D201 began with the placement of a thick stratum of mottled gray and brown clay (Stratum I in Figures 3.2–3.4). Presumably this layer was deposited on the natural ground surface or premound cultural deposits. This assumption has not been verified, because we reached the water table in the units and the ad-

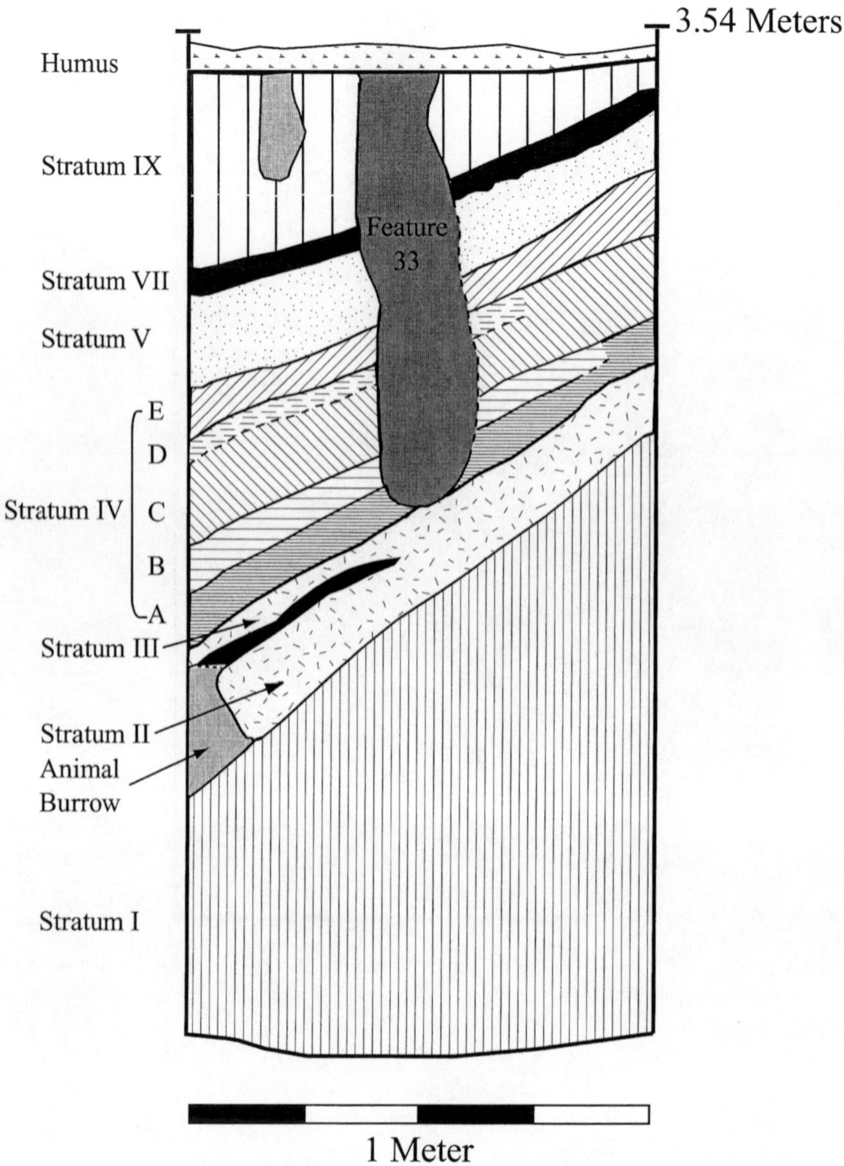

3.2. Section drawing of the south wall of Unit D201, Mound B terrace.

jacent borrow pit "pond" while removing the clay stratum and did not excavate any deeper. We encountered the water table about 2.45 m below the mound platform. Measuring from the base of the excavations, the clay base exposed at the southern end of D201 was 1.3 m thick, and it sloped gradually downward over 4 m to a thickness of 55 cm at the north end of unit D200. We initially screened the clay stratum until it was apparent that

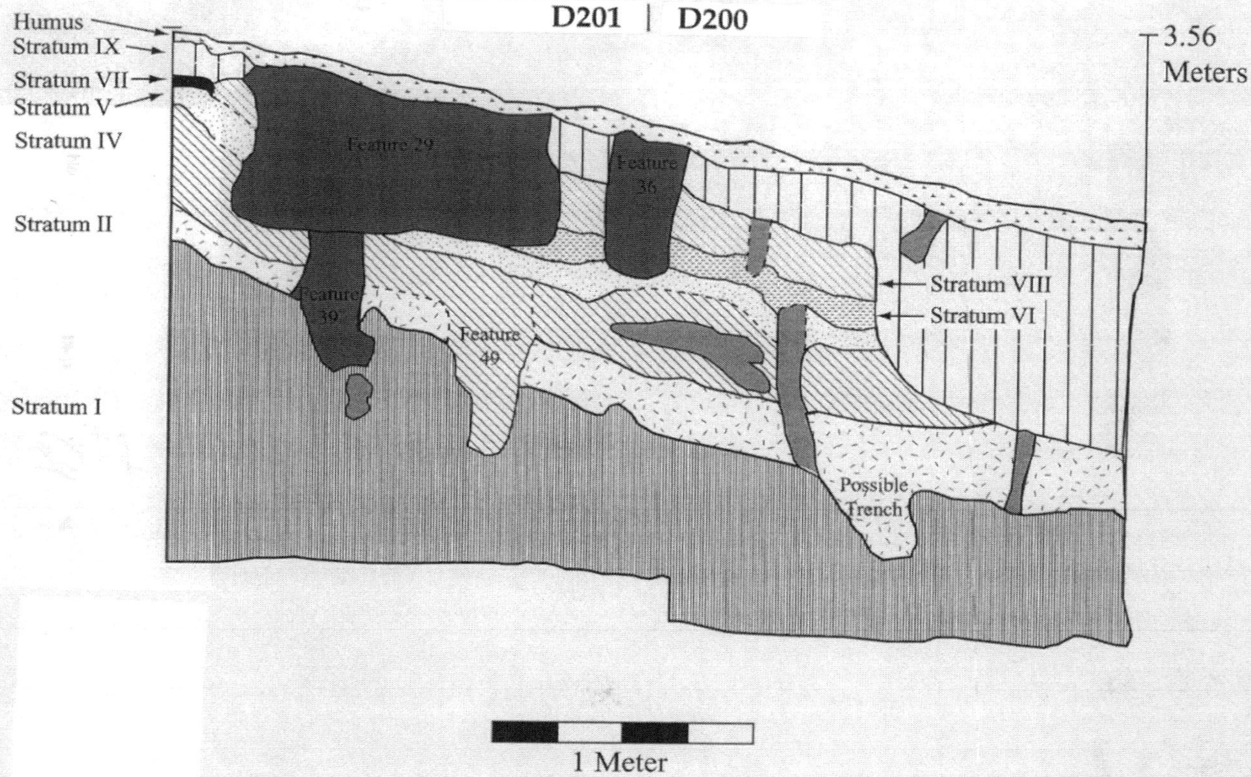

3.3. Section drawing of the west walls of units D200 and D201, Mound B terrace.

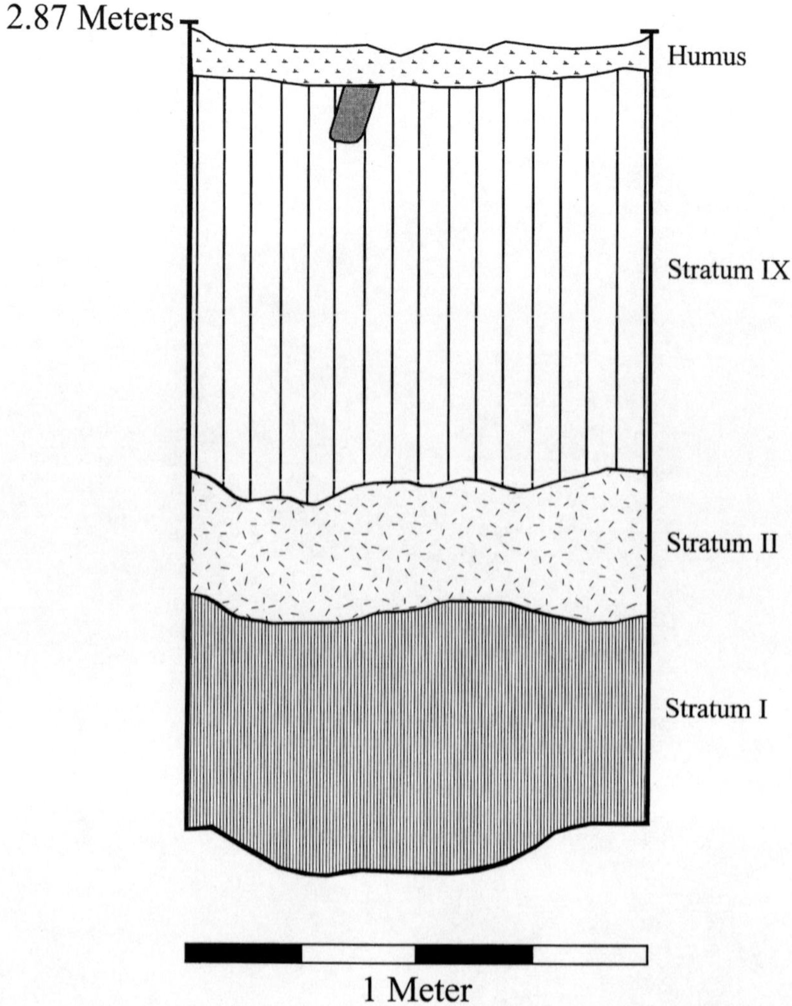

3.4. Section drawing of the north wall of Unit D200, Mound B terrace.

no artifacts were present. Then we removed the clay stratum without further screening.

We found a roughly linear arrangement of 10 postholes, each about 10 to 15 cm in diameter, within the lower portion of the clay layer in unit D201, and observed a possible wall trench cut into the clay after excavation in the west profile of unit D200 (Figure 3.3). The line of posts was situated perpendicular to the long axis of the trench and extended across the middle of the unit from east to west (Figure 3.5). The locations of this line of posts and the possible wall trench correspond well with the inflection point of the slope of the clay platform's surface (Stratum I in Figure

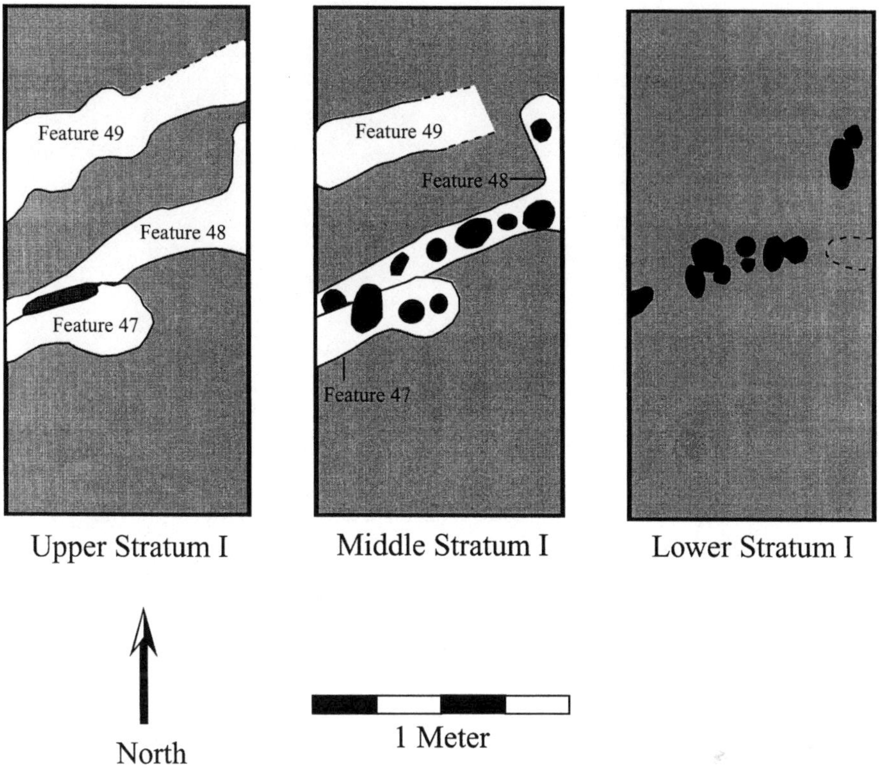

3.5. Plan view drawing of lower, middle, and upper levels of Stratum I (clay base) in Unit D201, Mound B terrace.

3.3). North of this post and trench arrangement the clay base is relatively level. South of the line of posts the clay base slopes sharply upward at about a 25- or 30-degree angle. I hypothesize that these post and possible trench features could have served two purposes: 1) to outline on a relatively flat clay base the desired shape of the mound, and 2) to serve as a retaining wall as clay was heaped on their interior, southern side as the next step in achieving this desired shape.

The people who built Mound B pulled the 10 posts from the ground sometime later, to judge from the absence of post molds and the presence of feature fill that consists of the overlying matrix. When they removed these posts is unclear. It could have occurred after the clay base was shaped and prior to the next construction episode, or the retaining wall of posts could have remained in place until the builders completed the next construction stage.

Regardless, new mound construction began once the clay platform was mounded on the south side of the barrier of posts. The builders deposited a layer of heterogeneous yellow and brown sand and sandy silt about

25 cm thick in basket loads on top of the clay platform (Stratum II in Figures 3.2–3.4). This stratum appears to have remained exposed for an indefinite amount of time, since the sand and silt appear to have been water-sorted. A thin patch of this soil immediately above the clay in the south section of D201 was reddish in color and contained mineralized bone that also may be the result of percolation of rain or groundwater through the layer.

The source of this soil may be one of the two borrow pits flanking the northern and southwestern sides of Mound B (Figure 1.3). Wherever its origin, this stratum consists of presumably redeposited cultural material. The majority of the artifacts are potsherds, most of which are Mississippian (n=65), including Moundville Engraved, L'Eau Noire Incised, Pensacola Incised, and others. A smaller amount of Late Woodland pottery also is present (n=34), including sherds of Mobile Cord Marked and Weeden Island Plain vessels.

People apparently were using the surface of Mound B as they dumped Stratum II onto the clay platform. The sand and silt in the middle portion of Stratum II in the southernmost section of D201 were oxidized. They were orange in color and possessed a distinctive "crunchy" texture that may be the result of burning. Furthermore, this area of orange soil was associated with a thin layer of midden debris that accumulated on the slope of the mound (Stratum III in Figure 3.2). The midden and oxidized soil were covered later by the same sand and silt making up the underlying portions of Stratum II, implying that the midden formation interrupted this construction stage only briefly.

Stratum III is one of two midden deposits encountered in the excavation, so it is critical both for understanding construction chronology and mound function. The sparseness of the midden and the small quantity of artifacts within it, however, did not provide much information. We recovered three plain shell-tempered sherds, four pieces of fired clay, three pieces of ocher, and small fragments of unidentified bone from the midden. Of the sherds, only two—Bell Plain *var. Stockton* and Mississippi Plain *var. Devils Bend*—are temporally sensitive (Fuller 1996:2, 4). Both are markers for the Bottle Creek I and II phases (A.D. 1250–1550), confirming what Brown and Fuller had suspected based on the surface collection in 1991. That this midden and associated burned soil accumulated in the midst of a formal construction episode hints that they represent something more than the ordinary refuse of everyday life. These deposits are interpreted as the debris from an instance of ritualized burning and feasting that perhaps commemorated the first covering of the mound's base. These activities would have occurred on the mound platform, and the midden and burned soils could have developed on the mound's slope, as its surface was swept clean.

Such an interpretation is not without precedent. Knight (1989) has summarized succinctly the symbolic role of ritual sweeping and purification as part of the process of mound construction, and he thinks that an episode of ritualized feasting similar to the one hypothesized here for Mound B took place on Mound Q at Moundville (Knight 1992:9–10). At Mound Q, a level area about 3.5 m in diameter had been burned heavily during the middle of a construction stage. This area was associated with abundant faunal remains, most of which were deer, and a sherd of a Moundville Engraved bottle encrusted on the interior with glauconite, a bright green pigment. Although Stratum III at Mound B bore few artifacts and likely is a secondary deposit, the presence of bone and ocher, the evidence for burning, and the stratigraphic placement of these deposits within a construction episode is suggestive of a similar event.

The use of lines of posts to retain basket-loaded soils characterized the remainder of the construction of Mound B. After the builders deposited Stratum II, they dumped five additional strata of heterogeneous yellow-brown silt and sand in place, in association with four construction barriers (Strata IV A–E in Figure 3.2 and Stratum IV in Figure 3.3). The source of this fill is presumably different from the initial layer of yellow-brown silt and sand (Stratum II) deposited on top of the clay base, as Strata IV–VIII combined yielded only five artifacts.

It is possible that the four associated construction barriers could be part of structures, palisades, or other architectural features, but they seem instead to have served as a way of holding layers of soil in place as the mound was built. The barriers consisted of posts about 10 cm in diameter set within linear trenches. The strata south (upslope) of the post trenches were distinct and well defined, while those north (downslope) of the post barriers were much more heterogeneous and interbedded. This distinction is paralleled by differences in soil color and composition, too. Often, soil within the same stratum varied depending on whether it was upslope or downslope of the barriers. Stratum IV, for example, consisted of a blending of silts and sands upslope of the barriers, while it was composed of yellowish brown silt downslope of the barriers (Nos. 34 and 41 in Figure 3.6). Also, the trenches and post lines, while associated with different mound surfaces, all were superimposed, implying that the builders worked to maintain over time the basic shape outlined by the clay base and the original set of retaining posts. This hypothesized construction technique echoes the method thought to have been used to build Mound L (Brown and Fuller 1993b:159), and it is a technique similar to that reconstructed for the Snodgrass site, a Mississippi period mound center located in the Guntersville Basin of the Tennessee River (Krause 1988:33–37).

We encountered three of the wall trenches and associated post features first within the intermediate and upper portions of the clay base (Features 47–49 in Figure 3.5). Features 47 and 48 both were directly above the line of single-set posts observed in the lower portion of the clay base, and they

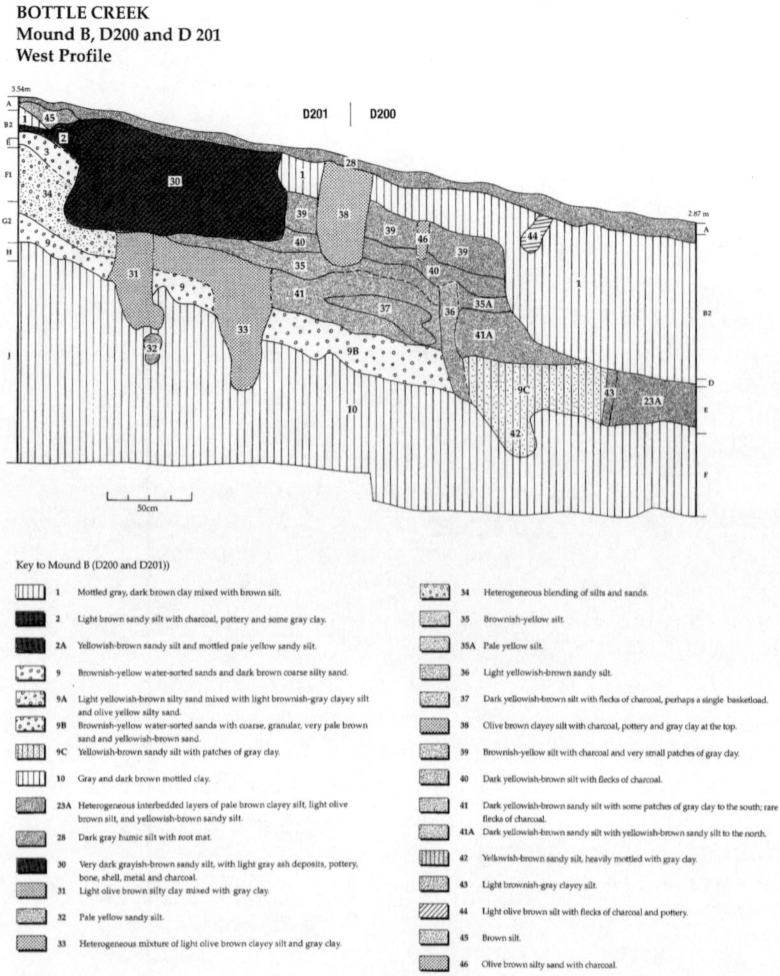

3.6. Section drawing of the west walls of units D200 and D201, Mound B terrace, showing soil colors and composition.

were associated with two and six posts, respectively. These more recent wall trenches were aligned slightly differently from the older line of posts, reinforcing the impression that these are indeed separate features, not merely postholes seen at different excavation levels. The third wall trench, Feature 49, was oriented parallel to the other two, but it was located about 50 cm further downslope (north) (Figures 3.3 and 3.5). We noted no post features in association with this wall trench.

Feature 49 appears to have been associated with the first of the five overlying strata of yellow-brown sand and silt, and Features 47 and 48 appear to have been associated with the second and third of the five overlying strata. Of these two features, Feature 48 is the oldest, as Feature 47 was dug into Feature 48. As with the line of posts associated with the lower portion of the clay base, the location of these three more recent wall trenches also was associated with a mound slope inflection point. South of the wall trenches the associated strata sloped gently upward, and north of the wall trenches the strata lay flat (Figure 3.3). Unlike the line of posts in the lower portion of the clay, however, the post features associated with wall trench Features 47 and 48 consisted of both the postholes and post molds, implying that the posts were left in place to rot.

After depositing the five yellow-brown silt and sand layers, the builders then covered the mound with a stratum of light tan sand (Stratum V in Figures 3.2 and 3.3). Stratum V may have been associated with another episode of activity on the platform of Mound B. We recovered no artifacts from this stratum, but one portion of the southern section of D201 appears to have been oxidized. The sand in this locale graded in color from light tan at the top of the stratum to orange at the base. This area of orange sand lay in a depression in the underlying stratum of yellow-brown silt and sand, and it contained small fragments of charcoal and fired clay. A fire in the depression may have oxidized sand used to extinguish the fire and cover the mound, or oxidized soil and carbon flecks from a fire on top of the mound platform may have been swept or washed down the mound slope, accumulating in a natural depression.

A very thin midden stratum accumulated on top of Stratum V in the southern portion of unit D201 (Stratum VII in Figures 3.2 and 3.3). Although its location near the end of the mound building sequence gave this stratum the potential for providing important chronological information, it possessed even fewer artifacts than the midden near the beginning of the construction sequence (Stratum III). Only small bone fragments and unclassified pottery sherd fragments smaller than 1.27 cm (.5 in) were recovered in Stratum VII, and the processes resulting in the deposition of this layer of debris are unknown. This sparse midden may be formed of the debris of people living on top of the mound. Alternately, if it formed soon after the burned, underlying sand stratum was deposited, the midden may be better interpreted as a second episode of ceremonial activities.

After the midden deposit formed, layers of yellow-brown silt (Stratum VI) and dark brownish-yellow silt (Stratum VIII) were added to the mound (Figures 3.2 and 3.3). These layers were visible only in the west-central portion of the unit, and the precise stratigraphic relationship between strata VI, VII, and the midden is unclear because of their limited representation in the excavation. Although they are treated separately here, the midden may be the same stratum as VI or VIII, but it is impossible to link the strata physically because a pit (Feature 29) dug into the mound platform in the late nineteenth or early twentieth century disturbed the area in question.

The inhabitants built a fourth barrier (Feature 37), consisting again of a wall trench and posts, in association with the dumping of Strata VI, VII, and VIII. One of the posts in this trench is visible in the west profile drawing (Feature 39 in Figure 3.3). The barrier's precise stratigraphic affiliation is unknown, as Feature 29 destroyed the upper portion of the wall trench. Nevertheless, it is apparent that Feature 37 was in the same general position as the other construction barriers, and its alignment across the mound slope also was the same.

After depositing the last of the fill strata, the builders then covered the mound with a layer of mottled gray and dark brown clay (Stratum IX in Figures 3.2–3.4). Like the clay layer comprising the base of the mound, the clay cap on Mound B was thick in places. Near the base of the mound slope, in Unit D200, the cap was about 85 cm thick. The depth of this clay layer was relatively uniform across D200, but in the southern (upslope) section of the unit the thickness of the clay stratum decreased precipitously. Along the western side of D201 the layer was about 25 cm thick, while it was about 40–50 cm thick along the eastern side of the unit.

The clay cap was not limited to the slope of the mound, although it no doubt functioned to keep the silt and sand fill in place. We dug a line of four shovel tests on top of the platform at 5 m intervals south of unit D205 in order to examine the upper stratigraphy of the mound platform. The three tests nearest unit D205 revealed the clay cap at depths ranging from 37–62 cm below ground surface. The clay stratum varied from 7 to 22 cm thick in these locations. These findings suggest that all, or at least major portions, of the mound summit also were blanketed in clay.

MOUND USE AFTER CONSTRUCTION

People continued to use the mound after capping its northern slope and its summit with clay. Excavation on top of the mound platform began in Unit D205 (Figure 3.7). Removing the root mat and humus in this unit exposed a stratum of tan silt. At the base of this silt stratum, at a depth of about 15 cm below ground surface (elevation of 3.75 m), shoveling and troweling revealed a wall trench (Feature 5) and associated post features dug into an underlying stratum of orange-tan sandy silt. We then removed the overburden and tan silt stratum in units D202–D204 to expose Feature 5 and its posts. In the process, we also uncovered a second wall trench (Feature 9) and associated post features. These, too, lay beneath the tan silt stratum and were cut into the underlying orange-tan sandy silt stratum. The two wall trenches were linear in shape and lay parallel to each other, aligned across the excavation unit from southeast to northwest (Figure 3.7). The builders dug trenches into the orange-tan sandy silt stratum, after which they lined them with posts and then filled them solidly with

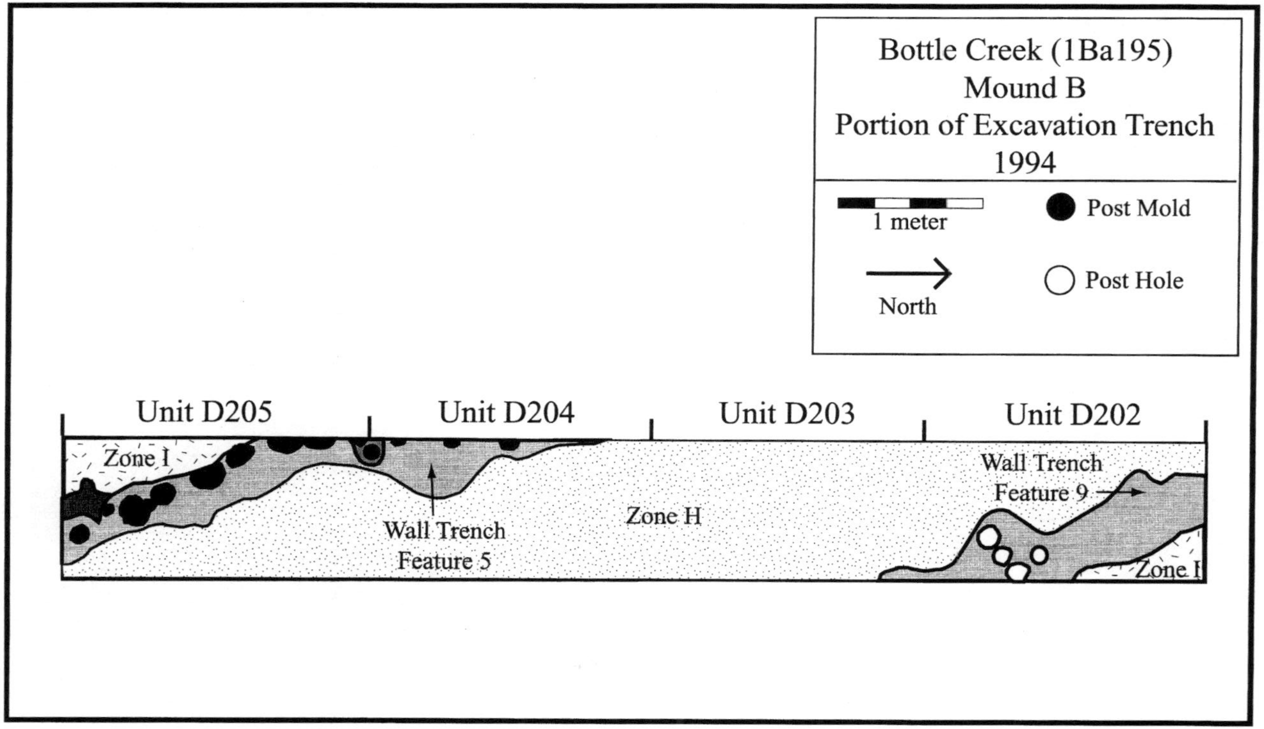

3.7. Plan view drawing of the wall trench and post features visible in units D202–D205, Mound B terrace.

densely packed gray clay identical to that forming the clay cap along the mound slope.

Fourteen post features are associated with wall trench Feature 5 (Features 12–25). Thirteen of these posts clearly are part of the wall trench. The other is believed to be intrusive, because it differs from the rest in terms of its size and fill. All 13 contemporary posts were placed flush against the western wall of the trench prior to being packed in place with clay. These timbers apparently were left in place to rot, as they all consist of postmolds.

This pattern is not so regular in wall trench Feature 9. A total of four post features were found in this wall trench (Features 10, 11, 27, and 28). They were not distributed along the length of the wall trench, as were those in Feature 5, but instead were clustered together in the southeastern portion of Unit D202. Also unlike the post features in the other trench, those in Feature 9 consisted of postholes rather than postmolds, suggesting the posts were pulled.

I interpreted these posts and trenches as the walls of two separate structures. The basis for this interpretation comes from several observations. First, the post feature patterns in each of the trenches vary, as described above. One wall trench is filled with postmolds aligned along its western margin, while the other trench contains only a few postholes. Second, the soils surrounding each wall trench differ subtly. Both trenches cut into a matrix of orange-tan sandy silt, but the soil matrix between the wall trenches, designated Zone H, was homogenous, while that on the opposite side of each trench, designated Zone I, was mottled with charcoal and small potsherds (Figure 3.7). It is possible that the trenches represent a palisade or other physical barrier against which material debris accumulated differentially, but it seems more likely that Zone I represents the interiors of two separate, probably contemporaneous, structures, and Zone H represents the space between the two.

We found a few chronologically significant artifacts in the trenches and their post features. Most date to the Bottle Creek phase, including sherds such as Moundville Engraved *var. unspecified,* Middle River Incised *var. Middle River*, and Moundville Incised *var. Snows Bend.* Assessing the age of the features, however, is complicated by the potential intrusion of artifacts from the ground surface located only 15 cm above. This difficulty is evidenced by the presence of an iron fragment and piece of brick mortar in the wall trenches. Historic period artifacts were plentiful in the tan silt stratum overlying the orange-tan sandy silt and its associated features, so the possibility of other less obvious intrusions as a result of plowing and animal burrowing is to be expected.

Assuming the Indian pottery is not intrusive, the *terminus post quem* of the trench and post features is derived from a sherd of Bell Plain *var.*

Ft. Conde pottery. This plainware is part of the Port Dauphin pottery complex and dates to the early historic period (Fuller 1996:2). If intrusive, the next most recent artifact is an unidentified, undecorated sherd tempered with shell and fashioned with a "Gasque" rim mode. This distinctive mode would date these features to no earlier than the Bottle Creek II phase (A.D. 1400–1550) (Fuller 1996:22; Fuller and Brown 1998:36, Table 2).

The platform of Mound B was used again after these structures were built. As mentioned above, we encountered a large pit about 1.3 m wide and about 60 cm deep in the central and western portions of unit D201 (Feature 29 in Figure 3.3). The soil within this feature was very dark grayish-brown sandy silt mottled by light gray ash deposits, pottery, bone, shell, metal, and charcoal. Nearby, at the same stratigraphic level and intruding into the underlying clay cap and yellow-brown sand and silt strata, were two posts thought to be associated with this pit (Features 33 and 36 in Figures 3.2 and 3.3). These posts were located just to the north and south of the pit, respectively. Each was about 20 to 30 cm in diameter. The northern post extended to a depth of about 50 cm below the humus layer, while the southern post extended to a depth of about 90 cm. I have interpreted this pit as a privy based on the presence of associated posts, the artifact content of the pit, and the dark, organically stained matrix of the pit fill. Abundant artifacts, including pipe fragments, buttons, square-head cut nails, and pottery, date the privy to the late nineteenth and/or early twentieth centuries. Oral tradition in the delta area maintains that these artifacts may have been the belongings of an African-American named Charles Walker.

HISTORIC MODIFICATIONS TO THE MOUND

As described in the introduction, Mound B consists of a main platform that is about 3.5 m high. This platform slopes downward to the east and southeast, and it climbs sharply on the western side to form a terrace, the apex of which stands at about 7.7 m. Because of the decline to the east and southeast, the north and northeast sections of the platform have the appearance of an embankment or ramp that extends toward Mound A. Andrew Bigelow (1853:189, Figure 2) made the first map of the site, and his description of the mound in 1853 varies considerably from its current shape (Figure 3.8). Did Bigelow make an inaccurate sketch, or has the mound's shape been altered since the mid-nineteenth century? Answering this question was one goal of the Mound B excavations in 1994.

When Bigelow made his map he took great pains to be precise. He sketched the shapes of the mounds in relation to magnetic north, described their alignments and positions relative to one another, and provided measurements of their bases and heights. When compared with Waselkov's

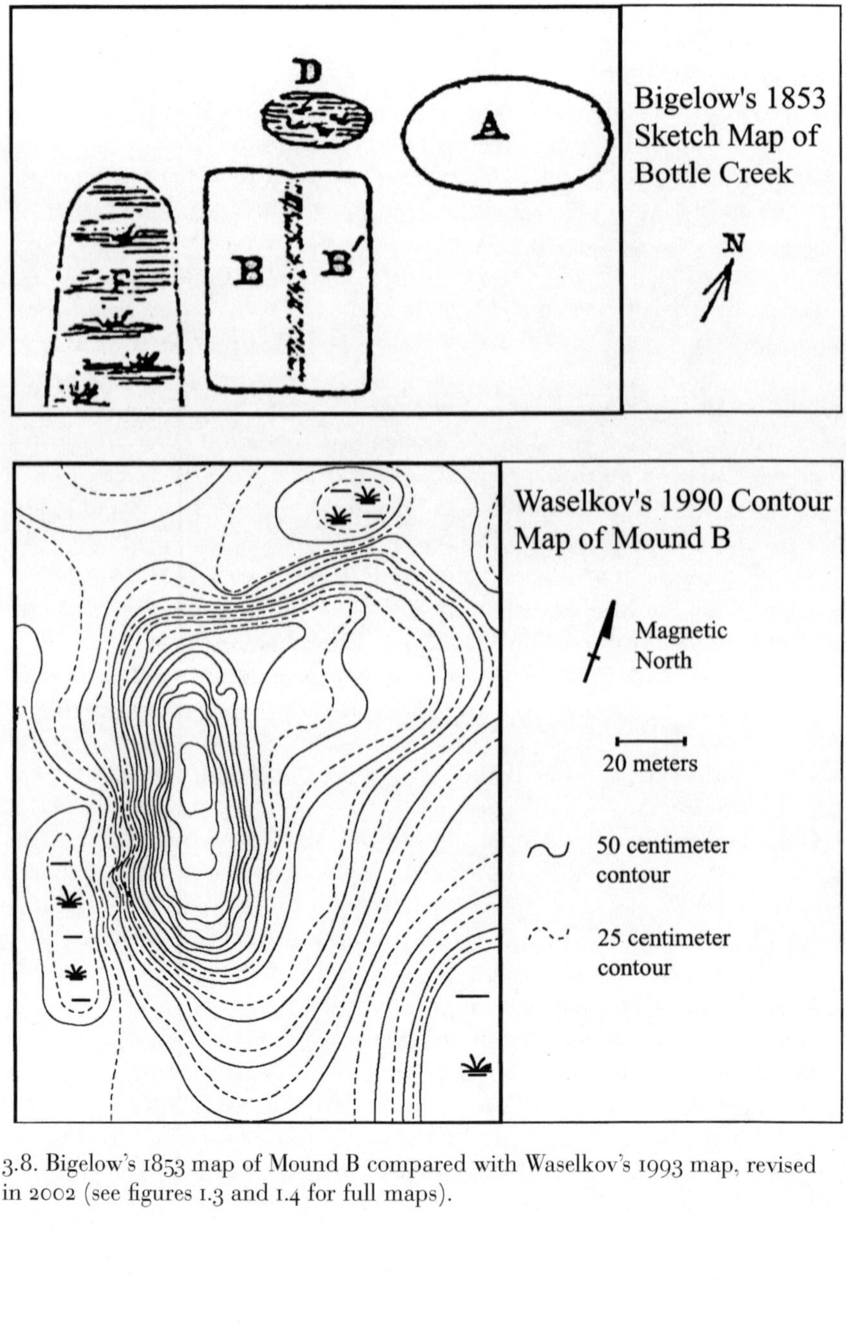

3.8. Bigelow's 1853 map of Mound B compared with Waselkov's 1993 map, revised in 2002 (see figures 1.3 and 1.4 for full maps).

instrument survey of Bottle Creek about a century and a half later, it becomes apparent that Bigelow's mid-nineteenth-century sketch is, "in a general sense . . . surprisingly accurate" (Waselkov 1993:30). Bigelow sketched all of the mounds as ovals except Mound B. Mound B he drew as a rectangle bisected down its long axis by a dividing line. East of the dividing line was labeled B′, and west of the dividing line was labeled B. Bigelow (1853:188) first mentioned the mound relative to its location near Mound A:

> Near to this is a large rectangular mound of small elevation, one-half its breadth, about five feet higher than the other, and about six feet above high water.

That Bigelow's B and B′ were intended to represent this height difference is more apparent from his description later in the article:

> B B′ is the large rectangular mound; B is about five feet higher than the part B′, it is 344 feet long by 250 feet wide. I think, from its situation and appearance that the builders designed to bring up the whole to the same elevation, so as to have more room and greater security. Upon this are found great quantities of broken crockery. (Bigelow 1853:189–190)

The biggest discrepancy between Bigelow's depiction of the mound and its appearance in the early 1990s is that the mound is not as precisely rectangular as Bigelow described. If Bigelow's description was accurate in 1853, then the southeastern side and possibly the northeastern side of the mound have been modified. To complicate the picture further, there was ample opportunity for the prehistoric shape of the mound to have been altered even before Bigelow recorded it.

During the nineteenth century the Bottle Creek site was part of a plantation's fields. Bigelow (1853:188) mentioned the presence of a plantation in the area and he described specifically how its owners planted corn on the slopes of Mound A. Bigelow believed that plowing had disturbed many of the accretionary mounds north of Mound A. Mound B, with its flat surface and relatively low elevation compared to Mound A, also may have served as a cultivated field, although Bigelow never explicitly mentioned this possibility.

If the shape of Mound B in 1853 was as Bigelow described, then much of the mound's current shape is a result of modifications that occurred during the late nineteenth or early twentieth century. Charles Walker, reputedly associated with the pit excavated in unit D201, may be the most likely suspect behind these hypothetical modifications. Walker is said to have lived at the site around the turn of the twentieth century, where he farmed and kept livestock.

That someone was using or living on Mound B is clear from several pieces of evidence. First, as already discussed, excavations on the northern slope of Mound B revealed a late-nineteenth-century and/or early-twentieth-century pit interpreted as a privy. Second, in addition to the pit feature, large hunks of rusted iron—possibly stove parts—are scattered on the platform of Mound B. Third, photographs taken in 1931 and 1932 as part of David L. DeJarnette's investigations at Bottle Creek (Jones and DeJarnette 1933), corroborate the archaeological evidence. A metal building is visible in the background of one photo, although the location from which this photograph was taken is unclear. Since DeJarnette was excavating in the vicinity of Mound A, it is possible that the metal building in the photograph was situated on or near Mound B. Finally, the original site card filed by W. B. Jones refers to a "Barn Mound" located on an elevated area between mounds A and B. There is no mound between these two earthworks. Jones probably was referring to the northeastern portion of the platform of Mound B, since it extends into the space between Mound A and the western, higher terrace of Mound B. If so, then his choice of labels gives credence to the idea that the metal building in the photograph was located on Mound B.

MOUND SHAPE

It seems likely that the current shape of Mound B is similar to its shape about 70 or 80 years ago, but the prehistoric shape of the mound remains unclear. Shortening the length of the trench excavated into Mound B made it difficult to resolve this issue confidently. However, the stratigraphy exposed in the 1 × 4 m trench does provide some working hypotheses. The strata exposed in the east and west profiles (the long axis) of units D200 and D201 dip downward from the top of the platform to its base, as one would expect for a cross-section of the mound's northern shoulder (Figure 3.3). The northern profile of the trench shows that the clay base and cap come within about 25 cm of meeting, with no perceptible dip from east to west (Figure 3.4). The southern profile of the trench, in contrast, exhibits strata that dip downward sharply from west to east (Figure 3.2). If Bigelow's sketch was accurate, then this finding is unexpected, as the south end of the trench was positioned in what would have been the northern edge of the middle of the Mound B′ platform. I would expect the strata in the middle of B′ to lie relatively flat, not dip from west to east at an angle of about 40 to 60 degrees. In short, it appears as if the trench exposed a corner of the mound platform, even though the approximate current platform edge lies further northeast of the trench.

There are several ways to interpret this stratigraphy. One way is to assume that Bigelow's map was accurate, and that the current eastern edge of the platform is what he recorded. The corner revealed in the excavations west of the current edge of the platform would have to predate Bigelow's map. If so, then it implies that the platform of Mound B (Bigelow's B′) was built in two or more stages. The northeastern corner of the first stage is what is apparent in units D200 and D201, and this initial prehistoric platform was extended subsequently to the dimensions Bigelow recorded.

Another way to explain the stratigraphy is to again assume that Bigelow sketched Mound B accurately, but that the eastern edge of the platform B′ is what has been exposed in the excavations. If this is the case, then the current embankment extending northeast toward Mound A must postdate 1853. The "deflated" south and southeastern edges of Bigelow's B′ could have been the source of the dirt needed to create an incline from ground level to the surface of Mound B. This incline—Jones's "Barn Mound"—may have been constructed in the late nineteenth or early twentieth century as a convenient ramp providing access to the Mound B platform, where one or more structures were located.

A third interpretation combines elements of the first two. The excavations in 1994 may have exposed the corner of an inner platform, as suggested in the second interpretation, but the origins of the ramp may be prehistoric. Once the first platform was created, at a later date the prehistoric builders may have added a ramp by adding dirt to the northeastern slope of the mound, extending it by basket-loads toward Mound A. Prehistorically, there may never have been more than an original platform upon which the 7.7 m mound terrace rests, with the later addition of a ramp. Bigelow may have sketched Mound B to provide a rough approximation of this platform, neglecting to show the more subtle elevation differences in the northeast and southeast. Later, Walker may have placed structures, including his barn and privy, on top of the Mound B ramp. He even may have chosen to use Mound B because of the pre-existing ramp that provided easy access to the platform for both him and his livestock.

What construction or destruction occurred in the southeastern area of the mound is pure speculation. The only directly pertinent evidence is cartographic, and the maps of Bigelow and Waselkov disagree. It is uncertain that there ever was a southeastern corner to a rectangular platform, as Bigelow indicated. Assuming Bigelow was as accurate with Mound B as he was with the Bottle Creek site map in general, then the deflated appearance of the southeastern corner must be explained. Mounds in the Southeast typically were not excavated prehistorically in order to make modifications or to use as backfill for new mounds, so a historic origin for the current platform shape seems likely.

Either the southeastern portion of the mound was used as fill for the northeastern ramp, or, equally likely, the destruction may have resulted from erosion. It is reasonable to assume that the owners of the plantation grew crops on Mound B. It also is possible that Walker or others had parts of the site, including Mound B, in cultivation. Decades of plowing could have broken through the clay stratum capping the platform of Mound B. If Walker situated his barn and other structures on the northern and northeastern edges of the mound, this portion of the platform may not have been plowed and the clay cap may have been preserved intact. Once the clay cap was broken on the southeastern portion of the mound, the annual floodwaters of the delta easily could have eroded the underlying sand and silt. The protective covering of clay along the northern and northeastern edge of the platform would account for different rates of erosion.

SUMMARY AND CONCLUSIONS

The construction of Mound B began sometime during the Bottle Creek I or II phases. The builders first deposited a thick base of clay. Then they set small posts into the clay base to serve as both a blueprint and a construction barricade. They heaped more clay to the interior of these barriers until they achieved the desired basal shape. Afterward, the builders dumped a layer of sand and silt on top of the mounded clay base. Then they dug a series of wall trenches lined with small posts into the existing strata as they added successive layers of sand and silt. They positioned each set of construction barriers at similar orientations and locations along the slope of the mound, indicating that these walls continued to mold the basket-loaded fill into a desired form. After adding the final layer of fill, the builders used a thick layer of clay to cover the mound.

People used Mound B briefly for at least two periods during and between episodes of construction. Activities took place on the surface of the mound platform that involved burning and resulted in the accumulation on the mound slope of small amounts of bone, pottery, and charcoal. The first episode occurred as the first stratum of sand and silt was placed over the clay base, and the second occurred before the clay cap was used to seal the mound. It is possible, based on analogy with other mound sites in the Southeast, that these were instances of ritualized feasting and purification timed to commemorate episodes of mound construction.

After construction of the mound ceased, the residents of Bottle Creek built several different structures on the platform of Mound B. They placed two structures—recognized by their wall trench and post architecture—on the platform during either Bottle Creek II or the early historic period. Site residents placed the second set of structures on the mound during the late nineteenth century and/or early twentieth century. A barn was present on or near Mound B at that time, as documented photographically and on the original site file form. Excavations revealed the presence of a large, trash-filled pit with associated posts, interpreted as a privy.

The puzzle of Mound B's unusual shape remains unsolved. It may have been built prehistorically as a rectangular platform, but was subject to subsequent historic modifications, including the construction of a ramp. Alternately, Bigelow's sketch in 1853 of Mound B as a rectangle may be inaccurate, and the ramp may have been built prehistorically. Regardless, if buildings and the clay cap protected the northern portion of the mound during the late nineteenth and early twentieth centuries, plowing during the historic period may have destroyed the clay cap in the southeastern portion of the mound, and differential erosion may account for the current shape of the platform. A combination of all these factors likely is responsible for Mound B's enigmatic shape. Further excavations are required to establish firmly the chronology and construction history of this earthwork.

4 / Historic Aboriginal Reuse of a Mississippian Mound, Mound L at Bottle Creek

Diane E. Silvia

INTRODUCTION

In 1991 the Gulf Coast Survey conducted test excavations on the summit of Mound L at the Bottle Creek site (Figure 1.3). Brown and Fuller (1993b) excavated two 1 × 2 m units that contained numerous overlapping features, to a depth of more than 2 m. This work indicated the presence of several superimposed structures and details on mound construction (Figures 4.1–4.5). Some of the artifacts in the upper levels were historic, documenting a little known component of the site. During the summers of 1993 and 1994, we continued excavations at Mound L to investigate the mound's structures, with particular emphasis on the later components. These are the first intensive excavations of aboriginal structures in southwest Alabama (Silvia 2000:255–300).

METHODS

Using the 1991 datum, we established a 2 m grid over the entire mound summit. We maintained distances and elevations in reference to this datum. Our next task was to use a manual soil auger to take soil cores from the mound slope to search for buried midden. We obtained 29 cores in a zigzag fashion all around the mound. We measured and recorded soil profiles and noted and collected any artifacts. Maximum core depth was 96 cm, with an average depth of about 80 cm. Typically, soil profiles consisted of brown sandy humus over tan sandy clay. These layers were underlain by brown and gray mottled sandy clay. Three sherdlets, a fragment of daub, and small fragments of charcoal were the only materials recovered. Surprisingly, the midden we expected to be associated with this mound was not located in the typical fashion, along the mound slope.

We also obtained soil cores at each grid point on the mound summit to determine the extent and density of an extensive daub deposit that was

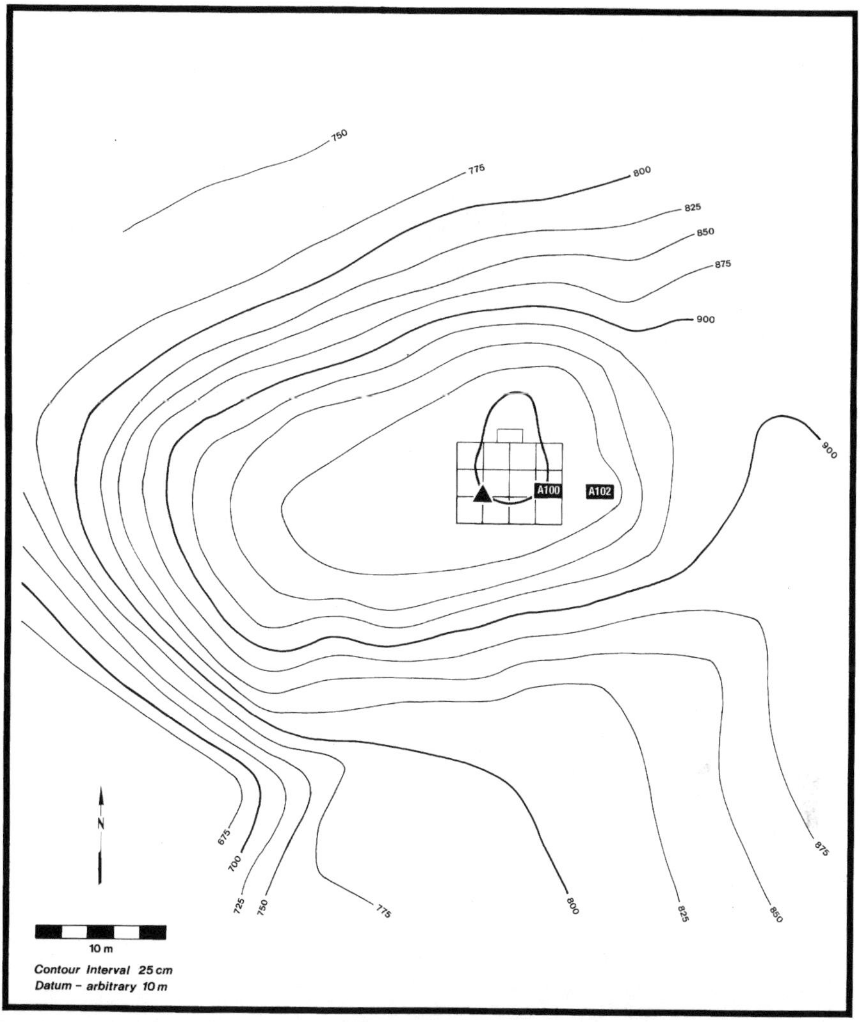

4.1. Map of Mound L, showing excavation units.

recorded as Feature 2 during test excavations (Figure 4.2). Coring indicated that most of the daub was concentrated in the southeast quarter of the summit. We also conducted a metal detector survey over the area to be excavated to get some idea about the density and extent of metal artifacts. We plotted signals and marked them with pin flags for reference during excavation. We wet or dry screened all excavated fill through 6.4 mm (.25 in) hardware cloth. We added a 3.2 mm (.13 in) screen to the water screen after recovering the first glass bead. We piece-plotted artifacts that were especially diagnostic.

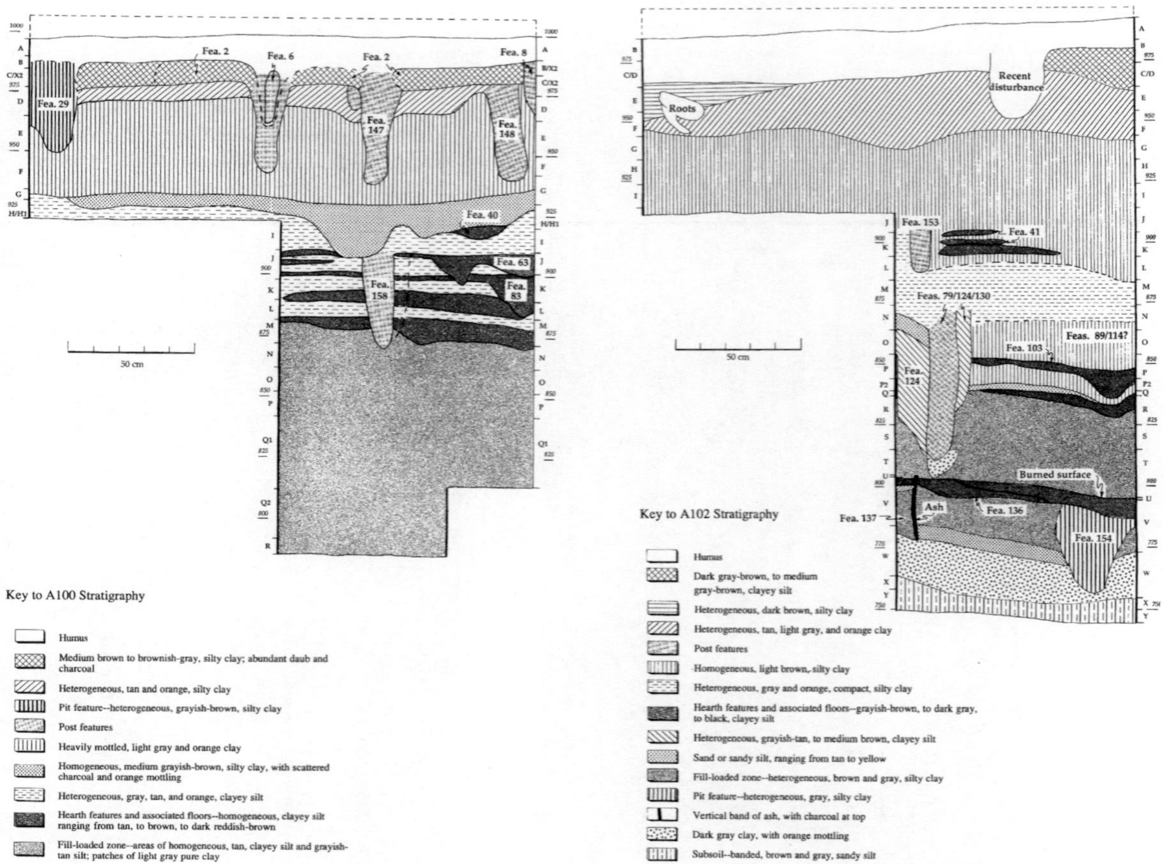

4.2. Section drawings of the south walls of units A100 and A102, Mound L (from *Bottle Creek Research*, edited by Brown and Fuller, copyright 1993 by the Alabama Archaeological Society, used by permission).

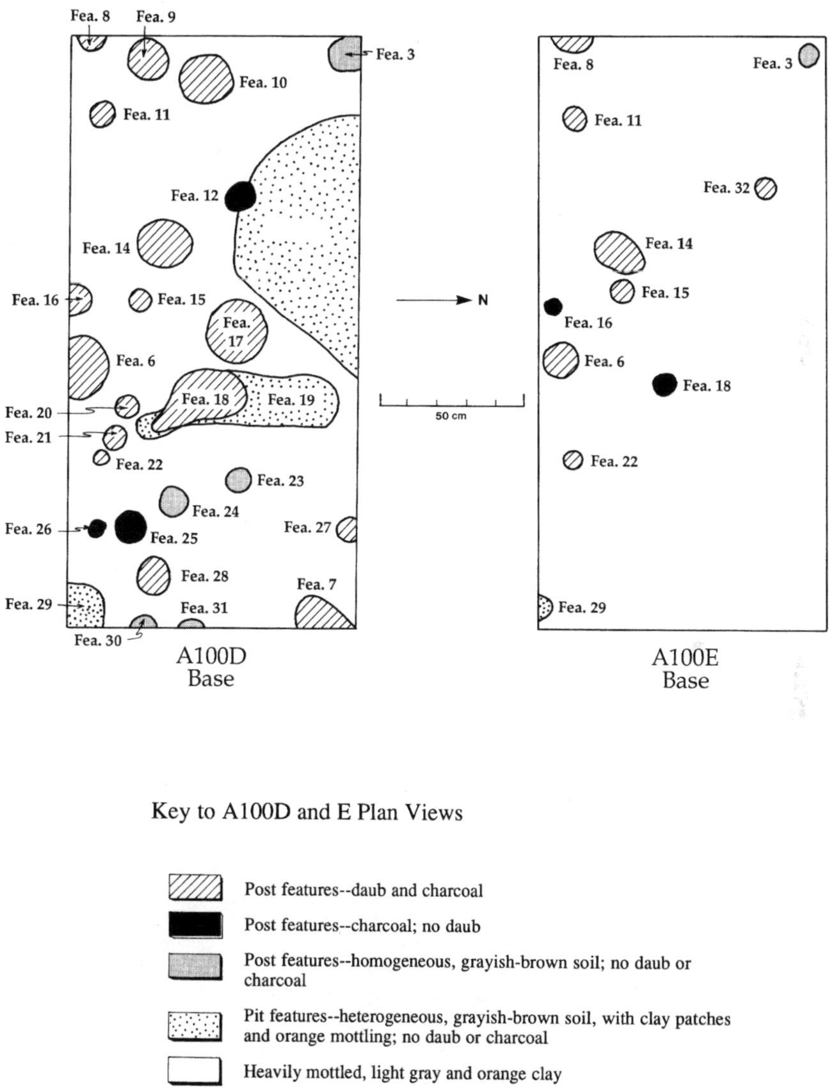

4.3. Plan views of the bases of levels D and E in Unit A100, Mound L (from *Bottle Creek Research*, edited by Brown and Fuller, copyright 1993 by the Alabama Archaeological Society, used by permission).

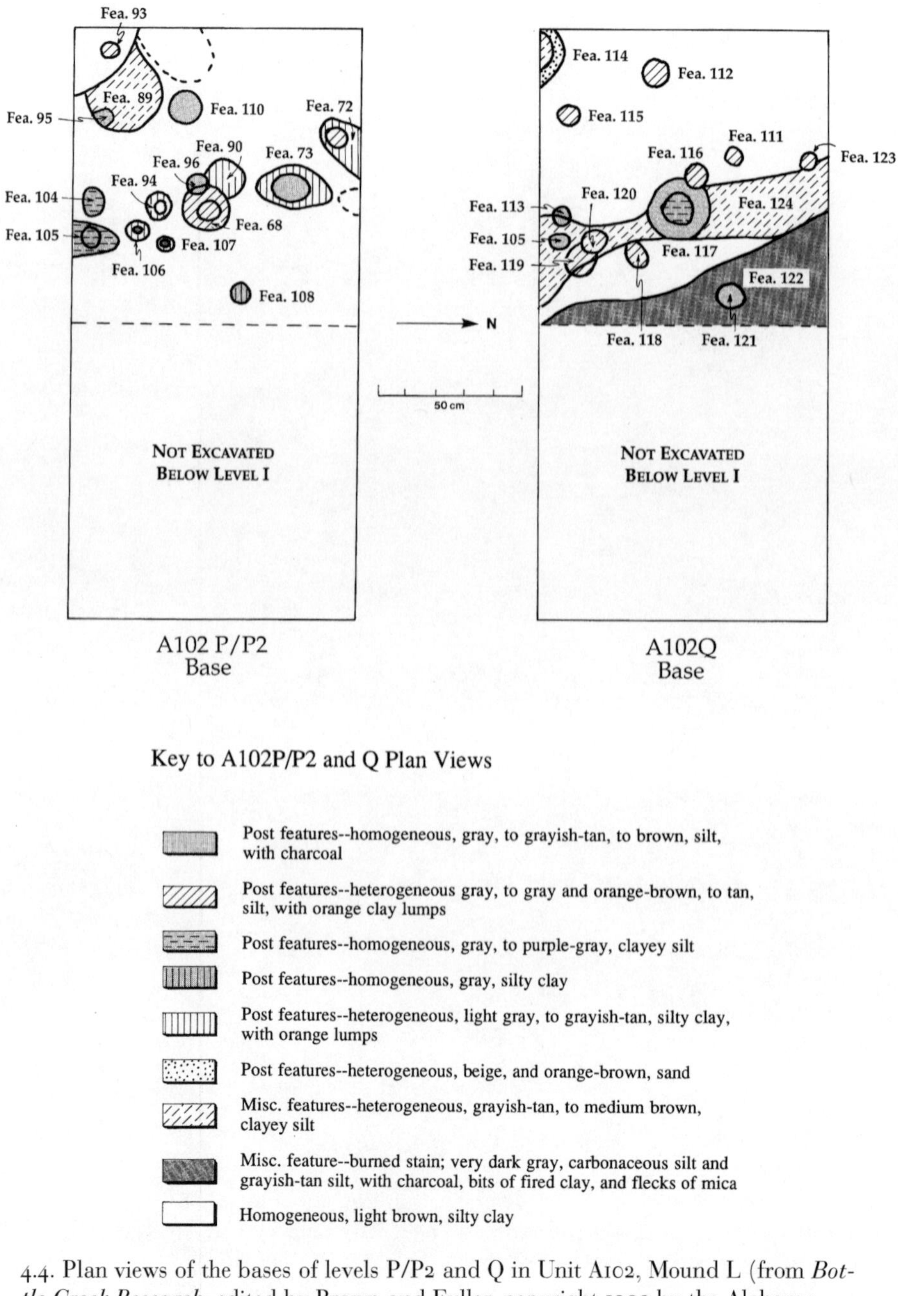

4.4. Plan views of the bases of levels P/P2 and Q in Unit A102, Mound L (from *Bottle Creek Research,* edited by Brown and Fuller, copyright 1993 by the Alabama Archaeological Society, used by permission).

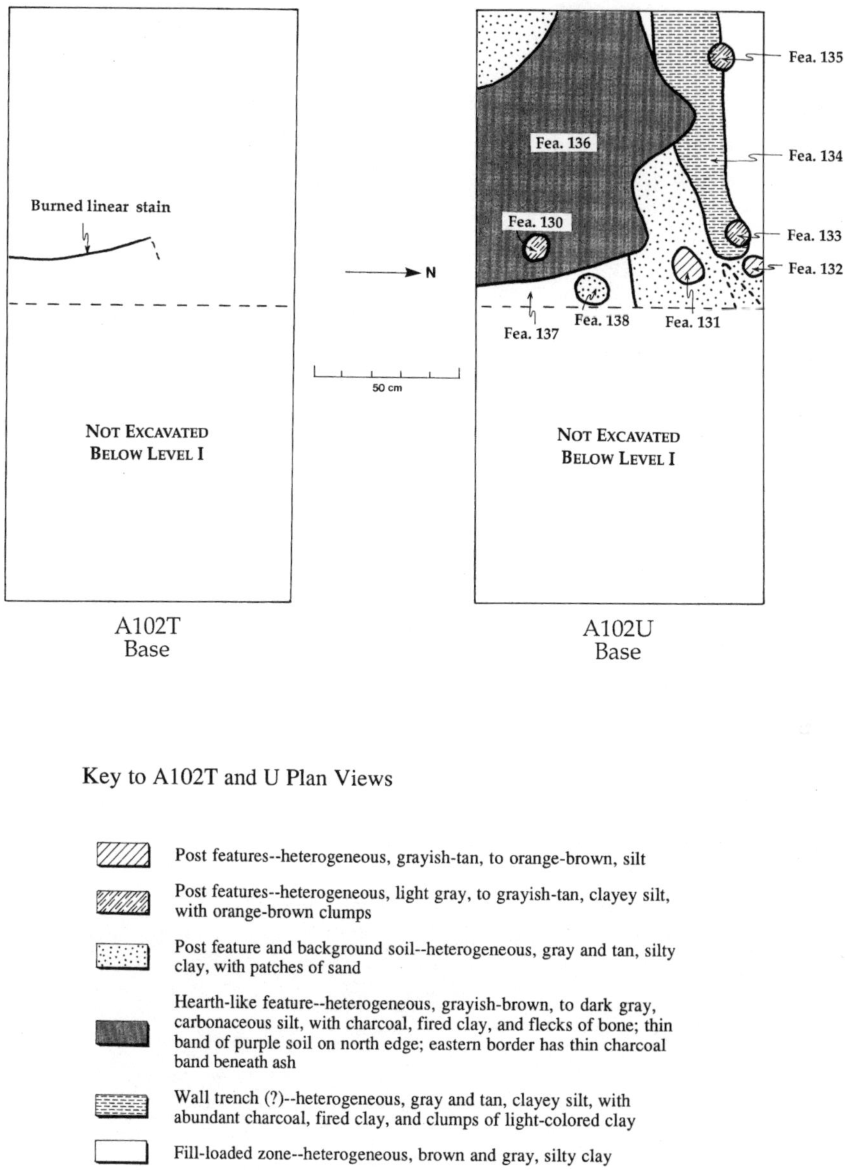

4.5. Plan views of the bases of levels T and U in Unit A102, Mound L (from *Bottle Creek Research*, edited by Brown and Fuller, copyright 1993 by the Alabama Archaeological Society, used by permission).

The most abundant artifact type found was daub. We plotted the relative density of daub by weight for each level (Table 4.1). This distribution is important because it helps correlate the nature of the structure's orientation and final collapse with post-depositional change. We also analyzed daub greater than one inch in size in terms of characteristics such as temper, degree of oxidation, and form, such as the presence of cane impressions, mat impressions, flat surfaces, etc., according to a classification system created by Richard Fuller (personal communication, 1993). We measured cane impression diameters, providing further evidence of structure framework.

EXCAVATIONS

We began excavations at the east end of the summit by removing the loose, brown, sandy humus layer as Zone A. Zone B consisted of light brown to light brown and gray mottled clayey silt. At the base of Zone B, which ranged from 3 to 16 cm below the ground surface, we encountered a thick concentration of daub in units in the southeast portion of the excavation block. As noted above, we designated this daub layer Feature 2 (Figure 4.6). We found that the daub concentration thinned out west and north of an east-west running trench that lay beneath Feature 2, along the south end of the excavation block. This trench, designated as Feature 264 (Figure 4.7), appears to represent the base of a wall from the latest house on the mound, which dated to the middle of the eighteenth century. Feature 2 is probably dispersed daub from this burned structure.

A variety of features began to show up at the base of Feature 2. One of these, Feature 171, was a historic period pit feature. It was located at the juncture of two units in the center of the north wall of the excavation block. As this feature extended into the north profile, a thirteenth unit (D250, 1 × 2 m) was added to include the remaining portion of the pit (Figure 4.1). This pit contained a variety of aboriginal sherds, including numerous sherds from a single Moundville Incised, *var. Douglas* globular jar with small handles, a number of sherds from a small Bell Plain, *var. unspecified* open bowl with a single incision below the rim, as well as other sherds such as Port Dauphin Incised. Many of the large sherds from the *Douglas* vessel were stacked horizontally on top of one another, in the center of the pit. A smudge pit or corn cob pit (Feature 172) was located at the edge of Feature 171.

Zone C was relatively hard-packed and varied from 4 to 8 cm in thickness. Feature 264 became very distinct in those units located along the south end of the block, especially after the removal of Zone C. All of these units contained burned soil and reduced daub along the north edge of this daub trench feature, indicating that this was the base of a wall. Just

Table 4.1. Daub weight (gm) in various levels and features from the Mound L excavations

Units	Levels A–B	Feature 2	Provenience Level C	Feature 264	Level D
C141	100	125	395	0	297
C142	320	3925	595	0	445
C143	2225	9250	2798	18854	2298
C148	825	1347	697	0	244
C149	1650	9150	403	0	44
C150	1950	17370	4188	41877	796
C155	97	296	1095	0	447
C156	630	3497	497	0	247
C157	1451	5825	2694	14057	499
C162	297	195	997	0	1139
C163	552	397	2248	297	697
C164	675	3296	1947	13858	27
D250	747	497	–	–	–

north of this wall trench, a concentration of post features occurred. It is interesting to note that several large sherds were oriented vertically in the Zone C fill, suggesting intentional movement of upper fill to level the surface prior to reuse of the mound summit. We noted Bottle Creek phase ceramics such as D'Olive Incised, *var. unspecified*, Pensacola Incised, *vars. Gasque* and *Jessamine*, Mound Place Incised, *vars. McMillan* and *Waltons Camp*, Moundville Engraved, *var. Hemphill*, and Mississippi Plain, *var. unspecified*, along with Coastal Plain agate flakes and a few bone fragments. We recovered a Pensacola Incised, *var. Bear Point* sherd near the center of the west end of the block. Within Zone C, in the northwest end of the block, we discovered a small pit feature (Unit 162, Feature 329) that contained a bail from an iron kettle. The bail was oriented vertically in the ground, perhaps left in situ after being used secondarily as a pot hook of sorts. The weight of daub recovered in Zone C is also shown by unit in Table 4.1 and reflects the daub concentration in the southeast quarter of the summit.

Next, we excavated Feature 264 (Figure 4.7). This substantial trench feature contained numerous large chunks of daub. We observed a charred log just north of the daub wall in Unit C150. The daub feature is deepest in C150, dipping down along the southern edge into a pit-like depression. Aside from daub, we recovered relatively few artifacts from Feature 264. We discovered Bottle Creek phase ceramics such as Bell Plain, Mississippi Plain, and a sherd of Pensacola Incised, *var. Gasque.*

With the completion of Zone C and Feature 264, we were still just above the gray, tan, and orange clay mound cap, where features were most distinct. We removed this remaining heterogeneous layer as Zone D. At the base of Zone D, features were now apparent everywhere, and those noted previously showed up quite distinctly against the clay matrix (Figure 4.8). Within Zone D, we noted a faint trench (Feature 495) in units in the center of the north end of the block (C148 and C155). This trench is parallel to the

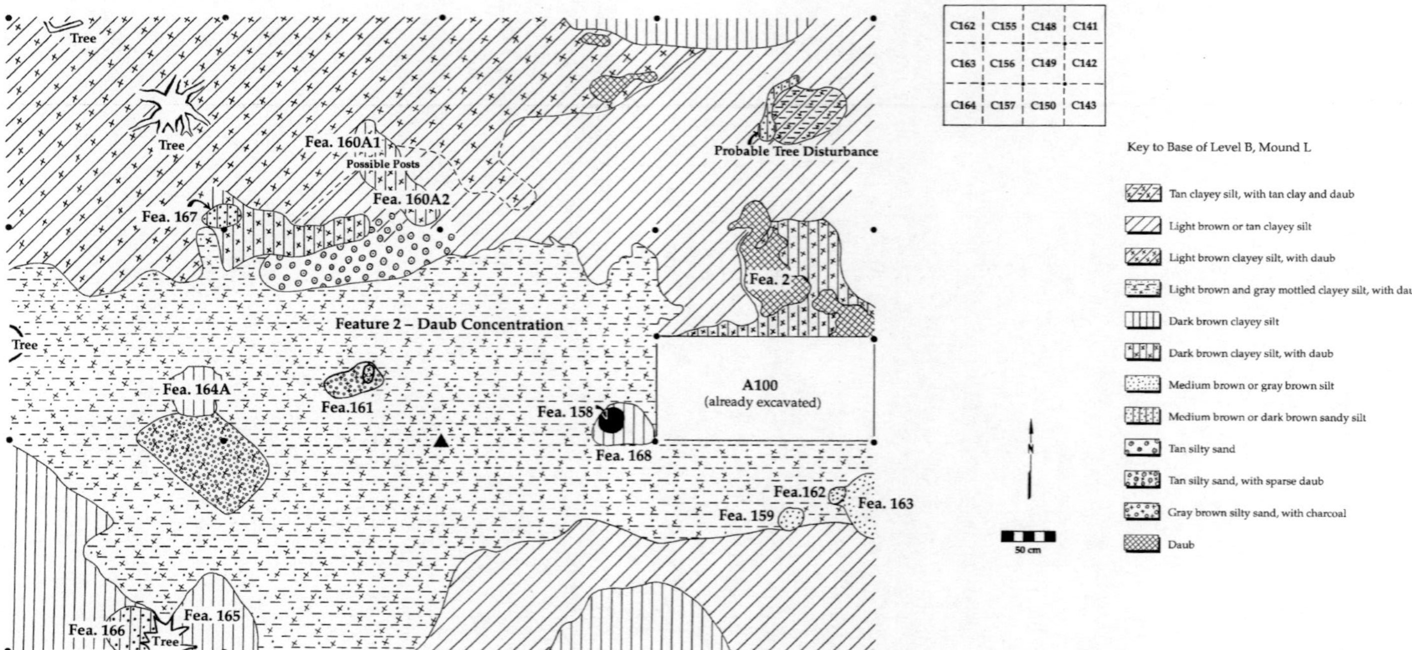

4.6. Plan view of the base of Level B, Mound L, showing the heavy concentration of daub (Feature 2).

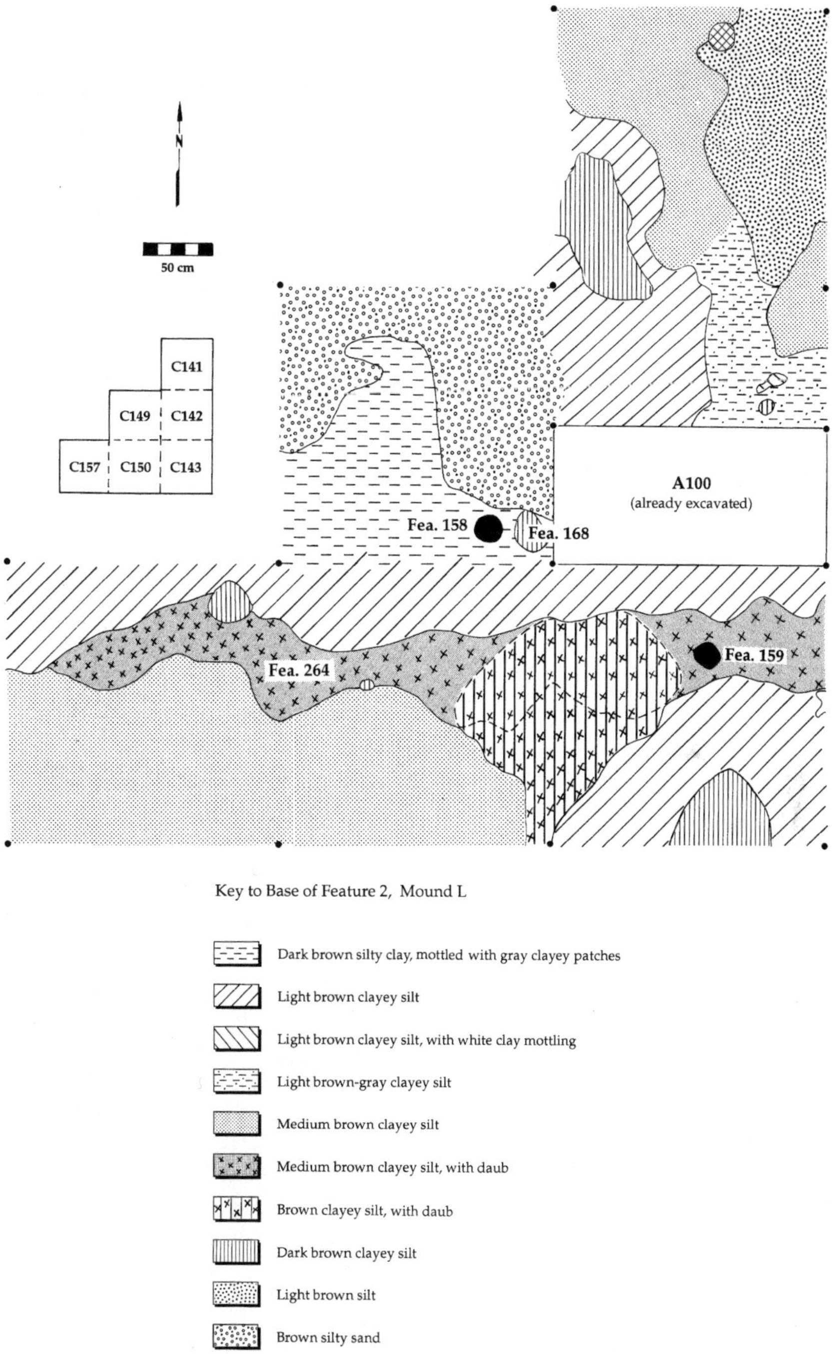

4.7. Feature 264, the daub-filled trench in Mound L, located below Feature 2.

4.8. Base of Zone D, Mound L, facing west. Note the plethora of post features (GCS/94/P8/4).

trench at the base of the daub wall feature (Feature 264). Daub weights for Zone D are shown in Table 4.1. Once Zone D was recorded, we focused our attention on the 689 remaining features, most of which were postholes and postmolds.

The most recent structure at Mound L has been identified as an Indian house that dates to the middle of the eighteenth century. The outline of this structure became evident at the base of Feature 2. Evidence for this component comes from a limited collection of European goods mixed with historic period native ones. The paucity of historic period aboriginal and European artifacts suggests the structure was occupied for only a short period. Perhaps the best evidence for short-term occupation structures may come from the site of Old Mobile where a number of French houses that date to the turn of the eighteenth century have been investigated (Waselkov 1991; 1993). Based on the known occupation of the site, the longest period of occupation at any one of these Old Mobile houses does not exceed nine years. It is probable that most of the Old Mobile structures were occupied for a much shorter period, and yet they contain very dense assemblages, even when considering only the aboriginal artifacts. This is in marked contrast to the historic period structure on the summit of Mound L.

The latest Bottle Creek Mound L structure appears to have been built over rubble from the preceding one, as the builders used daub as trench fill. The structure was rectangular in shape, and measured about 5.5 m east-west, by 3.5 m north-south. It appears very similar in size and construction to an excavated early-eighteenth-century aboriginal structure at a site (1Mb147) adjacent to Old Mobile (Silvia 2000:218–254; Waselkov 1999:41). The low artifact density, artifacts such as a French gunlock plate and a clasp knife, along with the total absence of European ceramics, suggest that this particular structure on Mound L was used over a short time period and may have served as a hunting camp.

ARTIFACTS

We recovered historic period artifacts from zones A and B, and within some of the features. We found most of the recovered iron, which is in very good condition, less than 10 cm below the ground surface. One of the most interesting pieces was the French gunlock plate that we found about 2 cm below the surface, above the structure floor. It is a Type C French trade gun that dates between 1680 and 1730 (Hamilton 1980:29, 32). As noted above, one very large iron spike, intentionally bent to form a hook, was recovered near the northwest corner of the latest structure. It probably functioned for hanging items within the building (Waselkov 1999:41). The blade of a clasp knife and three hand-wrought nails were also recovered. The only brass found was a French military button, which is in excellent condition. It is a simple dome button with a finished edge and attached shank. It is identical to Brain's (1979:189) type IIIa. Outside of southwest Alabama this type has been recovered from a number of sites, including Fort St. Pierre (Brown 1979), Fatherland (Neitzel 1965), Haynes Bluff (Brain 1988), and Fort Toulouse (Heldman 1973). In southwest Alabama the sites of Port Dauphin (Stowe n.d.), Fort Conde (Harris 1971), and Old Mobile (Waselkov 1991) have yielded these buttons. In this region of Alabama, a date range of 1702 to 1763 is suggested for this button type, corresponding with the French occupation. Lead artifacts included a smashed musket ball, a piece of shot, and a sprue. Glass was limited to a few fragments of dark green bottle glass.

Despite using 3.2 mm screen to process a large sample of the excavated fill, we recovered only four glass beads. This stands in contrast with the thousands recovered at Old Mobile (Waselkov 1999:43–44). All of the beads from Mound L appear to have originated in Amsterdam. Two are oblong dark blue beads, classified as type IIA6 (Brain 1979:98, 102). They are simply constructed with rounded ends. The date range for these beads is 1600–1890, with a mean date of 1749. A single pale blue, large, round, wire-wound bead was classified as WIA1. The date range for this type is given as 1680 to 1890, with a mean date of 1764 (Brain 1979:99, 107). The fourth bead fits Brain's type WIIIA6 (1979:112–113) or Karklins and Barka's type WIIIb*(a) (1989:65, 74). It is a portion of a large burgundy bead with bright yellow wavy lines forming diamond patterns around the surface. This bead type has a date range of 1699–1799, with a mean date reported between 1730 and 1734.

Lithic artifacts were relatively abundant throughout the excavations. Most of this material is Coastal Plain agate. We also recovered a small number of Tallahatta sandstone, coarse sandstone, quartz, and chert artifacts. The lithic assemblage consists mostly of microliths (Chapter 9). These tools are bifacially or unifacially worked and include scrapers or knives, burins, drills, and retouched flakes. We also found a number of utilized and unmodified, small, tertiary flakes. Cores, decortication flakes, and more usual sized tools were relatively scarce.

The only projectile point found was a Mississippian Triangular, *var. Madison* point of gray and tan banded chert. It was recovered near the northwest corner of the structure. This point is in perfect condition and does not appear to have been used. It is interesting to note that archaeologists performing structure excavations at the site of Old Mobile have recovered several similar points that also appear to have been curated (Waselkov 1991; 1999:39).

We recovered three ground stone artifacts of hematitic sandstone. One of these has an incised design, while another was simply a triangular chunk. The third example was tabular in shape with striations from sawing, and appears to have been ground flat on the bottom and sides; the top was rounded. It resembles the prow of a catlinite pipe and may represent an attempt at reproducing one. Investigators at Old Mobile have also found a number of worked catlinite fragments and portions of pipes (Waselkov 1991, 1999:41–43). A fragment of ground greenstone or schist with a square corner was also recovered at Bottle Creek.

All of the ceramics recovered to date are aboriginal. This fact is a little surprising given that we had encountered other kinds of European materials. Aside from daub, aboriginal ceramics comprise the bulk of the artifact collection. We obtained good diagnostic assemblages for the two uppermost components, with historic aboriginal types including Fatherland Incised, *vars. Nancy*, *Snyders Bluff*, and *unspecified*, Old Town Red, *var. Fort Louis*, Mission Red Filmed, *var. unspecified*, Port Dauphin Incised, *var. unspecified*, and Chickachae Combed, *var. unspecified*. The collection includes simple open bowls, colono-ware brimmed plates, and collared globular jars. Middle Mississippian Bottle Creek phase markers include Pensacola Incised, *vars. Gasque* and *Jessamine*, Mound Place Incised, *var. McMillan*, Moundville Incised, *vars. Bottle Creek* and *Moundville*, and D'Olive Incised, *vars. Dominic* and *unspecified*. Grog- and grog-and-sand-tempered sherds that fall under the type Baytown Plain are most common at Old Mobile, typically comprising about 65 percent of the ceramic as-

4.9. Plan view of the base of Zone D, Mound L.

semblages associated with structures. At Mound L, however, this percentage is much lower. Shell tempering is much more common, suggesting that the inhabitants were descended from a local group such as the Tomés, Pensacolas, or Mobilians (Waselkov and Gums 2000:6–23, 121–131).

We found a tubular pipe stem and portions of at least three pottery pipe bowls in the Mound L excavations. Six of the pipe bowl fragments were plain, one is incised around the rim exterior, and one has small vertical ticks on the rim exterior. All of these are of very fine ware and probably date to the historic component. They resemble European white clay tobacco pipes and are similar in size and form to pipe fragments from Old Mobile (1Mb94) (Waselkov 1991), Conde Village (1Mb132) (Silvia and Waselkov 1993b), the Courthouse Annex (1Mb156) (Sheldon and Cottier 1983), and Dog River (1Mb161) (Silvia and Waselkov 1993a).

STRUCTURE RECOGNITION

As revealed in the plan view at the base of Level D (Figure 4.9), it is apparent that there are a number of earlier structures represented by the

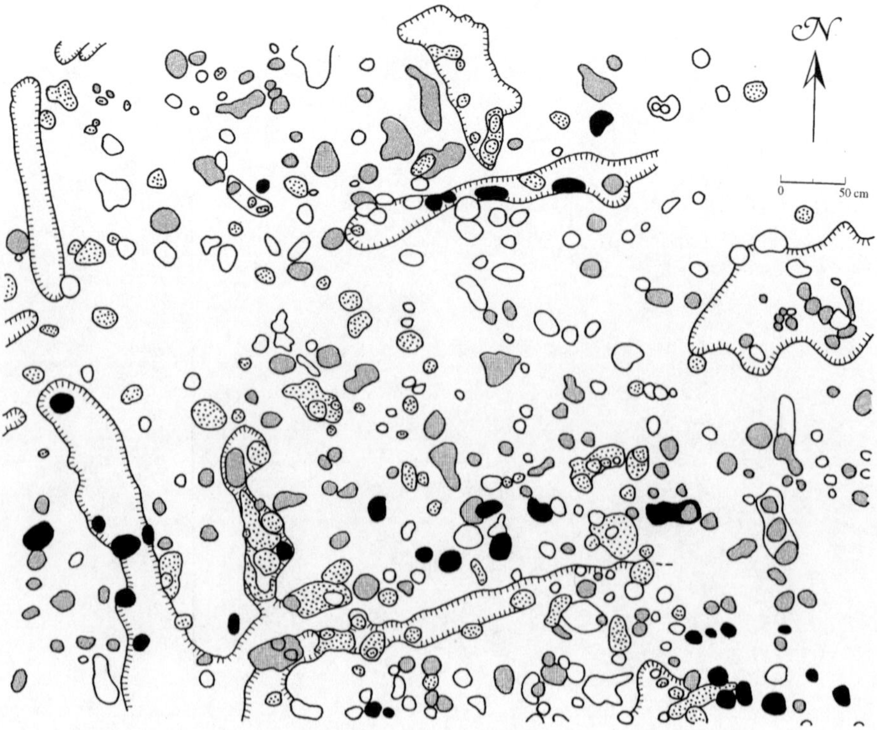

4.10. Plan view of the base of Zone D, Mound L, showing post features with daub (black—abundant daub; shaded—moderate; stippled—sparse).

numerous post features and trenches. One means of deciphering this picture is to look at feature fill type. We color-coded all features to search for patterns, but unfortunately this method failed to clarify the situation. The next approach was to simplify matters, by coloring only those features that contained daub (Figure 4.10). This technique revealed several linear patterns. The blackened posts that represent very abundant, large daub fragments essentially follow the line of Feature 264 (Figure 4.7). These may represent pulled posts, which filled in with the overlying Feature 264 fill. Figure 4.11 highlights the trench features present at the base of Zone D. The three easternmost trenches are believed to represent a structure that existed immediately below the mid-eighteenth-century structure. It is composed of posts set in trenches, but the location of its corners is uncertain. If the pattern is recognized correctly, the building would have measured about 4.25 m long by 3.25 m wide. The trenches to the west appear to be prehistoric and probably belong to structures that lie largely outside the excavation block.

There are several other possible rectilinear and curvilinear structures

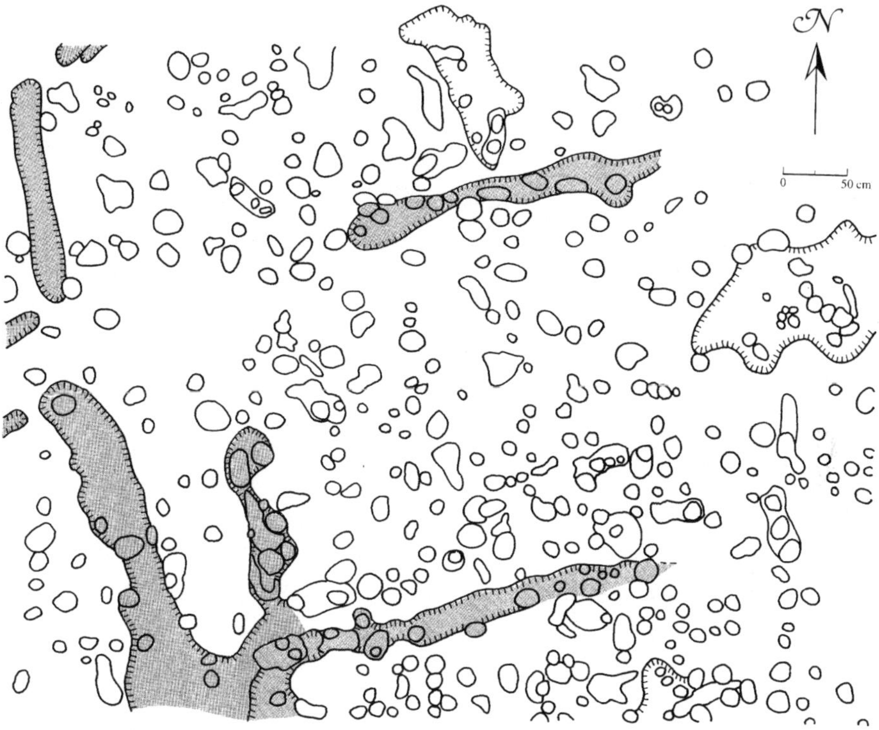

4.11. Proposed structure pattern 1 on Mound L.

that may have existed, constructed with single or double set posts. The rectilinear structure in Figure 4.12 measured about 4.5 m long by 4 m wide. Another possible rectilinear structure was about 5 m long by 4.5 m wide (Figure 4.13). The structure in Figure 4.14 appears to have been round, with a diameter of about 9.25 m. This structure is similar to a round structure excavated at the Lookout site in the Natchez Bluffs region, which had a diameter of 9.5 m (Brown 1985:274). The delineation of these earlier structures obviously is very tentative, as it is based simply on pattern recognition. The artifact assemblage does suggest, however, that all of the buildings that the inhabitants erected at the base of Zone D date to the Bottle Creek I and II phases (A.D. 1250–1550) and were occupied over a relatively narrow time range.

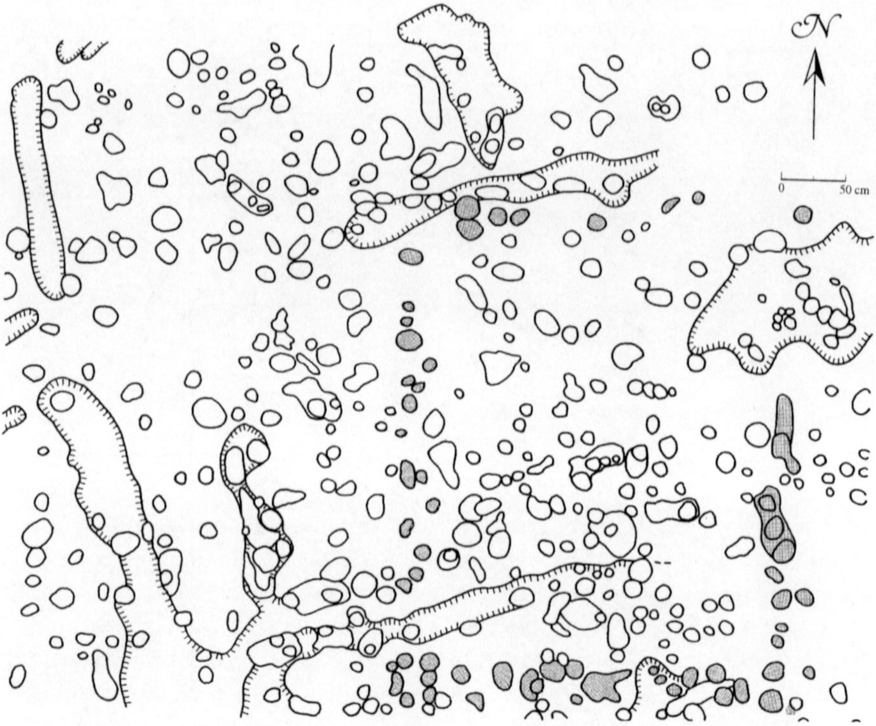

4.12. Proposed structure pattern 2 on Mound L.

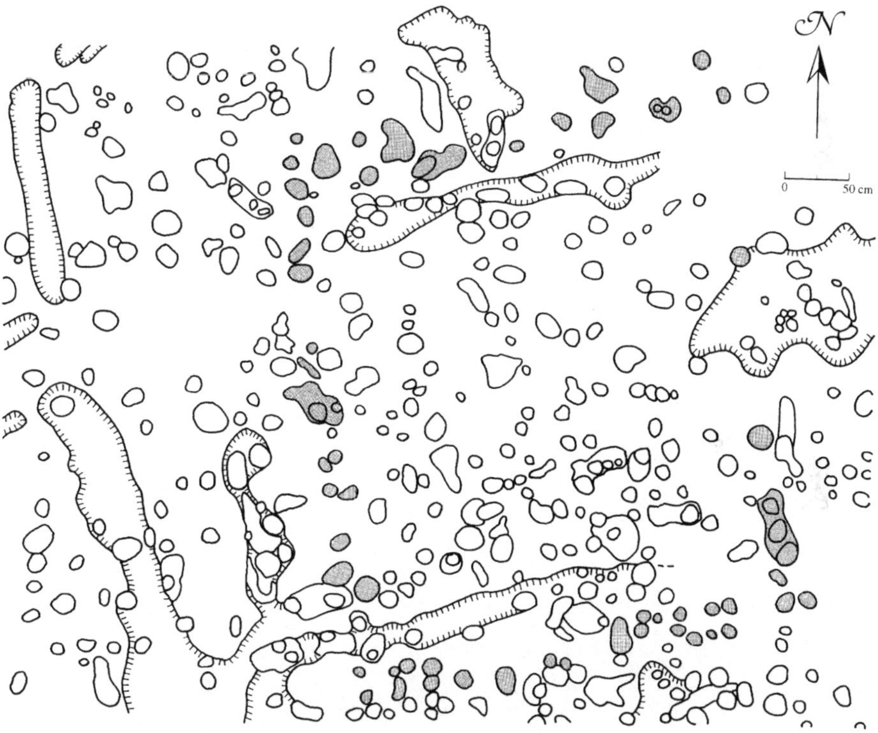

4.13. Proposed structure pattern 3 on Mound L.

4.14. Proposed structure pattern 4 on Mound L.

5 / Food Plant Remains from Excavations in Mounds A, B, C, D, and L at Bottle Creek

C. Margaret Scarry

INTRODUCTION

The archaeobotanical analyses of the Bottle Creek materials were designed to investigate how the people who lived at the site procured and produced plant foods. Specifically, our goal was to collect data that could be used to determine what plant resources the inhabitants chose to use, to assess the relative importance of cultivated and wild plants in their diets, and to compare the subsistence practices of the Bottle Creek residents to those of people who were part of contemporaneous Mississippian societies of the interior Southeast, such as Moundville.

The following pages describe the results of my analyses of the plant data from the 1993 and 1994 excavations at Bottle Creek. The plant data collected from test excavations in mounds A, B, C, D, and L provide a picture of late prehistoric plant use at Bottle Creek and yield information relevant to the issues noted above.

FIELD AND LABORATORY METHODS

Because we wanted to recover fine-grained subsistence data, we collected flotation samples from both midden and feature contexts encountered during the excavations in the various mounds. Generally the samples were 10 liters in volume, although some were smaller or larger depending on the nature of the deposit. We took the soil samples to the laboratory at the University of South Alabama where we floated them to separate the plant remains from other materials. The system we used to process the samples was a flotation machine manufactured by R. J. Dausman Technical Services. (We are indebted to Dr. Greg Waselkov for the loan of this machine, which made processing the flotation samples a comparatively efficient task.) The light fractions from the flotation samples were caught on fine-mesh nylon cloth. The heavy fractions were caught on a 1 mm mesh screen.

Table 5.1. Analyzed flotation samples from mounds A, B, C, D, and L

Unit	FS	Volume (liters)	Plant wt./vol. (grams/liter)	Wood wt./vol. (grams/liter)
Mound A				
D100 F1	1	12.0	0.06	0.03
D100 F3	2	10.0	0.13	0.08
D100 M	5	15.5	0.13	0.12
D100 S2	6	10.5	0.43	0.38
D100 S2	7	11.0	0.49	0.45
D100 GG	8	8.0	2.76	2.34
D100 EE	9	14.0	0.23	0.21
D100 FF	10	18.0	0.03	0.03
D100 Fea. 3	4	5.5	0.11	0.09
Mound B				
D201 Fea. 29	1	9.5	0.64	0.61
Mound C				
C100 J	13	20.0	0.36	0.35
C100 N	27	10.0	0.81	0.77
C100 Z	45	33.0	0.96	0.78
C100 Fea. 2A	35	2.0	0.46	0.43
C100 Fea. 5A	11	10.0	0.65	0.34
C100 Fea. 5B1	12	11.0	0.77	0.37
C100 Fea. 5C	15	10.0	0.41	0.38
C100 Fea. 6	14	16.0	1.24	0.64
C100 Fea. 7A	16	10.0	9.19	4.72
C100 Fea. 8A	18	5.0	4.38	3.02
C100 Fea. 10B1	25	4.0	2.41	2.39
C100 Fea. 17B	30	10.0	0.73	0.72
Mound D				
C101 J	17	10.0	0.54	0.52
C101 Fea. 3F2	10	10.0	0.34	0.33
C101 Fea. 13B	9	10.5	0.12	0.10
C101 Fea. 17A	15	10.0	0.24	0.23
C101 Fea. 20A	16	13.0	0.36	0.34
Mound L				
C155C	9	9.0	0.05	0.05
C155 Fea. 171	12	9.0	0.03	0.02
D250 Fea. 171	14	55.0	0.06	0.06
C148 Fea. 171	10	9.0	0.05	0.04
C148 Fea. 172	11	3.0	28.86	0.00
C155 Fea 174	13	8.0	0.07	0.02
C157 Fea. 296	17	7.0	3.63	3.63
C142 Fea. 336	15	11.0	0.31	0.30
C148 Fea. 499	16	10.0	0.76	0.73

Since our goal was to collect evidence about subsistence practices, we selected for analysis samples from midden and feature contexts that seemed most likely to contain food plant remains. In all, I analyzed 36 samples from five mounds, representing 31 different contexts. Table 5.1 provides basic information about the quantities of wood and plant material (wood plus food plant remains) in each sample. The samples that were floated but not analyzed for this report are held in reserve.

The methods I used to sort and identify the plant remains were the same for all samples except Mound L Feature 172 (see below). I weighed the samples and then sieved them through geological screens (2 mm, 1.4 mm, and .7 mm) to make sorting easier. I inspected each size fraction, including the material that passed through the .7 mm screen, with the aid of a binocular stereoscopic microscope (10–20x magnification). I sorted all plant fragments greater than 1.4 mm in size and scanned the plant materials in the fractions smaller than 1.4 mm. I removed and identified seeds or seed fragments found in these small fractions, but did not otherwise sort the materials.

My sorting procedures differ from those generally used on plant remains from the eastern United States in one way. It is standard practice to use 2 mm as the dividing point between complete sorting and scanning. In my analyses of remains from the Moundville system in the Black Warrior Valley of Alabama (Scarry 1986:186–188), however, I used 1.4 mm as the dividing point between sorting and scanning. I chose to sort to a finer level because experiments by Neal Lopinot (1984:111–112) had demonstrated that acorn was underrepresented when sorting stopped at the 2 mm level. For this study of the Bottle Creek remains, I chose to sort remains greater than 1.4 mm in size. This makes the data from Bottle Creek directly comparable to those from sites in the Moundville system and insures that acorns are not underrepresented in the analysis.

Several of the light fractions were quite large. For these samples, I used a riffle splitter to halve or quarter the materials. Once the subsample was sorted, I used the quantities of plants identified in the subsample to estimate the quantities in the sample as a whole.

Seeds and other non-wood plant parts were identified to the lowest possible taxonomic level. Size, shape, and surface texture were the primary characteristics I used to classify the seeds. I made initial identifications by reference to pictorial seed manuals (e.g., Martin and Barkley 1961). When possible, I confirmed identifications by reference to modern comparative specimens. I divided seeds that I could not identify into two categories. Unidentified seeds are ones for which taxonomic affiliations have not been determined. Unidentifiable seeds are fragments or damaged specimens that lack diagnostic characteristics. Table 5.2 gives the common and taxonomic names of the plants identified in the samples.

For the purposes of analysis, I quantified the nutshell and corn remains by count and weight; I counted seeds but not did not weigh them, and I counted each seed and nut fragment separately. I made no attempt to determine the actual number of nuts or seeds represented in the remains.

To compare taxa abundances between contexts, I standardized the data by dividing the raw count for each taxon in a sample by the weight of plant remains from that context (N. Miller 1988; Scarry 1986:195–196) (Tables 5.3–5.5). The standardized counts measure a taxon's abundance relative to the amount of plant material in a sample. This provides a good basis for examining the representation of taxa in various contexts.

I processed the sample from Mound L Feature 172 in a different way from the other 35 samples. This sample, which came from a smudge pit, contained 27 fragments of corncobs and thousands of corn cupules, the sockets on the cobs that hold the kernels. I pulled and measured the cob

Table 5.2. Plants identified in the Bottle Creek flotation samples

Common Name	Taxonomic Name	Mound A	Mound B	Mound C	Mound D	Mound L
Introduced Crop						
Corn	*Zea mays*	X	X	X	X	X
Native Crops						
Chenopod	*Chenopodium berlandieri*	X		X	X	X
Knotweed	*Polygonum* sp.	X				X
Little barley	*Hordeum pusillum*	X				
Maygrass	*Phalaris caroliniana*	X		X		
Sunflower	*Helianthus annuus*		X			
Nuts						
Acorn	*Quercus* sp.	X		X	X	X
Hickory	*Carya* sp.	X		X	X	X
Fruits						
Persimmon	*Diospyros virginiana*			X	X	X
Blackberry	*Rubus* sp.			X	X	
Maypop	*Passiflora incarnata*				X	
Miscellaneous						
Yaupon	*Ilex vomitoria*			X	X	
Wild rice cf.	*Zizania aquatica*	X		X		
Amaranth	*Amaranthus* sp.			X		
Morninglory	*Ipomoea/Convolvulus*	X				
Nightshade	*Solanum* sp.		X			
Sida	*Sida* sp.					X
Smartweed	*Polygonum* cf. *pennslyvanicum*	X				
Purslane	*Portulaca* sp.			X		
Verbena	*Verbena* sp.	X				
Bulrush	*Scirpus* sp.			X	X	
Bean family	Fabaceae	X				X
Composite family	Compositae	X				
Grass family	Poaceae	X		X	X	X
Mallow family	Malvaceae	X				X
Saw palmetto root	*Serenoa repens*					X

Table 5.3. Standardized counts for plants identified in the flotation samples from Mound C at Bottle Creek (data are taxon count/grams plant weight)

Common Name	C100J	C100N	C100Z	C100 Fea. 2A	C100 Fea. 5A	C100 Fea. 5B1	C100 Fea. 5C	C100 Fea. 6	C100 Fea. 7A	C100 Fea. 8A	C100 Fea. 10B1	C100 Fea. 17B
Crops												
Corn cupule	7.54	4.47	10.10	6.45	5.16	2.91	5.33	90.53	59.33	67.90	1.35	0.87
Corn kernel	10.14	13.41	37.86	6.45	93.23	72.48	14.20	1.42	3.80	1.81	0.58	3.48
Chenopod	1.16	1.63	0.35	—	—	—	1.18	—	0.04	0.10	—	—
Maygrass	—	2.44	0.07	—	—	0.19	—	—	—	—	—	—
Nuts												
Acorn	0.29	—	1.11	—	—	0.19	—	—	—	—	—	—
Hickory	—	—	0.07	—	0.32	—	—	—	—	—	0.39	—
Fruits												
Blackberry	—	—	0.07	—	—	—	—	—	—	—	—	—
Maypop	—	—	—	—	—	—	—	—	—	—	—	—
Persimmon	—	—	0.10	—	—	—	—	—	—	—	—	—
Miscellaneous												
Wild rice cf.	2.03	—	0.69	—	0.65	0.39	0.59	—	—	—	—	—
Yaupon	0.29	0.41	0.17	—	—	—	0.59	—	—	—	—	—
Amaranth	—	0.41	—	—	—	—	—	—	—	—	5.97	—
Purslane	0.29	—	—	—	—	—	—	—	—	—	—	—
Bulrush	—	0.41	—	—	—	—	—	—	—	—	—	—
Grass family	—	0.41	—	—	—	—	—	—	—	—	—	—
Unidentified	—	1.22	0.10	—	—	0.19	1.18	—	0.04	—	—	—
Unidentifiable	1.16	1.22	1.21	—	2.26	0.58	1.78	0.16	0.04	0.10	—	—

Table 5.4. Standardized counts for plants identified in the flotation samples from Mound D at Bottle Creek (data are taxon count/grams plant weight)

Common name	C101J	C101 Fea. 3F2	C101 Fea. 13B	C101 Fea. 17A	C101 Fea. 20A
Crops					
Corn cupule	3.53	0.85	—	3.90	3.35
Corn kernel	1.18	9.79	8.33	10.39	8.38
Chenopod	2.35	0.43	1.19	1.30	0.56
Maygrass	—	—	—	—	—
Nuts					
Acorn	—	2.13	1.19	2.60	2.23
Hickory	—	0.85	—	—	1.12
Fruits					
Blackberry	—	0.43	—	—	—
Maypop	1.18	—	—	—	—
Persimmon	—	0.85	—	—	—
Miscellaneous					
Wild rice cf.	—	—	—	—	—
Yaupon	—	—	—	1.30	—
Amaranth	—	—	—	—	—
Purslane	—	—	—	—	—
Bulrush	—	—	—	1.30	—
Grass family	—	—	1.19	—	—
Unidentified	—	—	—	5.19	0.56
Unidentifiable	—	—	7.14	—	2.79

fragments that had complete cross-sections and scanned the remainder of the material. The scanning resulted in the identification of a few kernel fragments, but I found no other food remains. Because counting the fragmentary corn remains would have been excessively time-consuming, I weighed the plant remains from this sample but did not attempt to count the cupules and cupule fragments.

RESULTS

The samples from all mounds produced more than ample plant remains. There is, however, considerable variability from sample to sample in the quantity and variety of such remains. Some samples produced relatively modest quantities of plant remains, while others produced an abundance of the same. In general, plant remains are more abundant in the midden and feature samples from Mound C than in those from the other mounds. This pattern is consistent with field observations about the nature and richness of the deposits in the various mounds. In all, I identified 26 plant taxa in the samples from Bottle Creek (Table 5.2). The range of plants represented is comparable to that found at many other late prehistoric sites in the lower Southeast.

The composition of the food plant assemblage leaves little doubt that the inhabitants of Bottle Creek depended on farming for a substantial portion of their diet. Corn remains are, by far, the most abundant food plant

Table 5.5. Standardized counts for plants identified in the flotation samples from mounds A, B, and L at Bottle Creek (data are taxon count/grams plant weight)

Common Name	Mound A								Mound B	Mound L							
	D100 EE	D100 F1	D100 F3	D100 FF	D100 GG	D100 M	D100 S2	D100 Fea. 3	D201 Fea. 29	C142 Fea. 336	C148 Fea. 171	C155 Fea. 171	D250 Fea. 171	C148 Fea. 499	C155 C	C155 Fea. 174	C157 Fea. 296
Crops																	
Corn cob	—	—	—	—	—	—	—	—	—	—	—	—	—	—	—	—	—
Corn cupule	3.13	28.00	34.38	3.39	33.82	7.61	23.98	13.79	2.81	3.53	2.44	4.00	4.32	0.92	4.76	—	—
Corn kernel	12.23	9.33	26.56	30.51	3.99	3.55	12.26	20.69	7.28	2.06	19.51	8.00	4.32	0.92	9.52	5.66	—
Chenopod	—	—	—	—	0.09	1.02	0.22	—	—	—	—	4.00	0.62	—	—	—	—
Knotweed	—	—	—	—	—	0.51	—	—	—	0.29	2.44	—	—	—	—	—	—
Knotweed cf.	—	—	—	1.69	—	—	—	—	—	—	—	—	—	—	—	—	—
Little barley	—	—	—	1.69	—	—	—	—	—	—	—	—	—	—	—	—	—
Maygrass	—	—	—	—	0.32	—	0.22	—	—	—	—	—	—	—	—	—	—
Sunflower	—	—	—	—	—	—	—	—	0.17	—	—	—	—	—	—	—	—
Nuts																	
Acorn	0.31	1.33	4.69	—	1.63	1.02	—	—	—	—	—	—	—	—	2.38	—	—
Acorn meat	—	—	—	—	—	—	—	—	—	—	—	—	—	—	—	32.08	—
Hickory	—	—	2.34	—	0.41	—	—	—	—	—	—	—	—	0.13	—	—	—
Fruits																	
Persimmon	—	—	—	—	—	—	—	—	—	—	—	—	—	0.26	—	—	0.04
Miscellaneous																	
Wild rice	—	—	—	—	—	—	—	1.72	—	—	—	—	—	—	—	—	—
Sida	—	—	—	—	—	—	—	—	—	—	—	—	0.31	—	—	—	—
Smartweed	—	—	—	—	0.05	—	—	—	—	—	—	—	—	—	—	—	—
Morninglory	—	—	—	—	—	0.51	—	—	—	—	—	—	—	—	—	—	—
Nightshade	—	—	—	—	—	—	—	—	0.17	—	—	—	—	—	—	—	—
Saw palmetto root	—	—	—	—	—	—	—	—	—	—	—	—	—	—	—	—	0.04
Verbena	—	1.33	—	—	—	—	—	—	—	—	—	—	—	—	—	—	—
Bean family	—	—	—	—	—	0.51	—	—	—	—	—	—	—	—	—	1.89	—
Composite family	—	—	—	—	—	0.51	—	—	—	—	—	—	—	—	—	—	—
Grass type 1	—	—	—	—	—	—	—	—	—	—	—	—	14.2	—	—	—	0.12
Grass type 2	—	—	—	—	—	—	—	—	—	—	—	—	5.86	—	—	—	0.12
Grass type 3	—	—	—	—	—	—	—	—	—	—	—	—	0.62	—	—	—	—
Grass family	—	—	—	—	0.09	—	0.22	—	—	—	9.76	—	—	0.53	—	3.77	—
Mallow family	—	—	—	—	0.05	—	—	—	—	—	—	—	—	0.26	—	—	—
Unidentified	—	—	2.34	1.69	—	2.54	0.19	—	—	—	—	—	3.71	0.92	—	1.89	—
Unidentifiable seed	1.57	8.00	—	20.34	—	—	—	—	—	—	—	—	—	—	—	—	—
Unidentifiable	—	—	—	—	0.14	4.57	0.22	—	—	—	—	—	—	—	—	41.51	0.16

remains in the assemblage. Kernels and cupules are present in all but two samples. One of the latter, Mound D Feature 17, had kernels but not cupules. The other, Mound L Feature 296, contained substantial quantities of wood charcoal, but virtually no food plants of any kind. In the samples containing both kernels and cupules, the quantity of kernels equals or exceeds that of cupules in 21 of the 34 samples. In some cases (e.g., Mound C C100xZ, C100 Feature 5A, C100 Feature 5B1) the abundance of kernels relative to cupules is truly dramatic. Cupules do, however, greatly outnumber kernels in the samples from Mound C features 6, 7a, and 8a, which were identified in the field as possible smudge pits, and in the definite smudge pit from Mound L Feature 172.

The fact that kernels outnumber cupules in many samples is interesting. At most sites cupules, which are inedible by-products discarded during food processing, are more abundant than kernels, which are generally cooked and consumed. The low to moderate quantities of cupules in many of the samples suggests that the grains were removed from the cobs at off-mound locations on the site or at nearby sites associated with Bottle Creek. This raises the possibility that some of the food remains in the mound deposits are derived from feasting or from foodstuffs provided as tribute to the Bottle Creek elite. It is worth noting that the proportions of kernels relative to cupules are higher in the samples from Mound C than in the samples from the other mounds. This may indicate that the midden deposits on this mound derive from different activities than do those of the other mounds.

Besides corn, the samples from Bottle Creek produced small numbers of seeds from five indigenous plants—chenopod, knotweed, sunflower, maygrass, and little barley—that were grown as crops in parts of the Eastern Woodlands. It is disappointing to have to note that the evidence for whether the seeds at Bottle Creek came from wild or cultivated stands of these plants is ambiguous. Seeds from domesticated chenopods have coats that are thinner than those of wild types and margins that are truncate rather than rounded or convex (Smith 1985a). The chenopod seeds from Bottle Creek popped when they burned and most lack any trace of seed coat. While it will take further analysis to be sure, there is a distinct possibility that the seeds are from the domesticated testa-less variety described by Smith (1985b:130). Populations of domesticated knotweeds can be recognized by a combination of two characteristics. The seeds are generally longer than those from wild plants, and most seeds have thin, smooth coats rather than thick, rough ones (Asch and Asch 1985; Fritz 1987). There were only a few knotweed seeds in the samples and those that were present lacked their seed coats. Thus, it is not possible to determine whether they came from domesticated or wild plants. Domesticated sunflowers produce seeds that are larger than those of wild plants, but we recovered only a single fragment of a sunflower seed from Bottle Creek and it was not sufficiently intact to estimate its size. Although maygrass and little barley were clearly part of the indigenous crop complex, no morphological changes attributable to domestication have been identified for these taxa. Thus, context is the only criterion we have for distinguishing seeds from wild plants from those of cultivated plants. Maygrass is native to the Black Belt prairies of Alabama but does not naturally occur in the Mobile-Tensaw Delta (Harper 1944:67). Little barley is also a native of Alabama, but it is found in dry habitats (Harper 1944:74–75) quite unlike the conditions at and around Bottle Creek. Given that Bottle Creek is outside the natural range of maygrass and is an unlikely place to find wild stands of little barley, it is possible that the seeds from both taxa came from plants that were cultivated.

While seeds from these potential native crops occur in 20 of the 36 samples from Bottle Creek, they are much less abundant than corn remains. If the people of Bottle Creek grew them, the evidence suggests that they were minor crops in comparison to corn. This pattern is similar to that found at other late prehistoric sites in the lower Southeast, where native crops do not seem to have been as important as they were to contemporaneous societies of the Midwest and Midsouth (Johannessen 1993; Scarry 1993b).

Both acorn and hickory shell are present in the Bottle Creek samples. Acorn occurs in more samples and in slightly higher quantities than hickory, but neither is abundant. Indeed, given that nuts were major foods for many prehistoric peoples of the Southeast, nutshells are surprisingly scarce at Bottle Creek. The paucity of nutshells in the deposits from the mounds may be a result of a markedly greater reliance on cultivated over gathered plant foods by the site's inhabitants. Alternatively, nutshells may be scarce because nuts were processed for their starch or oil elsewhere on the site or at other sites in the region.

Seeds from three wild fruits—blackberry, persimmon, and maypop—are present in the samples. None is frequent or abundant, however. Beyond noting their presence, little can be said about fruit use at Bottle Creek.

The plants listed in the miscellaneous category in the various tables are ones that do not fit into the other groups. Most taxa in this category are represented only by one or two specimens, which may be incidental inclusions in the deposits. Several plants, however, deserve special comment.

Seeds from a member of the holly family are present in five samples—four from Mound C and one from Mound D. These compare well with the seeds of yaupon (*Ilex vomitoria*). Leaves of the yaupon holly were the principal ingredients in the black drink, a beverage that was consumed in large quantities on many important ceremonial occasions (Hudson 1979). Yaupon berries were not used in the black drink, but the seeds in the samples were probably a by-product of brewing the beverage. Yaupon berries have short stalks and grow singly or in small clusters distributed along the branches of the shrub. The fruit is persistent, remaining on the plant for long periods after it is ripe (Grimm 1966: 172). If yaupon leaves were harvested by cutting branches, then sometimes the persistent berries would have been unintentionally collected and brought to where the beverage was prepared. Likewise, if leaves were harvested by hand-stripping, it would be more efficient to collect both the leaves and the berries—which could be discarded later—than to try avoiding the berries. In either case, the presence of the seeds strongly suggests that the beverage was brewed on some of the mounds at Bottle Creek.

Specimens from a large-seeded member of the grass family occur in five of the samples from Mound C and in one sample from Mound A. I have identified these seeds as wild rice. We know that wild rice was an important food for Native Americans who lived in the upper Midwest. Its distribution, however, extends to brackish and freshwater marshes throughout much of the Eastern Woodlands including the Gulf Coast. The identification of wild rice seeds at sites in Tennessee (Chapman and Shea 1981), as well as at Bottle Creek and Moundville (see Chapter 6) attest to the occasional use of wild rice for food in the Midsouth and lower Southeast.

In addition to maygrass, little barley, and wild rice, there are at least three other members of the grass family represented in the samples. One of these grasses has seeds that resemble those of the panicoid group that includes the *Panicum* and *Setaria* genera. Another has minute seeds that resemble those of the *Digitaria* genus. The grass family is, however, an enormous group containing numerous species with seeds that can be difficult to distinguish. For now I merely note the presence of several grass taxa in the miscellaneous category.

COB MEASUREMENTS

Besides the fragments of cupules and kernels found in most samples, we recovered portions of 27 corn cobs from the smudge pit (Feature 172) in Mound L. These portions are of interest because cob morphology differs between corn cultivars (Nickerson 1953). The number of rows of grain per ear is an important diagnostic trait. In addition, cupule size and shape, cob shape, and row alignment vary by cultivar.

Ideally, we would use observations on the cobs from Feature 172 to identify the type or types of corn raised at Bottle Creek and its associated sites. We know from ethnohistoric accounts that Native Americans elsewhere in the Southeast grew several distinct varieties, which they planted at different times and used for different purposes (Swanton 1946:268, 274, 290; Williams 1930:437). Unfortunately, the standard typology (North American Pop, Midwestern 12-row, Eastern 8-row) that has been used for archaeological corn from the Eastern Woodlands does not adequately describe variation that is present in collections (King 1994; Scarry 1994; Wagner 1994). While this problem is widely recognized, no one has yet devised a satisfactory new classification. For the present, it seems best to describe the cob remains from Mound L Feature 172 in detail, but to postpone assigning them to types until larger collections and better classification schemes are available.

Because row number is an important attribute, only the 18 cobs from Feature 172 with complete cross-sections from which I could determine row number are described here (Table 5.6). For each cob, I made observations on eight morphological attributes. The procedures used followed the general methods described by Ford (1973:188–189). The attributes recorded include, among others, those that experiments by King (1987:118)

Table 5.6. Attributes of cobs from the smudge pit in Mound L, Feature 172

Cob Type	Row No.	Row Pairing	Cob Form	Maximum Diameter (mm)	Minimum Diameter (mm)	Cupule Height (mm)	Cupule Width (mm)
M	8	W	S	7.27	7.24	3.88	5.06
M	10	W		7.37	7.01	3.14	4.98
M	8	W	S	7.55	6.25	2.82	4.86
M-T	8	W	S	7.60	7.40	2.59	4.58
M-T	10	W	S	8.00	7.56	3.09	4.30
T	10	W		9.05	7.36	2.87	4.93
M	8	W	S	9.42	8.89	2.59	5.51
M	10	W	S	10.22	9.77	3.01	6.11
M	10	W		10.51	9.64	3.57	5.90
M-B	10	W	S	11.09	10.81	3.18	5.63
M	8	W	S	11.31	10.11	3.47	6.71
M-B	10	W	S	11.31	11.49	3.29	5.30
M-B	10	W	S	11.42	8.83	3.48	4.97
M-B	10	W	S	11.49	11.25	3.39	5.87
M	8	W	S	11.55	10.19	3.11	7.38
M-B	8	W	S	12.01	10.69	3.12	7.32
M	8	W	S	12.79	12.74	3.30	7.20
M	10	W	S	13.49	11.42	2.71	7.21
Mean	9.11			10.19	9.37	3.15	5.77
SD	0.99			1.92	1.83	0.34	0.98

have shown to be among the most useful for distinguishing corn cultivars grown in the Eastern Woodlands. They are also the attributes that I used in my analyses of cobs from the Moundville area (Scarry 1986). Thus, cobs from Bottle Creek can be readily compared to those from Moundville.

Three of the observed attributes are qualitative characteristics. I coded cob section as whole, midsection, tip, or butt. I used combinations, such as midsection-tip, to indicate segments present on larger fragments. I recorded cob shape as tapered when a fragment decreased in diameter toward the tip; and straight, or cigar-shaped when a fragment tapered toward both ends or toward the butt. I coded strength of row pairing as weak when cupule wings overlapped, moderate when a narrow groove separated adjacent cupules, and strong when the groove between cupules was wide.

Besides the qualitative characteristics, I recorded five quantitative attributes for each cob. I counted row number as close to the midsection as possible to avoid distortions caused by irregular rows at either end of a cob. I also measured maximum and minimum diameter at the midsection, and measured the width and height (internode length) of the largest cupule near the midpoint of the cob in millimeters.

Table 5.6 lists the attributes of each cob from Feature 172; mean values and standard deviations for the quantitative measures are given in the last two rows of the table. The cob assemblage is composed of cobs with

8 (39 percent) or 10 (61 percent) rows of grain. Most cobs are straight and exhibit weak row pairing. Mean cupule width is 5.77 mm and mean cupule height (internode length) is 3.15 mm.

SUMMARY AND CONCLUSIONS

The Bottle Creek plant samples provide insights about the subsistence practices of the site's residents. Crops, or at least corn, dominate the plant assemblage. It is clear that agricultural products played a major role in feeding the population. Wild plants, with the possible exception of wild rice, either were relatively unimportant in the diet or were processed elsewhere and brought to activities on the mounds in forms (e.g., acorn meal, hickory oil) that left few traces in the archaeological record. The abundance of corn and the paucity of nutshell in the deposits are similar to the situation that Gremillion (1993) found in her analysis of materials from Waselkov's test excavations at Bottle Creek. Based on the results of these analyses, it would appear that the people of this site were as reliant on agriculture as were their contemporaries living in the interior river valleys. I think it is also quite possible that if we examine plant remains from sites associated with Bottle Creek, we will find evidence that its neighboring communities provisioned the elite at this center.

6 / The Use of Plants in Mound-Related Activities at Bottle Creek and Moundville

C. Margaret Scarry

INTRODUCTION

Bottle Creek, located in the Mobile Delta, and Moundville, located in the Black Warrior Valley of Alabama, are the two largest Mississippian sites in Alabama (Figure 6.1). As discussed by Fuller (Chapter 2), ceramics recovered from the two sites suggest interaction and exchange between the polities, although neither community seems to have been under the direct control of the other. Excavations in midden deposits on the mounds at both sites have yielded plant remains. This chapter summarizes what we know about the production and use of plant foods at the two sites and explores the use of plants in mound-related activities.

Bottle Creek and Moundville are arguably the most impressive Mississippian mound centers in the lower Southeast. The sheer scale of monumental architecture at these two sites speaks to us of the commanding authority of the paramount chiefs who ruled them. Undoubtedly many factors contributed to the dominant role these centers achieved in regional politics, but we can be certain that the power of the elite was based in part on productive agricultural economies capable of generating substantial surpluses.

For several reasons Bottle Creek and Moundville make a logical pairing for examining late prehistoric subsistence practices in the lower Southeast. Although the sites are located on the same drainage system, they are in vastly different environmental settings. Moundville was built on a high terrace overlooking the Black Warrior River, while Bottle Creek was built on Mound Island, surrounded by the swamps and rivers of the Mobile-Tensaw Delta. The occupation histories of the two sites overlap, but they show different developmental trajectories (Figure 6.2). A basic commonality is that both sites are believed to have been paramount centers of polities that dominated the surrounding countryside.

In this chapter I present the results of analyses of plant remains recovered from mounds at Bottle Creek and Moundville, and I place the results

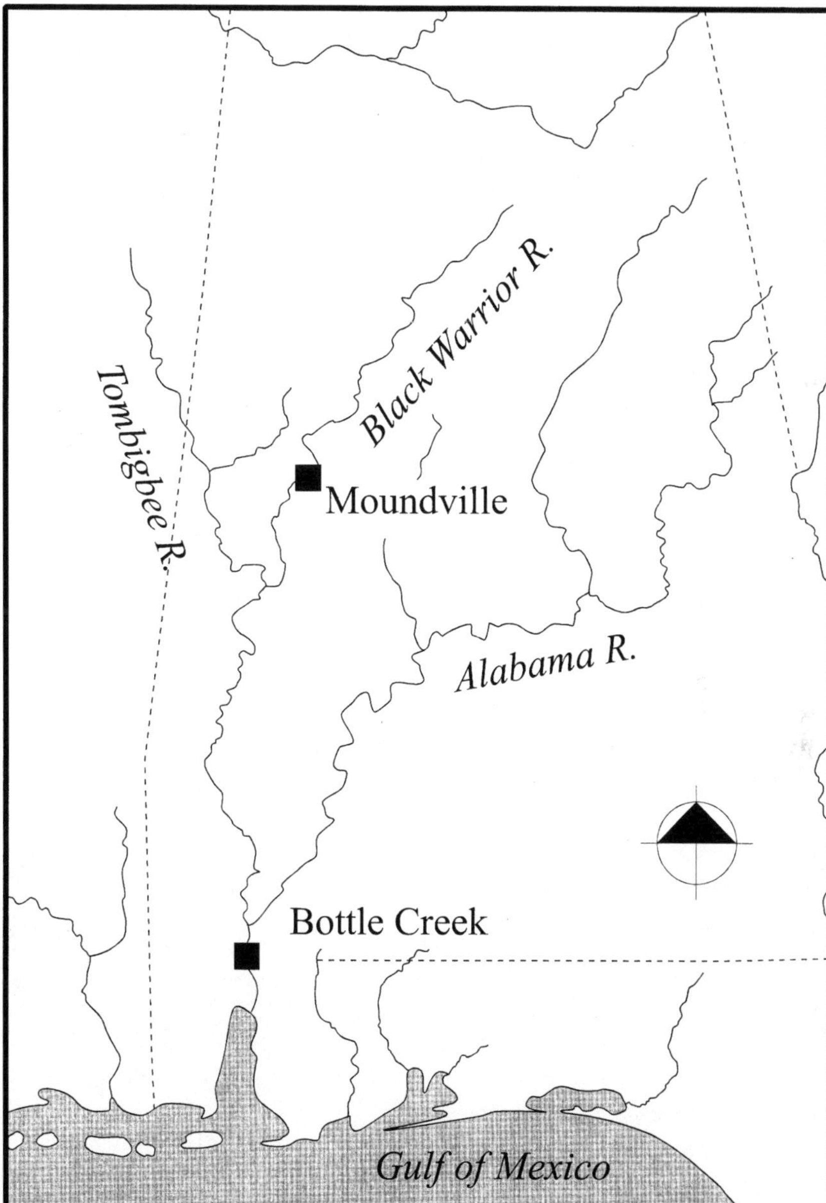

6.1. Location of the Moundville site on the Black Warrior River, relative to the Bottle Creek site in the Mobile-Tensaw Delta.

Date	Period	Bottle Creek	Moundville
1750			
1700	Early Historic	Port Dauphin	
1650			Alabama River
1600	Protohistoric	Bear Point	
1550			
1500	Late Mississippi	Bottle Creek II	Moundville III
1450			
1400			
1350			Late Moundville II
1300	Middle Mississippi	Bottle Creek I	
1250			Early Moundville II
1200		Andrews Place	Late Moundville I
1150	Early Mississippi		
1100			Early Moundville I
1050			

6.2. A comparison of late prehistoric chronologies at Moundville and Bottle Creek.

in the context of previous studies from the two polities. For Moundville, this entails fitting them into the larger picture I have developed over the last twenty or so years. For Bottle Creek, we are dealing with baseline studies that build on those done by Kristen Gremillion (1993) and myself (Chapter 5). In addition to characterizing the plant assemblages, I will examine evidence for provisioning of plant foods from outlying sites to the centers and provide a glimpse of ceremonial uses of plants in mound-related activities. The plant remains from both sites were recovered using flotation and for most samples I examined both the light and heavy fractions. I used standard procedures to sort and quantify the remains, and the procedures were consistent for all samples, including those from earlier analyses (see Chapter 5). In order to have sample populations large enough to make quantitative comparisons, I combined materials spanning several phases. Although this is far from ideal, it is unavoidable until we have additional collections from mound contexts.

MOUNDVILLE

I do not intend to put Bottle Creek in Moundville's shadow (Chapter 2), but it makes sense to discuss the plant data from Moundville first. By doing so we can use the better documented foodways from Moundville as reference points for examining those from Bottle Creek.

Over the last few years we have substantially revised our interpretations of the development of Moundville as a political center (Figure 6.3). The Mississippian presence at Moundville begins about A.D. 1050 with a dense cluster of farmsteads and two mounds. The inhabitants began a massive construction project around A.D. 1150 and, by A.D. 1300, the mound-and-plaza complex, as we know it today, was in place (Knight and Steponaitis 1998). The monumental architecture was clearly built according to a plan. A palisade enclosed the ceremonial precinct, which exhibits bilateral symmetry on its east-west axis, pairing of mounds around the plaza, and a status-related division of space along its north-south axis. Knight (1998) has argued that this town plan was a sociogram designed to mark the social order among ranked clans. During this period of intense activity, the resident population at Moundville reached its peak and the regional polity was consolidated. After A.D. 1300, Moundville changed from a bustling community to a "vacant ceremonial center." It remained home for the highest elite and a mortuary place for people from the surrounding region, but the resident population dropped dramatically (Steponaitis 1998). There was limited new construction on the mounds and some mounds, particularly those along the southern periphery of the plaza, dropped out of use.

The plant data that are the focus of this discussion come from Knight's excavations in mounds Q and G (Knight 1992, 1995, 2001). Both mounds were constructed during Late Moundville I and Early Moundville II and both had later stages added in Moundville II and III. The plants from Mound Q come from 15 contexts, the majority of which were slope middens associated with the Moundville II and III stages. The plants from Mound G come from five slope midden contexts dating to the Late Moundville II phase. Mound Q contains burials and has generally been considered a "mortuary-temple" mound. Mound G lacks burials and has been considered an elite residential mound. Knight's (2001) investigations, however, demonstrate that whatever their other differences, both mounds supported structures in which domestic activities took place. My previous analyses of plants from an elite residential district North of Mound R (NR on Figure 6.3), a residential district on the Riverbank, and two farmsteads provide a source of comparative data for the mound samples (Scarry 1986, 1993a, 1995). Note, however, that the Mound Q and G plant remains date to the Moundville II and III phases, while most of the comparative data come from Moundville I contexts.

Table 6.1 compares the food plants identified from mounds Q and G to those identified from non-mound contexts at Moundville. There is substantial overlap in the assemblages, especially those from Mound Q and the non-mound contexts. The apparently limited array of plants from Mound G is probably a result of the small sample size.

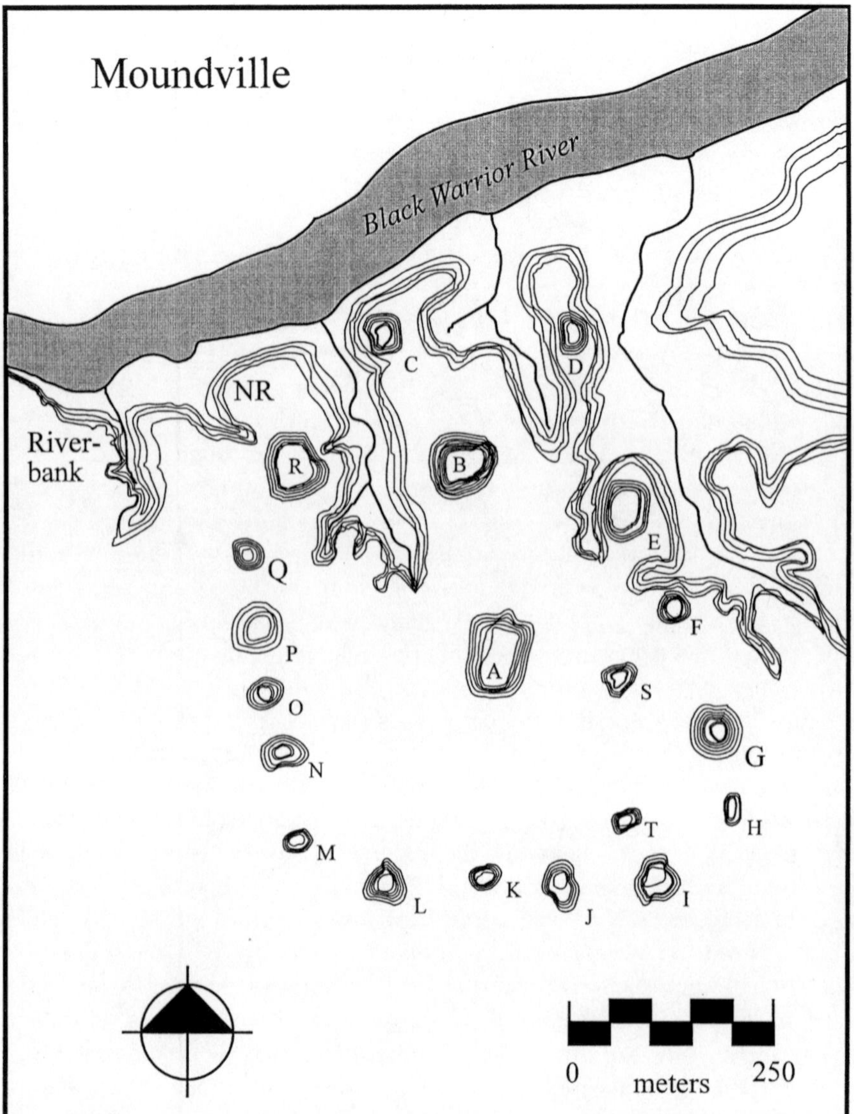

6.3. Plan of Moundville, showing the arrangement of its mounds.

If we consider frequency and abundance as well as presence, we find that the pattern of plant use on the mounds is, in most respects, similar to that seen in non-mound contexts. Corn remains dominate the mound samples. Kernels and cupules are ubiquitous and are consistently the most abundant plant food remains. Seeds from native crops occur in low num-

Table 6.1. Comparison of plants identified from various contexts at Moundville

	Mound Q		Mound G		Non-mound	
	count	count/gm plants	count	count/gm plants	count	count/gm plants
Crops						
Corn cupule	849	3.77	65	1.77	2859	2.91
Corn kernel	248	1.10	22	0.60	4169	4.24
Bean	7	0.03			37	0.04
Tobacco	1	>0.01				
Chenopod	38	0.17	13	0.35	529	0.54
Knotweed	2	0.01			21	0.02
Little barley	4	0.02			3	>0.01
Maygrass	26	0.12	25	0.71	206	0.21
Squash/gourd	2	0.01			1	>0.01
Squash/gourd rind	3	0.01			1	>0.01
Sunflower					4	>0.01
Nuts						
Acorn shell	36	0.16	1	0.03	3150	3.21
Acorn meat	11	0.05	2	0.05	41	0.04
Hickory	246	1.09	16	0.44	2108	2.15
Other nut	1	>0.01			28	0.03
Fruits						
Blackberry					6	0.01
Blueberry	2	.01	2	0.05	17	0.02
Elderberry					15	0.02
Grape	1	>0.01			24	0.02
Maypop	2	0.01	1	0.03	14	0.01
Persimmon	72	0.32	3	0.08	752	0.77
Plum/cherry	3	0.01			2	>0.01
Sumac					2	>0.01
Miscellaneous						
Wild bean	1	>0.01			2	>0.01
Wild rice			1	0.03	29	0.03
Yaupon					2	>0.01

bers, indicating the minor role these crops played compared to corn. Although never abundant at Moundville, nutshells, particularly those from acorns, are less common and less numerous in the mound samples than they are elsewhere at the site. In short, we are presented with a classic picture of a Mississippian agricultural economy, in which nuts, fruits, and native crops supplement a diet in which the preeminent plant food is corn.

Although a general pattern of plant use can be described for the Moundville polity, there is variation in the proportions of plant remains from different contexts at Moundville and its associated sites. I compared assemblages from elite residential districts at Moundville to those from a single-mound center and two farmsteads (Scarry and Steponaitis 1997). Specifically, I examined the distribution of nutshells and cupules, which indicate primary processing, to the distribution of kernels, which indicate cooking and consumption. My analyses showed that farmsteads had higher levels of processing debris than the single-mound center and the elite residential districts, but that levels of consumables were similar in all contexts. I argued that these results suggest that commoners living on farmsteads provisioned the elite with processed plant foods in the form of shelled corn, nut oils, and perhaps other nut products.

The data from mounds Q and G make it possible to add mound contexts from Moundville to my investigations of social variation in foodways. I use boxplots to compare and display the patterns of plant abundances (Figure 6.4). The data plotted are the natural logs of ratios derived from taxon counts. On these plots the vertical line within the box indicates the median, while the vertical lines at either end of the box approximate the twenty-fifth and seventy-fifth percentiles. The horizontal lines extending from the boxes indicate the tails of the distribution. Asterisks and circles indicate values that are outliers and extreme outliers, respectively. Areas where the boxes are constricted like hourglasses define confidence intervals for the medians. If the notches of boxplots on the same graph do not overlap, then the sample medians are significantly different at the 9.95 level (Tukey 1977; Velleman and Hoaglin 1981; Wilkinson 1990). In these plots, I used Moundville I data from farmsteads and from the elite residential district North of R as a basis for examining the Moundville II/III data from mounds Q and G.

When we examine the relative proportion of corn cupules to hickory nutshells, we find significant differences between contexts. The elite living on mounds Q and G were processing more corn relative to hickory nuts than the elite residing North of R, who in turn were processing more corn relative to nuts than the people living on farmsteads.

Keeping in mind that we are comparing deposits that span a period in which marked changes took place at Moundville, we can interpret the difference in cupule-to-nutshell ratios in several ways. It may be that the residents of Moundville ate more corn relative to nuts than their contemporaries living on farmsteads and that that disparity increased over time. This interpretation is certainly plausible given that bone chemistry analyses by Margaret Schoeninger and Mark Schurr (1998) indicate an increase in corn consumption between Moundville I and Moundville II/III. Alternatively, we may be seeing differences in levels of access to provisioned nut products. By this logic, the elite on mounds Q and G had greater access to, or made more use of, such products than did the elite living North of R.

Turning now to corn (Figure 6.5), we can use ratios of kernels to cupules to measure the amount of corn being consumed relative to the amount being processed. When we plot kernel-to-cupule ratios, we get results that appear problematical. The ratio of kernels to cupules from North of R are significantly higher than those of the farmsteads, and significantly higher than those of mounds Q and G. In fact, the ratios from the mounds do not differ significantly from those of the farmsteads.

These results seem counterintuitive. If the elite were provisioned, then we would expect the highest status contexts—those from the mounds—to have the highest ratios of consumption relative to processing. By looking more closely at the contexts from which the data are drawn, however, we can find an explanation for these apparently anomalous results. Although the households North of R were not located on a mound, their position

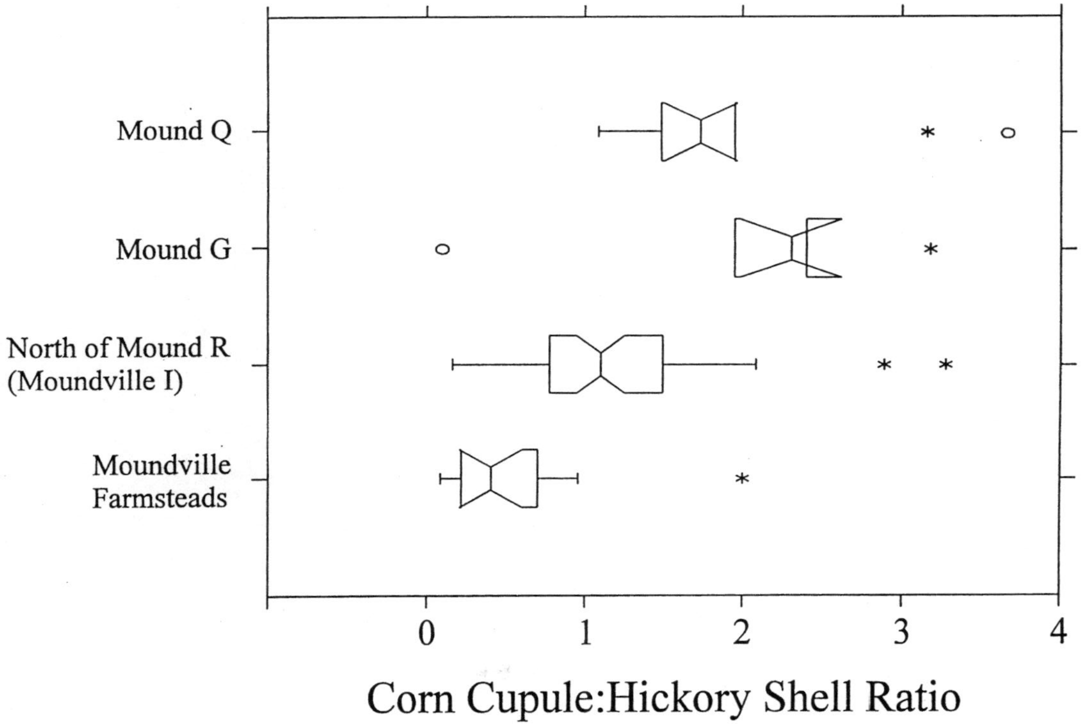

6.4. Box plot of the ratio of corn cupules to hickory shells at Moundville and Black Warrior farmsteads.

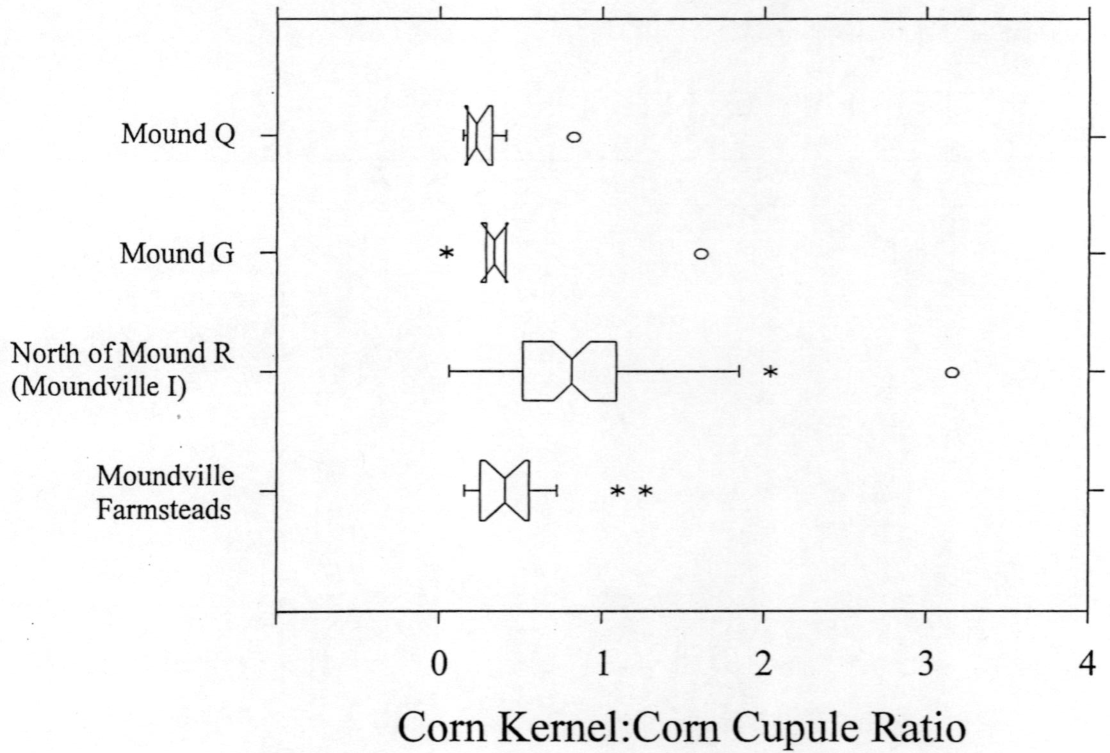

6.5. Box plot of the ratio of corn kernels to corn cupules at Moundville and Black Warrior farmsteads.

near the plaza at the extreme north edge of the site suggests the inhabitants were among the highest elite. We should also note that the ratios from North of R are a result of activities that took place during Late Moundville I when the site was densely populated and centralized control was at its height. The residents of mounds Q and G were undoubtedly high status, but the data come from activities that took place during Moundville II and III when the resident population was low. Moreover, Knight and Steponaitis (1998) have suggested that the fact that some mounds fall out of use at this time may indicate the lesser elite were contesting the power of the highest-ranking clans.

It is possible that the differences between the ratios from the Moundville I deposits North of R and those from the Moundville II/III deposits on mounds Q and G are a product of the lower population density in the later phases. In other words, with the decrease in the resident population at Moundville it may have been possible to meet demands for corn with grain raised in nearby fields. Since transport costs would be less of an issue and husked corn can be stored longer than shelled corn, more of the grain may have arrived at Moundville in an unprocessed form.

Alternatively, the differences between the ratios may be a result of changing social and political relations at the center. If power of the high elite was contested in Moundville II and III, then their ability to command tribute, particularly processed food from more distant farmsteads, may have been undermined.

BOTTLE CREEK

Let us turn now to Bottle Creek. As described by Fuller (Chapter 2), the Mississippian presence at Bottle Creek begins about A.D. 1100 in the Andrews Place phase. As far as we know, mound construction began about A.D. 1250 in the Bottle Creek I phase and continued unabated through the end of the Bottle Creek II phase, circa A.D. 1550. The mound complex, or at least part of it, was occupied in the protohistoric Bear Point and early historic Port Dauphin phases. As it exists today, the site has a ceremonial precinct with a central plaza bounded by mounds A, B, M, and L (Figure 1.3). The small mounds on the periphery of the precinct are composed of accumulated midden and are believed to have been the locations of the households of the chief's retainers and/or lower ranking elite.

The plant data that I use here come from excavations in mounds A, C, and L (Chapter 5). The plants from Mound A come from two premound midden deposits dating to the Andrews Place and Bottle Creek I phases, and from three deposits of midden associated with mound stages dating to the early Bottle Creek II and early Bear Point phases. The plants from Mound C come from 12 contexts including midden deposits, hearths, and three cob concentrations. Three of the contexts date to the Andrews Place phase, eight date to the Bottle Creek I phase, and one to Bottle Creek II. The plants from Mound L come from seven contexts, all of which probably date to the early historic Port Dauphin phase. I have also examined plants from mounds B and D, but I mention them only in passing since their chronological contexts have yet to be worked out. The only other plant data from Bottle Creek come from Gremillion's (1993) study of materials from Waselkov's tests on mounds G and E.

Table 6.2 presents summary data on the plants identified in the Bottle Creek samples from midden and refuse-pit contexts; smudge pits have been excluded. There appears to be considerable variability in the assemblages from the several mounds, but much of it is probably due to small sample sizes. It is interesting to note, however, the differences between the two largest assemblages, those from mounds A and C. The samples from Mound A, the big mound, contained mostly crop and nut remains. The nutshells occurred primarily in the samples from the premound middens and in the Bear Point midden. Crops, more specifically corn, overwhelmingly dominated the midden deposits associated with the Bottle Creek II stages of the mound. Although also dominated by corn, the assemblage from Mound C, a house mound, contained a variety of fruit seeds as well as the crop and nut remains. In addition, more than a third of the contexts from Mound C produced yaupon seeds (see Chapter 5).

Stepping back from the individual mounds and examining the Bottle Creek assemblage as a whole, it is possible to make some general statements about the frequency and abundance of the various plant foods. Corn occurs in every context and is, by far, the most abundant taxon. Native crops exhibit a typical pattern for the lower Southeast; they are sporadically present but never abundant (Johannessen 1993; Scarry 1993b). Hickory and acorn nutshells are present but surprisingly sparse. Both types of nutshell occur in fewer than half of the samples, and when present they are generally represented by only a few specimens. Gremillion's (1993) analysis of remains from mounds G and E produced similar results.

There has been considerable debate about whether late prehistoric people living in coastal environments raised crops on a scale comparable to their contemporaries living in interior settings (Knight 1984). A qualitative comparison of the plant assemblages from Moundville and Bottle Creek (Table 6.3) shows that the members of the two societies used quite similar sets of resources. Quantitatively, the greatest difference between the two areas is not the abundance of corn, but rather the lower frequency and abundance of nut remains at Bottle Creek. In sum, the Bottle Creek data indicate that at least in the Mobile-Tensaw Delta, the prehistoric people were unquestionably farmers as well as fisher/foragers.

Drawing on ethnohistoric descriptions of the Mobile and Tomeh subsis-

Table 6.2. Comparison of plants identified from various contexts at Bottle Creek

	Mound A		Mound C		Mound L	
	count	count/gm plants	count	count/gm plants	count	count/gm plants
Crops						
Corn cupule	963	23.88	494	5.89	37	0.90
Corn kernel	266	6.60	2227	26.56	45	1.09
Chenopod	5	0.12	20	0.24	3	0.07
Knotweed	1	0.02			2	0.05
Little barley	1	0.02				
Maygrass	8	0.20	9	0.11		
Nuts						
Acorn shell	46	1.14	42	0.50	1	0.02
Acorn meat			1	0.01	17	0.41
Hickory	12	0.30	7	0.08	1	0.02
Fruits						
Blackberry			2	0.02		
Cabbage palm			1	0.01		
Persimmon			3	0.04	3	0.07
Saw palmetto			2	0.01		
Miscellaneous						
Wild rice	1	0.02	32	0.38		
Yaupon			8	0.10		

Table 6.3. Comparison of plants identified at Moundville and Bottle Creek

	Moundville	Bottle Creek
Crops		
Corn	X	X
Bean	X	
Tobacco	X	
Chenopod	X	X
Knotweed	X	X
Little barley	X	X
Maygrass	X	X
Squash/gourd	X	
Sunflower	X	X
Nuts		
Acorn	X	X
Hickory	X	X
Other nut	X	
Fruits		
Blackberry	X	
Blueberry	X	
Cabbage palm		X
Elderberry	X	
Grape	X	
Maypop	X	X
Persimmon	X	X
Plum/cherry	X	
Saw palmetto		X
Sumac	X	
Miscellaneous		
Wild bean	X	
Wild rice	X	X
Yaupon	X	X

tence regimes, Knight and Adams (1981:41–42) have suggested that the prehistoric occupants of the Mobile-Tensaw Delta spent their summers at farmsteads located in the fertile bottomlands where they raised corn and other crops. Knight and Adams posit that in the fall people moved themselves—and presumably their harvested crops—to villages on high

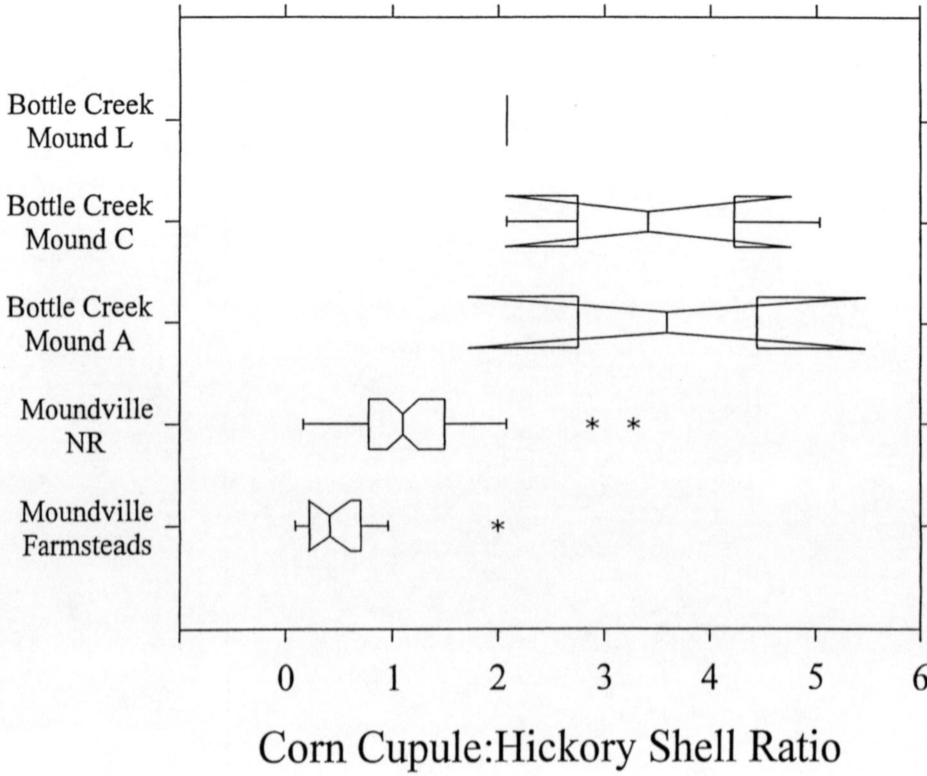

6.6. Box plot of the ratio of corn cupules to hickory shells at Bottle Creek, Moundville, and Black Warrior farmsteads.

ground where they were well above the winter and spring floods. The data from Bottle Creek fit well with this model.

Bottle Creek, like Moundville, is believed to have been the paramount center for a regional polity. Mound Island is surrounded by swamp and much of the dry land was taken up by the ceremonial precinct (Figure 1.2). Thus, it seems quite likely that many of the plant foods consumed at Bottle Creek were produced or procured elsewhere; that is, the elite and their retainers were provisioned. We do not have plant data from farmsteads or other sites associated with Bottle Creek, so we cannot compare levels of consumables and processing waste among different sites within the polity. We can, however, use the Moundville data as a baseline for investigating the question of provisioning.

The plots in Figure 6.6 compare the ratios of corn cupules to hickory nutshells from the mounds at Bottle Creek to the ratios from the Moundville I elite residential district and farmsteads. The comparisons emphasize

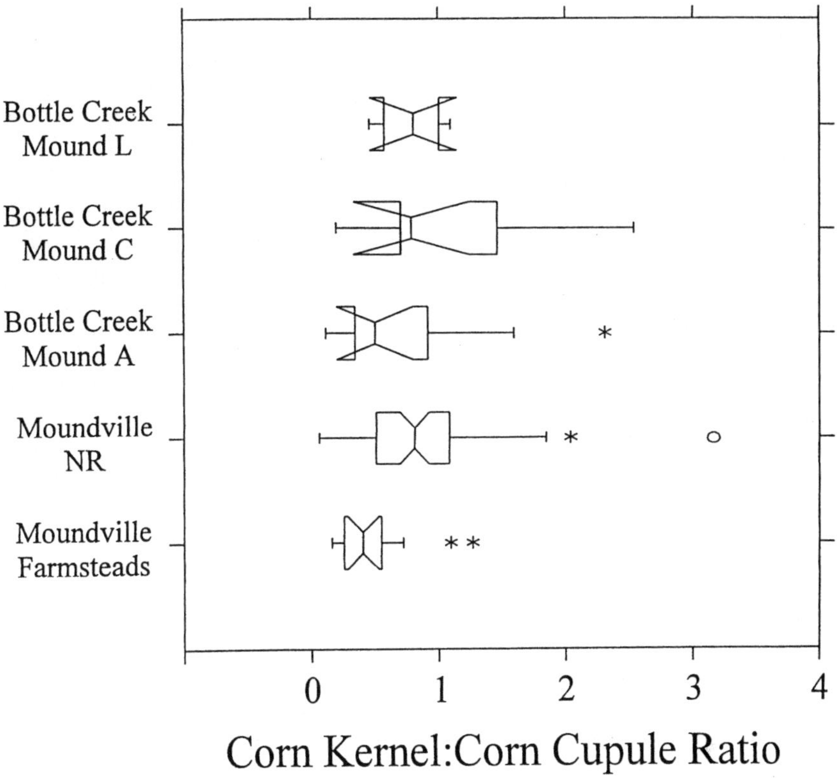

6.7. Box plot of the ratio of corn kernels to corn cupules at Bottle Creek, Moundville, and Black Warrior farmsteads.

the scarcity of nutshell at Bottle Creek. The ratios of cupules to nutshells from mounds A, C, and L are so much higher than those from the Moundville polity that the distributions do not even overlap.

The plots comparing kernel-to-cupule ratios from Bottle Creek and Moundville are equally intriguing (Figure 6.7). (Only ratios from refuse pits and midden deposits are plotted. Several smudge pits from Bottle Creek, which represent special episodes of deposition, are omitted.) The ratios from mounds C and L are comparable to those from the elite contexts North of R at Moundville and higher than those from the Moundville farmsteads. At first glance Mound A appears to be more like the farmsteads than the other contexts. What we are seeing here, however, is an effect of combining data from the midden deposits under Mound A with those from the actual mound stages. The ratios from the premound contexts are low, while those from the mound stages are comparable to the ratios from mounds C and L.

Both the cupule-to-nutshell ratios and the kernel-to-cupule ratios indicate that the residents of the mounds at Bottle Creek did little primary processing of plant foods. We do not know whether the residents of the mounds at Bottle Creek routinely consumed nut products, but clearly they ate corn. This raises the question of whether the primary processing was performed elsewhere on the site or whether shelled corn and perhaps nut products were sent to Bottle Creek from other sites in the polity. Both arable land and nut mast (particularly sweet hickories) are in short supply on Mound Island. Thus, I am inclined to argue for provisioning from farmsteads and villages rather than for processing in off-mound areas.

It is worth noting that at both Moundville and Bottle Creek the evidence for provisioning of plant foods coincides with periods of active mound construction and, presumably, highly centralized social and political control. For Moundville this period is Late Moundville I/Early Moundville II, that is, circa A.D. 1150–1300. For Bottle Creek the period seems to begin in Bottle Creek I circa A.D. 1250 and to continue through Bottle Creek II until at least A.D. 1500.

RITUAL/SYMBOLIC PLANTS

Thus far, I have discussed the use of food plants in various contexts of Moundville and Bottle Creek. The mounds at both sites, however, have produced evidence for the use of plants that were ritually or symbolically important.

I have examined plant remains from over two hundred distinct contexts from sites in the Moundville polity. These include midden and refuse deposits from farmsteads, subsidiary centers, residential areas at Moundville, and mounds Q and G. All of the remains were collected by flotation and all were sorted using the same procedures. The sole tobacco seed from the entire polity comes from Mound Q. Given that other non-mound contexts are much better represented in the assemblages, I would argue that tobacco use was at a minimum—more common in mound-related public/ceremonial activities and quite possibly limited to such situations.

Of equal or greater interest is evidence from both Bottle Creek and Moundville for the use of yaupon (*Ilex vomitoria*). This is, of course, the plant whose leaves were used to brew the black drink (Hudson 1979). To my knowledge, despite its ceremonial importance, yaupon is scarce in archaeological assemblages. Investigators recovered yaupon seeds from the hearth in the council house at the Apalachee mission of San Luis (Shapiro and McEwan 1992). Elsewhere, these seeds may lurk among the unidentified seeds, but if they were common I would expect them to be identified and reported.

The black drink is a tea made from the leaves, not the berries, of the yaupon plant. The berries, however, remain on the plant long after they are ripe (Grimm 1966) and may have been unintentionally collected along with the leaves. Since the berries are inedible, the presence of the yaupon seeds in a deposit is quite likely a result of processing harvested leaves prior to brewing the black drink.

Bottle Creek lies within the natural range of yaupon and the residents would have had ready access to the plants. Interestingly, yaupon seeds are present in the Bottle Creek assemblage but they are not evenly distributed. They occur in roughly a third of the samples from Mound C, the house mound, but do not occur in the samples from mounds A and L. It is tempting to speculate that while the retainers who lived on Mound C received processed foodstuffs they, in turn, were processing yaupon for use in the ceremonial precinct.

Yaupon is considered to be a native of the coastal areas of the Southeast, but the plant is one of the dominant shrubs in the ravines and thickets at Moundville today. Fifty years ago the botanist Roland Harper (1944:148) wrote of yaupon, "Away from the coast it is scattered so erratically as to suggest that it might have been planted by the Indians, who brewed a beverage from its leaves." I identified a single yaupon seed from the deposits North of R, which provides tenuous evidence for the preparation of the black drink in elite households at Moundville.

The samples from mounds Q and G did not produce any seeds from yaupon, but Mound Q did produce tantalizing indirect evidence about the symbolic importance of this plant. Vernon J. Knight (personal communication, 1995) recovered several whole and fragmentary anthropomorphic ceramic figurines. Inspection of the paste of one of the fragmentary figurines reveals that the clay was mixed with yaupon leaves. The firing process destroyed the leaves but their impressions are clear and the identification is secure. In addition to the figurines from Mound Q, similar figurines have been found in Mound F and near Mound G. Although we do not know if all are tempered with yaupon, the association of yaupon with these figurines and with mound contexts suggests that the leaves were symbolically imbued as well as brewed.

7 / Zooarchaeological Remains from Bottle Creek

Irvy R. Quitmyer

INTRODUCTION

Archaeologists have known of the Bottle Creek site for more than a century, but until the current project there has been very little information on the diet of its people. In addition to its abundance of artifacts and plant food resources, Bottle Creek contains a dense concentration of zooarchaeological remains from subsistence activities. These animal remains present the first opportunity to study systematically well-recovered Mississippian faunal remains on the north-central Gulf Coast. This chapter presents the first report of a zooarchaeological study of vertebrate and invertebrate faunal remains excavated from Bottle Creek. There are two goals to this study. First, because systematic zooarchaeological inquiries are rare for the region, it is important to establish a methodological foundation for this and future studies. Second, this analysis documents animals that are represented in the samples and their relative abundances, thus revealing which animals were at the core of the economy of the Bottle Creek people. Based on these data, I make interpretations of the habitats that were exploited and the prehistoric technology needed to obtain these resources.

METHODS

Investigators excavated three faunal samples from the Bottle Creek Site during the 1993–1994 summer field seasons: C100Z, FS45 from Mound C; and D100EE, FS9 and D100FF, FS10 from Mound A (Figure 2.1). Sample C100Z comes from a 50 × 50 × 10 cm column sample of approximately 33 liters. Sediments from D100EE are from a 10.5 liter volumetric sample, while sediments from D100FF are from an 8.5 liter volumetric sample. These samples represent subsistence refuse from occupations during overlapping time periods and mound structures. Mound C flanks the western edge of the site. The sample from it dates to Late Bottle Creek I–Early

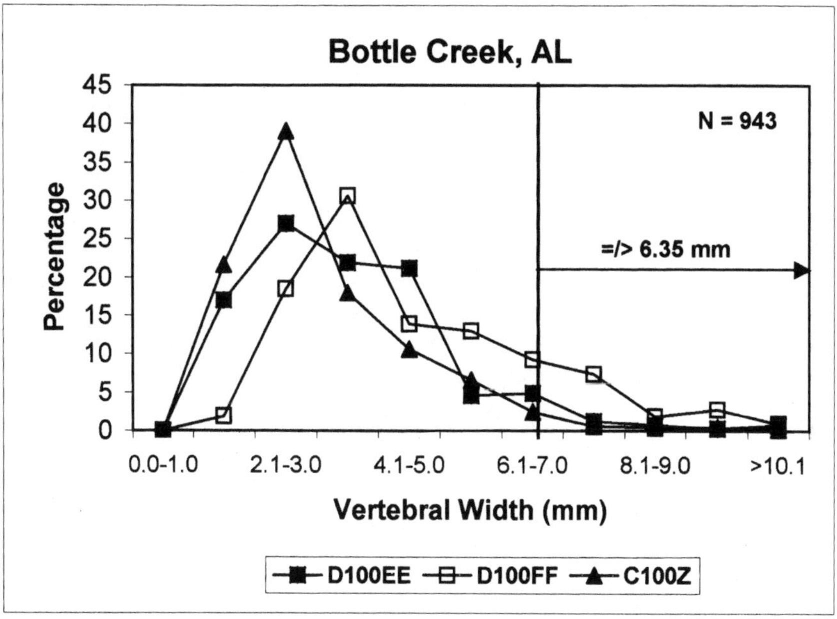

7.1. Line graphs of measured vertebral widths (mm) of fishes.

Bottle Creek II times (A.D. 1300–1450). Mound C is interpreted as a socially lower status area of the site when compared to larger, more centrally located structures like Mound A. Sample D100EE dates to the early Bottle Creek II phase (A.D. 1400–1500), while D100FF dates to Bottle Creek I (A.D. 1250–1400).

Investigators removed the samples from the field and water-floated them through screens measuring 1/4 in gauge and 1/16 in gauge. When the samples were dry, I re-screened the material from the 1/16 in gauge through 1/8th in gauge and 1/16 in gauge screens. This process produces three screen fractions of materials (1/4 in, 1/8 in, and 1/16 in). Fractionation of the fauna speeds identification and assures that all taxa, large and small, are recovered for study (Wing and Quitmyer 1985; Reitz and Quitmyer 1988; Reitz and Wing 1999).

The importance of using a fine gauge screen (1/16 in) recovery strategy at Bottle Creek is convincingly demonstrated in the three faunal samples by measurements of the vertebral centra of fishes. Figure 7.1 shows the percentage of measured vertebrae from the three Bottle Creek proveniences. Ninety-four percent of the fish vertebrae (n = 884) are smaller than 6.35 mm (1/4 in screen gauge) and could have been lost into the backdirt had we not used finer screens in their recovery. These data further confirm previous zooarchaeological observations throughout the southeastern United States. When fine gauge screen (1/16 in) is used to sample fauna from sites associated with aquatic habitats, small fishes dominate the vertebrate faunal (Bense 1985; Quitmyer 1985; Reitz 1982; Reitz and Quitmyer 1988; Russo et al. 1991; Walker 1992).

Perceived biases against rarely occurring taxa, such as mollusk and large mammals, may be caused by analytical differences that exist between assemblages recovered with fine gauge screen (1/16 in) and animal remains recovered with traditional 1/4 in gauge screen (Milanich et al. 1984:276). Elizabeth Wing and I (1985) have demonstrated experimentally that the relative abundance of archaeological mammals, birds, and reptiles from estuarine sites significantly decreases when recovered with successively smaller gauge screens (1/16 in screen), while the relative abundance of fishes exponentially increases. In our experiment, only 36 skeletal fragments of the fish stardrum (*Stellifer lanceolatus*) were recovered in the 1/4 in gauge screen, while 5,019 fragments were added with the use of 1/8 in and 1/16 in gauge screen (Wing and Quitmyer 1985:57). The estimated contribution of meat from white-tailed deer was 23,595 gm, while stardrum was 853 gm of meat recovered in the 1/4 in gauge screen (Wing and Quitmyer 1985:51). When fauna recovered with 1/8 in and 1/16 in gauge screens was added to the assemblage, the estimated meat contributed by white-tailed deer remained at 23,595 gm, but the cumulative estimated increase of meat from stardrum was 24,353 gm (Wing and Quitmyer 1985:53). Additional fish species recovered in the finer gauges of screen further suppresses the relative importance of white-tailed deer. In the 1/4 in screen there are two mammals and 65 minimum number of individuals (MNI) fishes; with the use of the finer gauges of screen MNI of mammals remained at two, while fishes increased to 993.

Sample adequacy is an important aspect of faunal analysis that has a direct relationship with the selection of screen size for faunal recovery and the size of the sample. By definition, an adequate sample should be a representation of the population from which it was taken. Sampling can be geared to the search for rarely (rarefaction) occurring animals that are most obvious to the excavator (e.g., large mammal forms) or toward the most commonly identified species that are less obvious in the field. For example, the presence of small fishes (Figure 7.1) went undetected during the course of the field excavations at Bottle Creek, while skeletal remains of white-tailed deer (*Odocoileus virginianus*), large fish (*Osteichthyes*), and Atlantic rangia clams (*Rangia cuneata*) were commonly observed in the 1/4 in gauge screens.

The relationship of the number of species versus MNI is one method of testing sample adequacy (Reitz and Wing 1999:108). As individuals are identified, the number of species exponentially increases to a point of di-

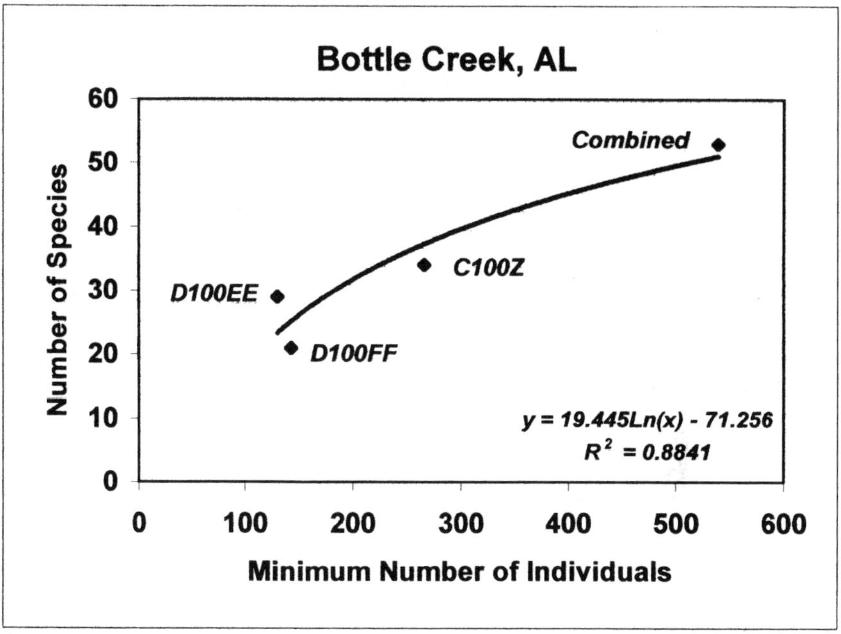

7.2. Scatter plot showing the relationship of minimum numbers of individuals and number of species identified.

minishing returns. Sample adequacy is attained at a point where further identification of MNI does not significantly add to the species count (Figure 7.2). In cases where samples are not adequate, rare taxa (MNI) may be overrepresented in the sample (Gingerich 1989:1). The point of diminishing returns may be affected by inter- and intrasite location, seasonality, selection of animal resources by prehistoric people, and faunal preservation. It is for these reasons that the point of diminishing returns has to be calculated for each archaeological site. Figure 7.2 shows the relationship of MNI to the number of species identified in the three Bottle Creek samples. Figure 7.2 also shows a combined total of the three samples to provide a theoretical maximum that might occur in the Bottle Creek site. These data seem to indicate that the point of diminishing returns occurs at about 500 MNI (vertebrates and invertebrates) and 50 taxa. Repeated sampling will be needed to fully develop this relationship at Bottle Creek.

All invertebrate and vertebrate fauna were identified to the lowest possible taxon (Table 7.1) by direct comparison with a series of reference specimens from collections of the Florida Museum of Natural History (FLMNH). I myself conducted the faunal identification, analysis, and preparation of this report.

Table 7.1. Scientific names, common names, and habitats of fauna identified

Scientific Name	Common Name	Habitat
Animalia	animals	
Bryozoa	moss animals	Estuarine
Mollusca	bivalves and gastropods	
Bivalvia	bivalves	
Mytilidae	marine mussels	Estuarine
Crassostrea virginica	Eastern oyster	Estuarine
Unionidae	freshwater mussels	Freshwater
Unionidae species 1	unknown species 1	Freshwater
Unionidae species 2	unknown species 2	Freshwater
Fusconaia ebena	ebonyshell	Freshwater
Quadrula sp.		Freshwater
Quadrula apiculata	southern mapleleaf	Freshwater
Rangia cuneata	Atlantic rangia	Estuarine
Polymesoda caroliniana	Carolina marshclam	Estuarine
Mercenaria sp.	quahog	Estuarine
Gastropoda	snails	
Pleuroceridae		Freshwater
Elimia hydei	gladiator elimia	Freshwater
Pleurocera canaliculata	silty hornsnail	Freshwater
Gastropoda (Terrestrial)		Terrestrial
Gastropoda (Terrestrial)	(1) undetermined	Terrestrial
Gastropoda (Terrestrial)	(2) undetermined	Terrestrial
Gastropoda (Terrestrial)	(3) undetermined	Terrestrial
Decapoda	decopod crabs	Estuarine
Brachyura	brachyura crabs	Estuarine
Balanus sp.	barnacles	Estuarine
Vertebrata	vertebrates	
Osteichthyes	bony fishes	
Lepisosteus sp.	gar	Freshwater
Amia calva	bowfin	Freshwater
Elops saurus	ladyfish	Estuarine
Clupeidae	herring	
Brevoortia sp.	menhaden	Estuarine
Notemigonus sp.	shiner	Freshwater
Siluriformes	catfishes	
Ictaluridae	bullhead catfishes	Freshwater
Arius felis	hardhead catfish	Estuarine
Centrarchidae	sunfishes	Freshwater
aff. *Ambloplites* sp.	bass	Freshwater
Lepomis sp.	sunfish	Freshwater
Lepomis macrochirus	bluegill	Freshwater
Lepomis microlophus	redear sunfish	Freshwater
Micropterus sp.	freshwater bass	Freshwater
Pomoxis nigromaculatus	black crappie	Freshwater
Archosargus probatocephalus	sheepshead	Estuarine
Sciaenidae	drums	
Aplodinotus grunniens	freshwater drum	Freshwater
Cynoscion sp.	seatrout	Estuarine
Micropogonias undulatus	Atlantic croaker	Estuarine
Sciaenops ocellatus	red drum	Estuarine
Mugil sp.	mullet	Estuarine
Paralichthys sp.	flounder	Estuarine
Serpentes	snakes	
Squamata	lizards	Terrestrial
Iguanidae	iguanid lizards	Terrestrial
Testudines	turtles	
Terrapene carolina	Eastern box turtle	Terrestrial
Anura	frogs/toads	
Aves	birds	
Aves (Large)	large birds, e.g., goose	
Aves (Medium)	e.g., coot	
Buteo sp.	hawk	Terrestrial
Anatidae	ducks and geese	Terrestrial
Anas platyrhynchos	mallard	Terrestrial
Fulica americana	American coot	Terrestrial
Mammalia	mammals	
Mammalia (small)	e.g., mice	
Mammalia (large)	e.g., deer	
Rodentia	rodents, e.g., mice	Terrestrial
Mustela vison	mink	Terrestrial
Odocoileus virginianus	white-tailed deer	Terrestrial
Homo sapiens	humans	Terrestrial

I used standard zooarchaeological methods to quantify the faunal remains (Bense 1985; Lee et al. 1984; Reitz and Quitmyer 1988; Reitz and Wing 1999; Ziegler 1973). I determined minimum numbers of individuals (MNI) by the use of the concept of paired elements and individual size. For example, four left opercula and five right opercula of bass (*Micropterus* sp.) would represent five MNI. Skeletal elements other than herring (Clupeidae) and mullet (*Mugil* sp.) vertebrae were less frequently identified. A count of herring vertebrae (n = 47) and mullet thoracic vertebrae (n = 10) was used to estimate the MNI of these species (Quitmyer 1985:37).

When animals of varying body mass are present in a faunal assemblage, the use of MNI does not fully characterize the relative importance, in terms of meat, of the various taxa. For example, meat from eight sunfishes (Centrarchidae) is not greater than that provided by a single white-tailed deer. Skeletal mass allometry used in conjunction with MNI can help to estimate the importance of the different species in the diet (Reitz and Wing 1999).

I used skeletal mass allometry to estimate the potential amount of meat provided by each species (Table 7.2) (Reitz et al. 1987; Wing and Brown 1979:127–129). For the purposes of this research, meat weight refers to just the animal's soft tissue estimated by the allometric constants used in this study. The principle of allometry is that growth is a nonlinear process through ontogeny (Peters 1983; Reitz et al. 1987; Schmidt-Nielsen 1984). The relationship between the weight of supportive tissue to meat is best described by the allometric formula of Y = aXb. For the ease of calculation, this formula is transformed to Log y = loga + b(logX). Skeletal mass allometry assumes that only the meat adhering to the bone was consumed. The same procedure is used to estimate meat weight of mollusks, but in this case the allometric relationship is between shell weight and weight of all of the soft tissue.

The diversity and evenness of the taxa present in a zooarchaeological assemblage differ as a function of human choice, diversity and evenness of the local resources, and the season of resource procurement (Reitz and Quitmyer 1988; Reitz and Wing 1999). The Shannon-Weaver Diversity Index (H′) was used to calculate species richness of the three samples (Shannon and Weaver 1949:14). The Shannon-Weaver Diversity statistic (H′) ranges from 0 to 5 where increasing values of H′ indicate greater faunal diversity. The Sheldon's Equitability Index (E) was used to characterize the evenness of animals represented in the three samples. Greater species evenness is indicated as (E) moves from 0 to 1. The diversity and equitability statistics represent one method of characterizing resource specialization and the range of resources used by people in a stratified society. For instance, higher status individuals might have access to a wider range (less specialized) of faunal resources when compared to people of lower status.

Atlantic rangia clams were the most frequently identified species from

Table 7.2. Allometric constants used to estimate proportional biomass (gm) of fauna

Species	n	a	Slope(b)	r2
Callinectes sapidus	11	0.99	0.82	0.58
Bivalvia	80	0.02	0.68	0.83
Geukensia demissa	100	-0.22	0.80	0.86
Unionidae	21	-0.35	1.07	0.87
Crassostrea virginica	100	-0.77	0.97	0.97
Rangia cuneata	86	-0.57	1.13	0.71
Polymesoda caroliniana	40	0.01	0.83	0.95
Mercenaria mercenaria	40	-0.50	0.94	0.95
Gastropoda	135	-0.16	0.92	0.89
Osteichthyes	80	1.38	0.90	0.96
Lepisosteus sp.	10	0.75	0.81	0.93
Siluriformes	16	1.15	1.05	0.96
Sparidae	15	1.23	0.88	0.99
Sciaenidae	35	1.34	0.99	0.94
Plueronectiformes	14	1.13	0.98	0.99
Bufo terrestrus	15	1.40	0.86	0.86
Serpenties	14	1.06	0.94	0.97
Testudines	9	1.65	0.53	0.74
Aves	39	1.24	0.84	0.98
Mammalia	40	1.41	0.81	0.91

Note: Key to Abbreviations.
Formula is $Y=aX^b$, where Y is the proportional biomass (soft tissue); X is the weight of the skeletal remains; a is the Y-intercept; b is the slope; n is the number of observations; and r^2 is the coefficient of determination (Peters 1986; Reitz and Cordier 1983; Reitz et al. 1987; Reitz and Wing 1999).

Bottle Creek. The age structures of living bivalve populations are known to be sensitive indicators of human harvesting pressure (Dodd and Stanton 1981:343–354; Quitmyer et al. 1985; Quitmyer and Jones 2000; Walker 1985; Walker and Tenore 1984). During the 1993 field season Atlantic rangia shells in Mound C appeared to be smaller than living specimens collected from nearby Little Lizard Creek (1Ba195) (Fuller and Brown 1998:45–53). It is noteworthy that the size of an animal may not always be a good proxy for ontogenetic age. Environmental constraints on animals can greatly affect their size (Arnold et al. 1991). I undertook a study of the age (years) and size (shell length) of Atlantic rangia shells from the three faunal samples to determine the effects of archaeological harvesting. I used structural and morphological techniques to determine the individual ages (years) of modern and archaeological Atlantic rangia (Aten 1981; Muniz 1994).

Richard Fuller and I collected a sample of living Atlantic rangia from the mouth of Little Lizard Creek near the Bottle Creek site during the summer of 1993. In this part of the estuary, state restrictions limit the harvest of most shellfish because of bacterial contamination. Furthermore, there appears to be little commercial demand for Atlantic rangia clams (Swingle and Bland 1974:10). For these reasons the living specimens should closely approximate the population age and size structure of unharvested Atlantic rangia.

I determined Atlantic rangia size class structure by measuring the shells anterior to posterior (mm) shell length with electronic calipers attached to a Gateway 2000 computer. I used the spreadsheet software Quatro Pro to manipulate the data statistically.

I exposed the growth structures of Atlantic rangia by cross-sectioning the shells from the umbo to the ventral margin along the greatest growth axis. I used a water-cooled lapidary saw equipped with an aluminum oxide blade for this procedure (Arnold et al. 1991; Muniz 1994; Quitmyer et al. 1985; Quitmyer and Jones 1992:249).

In the cross-sectioned Atlantic rangia shells a combination of one opaque and one translucent increment record one annual cycle of growth (Aten 1981; Wolf and Petteway 1968). A count of the number of gray (translucent) shell growth increments marks the number of years the individual lived. A prominent depression in the shell contour (morphological) identifies the gray growth increment seen in the shell cross-section. Correlating the internal growth structures with the morphological features on the shell surface helps to identify growth lines not associated with the annual cycle of shell growth (Aten 1981).

I calculated a 95 percent confidence interval for the age (years) and size of the modern and archaeological Atlantic rangia (Agresti and Agresti 1979:66–89). It is then possible to ascertain which samples are statistically different ($p \leq 0.05$) from one another by noting whether or not their confidence intervals overlapped. This is suitable to compare null hypothesis $H_0: X_1 = X_2 = \ldots$ of n samples. The null hypothesis is: the mean age or size of the modern specimens is not significant when compared to the archaeological sample. The procedure is straightforward, easily interpretable, and conservative.

I constructed two types of survivorship curves for the ontogenetic age structure of rangia: a) log-age frequency—a graph of the log of the number of survivors vs. age, in years; and b) age frequency curve—a graph of the percentage of survivors vs. age, in years. These curves illustrate the population age structure of the sampled Atlantic rangia (Dodd and Stanton 1981:337–365).

RESULTS

Mound C, C100Z, FS45 Faunal Assemblage

Fauna contained in C100Z is represented by 2,283 shell and bone fragments and 3731.04 gm of material. I identified 34 species and 266 MNI (Table 7.3). This does not include commensal species (e.g., landsnails) or human remains. It is worth noting that the human remains identified in this study were confined to a single molar fragment.

Table 7.3. Fauna identified from Mound C, C100Z–FS45

Species	Count	%	MNI	%	Weight (gm)	%	Meat (gm)	%
Animalia	8	0.35	–	–	0.58	0.02	–	–
Mollusca	5	0.22	–	–	1.74	0.05	–	–
Mollusca (marine)	3	0.13	–	–	0.11	0.00	–	–
Mytilidae	1	0.04	1	0.38	0.03	0.00	54.65	1.57
Crassostrea virginica	3	0.13	2	0.75	50.51	1.35	7.63	0.22
Unionidae	18	0.79	–	–	112.57	3.02	69.98	2.01
Unionidae species 1*	3	0.13	2	0.75	19.10	0.51	10.49	0.30
Unionidae species 2*	2	0.09	2	0.75	14.52	0.39	7.82	0.22
Quadrula sp.	19	0.83	–	–	14.34	0.38	7.72	0.22
Quadrula apiculata	4	0.18	2	0.75	28.47	0.76	16.08	0.46
Rangia cuneata	473	20.72	216	81.51	3452.61	92.54	2679.83	77.06
Gastropoda	2	0.09	–	–	0.09	0.00	0.08	0.00
Pleurocera canaliculata	3	0.13	3	1.13	2.37	0.06	1.53	0.04
Elimia hydei	1	0.04	1	0.38	1.07	0.03	0.74	0.02
Gastropoda (Terrestrial) species 1*	1	0.04	a	–	0.00	0.00	–	–
Gastropoda (Terrestrial) species 2*	56	2.45	a	–	0.03	0.00	–	–
Gastropoda (Terrestrial) species 3*	1	0.04	a	–	0.02	0.00	–	–
Brachyura	20	0.88	1	0.38	0.19	0.01	2.50	0.07
Balanus sp.	5	0.22	a	–	0.05	0.00	–	–
Vertebrata	62	2.72	–	–	9.65	0.26	–	–
Osteichthyes	1084	47.48	–	–	2.36	0.06	51.57	1.48
Lepisosteus sp.	65	2.85	1	0.38	1.91	0.05	9.50	0.27
Amia calva	1	0.04	1	0.38	0.02	0.00	0.74	0.02
Elops saurus	7	0.31	1	0.38	0.09	0.00	2.91	0.08
Clupeidae	211	9.24	2	0.75	2.86	0.08	61.10	1.76
Brevoortia sp.	8	0.35	5	1.89	0.09	0.00	2.84	0.08
Notemigonus sp.	1	0.04	1	0.38	0.00	0.00	0.05	0.00
Siluriformes	8	0.35	–	–	0.38	0.01	5.13	0.15
Ictaluridae	5	0.22	1	0.38	0.53	0.01	7.27	0.21
Centrarchidae	52	2.28	1	0.38	1.08	0.03	18.36	0.53
aff. *Ambloplites* sp.	1	0.04	1	0.38	0.05	0.00	0.93	0.03
Lepomis sp.	3	0.13	–	–	0.05	0.00	0.89	0.03
Lepomis microlophus	1	0.04	1	0.38	0.08	0.00	1.47	0.04
Micropterus sp.	10	0.44	1	0.38	1.90	0.05	31.64	0.91
Archosargus probatocephalus	3	0.13	1	0.38	0.81	0.02	14.11	0.41
Sciaenidae	5	0.22	–	–	0.36	0.01	7.85	0.23
Micropogonias undulatus	2	0.09	2	0.75	0.05	0.00	1.13	0.03
Sciaenops ocellatus	1	0.04	1	0.38	0.04	0.00	0.90	0.03
Mugil sp.	70	3.07	6	2.26	5.17	0.14	103.52	2.98
Paralichthys sp.	7	0.31	1	0.38	0.78	0.02	10.52	0.30
Serpentes	4	0.18	1	0.38	0.01	0.00	0.19	0.01
Iguanidae	2	0.09	1	0.38	0.00	0.00	0.06	0.00
Testudines	7	0.31	1	0.38	1.45	0.04	54.39	1.56
Aves	1	0.04	–	–	0.04	0.00	1.16	0.03
Aves (Large)	4	0.18	1	0.38	0.33	0.01	6.85	0.20
Aves (Medium)	12	0.53	–	–	4.73	0.13	64.07	1.84
Anatidae	1	0.04	–	–	2.60	0.07	38.78	1.11
Anas platyrhynchos	2	0.09	1	0.38	1.27	0.03	21.24	0.61
Fulica americana	2	0.09	1	0.38	1.31	0.04	21.80	0.63
Mammalia	5	0.22	–	–	1.18	0.03	15.77	0.45
Mammalia (small)	2	0.09	–	–	0.04	0.00	1.10	0.03
Rodentia	2	0.09	1	0.38	0.01	0.00	0.33	0.01
Mustela vison	1	0.04	1	0.38	0.19	0.01	3.60	0.10
Odocoileus virginianus	2	0.09	1	0.38	5.76	0.15	57.00	1.64
Homo sapiens	1	0.04	b	–	0.91	0.02	–	–
Total	2283	100	265	100	3731.04	100	3477.80	100

Note: Key to Abbreviations.
a = Commensal species not used in the calculations of MNI, weight, or biomass.
b = Human not used in the calculations of MNI, weight, or biomass.
* = Undetermined species.

Summary of Fauna Resources

	MNI	%	Biomass	%
Mollusk	230	86.5	2859.04	82.21
Fish	27	10.2	332.41	9.56
Reptile	3	1.1	54.65	1.57
Bird	3	1.1	153.90	4.43
Mammal	3	1.1	77.80	2.24
Total	266	100	3477.80	100
FW Mollusk	10	3.8	114.43	3.35
BW Mollusk	220	82.7	2742.10	80.23
FW Fish	8	3.0	70.10	2.05
BW Fish	19	7.1	204.87	5.99
Reptile	3	1.1	54.65	1.60
Bird	3	1.1	153.90	4.50
Mammal	3	1.1	77.80	2.28
Total	266	100	3417.86	100
Aquatic	256	96.6	3056.84	94.86
Terrestrial	9	3.4	165.47	5.14
Total	265	100	3222.31	100

Minimum Number of Individuals

Mollusks were the most frequently identified class of animals (86.5 percent) from the Mound C sample (Figure 7.3a). By the measure of MNI, Atlantic rangia clams dominate the faunal assemblage (81.5 percent). Eastern oyster (*Crassostrea virginica*, .75 percent), southern mapleleaf mussel (*Quadrula quadrula apiculata*, .75 percent), silty hornsnail (*Pleurocera canaliculatum*) (1.13 percent), and gladiator elimia (*Elimia hydei*) (.38 percent) were minor contributors to the assemblage.

I identified 16 species of fishes (10.2 percent) in C100Z (Figure 7.3a). In most cases the MNI of each species does not exceed .75 percent of the identified fauna (Table 7.3). The exceptions are menhaden (*Brevoortia* sp., 1.89 percent), Atlantic croaker (*Micropogonias undulatus*, .75 percent) and mullet (*Mugil* sp., 2.26 percent). The remaining classes of animals (reptiles, birds, and mammals) supply only 1.1 percent each of C100Z MNI (Figure 7.3a).

The calculation of MNI shows 96.6 percent of the MNI were aquatic species, while only 3.4 percent were terrestrial (Table 7.3). Furthermore, 82.7 percent of the fauna were estuarine brackish water (BW) mollusks and 3.8 percent were freshwater species (FW) mollusks (Figure 7.4a). Among the fishes, 7.1 percent were brackish water species from estuarine habitats, but only 3.0 percent could have been collected from freshwater habitats.

Estimated Meat

The relative estimated meat supplied by C100Z fauna confirm the trends seen in the frequency of MNI (Table 7.3). Mollusks contribute 82.2 percent of the estimated meat in the assemblage, while fishes contribute 9.6 percent (Figure 7.5a). Birds are ranked third (4.4 percent) in their relative meat contribution. Estimated meat from reptiles (1.6 percent) and mammals (2.2 percent) are less important constituents in the assemblage.

Meat from aquatic species accounts for 94.8 percent while only 5.2 percent of the meat came from terrestrial species (Table 7.3). Brackish water mollusks supply 80.2 percent of the estimated meat and freshwater mollusks provide 3.3 percent (Figure 7.6a). The importance of aquatic species is also seen in the contribution of fishes from brackish water (6.0 percent) and freshwater (2.1 percent) habitats.

Diversity and Equitability

The calculated Shannon-Weaver Diversity Index (H′) for the C100Z faunal assemblage is 1.10 while the Sheldon Index (E) is 0.31 (Table 7.4 and Figure 7.7). These data seem to indicate a somewhat specialized faunal assemblage where heavy reliance is placed on a few species.

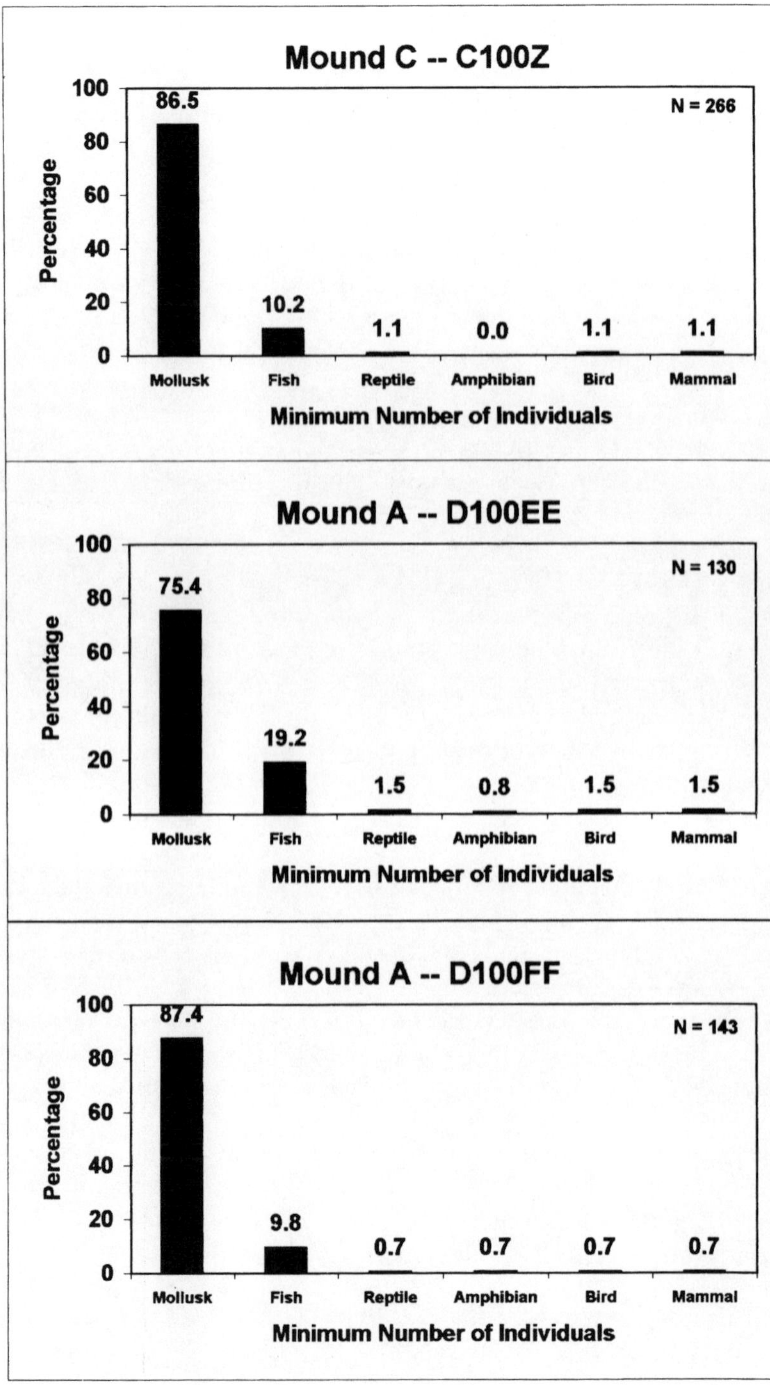

a

b

c

7.3. Histograms illustrating the relative frequency of the minimum numbers of individuals of six classes of fauna. a, Mound C, C100Z; b, Mound A, D100EE; c, Mound A, D100FF.

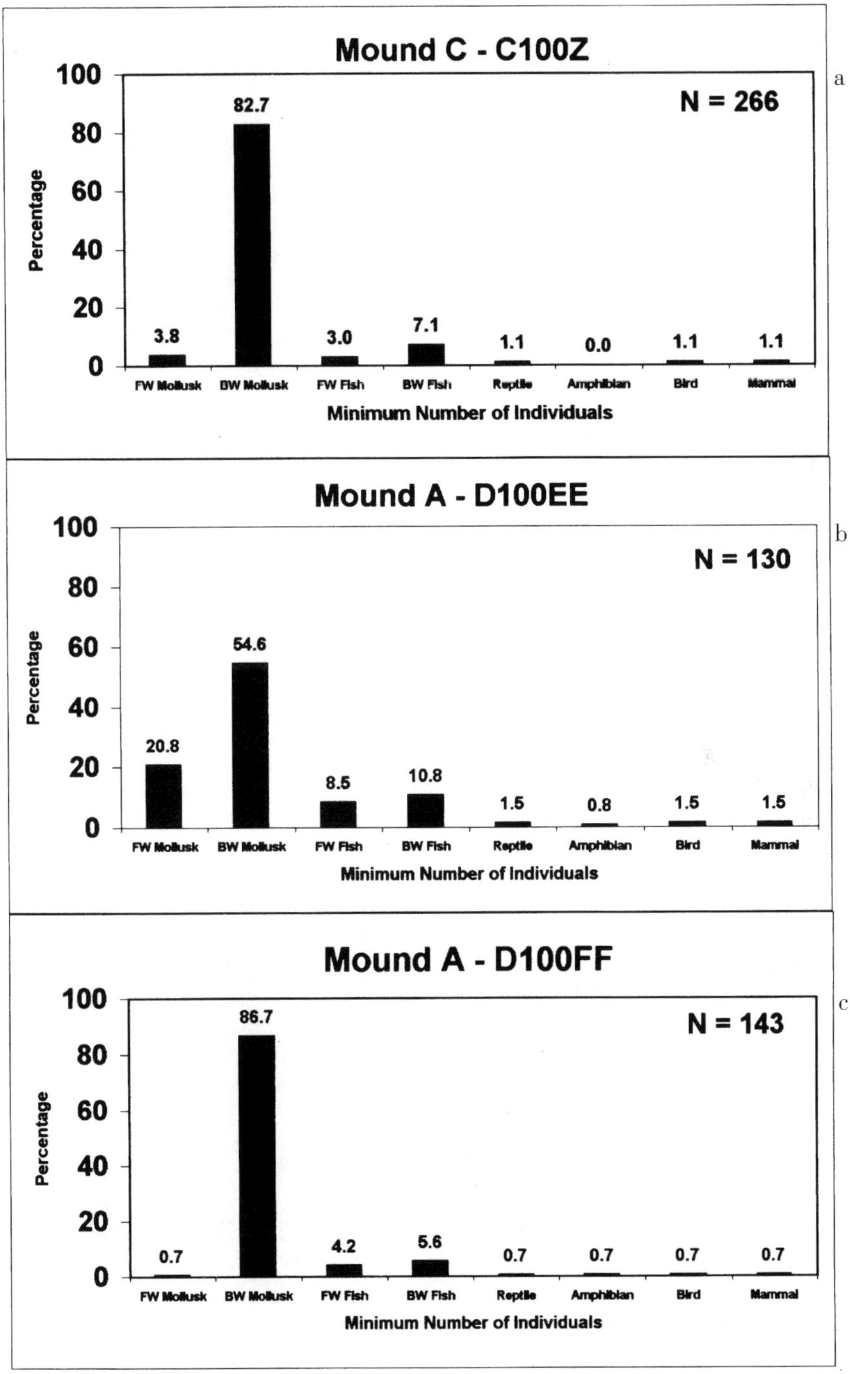

7.4. Histograms illustrating the relative contribution of the minimum numbers of individuals of fauna from brackish water (BW), freshwater (FW), and terrestrial habitats. a, Mound C, C100Z; b, Mound A, D100EE; c, Mound A, D100FF.

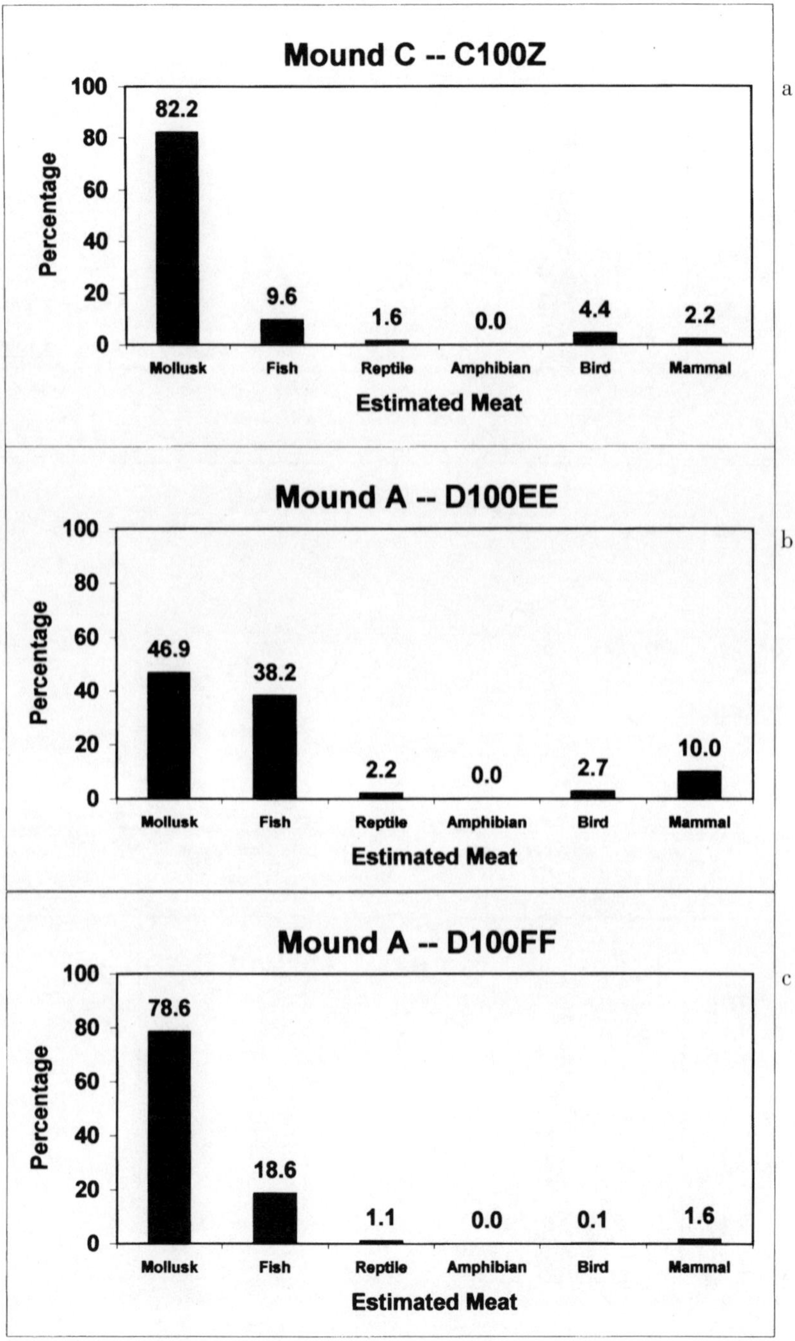

7.5. Histograms illustrating the relative frequency of meat contributed by six classes of fauna. a, Mound C, C100Z; b, Mound A, D100EE; c, Mound A, D100FF.

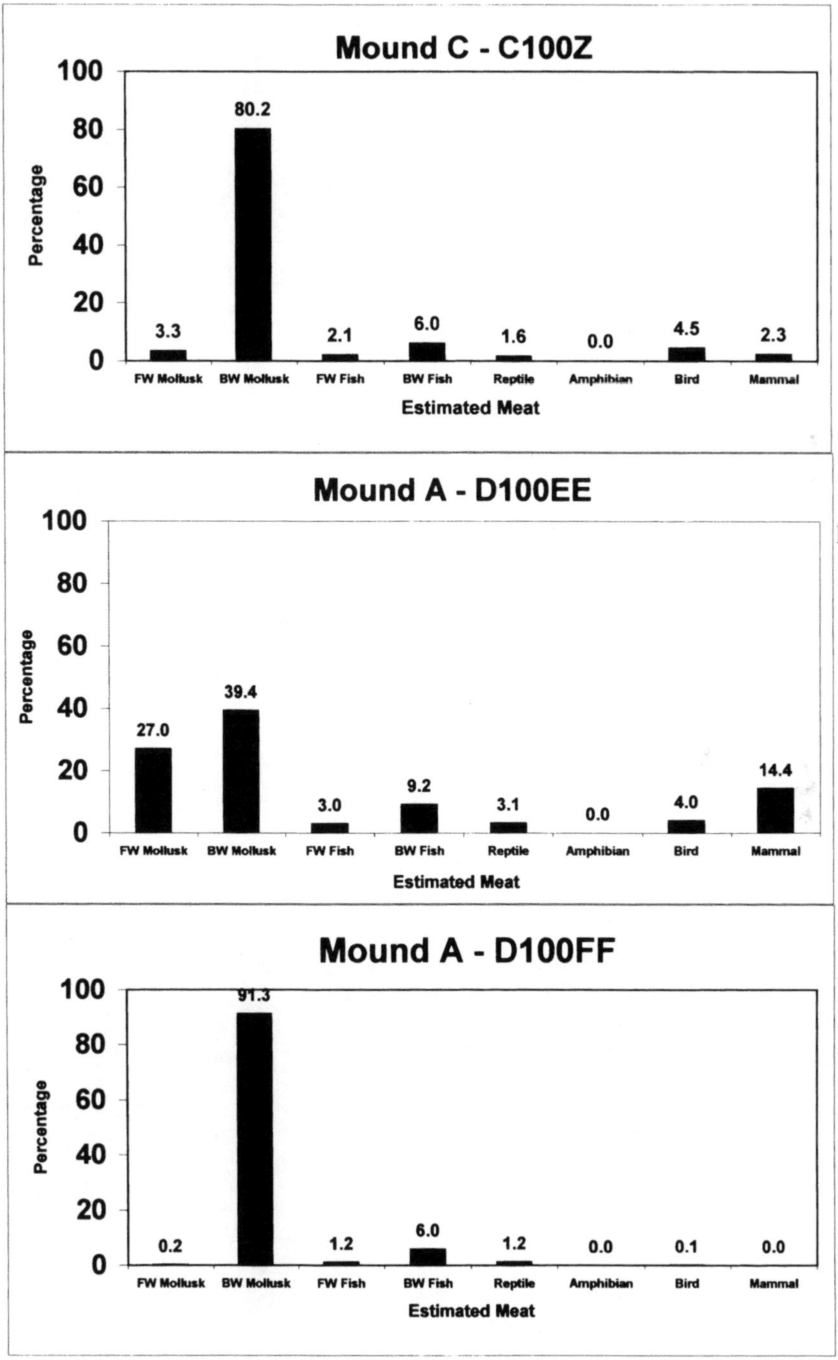

a
b
c

7.6. Histograms illustrating the relative contribution of meat from brackish water (BW), freshwater (FW), and terrestrial fauna. a, Mound C, C100Z; b, Mound A, D100EE; c, Mound A, D100FF.

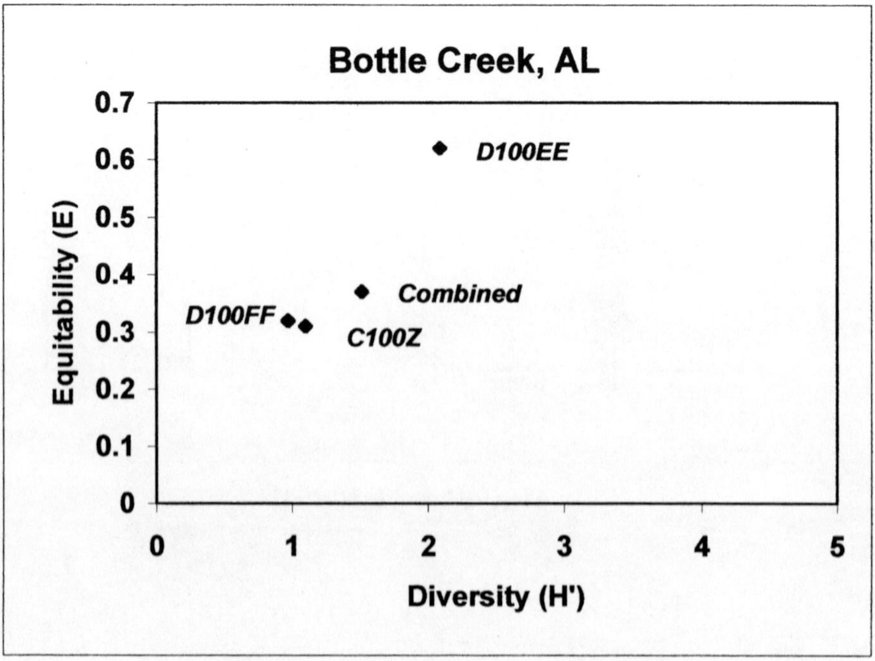

7.7. Scatter plot showing the relationship of species diversity (H′) to species equitability (E) of fauna identified.

Table 7.4. Species count, minimum numbers of individuals, diversity (H') and equitability (E) of zooarchaeological samples

Provenience	Species	MNI	H'	E
Mound A—D100EE— FS9	29	130	2.09	0.62
Mound A—D100FF— FS10	21	143	0.97	0.32
Mound C—C100Z—FS45	34	266	1.10	0.31
Combined Samples	53	539	1.52	0.37

Age and Size of Atlantic Rangia Clam

A statistical comparison of the size and age of the Atlantic rangia shows a significant difference between specimens in C100Z and the modern sample (Table 7.5). The Atlantic rangia shells from C100Z average 2.7 years of age (Standard Deviation—S^2 = 1.20) and have a shell length of 36.1 (mm) (S^2 = 7.2). The mean age of the modern individuals is six years (S^2 = .95) and the mean shell length is 60.4 (mm) (S^2 = 4.7). The null hypothesis that the mean age or shell length of the modern Atlantic rangia shell does not differ from the C100Z sample is rejected at the 95 percent confidence interval. Figures 7.8–7.9 show that the 95 percent confidence intervals about the mean for age and sizes do not overlap.

Table 7.5. Statistical tests for age (years) and size (mm) of *Rangia cuneata*

	Mound A—D100EE		Mound A —D100FF		Mound C—C100Z		Modern Bottle Creek	
	Age (yrs)	A/P (mm)	Age (yrs)	A/P (mm)	Age (yrs)	A/P (mm)	Age (yrs)	A/P (mm)
Sample n	16	10	57	58	146	130	81	81
Sample mean	4.06	48.10	3.65	44.79	2.69	36.08	6.04	60.43
Standard deviation	1.73	7.20	1.25	8.34	1.20	7.15	0.95	4.65
95 percent confidence interval	0.85	0.45	0.32	2.15	0.21	1.24	0.21	1.03

Note: Key to Abbreviations
A/P = Greatest anterior to posterior measurement of the shell (mm).

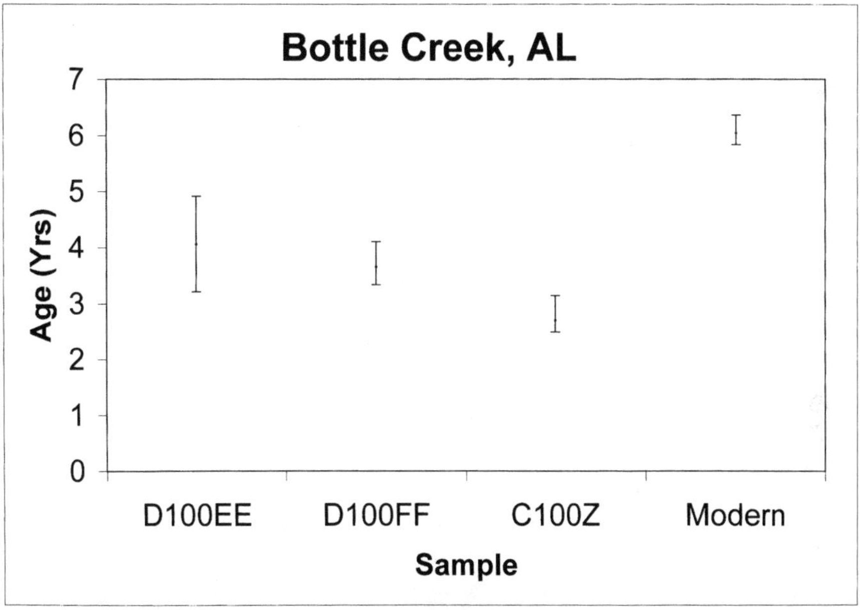

7.8. Statistical comparison of the ontogenetic age (years) at the 95 percent confidence interval of *Rangia cuneata* from archaeological and modern Bottle Creek contexts.

The log of the number of survivors versus age (years) illustrated in Figure 7.10 indicates increasing mortality with age for the living and archaeological samples (Table 7.6). The survivorship curve (log-age) for the living population shows that the greatest mortality occurs between five and seven years of age. C100Z Atlantic rangia suffer their greatest mortality after age two. Figure 7.11 further illustrates this trend in the percentage of survivors versus age curves. About 75 percent of the C100Z Atlantic rangia never attain four years of age, while 95 percent of the modern specimens live to four years.

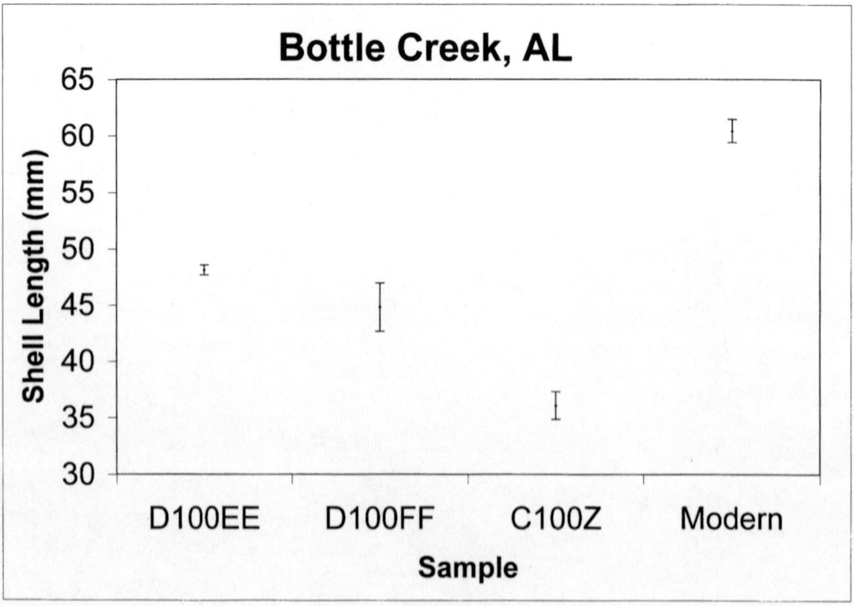

7.9. Statistical comparison of the mean shell length (mm) at the 95 percent confidence interval of *Rangia cuneata* from archaeological and modern Bottle Creek contexts.

Table 7.6. Survivorship curves for archaeological samples and modern samples of *Rangia cuneata*

Mound A—D100EE								
Age in years	1	2	3	4	5	6	7	8
Sample n	0	3	3	6	1	1	1	1
Number survivors remaining	16	16	13	10	4	3	2	1
Percentage of survivors	100	11.0	8.9	6.8	2.7	2.1	1.4	0.7
Log of survivors	1.2041	1.2041	1.1139	1.0000	0.6021	0.4771	0.3010	0.0000
Total sample n	16							
Mound A—D100FF								
Age in years	1	2	3	4	5	6	7	8
Sample n	3	5	18	19	8	3	1	
Number survivors remaining	57	54	49	31	12	4	1	
Percentage of survivors	100	37.0	33.6	21.2	8.2	2.7	0.7	
Log of survivors	1.7559	1.7324	1.6902	1.4914	1.0792	0.6021	0.0000	
Total sample n	57							
Mound C—C100Z								
Age in years	1	2	3	4	5	6	7	8
Sample n	18	60	33	23	9	2	1	
Number survivors remaining	146	128	68	35	12	3	1	
Percentage of survivors	100	87.7	46.6	24.0	8.2	2.1	0.7	
Log of survivors	2.1644	2.1072	1.8325	1.5441	1.0792	0.4771	0.0000	
Total sample n	146							
Modern Specimens								
Age in years	1	2	3	4	5	6	7	8
Sample n	0	0	1	3	16	37	20	4
Number survivors remaining	81	81	80	77	61	24	4	4
Percentage of survivors	100	100	98.8	95.1	75.3	29.6	4.9	4.9
Log of survivors	1.9085	1.9085	1.9031	1.8865	1.7853	1.3802	0.6021	0.6021
Total sample n	81							

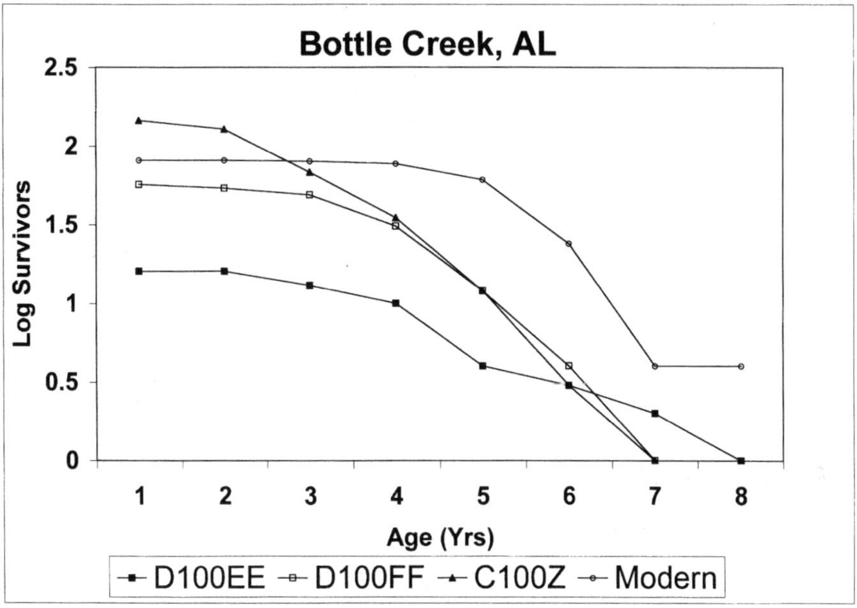

7.10. Survivorship curves of the log of the number of survivors of *Rangia cuneata* in relation to ontogenetic age (years) from archaeological and modern Bottle Creek contexts.

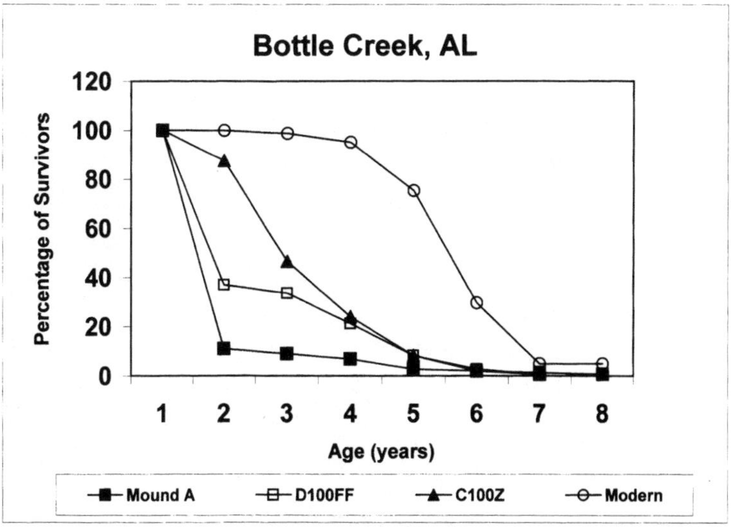

7.11. Survivorship curves of the percent of survivors of *Rangia cuneata* in relation to ontogenetic age (years) from archaeological and modern Bottle Creek contexts.

Mound A, D100EE, FS9 Faunal Assemblage

The D100EE faunal assemblage weighs 2,105 gm and contains 2,321 shell and bone fragments (Table 7.7). I identified 29 species representing 130 MNI. Commensal species, such as terrestrial snails and barnacles (*Balanus* sp.) are not included in this count.

Minimum Number of Individuals

Over 75 percent of the MNI contained in D100EE were mollusks (Figure 7.4b). Atlantic rangia account for nearly one half (47.7 percent) of the MNI. The freshwater mussels, ebonyshell (*Fusconaia ebene*) and southern mapleleaf (*Quadrula quadrula apiculata*) account for 16.2 percent and 3.1 percent respectively of the molluscan MNI. Eastern oyster (6.2 percent) and quahog (*Mercenaria* sp., .77 percent) are brackish water associates from the lower reaches of the estuary.

I identified 14 species of estuarine and freshwater fishes (19.2 percent) in D100EE (Table 7.7). Garfish (*Lepisosteus* sp., 1.5 percent), hardhead catfish (*Arius felis*, 1.5 percent), redear sunfish (*Lepomis microlophus*, 3.08 percent), and mullet (*Mugil* sp., 4.62 percent) are the main contributors of the fish fauna. The remaining 10 fish species do not exceed .76 percent of the identified fauna. Reptiles (1.5 percent), amphibians (.78 percent), birds (1.5 percent), and mammals (1.5 percent) are minor D100EE faunal constituents.

The species represented in D100EE indicate heavy reliance on aquatic fauna (Table 7.7). Ninety-five percent of MNI are aquatic species, while terrestrial animals account for 4.6 percent. Furthermore, 54.6 percent of the MNI are brackish water (BW) mollusks and 20.8 percent are freshwater mollusks (Figure 7.4b). MNI of brackish water fish species is represented by 10.8 percent of the MNI, and 8.5 percent could have been caught in freshwater habitats.

Estimated Meat

The relative contribution of molluscan meat accounts for 46.9 percent of the assemblage, while fishes contribute 38.2 percent (Figure 7.5b). Mammals rank third (10.0 percent) in their relative meat contribution, while reptiles (2.2 percent), amphibians (.01 percent), and birds (2.7 percent) are minor D100EE contributors.

Aquatic species contribute 78.6 percent of D100EE meat and terrestrial species 21.5 percent (Table 7.7). Brackish water mollusks supply 39.4 percent of the meat, while freshwater mollusks account for 27.0 percent (Figure 7.6b). Meat from brackish water (9.2 percent) and freshwater (3.0 percent) fishes further illustrate the importance of aquatic resources.

Table 7.7. Fauna identified from MoundA, D100EE—FS9

Species	Count	%	MNI	%	Weight (gm)	%	Meat (gm)	%
Animalia	9	0.39	–	–	1.10	0.05	–	–
Bryozoa	1	0.04	a	a	0.003	0.00	–	–
Bivalvia	b	b	–	–	74.91	3.56	19.62	0.77
Crassostrea virginica	26	1.12	8	6.15	206.34	9.80	29.86	1.18
Rangia cuneata	99	4.27	62	47.69	1001.78	47.59	662.02	26.09
Mercenaria sp.	1	0.04	1	0.77	5.62	0.27	1.60	0.06
Unionidae	9	0.39	–	–	199.07	9.46	128.81	5.08
Fusconaia ebena	34	1.46	21	16.15	435.14	20.67	297.39	11.72
Quadrula apiculata	8	0.34	4	3.08	81.35	3.86	49.44	1.95
Gastropoda (aquatic)	1	0.04	1	0.77	0.11	0.01	0.04	0.00
Pleuroceridae	1	0.04	1	0.77	0.24	0.01	0.19	0.01
Gastropoda (Terrestrial)	1	0.04	a	–	0.001	0.00	–	–
Balanus sp.	1	0.04	a	–	0.001	0.00	–	–
Vertebrata	66	2.84	–	–	2.17	0.10	–	–
Osteichthyes	1794	77.29	–	–	47.75	2.27	748.66	29.50
Lepisosteus sp.	11	0.47	2	1.54	2.93	0.14	13.29	0.52
Clupeidae	75	3.23	1	0.77	0.66	0.03	16.57	0.65
Brevoortia sp.	1	0.04	1	0.77	0.01	0.00	0.40	0.02
Siluriformes	5	0.22	–	–	0.55	0.03	7.54	0.30
Arius felis	3	0.13	2	1.54	0.24	0.01	3.16	0.12
Ictaluridae	5	0.22	1	0.77	0.80	0.04	11.17	0.44
Centrarchidae	30	1.29	–	–	0.53	0.03	9.17	0.36
Lepomis sp.	5	0.22	–	–	0.19	0.01	3.39	0.13
Lepomis macrochirus	4	0.17	1	0.77	0.13	0.01	2.35	0.09
Lepomis aff. macrochirus	1	0.04	1	0.77	0.04	0.00	0.75	0.03
Lepomis microlophus	11	0.47	4	3.08	0.46	0.02	8.00	0.32
Pomoxis nigromaculatus	1	0.04	1	0.77	0.09	0.00	1.64	0.06
Micropterus sp.	2	0.09	1	0.77	0.17	0.01	3.04	0.12
Archosargus probatocephalus	2	0.09	1	0.77	0.57	0.03	10.31	0.41
Sciaenidae	1	0.04	–	–	0.13	0.01	2.90	0.11
Cynoscion sp.	2	0.09	1	0.77	0.10	0.00	2.24	0.09
Micropogonias undulatus	2	0.09	1	0.77	0.12	0.01	2.68	0.11
Mugil sp.	67	2.89	6	4.62	5.18	0.25	103.69	4.09
Paralichthys sp.	4	0.17	1	0.77	0.79	0.04	19.45	0.77
Squamata	1	0.04	1	0.77	0.001	0.00	0.02	0.00
Testudines	7	0.30	1	0.77	1.50	0.07	55.38	2.18
Anura	1	0.04	1	0.77	0.01	0.00	0.26	0.01
Aves	2	0.09	–	–	0.14	0.01	3.33	0.13
Aves (large)	6	0.26	–	–	2.57	0.12	38.40	1.51
Aves (small)	1	0.04	1	0.77	0.03	0.00	0.91	0.04
Buteo sp.	1	0.04	1	0.77	1.70	0.08	27.14	1.07
Mammalia	10	0.43	–	–	1.18	0.06	15.78	0.62
Mammalia (small)	1	0.04	1	0.77	0.04	0.00	1.02	0.04
Mammalia (large)	17	0.73	–	–	10.07	0.48	89.63	3.53
Odocoileus virginianus	1	0.04	1	0.77	18.47	0.88	146.50	5.77
Total	2321	100	130	100	2104.98	100	2537.76	100

Note: Key to Abbreviations.

a = Commensal species not use in the calculations of MNI, weight, or biomass.

b = Crushed shell not counted.

Summary of Fauna Resources

	MNI	%	Biomass	%
Mollusk	98	75.38	1188.98	46.85
Fish	25	19.23	970.41	38.24
Reptile	2	1.54	55.39	2.18
Amphibian	1	0.77	0.26	0.01
Bird	2	1.54	69.79	2.75
Mammal	2	1.54	252.93	9.97
Total	130	100	2537.76	100
FW Mollusk	27	20.77	475.87	27.01
BW Mollusk	71	54.62	693.49	39.36
FW Fish	11	8.46	52.81	3.00
BW Fish	14	10.77	161.40	9.16
Reptile	2	1.54	55.39	3.14
Amphibian	1	0.77	0.26	0.01
Bird	2	1.54	69.79	3.96
Mammal	2	1.54	252.93	14.36
Total	130	100	1761.94	100
Aquatic	124	95.38	1383.83	78.54
Terrestrial	6	4.62	378.11	21.46
Total	130	100	1761.94	100

Diversity and Equitability

D100EE Shannon-Weaver Diversity Index (H′) is 2.09 while the Sheldon Index (E) is 0.62 (Table 7.4 and Figure 7.7). These numbers indicate that the D100EE faunal assemblage is less specialized than either of the other faunal samples presented in this report.

Age and Size of Atlantic Rangia Clam

The size and age structure of D100EE Atlantic rangia show a significant difference between the D100EE shells and the modern sample (Table 7.5). Atlantic rangia shells from D100EE average 4.1 years of age ($S^2 = 1.73$) and have a mean anterior to posterior size of 48.1 mm ($S^2 = 7.2$). The null hypothesis that the mean age or size of the modern specimens do not differ from the D100EE sample is rejected. Figures 7.8–7.9 show that the 95 percent confidence intervals about the mean for age and sizes do not overlap.

The log of the number of survivors versus age (years) illustrated in Figure 7.10 shows D100EE Atlantic rangia have their greatest mortality after age three. Figure 7.11 further portrays this trend in the percentage of survivors versus age curves. About 90 percent of the D100EE Atlantic rangia never attain three years of age.

Mound A, D100FF, FS10 Faunal Assemblage

The shell and bone identified in D100FF represents 1,468 fragments and weighs 3,904.3 gm. Twenty-one species representing 143 MNI were identified (Table 7.8). Commensal species such as barnacles are not included in this count.

Minimum Number of Individuals

Mollusks account for 87.4 percent of the identified D100FF animals (Figure 7.3c). Eighty-three percent of the mollusks are Atlantic rangia, while eastern oyster (*Crassostrea virginica*, .7 percent) and Carolina marsh clams (*Polymesoda caroliniana*, 2.1 percent) occurred less frequently.

About 10 percent of the D100FF MNI are fishes. Herrings, freshwater drum (*Aplodinotus grunniens*), and mullet (*Mugil* sp.) contribute 1.4 percent each to the total MNI (Table 7.8). The remaining species of fish do not exceed .7 percent each. Reptiles (.7 percent), amphibians (.7 percent), birds (.7 percent), and mammals (.7 percent) are minor components of D100FF.

Approximately 98 percent of D100FF MNI is aquatic species, while terrestrial animals account for just 2.1 percent (Table 7.8). Brackish water mollusks (86.7 percent) and brackish water fishes (5.6 percent) comprise the majority of the MNI (Figure 7.4c). Freshwater fish and mollusk species provide 4.2 percent and .7 percent respectively.

Table 7.8. Fauna identified from Mound A. D100FF—FS10

Species	Count	%	MNI	%	Weight (gm)	%	Meat (gm)	%
Mytilidae	1	0.07	1	0.70	59.76	1.53	15.89	0.42
Crassostrea virginica	8	0.54	1	0.70	3.03	0.08	0.50	0.01
Unionidae	10	0.68	1	0.70	11.26	0.29	5.96	0.16
Rangia cuneata	226	15.40	118	82.52	3774.06	96.66	2963.43	77.84
Polymesoda caroliniana	5	0.34	3	2.10	9.03	0.23	6.36	0.17
Decapoda	1	0.07	1	0.70	0.05	0.001	0.84	0.02
Balanus sp.	6	0.41	a	–	0.06	0.002	–	–
Vertebrata	11	0.75	–	–	0.79	0.02	–	–
Osteichthyes	1088	74.11	–	–	28.64	0.73	475.03	12.48
Lepisosteus sp.	20	1.36	1	0.70	0.69	0.02	4.16	0.11
Amia calva	1	0.07	1	0.70	0.02	0.00	0.74	0.02
Clupeidae	17	1.16	2	1.40	0.20	0.01	5.83	0.15
Siluriformes	2	0.14	–	–	0.08	0.00	1.00	0.03
Ictaluridae	2	0.14	1	0.70	0.04	0.00	0.48	0.01
Centrarchidae	10	0.68	1	0.70	0.55	0.01	9.51	0.25
Sciaenidae	1	0.07	–	–	0.10	0.00	2.24	0.06
Aplodinotus grunniens	7	0.48	2	1.40	1.05	0.03	22.96	0.60
Cynoscion sp.	2	0.14	1	0.70	0.31	0.01	6.86	0.18
Micropogonias undulatus	6	0.41	1	0.70	0.53	0.01	11.67	0.31
Sciaenops ocellatus	1	0.07	1	0.70	4.10	0.11	88.44	2.32
Mugil sp.	27	1.84	2	1.40	3.74	0.10	77.54	2.04
Paralichthys sp.	2	0.14	1	0.70	0.15	0.00	2.10	0.06
Testudines	1	0.07	–	–	0.12	0.00	14.52	0.38
aff. *Terrapene carolina*	1	0.07	1	0.70	0.36	0.01	25.99	0.68
Anura	1	0.07	1	0.70	0.03	0.00	0.12	0.00
Aves	1	0.07	1	0.70	0.12	0.00	2.93	0.08
Mammalia	8	0.54	–	–	2.33	0.06	27.39	0.72
Odocoileus virginianus	2	0.14	1	0.70	3.10	0.08	34.51	0.91
Total	1468	100	143	100	3904.30	100	3806.99	100

Note: Key to Abbreviations.
a = Commensal species not used in the calculations of MNI, weight, or biomass.

Summary of Fauna Resources

	MNI	%	Biomass	%
Mollusk	125	87.41	2992.97	78.62
Fish	14	9.79	708.56	18.61
Reptile	1	0.70	40.51	1.06
Amphibian	1	0.70	0.12	0.00
Bird	1	0.70	2.93	0.08
Mammal	1	0.70	61.90	1.63
Total	143	100	3806.99	100
FW Mollusk	1	0.70	5.96	0.18
BW Mollusk	124	86.71	2987.01	91.32
FW Fish	6	4.20	37.85	1.16
BW Fish	8	5.59	194.69	5.95
Reptile	1	0.70	40.51	1.24
Amphibian	1	0.70	1.00	0.03
Bird	1	0.70	2.93	0.09
Mammal	1	0.70	1.00	0.03
Total	143	100	3270.95	100
Aquatic	139	97.89	3225.50	98.61
Terrestrial	3	2.11	45.44	1.39
Total	142	100.0027	3270.94	100

Estimated Meat

Meat provided by molluscan species accounts for 78.6 percent of the assemblage, while fishes contribute 18.6 percent (Figure 7.5c). Species of reptiles (1.1 percent), birds (.1 percent) and mammals (1.6 percent) are minor contributors of meat in D100FF.

Aquatic species contribute 98.6 percent of D100FF meat and terrestrial species 1.4 percent (Table 7.8). Brackish water mollusks supply 91.3 percent of the estimated meat, while freshwater mollusks account for 0.2 percent (Figure 7.6c). Meat from brackish water (6.0 percent) and freshwater (1.2 percent) fishes further illustrate the importance of aquatic resources.

Diversity and Equitability

D100FF Shannon-Weaver Diversity Index (H′) is 0.97 while the Sheldon Index (E) is 0.32 (Table 7.4 and Figure 7.7). These statistical values characterize the D100FF samples as being the most specialized of the three Bottle Creek faunal samples. Such statistics indicate heavy reliance on a large number of individuals from few numbers of species.

Age and Size of Atlantic Rangia Clam

The size and age structure of D100FF Atlantic rangia shells are significantly different from the modern sample (Table 7.5). Atlantic rangia from D100FF average 3.7 years of age (S^2 = 1.25) and have a mean anterior to posterior size of 44.8 mm (S^2 = 8.3). The null hypothesis that the mean age or size of the modern specimens does not differ from the D100FF sample is rejected. Figures 7.8–7.9 show that the 95 percent confidence intervals about the mean for age and sizes do not overlap.

The log of the number of survivors versus age (years) illustrated in Figure 7.10 shows D100FF Atlantic rangia suffer their greatest mortality after age three (Table 7.6). Figure 7.11 further portrays this trend in the percentage of survivors versus age curves. About 90 percent of the D100FF Atlantic rangia never attain three years of age.

DISCUSSION

The Mound C and Mound A faunal assemblages represent three locations at Bottle Creek that contain part of the variability that may be observed across the site. Nevertheless, the analyses of these materials provide baseline data that may be compared to future faunal analysis at Bottle Creek. At this level of research, mounds C and A faunal assemblages show great consistency in their evidence of the habitats exploited and the technology used to obtain animal resources. The relative frequency of animal use exhibited in D100FF and C100Z is quite similar, while some differences exist in D100EE. Nonetheless, a general subsistence pattern among the assemblages exists. Evidence consistent with the over-harvest of Atlantic rangia clams is present in the Bottle Creek faunal samples.

The general Bottle Creek zooarchaeological theme shows a heavy reliance on aquatic resources. Mollusks and fishes were of primary importance. In all cases, the inhabitants used brackish water species most often. This conclusion is supported by the presence of estuarine fishes, such as menhaden, mullet, sheepshead (*Archosargus probatocephalus*) and Atlantic croaker (*Micropogonias undulatus*). Freshwater species, such as garfish (*Lepisosteus* sp.), freshwater bass (*Micropterus* sp.), and sunfishes are tolerant of low salinity conditions of the upper reaches of the estuary and would have occupied habitats near Bottle Creek (Swingle and Bland 1974). The presence of Atlantic rangia and freshwater mussels is further evidence of the use of the boundary between fresh- and saltwater. For example, Atlantic rangia needs some saltwater for reproduction (Swingle and Bland 1974), while freshwater mussels cannot survive exposure to brackish water. The diversity of species found shows the importance of aquatic resources to the Bottle Creek people.

Places like the upper reaches of the Mobile-Tensaw Delta serve as nursery grounds for invertebrates and vertebrates. Prehistoric Bottle Creek people living in the Mobile Estuary had access to a diverse range of high biomass zoological resources. Many of these species use the estuary as a nursery (e.g., menhadens, mullet, Atlantic croaker) and therefore are seasonally abundant. Maximum exploitation of seasonally available, high biomass resources (e.g., menhadens and mullet) establishes a reliable human food source (Smith 1979:156). In the event that one species fails to appear, alternatives are at hand. The strong reliance on aquatic resources at Bottle Creek indicates that the inhabitants may have used this subsistence strategy (Table 7.3). Mollusks and fishes were major contributors to the Bottle Creek diet, while terrestrial species were less often observed in the assemblages.

The technology used to exploit the environment was as diverse as the available resources. Atlantic rangia clams and freshwater mussels are evidence for simple harvesting in the shallow water zones. Open weave bags, baskets, and perhaps canoes would have facilitated their harvest. Atlantic rangia are most abundant around the mouths of creeks, where an occasional freshwater mussel may also be found. Freshwater mussels are more frequently collected where salinity is mitigated by freshwater runoff. Shallow inland creeks are ideal locations for mussel collection.

The overwhelming abundance of small schooling fishes is indicative of the use of fine mesh nets, traps, or weirs. For example, juvenile menhaden travel in large compact schools in the upper parts of the estuary (Dahlberg 1975:38). Such animals are most easily taken with fine mesh nets, open weave baskets, and dip nets. These devices would have maximized the catch of other schooling fishes, such as shiners (*Notemigonus* sp.), small sunfishes, Atlantic croaker, redfish (*Sciaenops ocellatus*) and mullet. The use of fine mesh nets is further supported by the identification of bowfin (*Amia calva*), catfishes, freshwater bass, and flounder (*Paralichthyes* sp.), which are known bottom dwellers and would have been caught in nets. The presence of predatory fishes (e.g., garfish, bowfin, freshwater bass, and flounder) that hunt smaller fishes may also represent individuals netted with schooling fish. Alternatively, the presence of predatory fishes may indicate the use of spears, hook, and line.

Access to natural resources and other people must have been important to the Bottle Creek inhabitants. The use of watercraft would have maximized the energy necessary to travel to distant locations while carrying provisions and exploited resources. Eastern oysters and quahogs identified at Bottle Creek indicate the movement of resources from the middle and lower zones of the Mobile Estuary. Connection with more northern localities is suggested by the identification of the gladiator elimia (*Elimia hydei*), which is endemic to the Black Warrior River of north-central Alabama (Burch 1989). Its presence at Bottle Creek could represent a food resource or an incidental stowaway brought by a visiting canoe.

Even though the relationships of the various faunal categories exhibit general trends in the three faunal samples, some specific differences exist. The MNI of mollusks in C100Z, D100EE, and D100FF dominate their assemblages. However, mollusks in D100EE are less important when compared to fishes. Nearly twice as many fishes were identified in D100EE and mammals (white-tailed deer) were more frequently identified in the assemblage.

By the estimate of meat provided by the various taxa, the two samples from Mound A contain relatively more meat from fishes than the sample from Mound C. Twice as much fish meat is observed in D100FF and nearly four times as much in D100EE. Relative to the other samples, D100EE has a greater percentage of meat from freshwater animals. D100EE freshwater mussels and freshwater fishes contribute proportionally more meat than either of the other samples. Estimated meat contributed by D100EE mammalian species (primarily white-tailed deer) is substantially greater. The differences existing between mounds C and A could be ascribed to either status differences or too few samples. For example, D100EE could represent refuse from a specific activity. Repeated sampling is needed to establish these trends.

Compelling evidence for the over-exploitation of Atlantic rangia is identified in the analysis of ontogenetic age (years) and size (age). The data may also identify a difference between the two mound areas. Statistical tests of rangia age (years) and size from D100EE and D100FF indicate Mound A shells could have been collected from the same population. D100EE and D100FF rangia populations are ontogenetically younger than the modern population, but slightly older than the Mound C specimens. Rangia shells from Mound C (C100Z) come from a population that is significantly younger in years than either Mound A or the modern collection. The survivorship curves show a precipitous decline in the ontogenetic age classes of the zooarchaeological Atlantic rangia shells. Prehistoric rangia harvesting occurred at such a rate that it did not allow for the replenishment of older individuals in the beds. It is noteworthy that smaller archaeological Atlantic rangia (average 32 mm) would have required greater energy to collect. The harvest of such small specimens could have been ineffective and required the use of rakes or open weave baskets. The ontogenetic age and size data also show that Mound A inhabitants had access to large Atlantic rangia when compared to Mound C.

SUMMARY AND CONCLUSIONS

The Bottle Creek zooarchaeological record indicates that the site was built at a boundary between fresh and salt water. This ecotone provided access to seasonally available high biomass resources. These resources were typically juveniles of fish species that use the estuary as a nursery during part of their life cycles. The strong presence of molluscan fauna also illustrates the importance of aquatic resources to prehistoric Bottle Creek people. Even though terrestrial resources were less frequently identified, their use provided the variability necessary to human subsistence.

The importance of aquatic resources provides indirect evidence of subsistence technology. Simple gathering of mollusks was a major enterprise requiring collecting bags or baskets. The small sizes of Atlantic rangia may indicate the use of rakes or open weave baskets for their efficient harvest. The catching of schooling juvenile fishes would have been maximized by the use of fine mesh nets, traps, or weirs.

Evidence of the movement of resources is found in the presence of species not common to the Bottle Creek environment. The occurrence of oysters and quahog suggest contact with areas to the south of the site. The presence of the gladiator elimia indicates contact with places along the Black Warrior River of north-central Alabama.

Status differences between mounds C and A are not well defined in the faunal assemblages, although greater amounts of fishes and perhaps mammals may be represented in the Mound A assemblages. Repeated sampling from across the site will help in identifying status differences.

Evidence for harvesting pressures on natural resources is rare in the zooarchaeological record. At Bottle Creek the age and size of zooarchaeological Atlantic rangia clams are significantly lower than that of modern populations. The data also show that people living in the higher status areas of the site had access to the oldest and largest specimens that could be obtained from the surrounding environment.

8 / A Functional Comparison of Pottery Vessel Shapes from Bottle Creek

Hunter B. Johnson

INTRODUCTION

In this chapter I explore the relationship between the central group of mounds and the peripheral mounds at Bottle Creek by examining primary pottery vessel shapes recovered in the Mound A (central) and Mound C (peripheral) excavations. In essence, this work complements Fuller's study of pottery sets (Chapter 2). The shapes that I present and discuss encompass most of the Bottle Creek I and II assemblages in our sample. My research recognizes that there are functionally distinct vessels within assemblages that can be explored to help understand social processes (Brown 1982:48–81; Hally 1983a, 1983b, 1986; Pauketat 1987a; Steponaitis 1983: 33–45). Because the Bottle Creek people used ceramic vessels in both the preparation and serving of faunal and floral components of diet, this research also contributes to an understanding of foodways at Bottle Creek. While it is not possible to give a detailed account of Bottle Creek people, through studies like this we can begin to get a flavor of daily life at the site.

The spatial layout of Bottle Creek (Figure 1.3), with its mound-plaza arrangement and an assortment of smaller surrounding tumuli, has parallels with other Mississippian mound centers in the Southeast (Lewis and Stout 1998a; Rogers and Smith 1995). If our understanding of the physical layout of the Bottle Creek site and its divisions is correct, then Mound A and its immediate surroundings would have supported principal elite activities at the site. The center of gravity for such proceedings would have been the space outlined by mounds A, B, L, and M. The plaza area for the site lies between these four mounds. Surrounding this centrally placed cluster of mounds is a series of small, accretionary house mounds (C–K and N) that were presumably occupied by lesser elites and/or retainers. These mounds would have risen over time through the continuous accumulation of refuse. Obviously there is a difference between the terms "lesser elites" and "retainers." We have no idea which of these terms actually applies, but the main argument is that the people who occupied the peripheral mounds were a step down (presumably a big step) from the principal elite. If this is so, their material culture—in this case pottery—should reflect the different statuses. It must also be mentioned that there are some outlying mounds (O–R) located along the eastern and western extremities of the Bottle Creek site. They are not part of this discussion as their function seems to have been more related to mortuary activities (Fuller and Brown 1998:100–103).

It is reasonable to believe that an established order of social rankings reflected in the spatial organization of the site might also be manifested in pottery assemblages. Presumably, as the site transformed into a major mound center, the size of the mounds and their location became important markers of social distinction (Knight 1998). This distinction allows a comparison of ceramic vessel assemblages by looking at excavated pottery from mounds A (unit D100) and C (unit C100). In comparing the vessel shapes from these units, information concerning mound activities should be revealed in the different assemblages. If indeed Mound A was occupied by the "primary elites" (Brown 1994:46), a large overall sherd percentage of serving vessels, such as plates, small bowls, beakers, and bottles should be found in Mound A deposits. The assumption is that the elite would have eaten the food that others cooked and served. As the peripheral mounds are believed to be the places where food preparation occurred, one would expect to find a greater percentage of cooking wares in the Mound C pottery assemblage, such as large jars, bowls, and pans.

In essence, if the spatial layout of the Bottle Creek site is indeed an indication of status, then one would expect variation in pottery between mounds A and C. I performed a vessel shape analysis on excavated rim sherds from these two mound assemblages to determine whether or not such a variation exists. As will be shown, there are indeed distinct variations in vessel shapes in the comparison of Mound A and pre-Mound A deposits on the one hand, and Mound A and Mound C deposits on the other.

MOUND C

As discussed in Chapter 2, after we conducted soil probe tests on and around the entire Mound C surface, we placed a 2 m square test unit (C100) in what we considered to be a prime midden deposit (Figure 2.1). As we carried out excavations, we found that stratified middens occurred throughout the entire unit. Only occasional post features showed up. Almost all of the soil zones in this unit consisted of a brown silt midden, but once we scraped the walls down, it was possible to identify different depositional zones. Large quantities of pottery and abundant food remains indicated midden concentrations. These rich midden zones are representative of important changes in the Bottle Creek assemblage between A.D. 1250 and 1550.

MOUND A

We also placed a series of soil probes around the base of Mound A, the goal once again being to find a rich midden area for a test unit. The best location was on the north side of Mound A's base, where we excavated a 2 m square test unit (D100). At about 2 m below the surface, we had to divide D100 into a 1 × 2 m unit for safety purposes. At its greatest depth, the unit reached approximately 2.5 m. The D100 unit revealed a series of mound construction stages, with intermittent midden zones (Table 2.1). Cultural deposits suggested over 400 years of occupation in this area between A.D. 1250 and the early eighteenth century. The lower premound levels in this unit consist of thin lenses of midden separated by equally thin alluvial deposits. These distinctions show an excellent chronological sequence for the premound deposits (Table 2.1 and Figure 2.4).

VESSEL CHARACTERISTICS

Mound C yielded an extremely large sample of sherds; 1,921 rims were recovered, 470 of which are classified as large fraction, 4 cm squared or larger. An arbitrary distinction had to be made between sherds that could be interpreted for form and those that could not. The Mound A assemblage is smaller, but still has an impressive total of 629 rim sherds, 158 of which fall into the large fraction category. Rims smaller than 4 cm squared are typically indistinguishable in terms of vessel form, so they were not considered in the analysis.

A previous study by Steponaitis at Moundville has shown that coarsely ground shell was used more in utilitarian wares, while finely crushed shell was used more in serving and ceremonial wares (Steponaitis 1983:33–45). This distinction holds true at Bottle Creek, too, where coarse wares were used almost exclusively for jars and large, open, basin-shaped pans. Whereas coarse-shell-tempered ware (Mississippi Plain) permits a high resistance to thermal stresses, fine-shell-tempered pottery (Bell Plain) is more resistant to mechanical stresses. Consequently, Bell Plain tends to be associated more with small open bowls, hemispherical bowls, bottles, and plates.

Researchers have also looked at burnishing as a way to differentiate between serving and cooking vessels. A common distinction holds that burnished pottery is associated with serving, ritual, and ceremonial type vessels, while cooking and storage vessels are mainly unburnished (Steponaitis 1983:23–24). At Bottle Creek ware distinctions seem to parallel variations found in vessel shapes.

Sooting, oxidation discoloration, and physical abrasion were all recorded as part of this study, following Hally (1983a). I noted that certain physical alterations appear more on specific vessel shapes than on others. Sooting, for example, occurs mainly on jars, collared bowls, and large plain bowls, while pitting and oxidation occur equally on jars and bowls. Burnishing appears mainly on fine wares, specifically bowls, bottles, beakers and plates. Jars and pans, on the other hand, lack burnishing.

The manner in which the Bottle Creek inhabitants cooked and served their food obviously influenced the shapes of vessels used in daily food preparation and consumption. The most common vessel shapes are the jar, bowl, plate, bottle, and saltpan (Figure 8.1). Each of these vessel shapes is believed to have played a different functional role in the lifeways of the inhabitants. Vessel morphology remains somewhat consistent for these vessel types, with varying size classes for each. Variations that occurred in a particular vessel shape class are almost always due to size and surface treatment.

VESSEL COMPARISON

A comparison of the pottery assemblages from mounds A and C has revealed certain formal differences, particularly between the Mound A and pre-Mound A deposits. By focusing on the analysis of rim sherds from mounds A and C, I was able to chart similarities and differences. When overall percentages are compared, there is little significant variation in vessel shapes between the Mound A (D100) and Mound C (C100) assemblages. However, because Mound A shows a distinct difference between mound-slope deposits and premound deposits (Table 2.1), it seemed more useful to divide the assemblage and calculate percentages separately (Table 8.1 and Figure 8.2). As shown by Fuller (Chapter 2), the pre-Mound A deposits mostly date to early in the Bottle Creek I phase (A.D. 1250–1300), with some occupation having occurred even earlier. The deposits on the Mound A slope, on the other hand, date to the late Bottle Creek I phase and later (post A.D. 1300).

When premound deposits and mound deposits are considered, a dramatic change in vessel shape frequencies can be seen. Although the vessel shape percentages differ greatly between Mound A and pre-Mound A deposits, actual form differs very little. All of the same types and varieties of Pensacola culture ceramics occur in the two contexts. Jars and pans are much more common in the premound assemblage for Mound A,

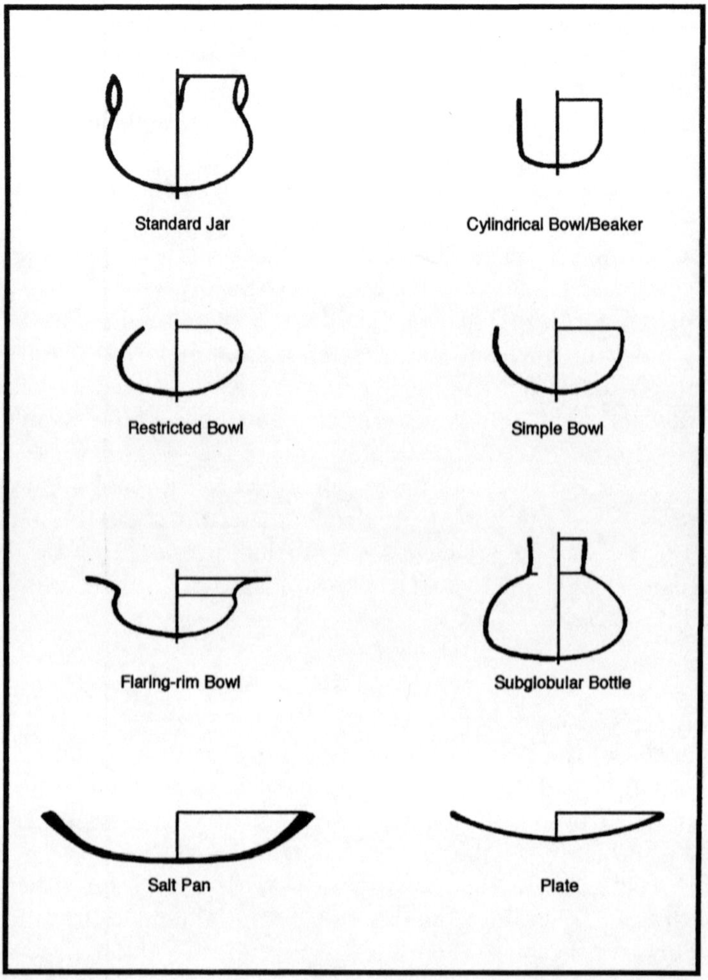

8.1. Typical vessel shapes represented at Bottle Creek (after Steponaitis 1983:Figure 22).

Table 8.1. Comparison of vessel shape percentages from mounds A and C

Provenience	Jars	Bowls	Bottles	Plates	Beakers	Saltpans	Unidentified	Total
Mound A—Mound Deposits								
Counts	34	45	6	19	1	10	2	117
Percentage	29	38	5	16	1	9	2	
Pre–mound A								
Counts	26	1	5	3	0	5	1	41
Percentage	63	3	12	7	0	12	3	
Mound C								
Counts	205	142	10	82	2	29	0	470
Percentage	44	30	2	17	1	6	0	
Total Counts	265	188	21	104	3	44	3	628

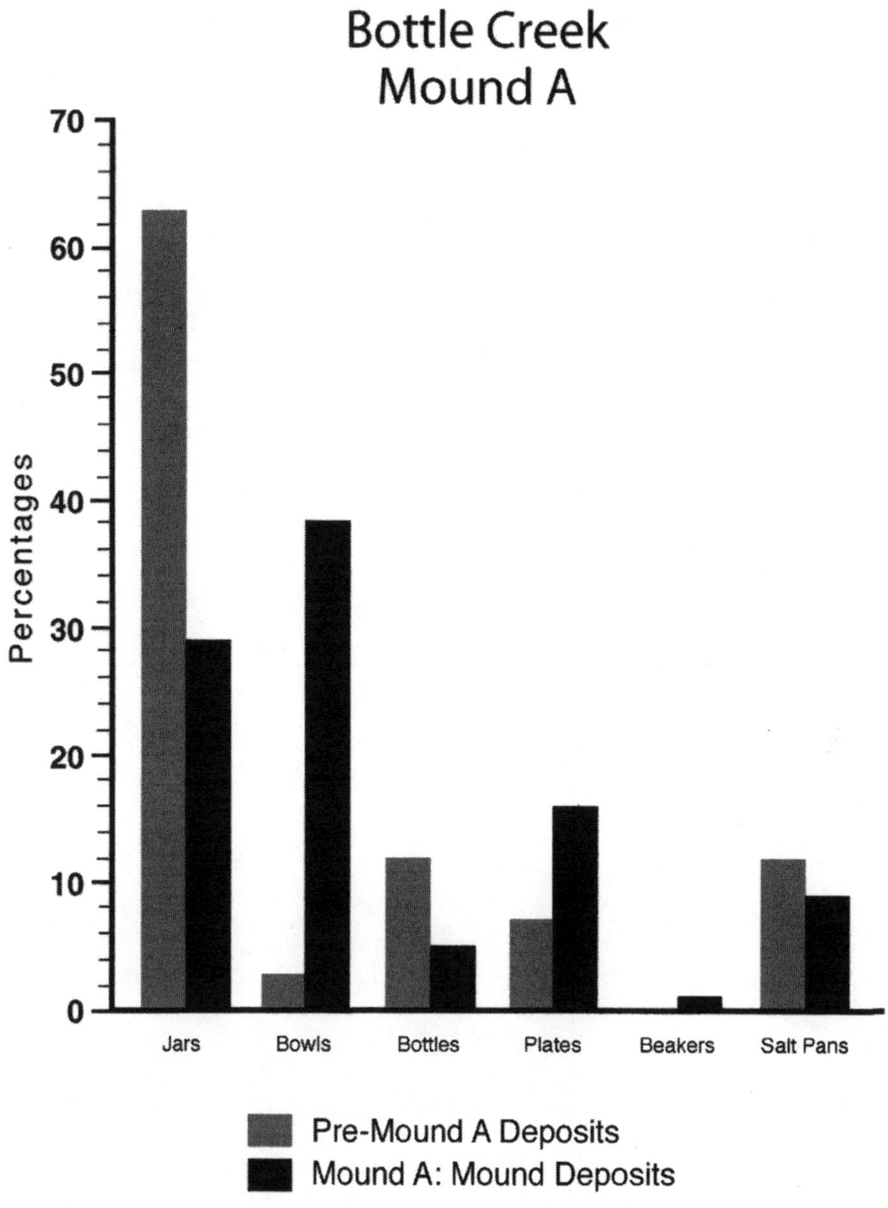

8.2. Percentage histograms of vessel shapes from Mound A and pre-Mound A deposits.

while bowls, plates, and bottles are more common in the mound deposits. These differences are suggestive of a marked social change at the site once mound-building occurred.

Jars

In Mississippian society the jar is believed to have been the everyday cooking pot. Jars at Bottle Creek are distinguishable by their coarse ground shell temper, handles, and a distinct color range of ware. The "standard jar" form is most typical (Figure 8.1). It has a globular body with a rounded base. Many of the jars are medium to large, with straight or excurvate rims and restricted necks. The lip is either rounded or pointed in most cases (Figures 8.3 and 8.4). These vessels are almost always unburnished, with an abundant amount of medium to coarse lamellar shell (Fuller 1996). Many of these jars have a more consolidated hardened interior surface treatment, presumably to prevent the flaking and leaching of vessel materials into food products. When decoration occurs on this vessel form, it is inevitably classified as Moundville Incised.

During the principal occupation of the Bottle Creek site (A.D. 1250–1550) there was a dramatic reduction in the use of jars in Unit D100. The jar percentage for the assemblage drops from 63 percent to 29 percent of the total vessel representation (Figure 8.2). This suggests that at least some food preparation activities shifted to another area of the site once Mound A started to be raised and used. As stated above, this shift came at the end or after the Bottle Creek I phase.

Bowls

Bowls have a wide range of variability at the Bottle Creek site, but certain common characteristics can be seen. Almost all have rounded flattened bases and rounded sides. Unless one has a large enough segment of the rim, cylindrical bowls and beakers are often difficult to distinguish. Bowls and beakers usually have vertical rims that are straight to incurvate in profile and are direct to expanded in cross-section. Bowls typically have flattened or round-flattened lips. For Mound A, the most common bowl form is the restricted bowl (Figure 8.1). With but one exception, bowls do not occur below the mound deposits in the D100 unit. Bowls are quite common in the Mound C assemblage, but for this context the cylindrical bowl/beaker is the most prevalent bowl vessel shape. This could mean that cylindrical vessels were used more in a food cooking/processing context, while restricted bowls were used more for elite subsistence purposes, with no pun intended.

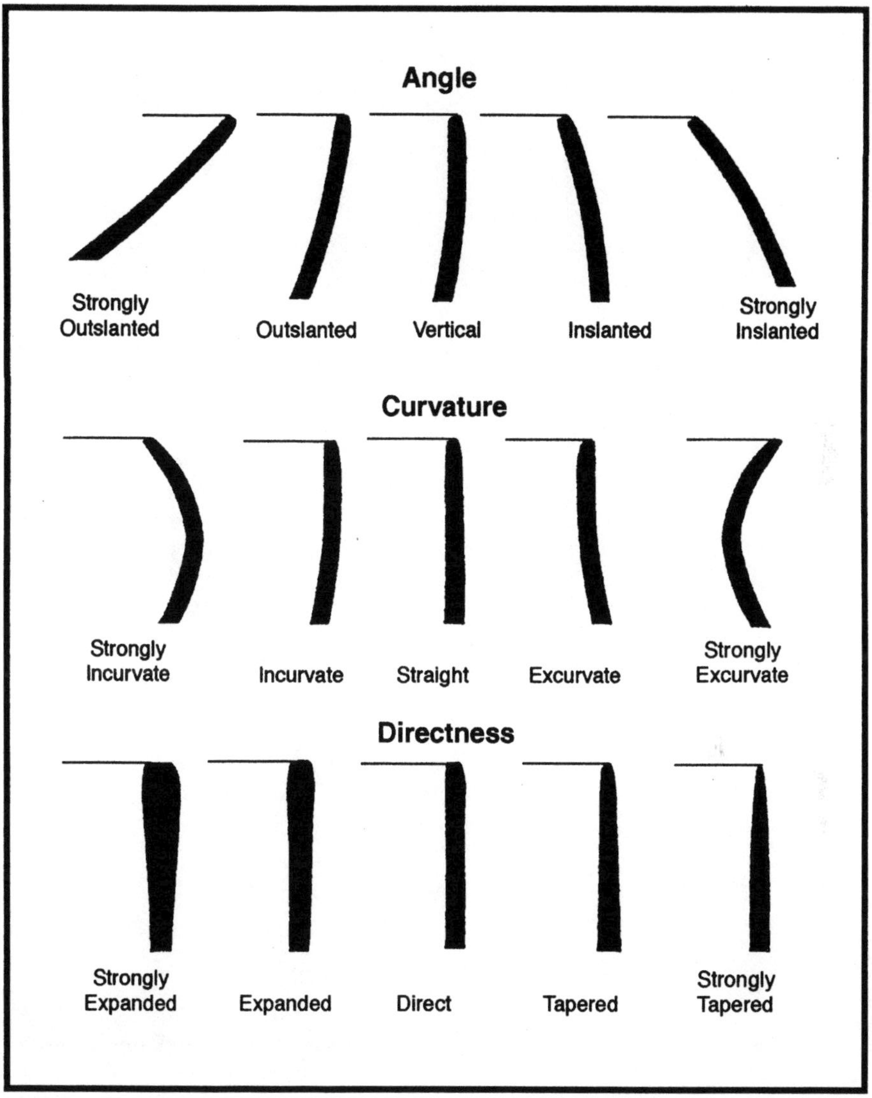

8.3. Attributes of rim cross-section.

Bottles

Bottle rims that occur in the pottery assemblage at Bottle Creek are comparable with bottle shapes in the coastal regions of Alabama and Florida. They generally have wide mouths and excurvate to straight necks, with a pointed to rounded rim. Their bodies tend to be subglobular and they are

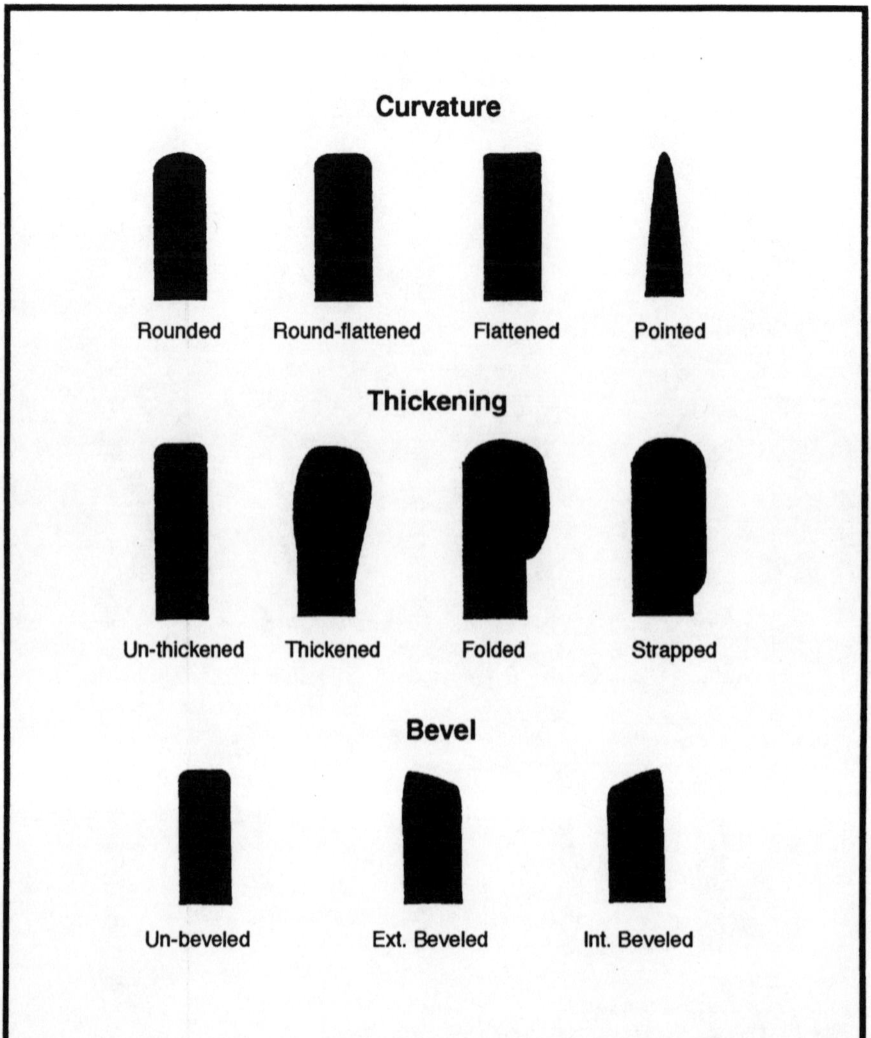

8.4. Attributes of lip cross-section.

medium to large in size (Figure 8.1). Because I observed very few flat slab bases in the collection, most of these wide-mouth bottles probably had rounded flattened bases. Some of the larger bottles are very similar to jars in shape, except at the base. Bottles would have acted as containers and serving vessels. At times, they were elaborately decorated, but this is not so evident at Bottle Creek. All of the bottles that occur in the assemblages from mounds A and C are on a Bell Plain ware, especially on Bell Plain, *var. Stockton* (Fuller 1996). Surprisingly, bottles have a greater representation in the pre-Mound A deposits than they do in the mound deposits for Unit D100. They have about equal representation in mounds A and C, but as we are only talking about 11 sherds in D100 and 12 in C100, the sample size is too small to say anything of relevance.

Plates

I expected the number of plates represented in the Mound A mound deposits to be greater than those from Mound C, but it turns out that the quantities are almost exactly the same. Plates represent 16 percent of the Mound A assemblage and 17 percent of the Mound C assemblage (Table 8.1). The premound plate assemblage for Mound A is much lower than that of both mound deposits, however, accounting for only 7 percent of the total assemblage. The increase in plate percentages for Mound A correlates well with mound-building stages.

Saltpans

Saltpans are large, strongly outslanting basin-shaped bowls with heavily thickened lips (Figure 8.1). They are generally believed to be utilitarian vessels (Brown 1980:28–30; Drooker 1992:33–36). They occur throughout the assemblages at Bottle Creek, from the early Kimmswick Fabric Impressed type to the later Salt Creek Cane Impressed type (Chapter 10). Salt Creek Cane Impressed, *var. Salt Creek* rim sherds are very thick in profile, sometimes three times as thick as the body of the vessel. These rims are flat on top and seem to have acted as a support for some kind of lid. In both C100 and D100 the saltpan is a rare but persistent vessel form. Unfortunately, the sample size of 44 sherds is too small to be significant.

SUMMARY AND CONCLUSIONS

It has been determined that Mound C is an accretional mound, built up slowly by the day-to-day discarding of food and household waste. No substantial earth deposit stages were obvious in the profiles of Mound C; instead we observed only thin lenses of sterile soil brought in to cover up undesirable smells or to cap off certain areas. The great abundance of *Rangia cuneata* found in unit C100 (Chapter 7) and the proximity of this mound to a potential water route, Dominic Creek, suggest that Mound C may have served as a food-processing area for shellfish and other foods coming into the site. This hypothesis is supported by a large number of utilitarian wares represented in the pottery from C100, with 44 percent of the Mound C assemblage made up of jars (Table 8.1).

Examination of the assemblages from mounds A and C has revealed a clear distinction reflected in the Bottle Creek phase materials. I believe that the Mound A midden deposits represent refuse of food and pottery containers used to serve primary elites, whereas the Mound C midden represents refuse that resulted from the process of catering to the elites' subsistence needs. It should be noted that the assemblages for these two mounds are very similar in terms of vessel shape representation. Both units reflect an early component dating to around A.D. 1200. A shift to Pensacola culture pottery occurs around A.D. 1250, and that change is clearly marked by stylistic variations in the pottery (Chapter 2). We at least know that this transition brought different amounts of vessel shapes to Mound A during a time that is also marked by a quick succession of mound-building stages. Although vessel shapes do not differ from mound to mound, percentages in the mound assemblages do vary, and I believe this to be related to the purpose (or purposes) that each vessel shape served.

The difference in mound assemblages is best reflected in the representation of jars in the two mounds. Mound C has a 44 percent jar representation for the total assemblage, while Mound A's total jar assemblage is 38 percent. If Mound A is divided into premound and mound deposits, however, jars constitute 63 percent in the former and only 29 percent in the latter. These findings suggest that prior to major mound construction this area served no specialized function. Presumably its inhabitants had the same social status as the occupants of Mound C at this time. Around A.D. 1350 the social context of this area changed as mound-building began. At this time, as Mound A became the focal point of the site, a shift occurred in the vessel assemblage in Unit D100, which correlates well with a marked change in the site's sociopolitical landscape. The marked change in vessel form percentages is all the more dramatic when compared with the vessel assemblage from Mound C, which remained consistent throughout the Bottle Creek I and II phases.

As these findings are based on small vertical windows into mounds A and C, the need for good spatial data is clear (Fuller and Brown 1998:54–105). One area that holds particular promise in addressing these questions further is situated along the northern flank of Mound A. This locale is well known for its rich midden deposits but unfortunately it has been heavily looted. Results of this research include the identification of spatially distinct activity areas recognized through cultural deposits. It is safe to say that Mound A was a center for elite activity at the site. Subsistence was a daily aspect of site occupants' lives, and pottery assemblages have helped us recognize certain activities and where they likely occurred. Food preparation was obviously a daily commitment. Foods were likely being brought into the site without need for much processing. Even so, these foods had to go through final preparation, which almost always required some form of cooking. Cooking requires fire and space. By comparing vessel shape percentages between two locales at Bottle Creek, mounds A and C, we see a distinction in assemblages. Within mound deposits in Mound A, we see more serving and presentation vessels, as opposed to Mound C deposits, which are dominated with vessels associated with food preparation.

While this chapter reflects important distinctions in pottery, we should remember that ceramics only represent a portion of the material culture used in the preparation and consumption of foods. What we do not see is how basketry, wooden, or leather containers figured in daily subsistence activities of the Bottle Creek Indians. But pottery does provide some tantalizing clues as to site usage. As the inhabitants of Bottle Creek began their major mound-building projects and the complexity of the site became greater, a change in social patterns occurred, a change that is reflected in the vessel assemblage from the site. Previously, the area on which Mound A now sits may have served, like Mound C, as a food-processing area. As social dynamics changed at Bottle Creek, a greater emphasis on status took place, one that is reflected nicely in the shapes of pottery vessels.

9 / The Bottle Creek Microlithic Industry

Paul D. Jackson

INTRODUCTION

In 1991 the Alabama Museum of Natural History conducted limited test excavations in Mound L at the Bottle Creek site (Chapter 4; Brown and Fuller 1993b). During the spring of 1992 I analyzed the microlithic collection from these excavations. My primary goal in this chapter is to present the raw data and to compare the Bottle Creek microliths to other related industries in the Southeast. Since these artifacts are from only two 1 × 2 m units in a single mound excavation (Figure 4.1), I can only offer limited information. It would have been nice to draw conclusions as to whether these materials represent full-time or part-time specialization, or even what the uses of the lithics might have been, but I can only offer several suggestions here.

In this chapter, following the format of Ensor's (1991) work at the Lubbub Creek site, I compare Bottle Creek to five southeastern sites and archaeological districts that have important microlithic industries. As with Bottle Creek, the principal sites of these districts are all mound complexes and represent some of the better microtool collections recorded to date. They include Cahokia, Lubbub Creek, Moundville, Cemochechobee, and Palm Court (Figure 9.1).

MICROLITHIC ARCHAEOLOGICAL DISTRICTS IN THE EASTERN WOODLANDS

Cahokia

The Cahokia site is best known as the largest mound center north of central Mexico (Fowler 1973; Yerkes 1983). In addition to playing an important role in the origin and development of Mississippian lifeways, Cahokia also has significant bearing on our understanding of microtools in Missis-

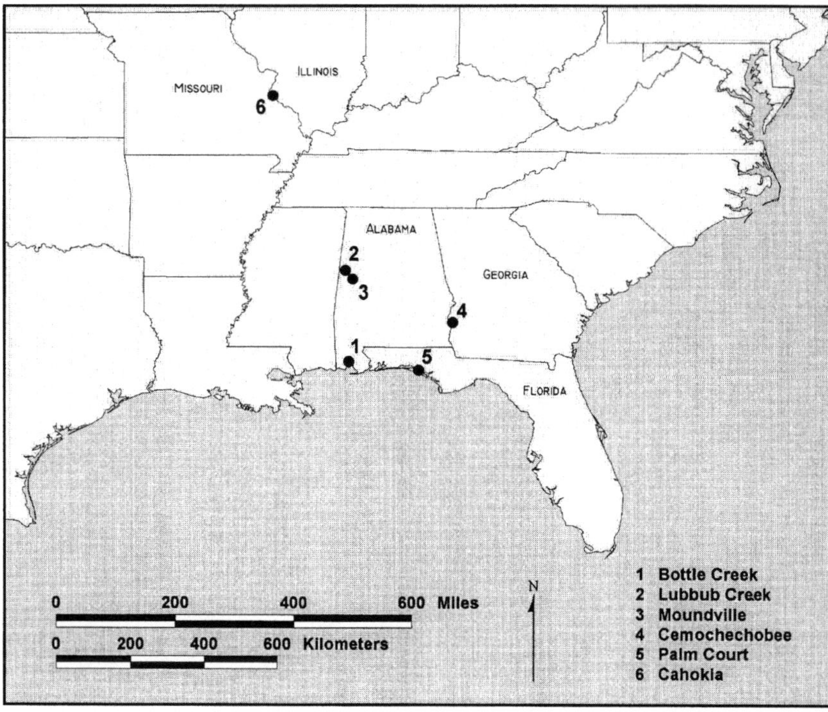

9.1. Location of certain microlithic industry districts in the Eastern Woodlands.

sippian society. The site itself is located in the American Bottom of the Mississippi River Valley in East St. Louis. Ever since Mason and Perino (1961) first described the microlithic industry present at the site, researchers have debated the role of these tools in the development of this complex society. More to the point, one issue archaeologists often discuss is whether microtools demonstrate some form of craft specialization related to developing Mississippian emergence (Yerkes 1983, 1989, 1991; Prentice 1985). Although this is an extremely important matter, I have little to contribute to that issue here. I concentrate instead on similarities and differences in tool attributes, production techniques, and material use, with the hope that this data will contribute to our knowledge of the range and distribution of this important tool industry.

Mason and Perino (1961) describe the microliths of Cahokia as part of a distinct collection consisting of cores, blades, and finished tools that were made from blades. There are single-ended drills, double-ended drills, side blades, and gravers at Cahokia. Yerkes (1983:514) suggests that the microdrills at Cahokia are specialized tools, specifically made for the production of shell objects. However, investigators found little shell refuse where the microlithic industry was most abundant (Mason and Perino 1961: 554). The majority of the microdrills are associated with ceramics that date between A.D. 900 and 1200 (Yerkes 1983:500), which would place the industry primarily during the Lohmann and Stirling phases (Emerson 1997:48–52).

Lubbub Creek

The Lubbub Creek archaeological locality, which includes a series of Late Woodland and Mississippian occupations, contains microlithic collections that scientists have thoroughly analyzed. Researchers originally recorded and defined the locality on the basis of a series of surface collections (Blitz 1983; Jenkins and Ensor 1981). In addition to conducting a wide collection of surface material, investigators also recorded a large Mississippian mound (1Pi85), situated within a palisade area. Excavations by the universities of Alabama and Michigan produced a substantial number of microlithic elements (Allan 1983; Ensor 1980, 1981).

Ensor (1991) described 195 micro-artifacts from the Lubbub Creek archaeological locality in his analysis. He noted a four-step process that was used in the production of these tools. The reduction process began with blade cores, then blades, then large and small microdrill preforms and, finally, with finished microdrills. Both the latter and possibly the microgravers appeared to have been used primarily to manufacture and decorate shell artifacts (Ensor 1991:23–32).

Moundville

Between 1978 and 1979 the University of Michigan Museum of Anthropology (UMMA) conducted a series of investigations around Moundville, the second largest mound center in the Eastern Woodlands. This site is located on the Black Warrior River in west-central Alabama. The UMMA survey included extensive surface inspections of agricultural fields in this valley. In addition to important work at the Moundville site (Scarry 1986; Steponaitis 1983), the survey also gathered information on several single-mound sites. Non-mound sites and smaller isolated sites, generally referred to as "farmsteads," were generally underrepresented in the UMMA survey, however (Pope 1989). The majority of the microtools recovered from survey and excavations are retouched blades that were extracted from cores. There is also a smaller group of drills that were made from retouched triangular arrow points. Pope (1986, 1989) analyzed this microlithic collection and called it the Black Warrior assemblage. Pope argues for an association with West Jefferson and Early Mississippian components dating to A.D. 900–1200. Sixty percent of the microliths in the Black Warrior assemblage are believed to have been used in shell-working, mainly for drilling and engraving. The remaining tools are thought to have been used on bone, wood, or hide (Pope 1989).

Palm Court

The Palm Court microlithic industry is associated with Weeden Island II sites in northwestern Florida (Morse and Tesar 1974:104–106). Most of the microliths are thought to have been used as drills, while some were employed as scrapers or gravers (Morse and Tesar 1974:97). This industry is believed to be similar to that seen at Cahokia, because of the emphasis on producing thick blades with triangular cross-sections (Ensor 1991:20).

Cemochechobee

The Cemochechobee microlithic industry occurs at a series of interrelated Mississippian sites located along the Chattahoochee River in southwest Georgia. Researchers recovered a small number of bifacially flaked microtools from investigations conducted at the Cemochechobee site itself, a Mississippian Roods phase (A.D. 900–1400) mound complex (Schnell et al. 1981:154–156, Plate 4.2s). The authors were hesitant to classify them as drill bits or perforators, because these objects lack visible discernible edge or tip wear. Ensor (1991:21), however, believes these microtools are similar to those found at Cahokia.

Bottle Creek Microlithic Industry

There are a total of 356 microlithic elements in the assemblage recovered from Mound L units A100 and A102 (Table 9.1). These objects started to appear in considerable quantities about 1.25 m below ground surface, and became quite common after 1.5 m. The greatest numbers of microliths were recovered from levels Q, Q2, R, and U in Unit A102, as well as from features 124 and 136 of this same unit (Figures 4.2, 4.4, and 4.5). The concentration in Feature 136 is directly associated with a wall trench (Feature 134) observed at the base of Mound L. The collection consists of 29 finished microdrills (Figure 9.2), 11 microblades (Figures 9.3a–d), six splinters, and 296 flakes and 14 shatter (Figures 9.3e–f and 9.4). There is also one core in the collection from A102Y. Size measurements and weights for microdrills, microblades, and splinters are offered in Tables 9.2–9.4, with summary statistics in Table 9.5.

The raw material for all of the chipped lithics at Bottle Creek is Coastal Plain agate. The color is generally tan or brown with several small intrusions of black, white, and gray. The quality of the stone overall appears to be poor. Coastal Plain agate is not an especially good material to produce

Table 9.1. Counts of microlithic elements in units A100 and A102

Provenience	Microdrills	Microblades	Splinters	Flakes	Shatter	Total
Unit A100						
Level A				1	1	2
Level C				2		2
Level D				1		1
Level G		1				1
Level H		1		3		4
Level K	1		2	9		12
Level L				2		2
Level M				7		7
Level N	1			9		10
Level O		1		6	3	10
Level P		1	1	8	1	11
Level Q1				4	1	5
Level Q2		2		3		5
Level R				1		1
Unit A102						
Level B				2		2
Level G				4		4
Level H	1			3		4
Level I	1			5	2	8
Level M				1		1
Level N	1	1		10	2	14
Level O		1		9		10
Level P	2		1	3		6
Level P2				4		4
Level Q	14	1		22	2	39
Level Q2		1		55	2	58
Level R	1			19		20
Level R1				10		10
Level S				3		3
Level U	1			22		23
Level V			1	2		3
Level Y	1			8		9
Level Z		1		1		2
Feature 124A	2		1	14		17
Feature 136	3			43		46
Total	29	11	6	296	14	356

blades because it breaks very unevenly. The only other type of material present in the collection is a very limited amount of quartz and sandstone.

At most sites in the Eastern Woodlands where inhabitants produced microdrills, they heat-treated cores first and then removed blade-like flakes from their sides. This is not quite the case for Bottle Creek, as the core recovered from A102Y was not heat-treated prior to use. The rocks used for lithic removal seem to have had very little preparation, perhaps because Coastal Plain agate itself lacks certain chipping qualities. As with the other microlithic localities discussed above, the Bottle Creek artisans bifacially retouched the microblades, generally along the entire body, after removing them from the core. The result is a drill-like form. The bipolar

Table 9.2. Microdrill sizes and weights

Provenience	Length (mm)	Width (mm)	Thickness (mm)	Weight (gm)
A100K/1	15.0	5.0	4.55	3.9
A100N/1	15.25	4.2	4.15	4.5
A102H/4	15.8	5.7	2.2	2.2
A102I/8	13.95	4.85	3.0	4.5
A102N/14	11.5	4.8	3.4	1.1
A102P/2	15.4	4.65	3.35	3.0
A102P/3	16.05	7.4	3.95	5.4
A102Q/A1	26.8	8.75	6.3	15.8
A102Q/A7	17.85	6.7	4.7	5.0
A102Q/A8	11.85	4.3	3.1	2.4
A102Q/A9	12.2	5.25	3.35	2.4
A102Q/A11	9.95	4.1	4.0	2.1
A102Q/A12	11.5	4.0	3.35	2.0
A102Q/A13	12.5	4.9	3.1	1.0
A102Q/A14	11.65	4.8	3.8	2.7
A102Q/A15	12.4	5.0	3.0	1.4
A102Q/A16	12.15	4.9	4.0	4.4
A102Q/A17	13.9	5.45	3.55	2.0
A102Q/A19	11.3	5.75	3.0	1.0
A102Q/A20	15.0	5.8	4.9	5.0
A102Q/A21	13.6	4.95	2.65	2.0
A102R/12	13.75	8.35	2.0	3.3
A102U/15	12.9	4.85	3.3	1.6
A102Y/7	13.35	6.2	2.55	4.0
A102x124A/1	13.25	4.6	3.2	2.3
A102x124A/3	11.8	5.7	4.25	2.2
A102x136/40	15.8	5.15	3.3	3.6
A102x136/41	12.65	4.5	3.6	2.4
A102x136/42	14.4	6.1	3.1	4.0

Note: Key to Abbreviations.
A100 = unit
K = level
x136 = feature
/1 = first microtool analyzed

technique seems to have been the typical way to produce suitable material for the microdrills at Bottle Creek. Putting a Coastal Plain agate cobble on a hard surface and repeatedly hammering its top would force splinters, small flakes, and miscellaneous shatter to pop off. This accounts for the frequency of burin-blows on many of the splinters and flakes in the collection, and it might also explain why microdrill preforms are so rare in the units. Once suitable lithic material was collected, a little bifacial flaking on the sides was all that was needed to produce the desired microdrills.

Two or possibly three types of microliths served as preforms for Bottle Creek microdrills. The first type is a splinter, which is a flake that has been knocked off the side of a larger flake. The splinters in this collection are thicker on one end and have the appearance of a thick wood splinter; they could serve well as microdrills. There are six unworked splinters present

Table 9.3. Microblade sizes and weights

Provenience	Length (mm)	Width (mm)	Thickness (mm)	Weight (gm)
A100G/1	19.55	10.3	4.7	5.9
A100H/4	9.7	1.9	4.1	7.7
A1000/1	25.6	5.5	2.65	3.5
A100P/3	16.85	15.8	3.4	4.1
A100Q2/3	13.25	6.85	3.0	2.4
A100Q2/4	20.0	10.3	4.95	6.9
A102N/4	19.55	8.5	3.25	5.6
A1020/9	11.7	5.15	2.0	1.2
A102Q/A2	20.85	6.5	6.15	7.0
A102Q/A31	13.0	7.6	2.65	3.5
A102Z/1	14.7	6.5	2.5	3.5

Note: Key to Abbreviations.
A100 = unit
G = level
/1 = first microtool analyzed

Table 9.4. Microlithic splinter sizes and weights

Provenience	Length (mm)	Width (mm)	Thickness (mm)	Weight (gm)
A100K/2	14.6	5.55	4.55	3.3
A100K/3	17.75	5.0	2.95	2.0
A100P/1	13.0	6.0	4.5	5.1
A102P/1	15.3	2.9	1.7	2.1
A102V/3	14.6	3.7	3.1	1.2
A102x124A/2	15.4	4.55	3.35	1.2

Note: Key to Abbreviations.
A100 = unit
K = level
x124 = feature
/2 = second microtool analyzed

in the Mound L collection. The second type of microlith is the microblade. At Lubbub Creek, the microblade itself is a stage in the four-step process of producing a microdrill, the resulting blades being triangular in cross-section (Ensor 1991:25). But at Bottle Creek, the blade-like flakes are rectangular to irregular in appearance. By using the bipolar technique, a lot of these blade-like flakes would have been byproducts of repetitive hammering. In terms of size and shape, most of the microblades would also have been suitable for future microdrills. There are 11 microblade-like flakes at Bottle Creek. Some use-wear was noted on several of the microblades and flakes. There also might have been a third type of microdrill preform. The striking platforms are missing on 16 flakes, although it has yet to be proven whether or not they were intentionally removed. Once

Table 9.5. Summary statistics for Bottle Creek microliths

Microdrills N = 29	Minimum	Maximum	Mean	Variance	Standard Deviation
Length	9.95	26.8	13.91	9.35	3.06
Width	4.0	8.75	5.4	1.35	1.16
Thickness	2.0	6.3	3.54	0.75	0.87
Weight	1.0	15.8	3.35	7.4	2.72

Microblades N = 11	Minimum	Maximum	Mean	Variance	Standard Deviation
Length	9.7	25.6	16.8	22.71	4.77
Width	1.9	15.8	7.72	12.84	3.58
Thickness	2.0	6.15	3.58	1.59	1.26
Weight	1.2	7.7	4.66	4.36	2.09

Splinters N = 6	Minimum	Maximum	Mean	Variance	Standard Deviation
Length	13.0	17.75	15.11	2.41	1.55
Width	2.9	6.0	4.62	1.34	1.16
Thickness	1.7	4.55	3.36	1.14	1.07
Weight	1.2	5.1	2.48	2.24	1.5

Note: Measurements are in millimeters and grams.

removed, the platform bodies would have been bulkier than the splinters and blade-like flakes and would have required more preparation before they would make a usable microdrill. I did not list this possible preform with the previous two preform examples, because there is not enough evidence to indicate it is a viable category. However, it is important to note its existence.

The microdrills at Bottle Creek have a limited amount of bifacial flaking along the entire length of the tool. Some have hafting applied to their proximal ends (Figure 9.2 M, R, S, W, X, Aa, Bb). The majority of the distal ends are broken off or very dull (Table 9.6). All of the microdrill bodies are cylindrical in shape. The wear usually is limited to the tip of the tool, but in some cases it extends along the length of the body. The wear along the lateral margins contributes to the cylindrical bodies of the microdrills. A total of 26 microliths are burned; three of these are tools.

SUMMARY AND CONCLUSIONS

The Bottle Creek microlithic industry, as represented in Mound L, consists of microdrills, microblades, splinters, flakes, shatter, and a core. Since we found no other tools, it is likely that Mound L served as some sort of microdrill workshop. The mound itself may have been designed with this activity in mind (Brown and Fuller 1993b; Fuller and Brown 1998:94–99). Bottle Creek is peculiarly different from the other Southeastern microlithic

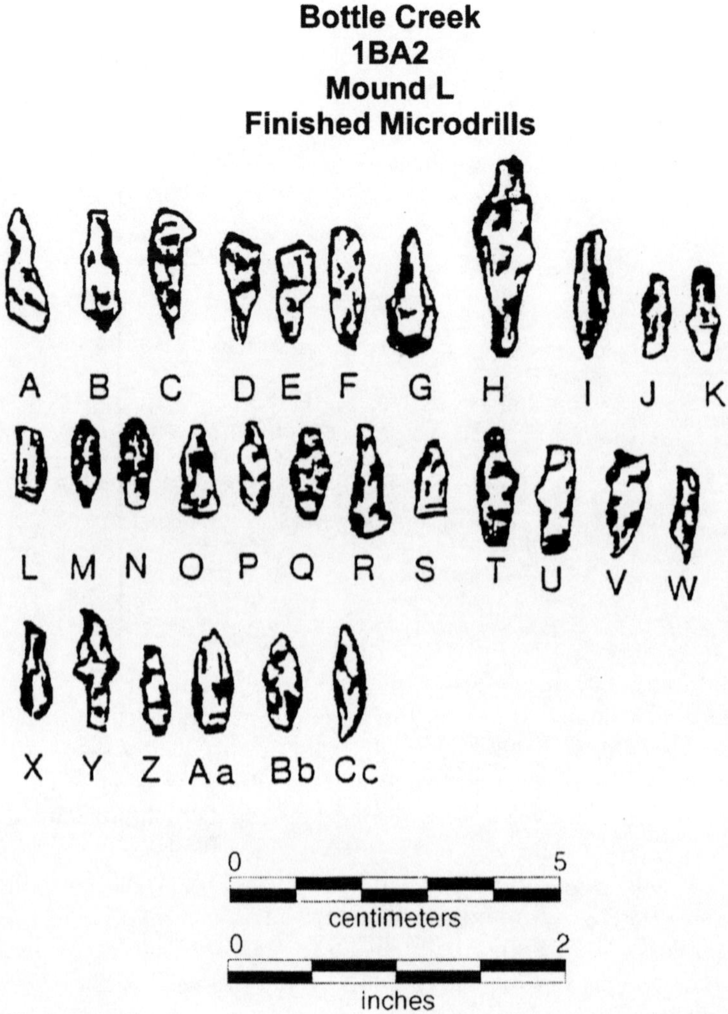

9.2. Drawings of finished Coastal Plain agate microdrills from Mound L.

industries in that there is very little evidence for the working of shell objects on Mound L. That does not mean that shell was not worked there, however, as shell does not survive particularly well in the acidic soil of the Mobile-Tensaw Delta unless it is deposited in some quantity. Small pieces of shell, the sort that might result from workshop activity, may not have much visibility in the archaeological record at Bottle Creek. At the same time, it is reasonable to assume that some shell debitage would have been observed in the various microlithic zones if shell had been worked in quantity. This was not the case. The fact that cut shell has been found else-

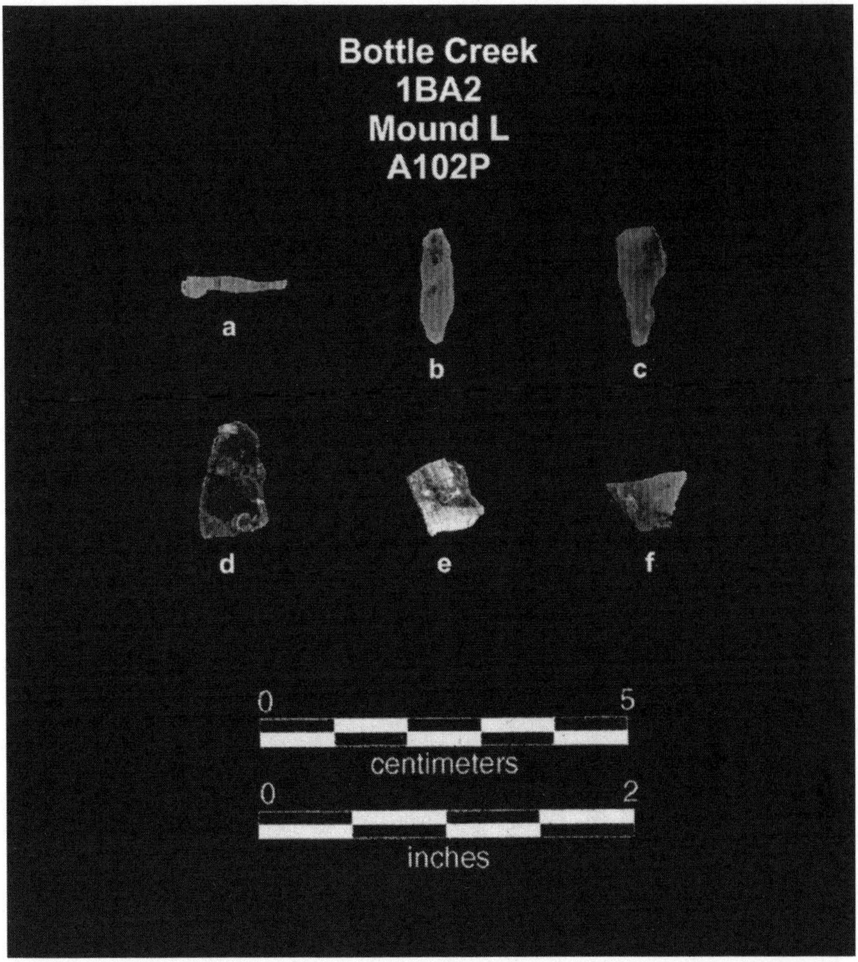

9.3. Examples of Coastal Plain agate microblades (a–d) and flakes (e–f) from Unit A102, Level P, Mound L.

where in the Bottle Creek excavations, including in a premound midden of Mound A (Table 2.1) keeps the issue alive.

It is also possible that the microtools at Bottle Creek may have been used to work mica. Although the sample is not particularly impressive, it should be mentioned that we found three small pieces of mica in Mound L (Brown and Fuller 1993b:158–159). It would have been nice if these pieces had been found in direct association with the microtools, but they were not. (The three pieces of cut mica were recovered in A100C, A100Q1, and A102G.) Nevertheless, a strong sharp tool would have been necessary to cut the straight edges that were observed in these mica artifacts. It is important to note that mica is not indigenous to the region. The piedmont

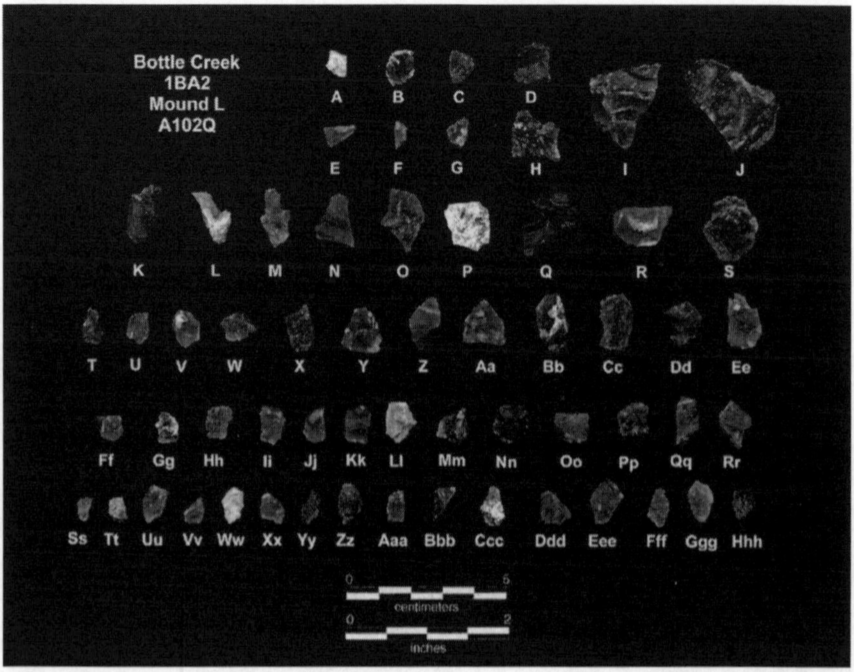

9.4. Examples of Coastal Plain agate flakes and shatter from Unit A102, Level Q, Mound L.

area of north Alabama and Georgia is the closest source. Although this is a long distance away, the transport of mica to Bottle Creek is certainly a conceivable accomplishment. It is worth noting that mica has been detected at Cemochechobee (Schnell et al. 1981:156), a site that occupies an intermediate location between Bottle Creek and the piedmont.

Microtools are the best represented stone artifacts at Bottle Creek. Despite extensive surface collections made in mound and non-mound contexts from all over the site (Fuller and Brown 1998:54–105), as well as the intensive testing program, no other part of the site has yielded much in the way of lithics of any sort. And even with the removal of more than 24 cubic meters in the block excavations in the upper levels of Mound L, microtools are only rarely seen (see Chapter 4).[1] Based on the location of

1. Out of a total of 396 objects made out of Coastal Plain agate that investigators recovered in the block excavations at Mound L, 51 tools, or 12.9 percent of the sample, are classified as microliths: Microdrills, 5; Biface Microliths, 7; Biface Microlith Fragment, 1; Bifacial Burin Microliths, 4; Burin Microliths, 9; Uniface Microliths, 11; Uniface Burin Microlith, 1; Uniface Burin/Graver Microlith, 1; Uniface Perforator Microlith, 1; Unifacially Retouched Microlith Flakes, 2; Unmodified Blade Microlith, 1; Utilized Microlith Flakes, 4; Microlith Cores, 4.

Table 9.6. Microdrill wear distribution

Provenience	Dull Tip	Broken Tip	Wear on Edges	Hafted	No Wear	Burned
A100K1	X	O	O	O	O	X
A100N1	X	O	O	O	O	O
A102H4	O	O	O	O	X	O
A102I8	O	O	X	O	O	O
A102N14	O	O	X	O	O	O
A102P2	O	O	X	O	O	O
A102P3	O	O	X	O	O	O
A102QA1	X	O	X	O	O	O
A102QA7	O	O	O	O	X	O
A102QA8	X	O	X	O	O	O
A102QA9	X	O	X	O	O	O
A102QA11	X	O	X	O	O	O
A102QA12	X	O	X	X	O	O
A102QA13	X	O	X	O	O	O
A102QA14	O	O	O	O	X	O
A102QA15	O	O	O	O	X	O
A102QA16	X	O	X	O	O	O
A102QA17	O	O	X	X	O	O
A102QA19	X	O	X	X	O	O
A102QA20	O	O	X	O	O	O
A102QA21	O	O	X	O	O	O
A102R12	X	O	X	O	O	O
A102U15	X	O	X	X	O	O
A102Y7	X	O	X	O	O	O
A102x124A1	O	X	X	X	O	O
A102x124A3	O	X	X	O	O	O
A102x136/40	O	X	X	O	O	O
A102x136/41	X	O	X	X	O	O
A102x136/42	X	O	X	X	O	O
Total	15	3	23	7	4	1

Note: Key to Abbreviations.
X = presence
O = absence

the microtools deep within Mound L, in levels dating to the Bottle Creek I phase (A.D. 1250–1400), it would appear that there was both a distinct place and time for the microlithic industry at Bottle Creek. Just why Mound L should have been chosen for this purpose we do not know. We also do not yet recognize why the manufacture and use of these lithics should have ceased to be important during the later history of Mound L. These questions certainly merit further study.

10 / Matting and Pliable Fabrics from Bottle Creek

Penelope B. Drooker

INTRODUCTION

Surface collections and excavations at Bottle Creek have produced 259 analyzable impressions of matting, pliable fabrics, yarns, and fibers on sherds from "saltpans"—large, shallow vessels often found at saline springs, where they would have been used to produce salt by evaporation (Drooker 1992:12–20). When I was asked to examine them, I anticipated learning much about the kinds of fabrics that people made and used for garments at this large ceremonial site. I had just spent several years looking at fabric impressions on saltpans at northern Early to Middle Mississippian sites such as Wickliffe, Kentucky, and Angel, Indiana. There, people usually lined their "saltpan" molds with worn skirts or mantles, some of them quite fine, and many decorated with designs made by manipulating the positions of warp and weft yarns (e.g., Drooker 1991, 1992:Figures 2, 25–29, 50–53). From reports by French missionaries and settlers, I knew that women in the Lower Mississippi Valley were producing fine yarn and cloth as late as the early eighteenth century (du Ru 1934:29; Le Page du Pratz 1763:230–232). I also knew that the Beckum Village site (1Ck24), about 60 km north of Bottle Creek as the crow flies, had produced impressions of many different kinds of fabrics, including twining, knotting, and interlacing (Wimberly 1960), as has the Lower Salt Works saline site (1Ck28) about 45 km away, so I had high hopes for the Bottle Creek fabrics.

However, as I found out, the use of skirts or mantles to line their molds was not the custom of "saltpan" makers at Bottle Creek. Apparently they preferred to employ cane or bark matting or very coarse, heavy fabrics. These are the materials I discuss here. I also will be tracing their connections to archaeological and ethnographic examples from the Gulf Coast and the larger Southeast.

BOTTLE CREEK FABRIC ATTRIBUTES AND THEIR FUNCTIONAL IMPLICATIONS

So far, impressions of five different fabric structures have been observed at Bottle Creek: interlaced matting[1] in plain weave and at least two different twill weave structures (Figures 10.1a and 10.1b); weft-faced[2] twined or interlaced fabric, where one set of yarn elements is completely covered by the other (Figures 10.1c and 10.1d); and one example of a somewhat more open twined fabric (Figure 10.1e). In addition to impressions on pottery, we found two impressions on fired clay and one on clay daub from a house wall (Drooker 1993; 1995). Numbers of each fabric structure type are summarized in Table 10.1. As can be seen, a large proportion of the impressions were difficult to analyze. Nevertheless, much information still can be obtained from them.

First, I shall discuss the clay daub. This held a very clear impression of thin slats interlaced over one, under one, around larger elements, which were about 7 mm wide (Figure 10.2). The impression on daub could have come from an actual house wall structure, or from a mat woven separately and then fastened to a framework. Because this impression is so deep and well-formed, it seems more likely that it was made from weaving to which wet clay was applied (i.e., a structure within a wall) rather than from weaving applied to the outside of a previously constructed wall. The woven structure obviously was very stiff and sturdy. The elements from which it was fabricated were relatively thick, and very sharp-edged and fresh. The stiffness and apparent newness of this woven material provide a strong contrast to the matting impressed on pottery, which was more flexible and often showed signs of wear.

Eighty-one percent of the analyzable impressions on ceramics were of interlaced bark, rush, or cane strips (Figure 10.3). On average, warp and weft elements were identical in width (Drooker 1995:Table 2), and most seemed to be least somewhat flexible. The most common recognizable structure was 4/1 broken twill, in which elements interlace over four, under

1. "Matting" is used throughout this chapter as a short-hand for either flat or shaped basketry. The former is more likely than the latter, but because investigators have found no whole vessels or very large sherds, the use of shaped baskets to form Salt Creek Cane Impressed "saltpan" vessels cannot be ruled out.

2. "Weft-faced" is used throughout this chapter as a shorthand for fabrics in which one set of elements completely covers the other. Only when a fabric edge can be examined is it possible to determine whether the fabric is weft-faced (with weft or active elements covering warp or stationary elements) or warp-faced. Because warp-faced fabrics usually are narrow, the probability is high that fabrics used in "saltpan" molds at Bottle Creek and elsewhere were weft-faced.

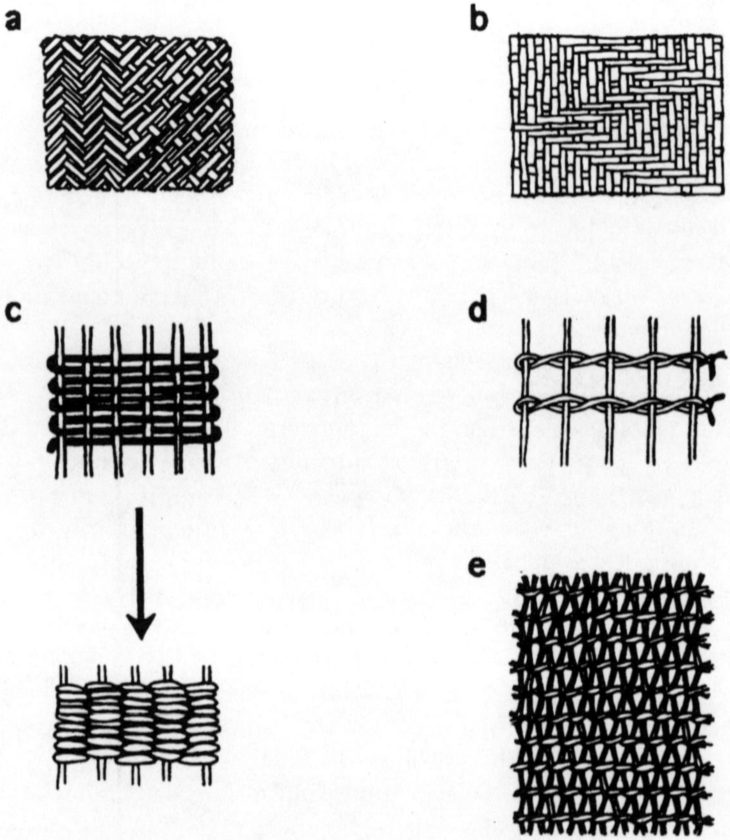

10.1. Fabric structures discussed in the text. a: Combination of 3/3 straight twill and 4/1 broken twill. b: 4/1 and 1/4 broken twill "damask," in which designs are formed by contrast between areas with long vertical and long horizontal floats. c: Plain weave (1/1 interlacing), showing compression of weft yarns to completely cover warp yarns in a weft-faced fabric. d: Plain twining structure. In an actual fabric, twining twist would be tighter. Twined fabrics can be made with widely spaced or closely packed weft rows. The latter would produce a weft-faced fabric. The two types of fabric are known as spaced or open twining and compact or close twining. e: Alternate-pair twining (after Brown 1976:Figures 2a–b; Drooker 1992:Figures 9a–b, 1993:Figure 1b).

Table 10.1. Fabric structures present at Bottle Creek

Fabric type	Count	Percentage
Open twined fabrics		
Alternate-pair twining (?)	1	0.4
Weft-faced fabrics		
Twined (?)	6	2.3
Interlaced (?)	8	3.1
Structure unknown	15	5.8
Subtotal	29	11.2
Interlaced matting		
1/1 plain weave (1 from daub)	3	1.2
3/1 twill (?)	1	0.4
4/1 broken twill	36	13.9
4/1 broken twill combined with straight twill	3	1.2
Twill, structure unknown	135	52.1
Interlacing, structure unknown	32	12.4
Subtotal	210	81.1
Structure unknown		
Parallel yarns (assumed to be warp)	8	3.1
Non-parallel yarns	3	1.2
Fibers	8	3.1
Subtotal	19	7.3
Total	259	100.0

Note: 81 Unanalyzable Sherds.

10.2. Cast of Bottle Creek daub impression (interlaced plain weave).

10.3. Casts of Bottle Creek interlaced twill matting, including 4/1 broken twill and one example of a combination of broken and straight twill.

one (Drooker 1995:Table 1). This structure has several advantages over plain weave made from similar materials, because it can be woven much more densely while still retaining flexibility. In some of the examples, the weaving was so tight that the elements bulged up in the middle. This would be unusual in shaped interlaced baskets, but not in flat matting. The end result would have been a thick mat, quite comfortable to sit or lie on.

In impressions on Bottle Creek "saltpan" sherds, this broken twill structure is found both alone and in combination with straight twill (Figure 10.1a). In a rare near-complete cane mat from a rockshelter in eastern Tennessee (Drooker 1992:Figure 21), straight twill was used as a border design, while 4/1 broken twill acted as a background texture. Combinations of these two structures, and variations of them, into more complex motifs (e.g., Figure 10.1b) are found in some southeastern archaeological and historical mats and baskets (see below). At Bottle Creek, matting containing two structures was finer than the single-structure examples. The average width of elements in the simple type was 4.7 mm, versus 4.2 mm in the two-structure type.

Besides impressions on pottery, there were two impressions of twill matting/basketry on fired clay. These materials were significantly finer than the total sample, fashioned from strips only 1.5–3.5 mm wide. The sample is too small to allow us to draw conclusions, but if this relationship continued in a larger sample it could indicate that the Bottle Creek people preferred to choose coarser, denser, sturdier mats for "saltpan" pottery making from a total range that included much finer specimens.

Five sherds showed impressions of what seemed to be the unfinished or torn edges of pieces of matting. Four of these were rim sherds, and in all cases the matting edge was aligned with the rim (e.g., Drooker 1993:Figure 3, top). No finished edges were encountered. The exclusively unfinished or damaged edges in the basketry/matting sample raise the likelihood that Bottle Creek potters used old, damaged mats or portions of mats to line "saltpan" molds, and that they positioned them in the mold by aligning one edge of the mat along the edge of the mold.

Eleven percent of the analyzable impressions from Bottle Creek consisted of a heavy fabric in which one set of yarn elements completely covered the other (Figure 10.4). In eastern North America, sometimes such fabrics were interlaced using a single weft, and sometimes they were twined using two wefts that twisted around each other while they enclosed the warp elements (Figures 10.1c and 10.1d). The difference is difficult to detect from impressions alone, particularly with the worn fabrics that were typical for Bottle Creek, but I believe that both types were present. The weft yarns were fairly large in diameter, averaging 2.5 mm (Drooker 1995:Table 2). More than half of them were two-ply, twisted together in the "S" direction that is a hallmark of virtually all Mississippian yarns (Drooker 1992:207, 218, 220, Figure 11; Miner 1936). Although twist direction could not always be determined, no "Z"-twisted yarns were recognized in these weft-faced fabrics.

It is worth noting that weft-faced fabrics are not only heavier and stiffer than open twined structures made from the same size yarns, but also are more labor-intensive to produce, since they require far more yarn. They would be made only with a particular function in mind. In the Southeast as elsewhere in North America, sturdy weft-faced structures often were used to make sandals or slippers (e.g., Kuttruff et al. 1998; J. Miller 1988; Scholtz 1975:141). The Bottle Creek fabrics, presumably large enough to cover the bottom of a "saltpan," could have been produced to serve as blankets, mats, or large bags.

One fabric from Bottle Creek (Figure 10.5) was a bit more like the pliable skirt fabrics used in the production of northern Mississippian "saltpans." It was twined of single-ply yarns, with pairs of twining elements twisting around each other in the typical Mississippian "S" direction. The twining rows were spaced at intervals of approximately one centimeter. Unfortunately, the ceramic impression was not large or clear enough for me to be certain of the fabric structure, but it probably was alternate-pair twining, in which weft yarns wrap around two warp yarns at a time (Fig-

10.4. Casts of Bottle Creek weft-faced fabrics.

10.5. Cast of open twined fabric from Bottle Creek, perhaps alternate-pair twined (see Figure 10.1e).

ure 10.1e). Warp and weft diameters were 1.5 and 1.9 mm, significantly smaller that those in Bottle Creek weft-faced fabrics.

Yarn size and fabric scale in the Bottle Creek open twined fabric (Drooker 1995:Table 2) are similar to average open twined fabrics impressed on pottery from the northern Mississippian sites I have studied (Drooker 1995:Table 2, 1992:Tables 6, 8, Figures 54, 55) and comparable to an alternate-pair twined skirt or mantle from a rockshelter in eastern Tennessee, although somewhat coarser (Drooker 1992:Figure 20, Table 3).

There were nineteen impressions that I could identify only as yarns or fibers. Most of them probably originated from weft-faced fabrics, but some could have been made by shredded bark or rush strips used in matting. One included single-ply yarns twisted in the "Z" direction, the only example of a non-"S"-twisted yarn in the site sample.

INTRASITE VARIATION AND CHRONOLOGICAL RELATIONSHIPS

The pottery type on which artisans impressed fabrics made of yarns is Kimmswick Fabric Impressed, *var. Langston.* At Bottle Creek, it is most strongly associated with a pre-Pensacola, Moundville-related component known as the Andrews Place phase, A.D. 1100–1250. The ceramic type on which potters impressed matting is Salt Creek Cane Impressed, *var. Salt Creek,* which is most strongly associated with the Pensacola culture Bottle Creek I and II phases, A.D. 1250–1550 (Figure 1.5). The chronological relationship between the two ceramic types at Bottle Creek is consistent with findings at Lower Salt Works (1Ck28), Salt Creek (1Ck222), and other saline sites north of Bottle Creek (Brown 2002; Fuller et al. 1984:220).

Unsurprisingly, the highest proportions of Kimmswick Fabric Impressed sherds at Bottle Creek came from mounds B and C, which had significant early components, and little was collected from the surface (Table 10.2). The non-elite residential Mound C, which was particularly rich in sherds, offers the best comparison of fabric-impressed pottery types and fabric types among excavation levels (Drooker 1995:Table 6). Upper levels A–L produced basketry/matting impressions exclusively, from both pottery and fired clay. Impressions on sherds in levels M, N, and O averaged 61 percent matting and 39 percent yarns and fabrics made from yarns, while the lowest levels P, Q, R, and S averaged 14 percent and 86 percent respectively.

It is possible that complex matting, combining more than one structure, was more common in later years. Two of the three examples came from surface collections, and the third from Mound C Level F. Unfortunately, the sample size is too small for definitive conclusions.

The primary conclusion that can be drawn from intrasite provenience

Table 10.2. Bottle Creek impressed fabric types by provenience (numbers of analyzable sherds)

Ceramic types:	Salt Creek Cane Impressed[a]		Kimmswick Fabric Impressed			Daub
Fabric structures:	Simple interlaced matting[b]	Complex interlaced matting[c]	Weft-faced fabric	Open twined fabric	Yarns/ fibers	Simple interlaced "matting"
Surface (1930s)	19	2	1	0	0	1
Surface (1990s)	17	0	0	0	0	0
Mound A	29	0	2	0	0	0
Mound B	19	0	3	1	1	0
Mound C	100	1	21	0	17	0
Mound D	23	0	2	0	1	0
Total	207	3	29	1	19	1

Note: Key to Abbreviations.
a = Including two impressions on fired clay
b = Single fabric structure
c = Combination of broken twill and straight twill

data is that for some reason there was a shift over time in the choice of materials used to line the molds in which "saltpans" were manufactured, from weft-faced fabric to interlaced matting. The relatively small sherd sample inhibits testing of more interesting anthropological hypotheses, such as might arise from a statistical correlation between elite contexts and finer, more complex fabrics and matting.

REGIONAL COMPARISONS

Both types and proportions of structures and materials impressed on "saltpan" pottery at Bottle Creek differ from those impressed on "saltpans" at other sites in the Southeast. This might in part be a temporal difference, since the Bottle Creek occupation extended later than most of the Mississippian sites that have produced fabric-impressed "saltpans." It might reflect availability of fabric and basketry types, or, more likely, preferences in their use for "saltpan" production.

Impressions of weft-faced fabrics on "saltpans" are fairly common in small percentages at most Mississippian sites with fabric-impressed pottery (Figure 10.6). I have found the highest proportions at Early Mississippian components and sites like Obion and Martin Farm, Tennessee, where the proportions were 17 percent and 10 percent respectively (Drooker 1992:142–143, Table 15). At most of the sites that I have investigated, the proportion of these fabrics compared to other types of fabrics made from yarn is only about 1–7 percent (Drooker 1992:211–212). At Bottle Creek, weft-faced fabrics represent 59 percent of all non-matting impressions, and 97 percent of all recognizable structures of fabrics made from yarn (Tables 10.1 and 10.2).

North of the Bottle Creek area, open twined structures appear to have

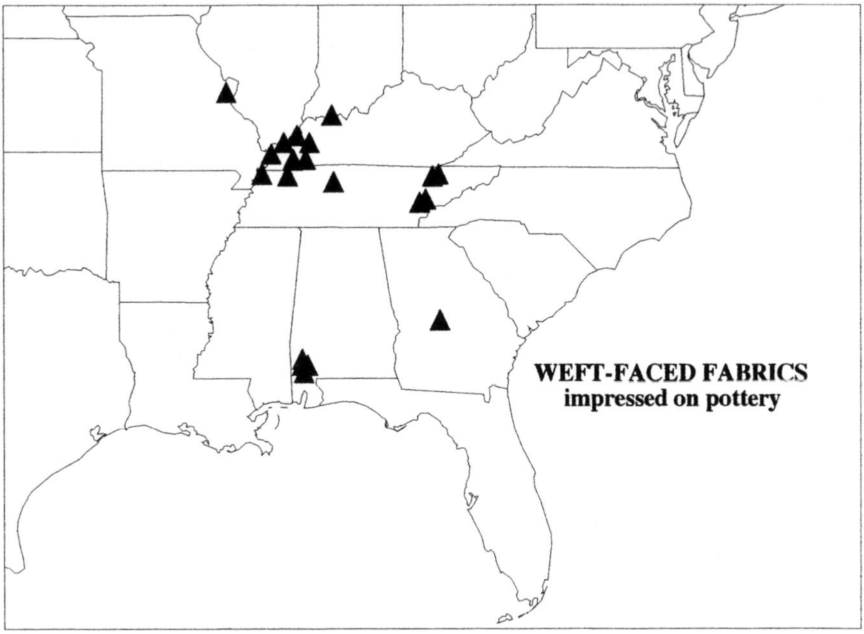

10.6. Distribution of Mississippian sites from which weft-faced fabric impressions on pottery have been reported (Drooker 1992:193, Table 13; Brandon and Mainfort 1995; Fuller et al. 1984:218–221). They include Beckum Village, Bottle Creek, Lower Salt Works, and Salt Creek, Alabama; Ocmulgee, Georgia; Kincaid and Saline River, Illinois; Angel, Indiana, Ml/14, Morris, Tolu, Tr/10, and Wickliffe, Kentucky; Kimmswick, Missouri; and Hiwassee Island, Mound Bottom, Norris Basin sites 5, 9, and 11, Obion, Oliver, and Toqua, Tennessee.

been the fabrics of choice for "saltpan" vessel production. They were in the overwhelming majority at Beckum Village (1Ck24), 60 km north of Bottle Creek, in a small sample from Lower Salt Works (1Ck28), about 45 km north of Bottle Creek, and at all sites that I have analyzed outside of southern Alabama (Brown 2002; Drooker 1992:177–197, personal examination of Beckum Village assemblage). Of 38 sites in six states from which impressed fabric data were available, only Salt Creek (1Ck222), about 35 km north of Bottle Creek, had no open twined fabrics at all, although the sample was tiny, consisting of only nine sherds (Drooker 1992:Tables 12, 13, 1993). At Alabama sites south of Bottle Creek, impressed "saltpan" sherds are exclusively Salt Creek Cane Impressed, which investigators take as an indicator that these areas were inhabited later (Chapter 2; Fuller et al. 1984:219).

In eastern North America generally, impressions on pottery of basketry or matting are much less common than fabric impressions. I have found

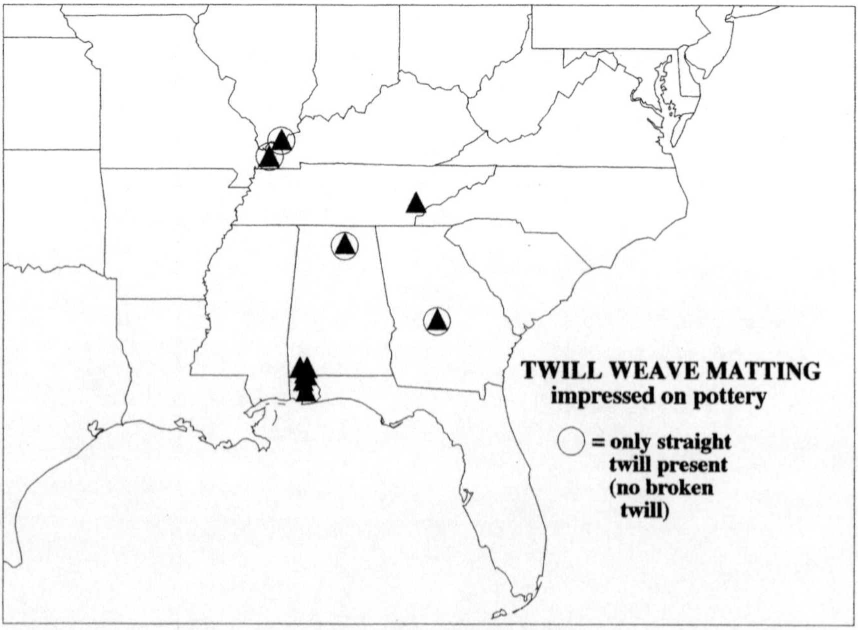

10.7. Distribution of Mississippian sites from which interlaced matting impressions on pottery have been reported (Drooker 1992:Table 13, 1993; Fuller et al. 1984:218–221). They include Ma4 (Tennessee River Wheeler Basin), Beckum Village, Boggy Gut, Bottle Creek, Lower Salt Works, Peavey's Landing, Salt Creek, Stimpson, and D'Olive Creek and three other sites in Baldwin County, Alabama; Ocmulgee, Georgia; Kincaid, Illinois; Wickliffe, Kentucky; and Bat Creek, Tennessee. Of the northern sites, only Bat Creek pottery has impressions of broken twill.

them at only five Mississippian sites north of the Alabama–Tombigbee River confluence area (Figure 10.7), represented by only one to ten examples at a given site. Because of their relative stiffness, mats (like weft-faced fabrics) would be less practical than flexible fabrics for lining deep vessel molds (see typical Mississippian saltpan shapes, Drooker 1992:Figure 3). Shapes of southern Alabama "saltpans" are not known, but because of their matting impressions it seems likely that Salt Creek Cane Impressed vessels would have been comparatively shallow, with gradually sloping sides.

At almost all of the northern sites, matting impressions on pottery, like the single example in the 1,574-sherd sample at Wickliffe (Drooker 1992:Figure 32), are of simple 2/2 or 3/3 straight twill, rather than broken twill or complex structural combinations. With the possible exception of two sherds from Bat Creek, Tennessee, described as impressed with broken twill (Schroedl 1975:Figure 58), only in southwestern Alabama have 4/1 broken twill matting impressions been reported. Southern Alabama also is the only region where archaeologists have excavated sherds with impressions of basketry that combine more than one structure.

Although rarely found in pottery impressions, 4/1 broken twill is not an uncommon structure in organic matting and basketry fragments from southeastern archaeological sites. It also was utilized in eighteenth-century/early-nineteenth-century Cherokee and late-nineteenth-century/twentieth-century Chitimacha mats and baskets. Extremely complex designs are known from both archaeological and historical examples.

Cane matting and baskets in 4/1 broken twill have come from a number of mound and rockshelter sites south of Missouri and Kentucky (Figure 10.8). West of the Mississippi, the 4/1 broken twill structure dates back almost a millennium. For instance, basketry in this structure came from a burial feature at the Mounds Plantation site in Louisiana radiocarbon dated to circa A.D. 1050, which calibrates to the twelfth century (Webb and McKinney 1975:39; Stuiver and Reimer 1986). This twill structure was used to make intricate designs, usually by setting up a contrast between sections where the long structural floats were horizontal versus sections where they were vertical, the same principle used to make damask fabrics (Figure 10.1b). Archaeological examples are known from Ozark bluff rockshelters in Arkansas and from burials at Spiro, Oklahoma, and Mounds Plantation, Louisiana (e.g., Brown 1976:Figure 2.b; Scholtz 1975:Figure 86; Webb and McKinney 1975:Figure 17). Broken twill also was used in combination with straight twill to produce designs, with archaeological examples coming from Mounds Plantation and the eighteenth-century Tunica Indian Trudeau site, also in Louisiana (Webb and McKinney 1975: Figure 20; Brain 1979:253).

Intricate patterns incorporating uni-directional or bi-directional 4/1 broken twill with straight twill still were being utilized in the nineteenth and twentieth centuries by Chitimacha women in St. Mary Parish, Louisiana, to make cane mats and baskets (e.g., Fundabark and Foreman 1957:Plate 134; Gregory and Webb 1975:Figure 1.d; Medford 1977:Figures 1, 8). The Chitimacha name for the broken twill structure, collected by John Swanton in the early twentieth century, translates to "spots or dots distributed over the surface of a basket to fill in" (Swanton 1911:caption to Plate 26).

Although organic matting in 4/1 broken twill has come from archaeological sites east of the Mississippi, to date I have found no examples of complex damask-like patterns. Archaeological specimens, all from burial contexts, either consist of fragments of broken twill alone, as in examples from Cooper Farm, Alabama, and Etowah, Georgia (Lindsey 1964:Figure 7; Robert S. Peabody Museum, Andover, MA, Catalog No. 61507), or include simple designs formed by lines of straight twill against a back-

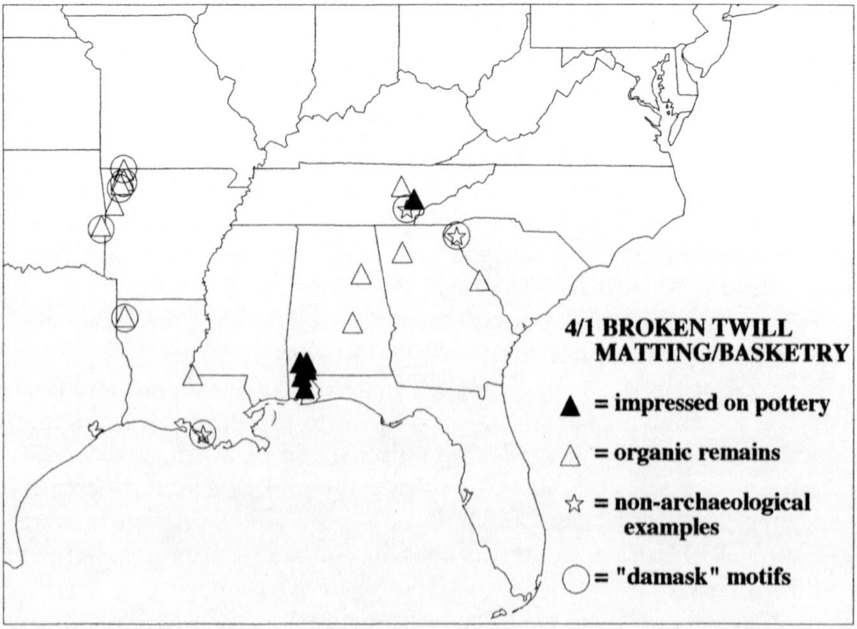

10.8. Distribution of Southeastern archaeological and historical locations from which 4/1 broken twill basketry/matting is known (Drooker 1992:86, 214, 1993:121–125; Duggan and Riggs 1991:Figure 2; Holmes 1896:36–37; Lindsey 1964; Moore 1899:Figure 65; Scholtz 1975:72–74, 87–91, 95–97; Etowah Mounds Historic Site museum display; R. S. Peabody Museum, Andover, Massachusetts). Sites with pottery impressions include Beckum Village, Boggy Gut, Bottle Creek, Lower Salt Works, Peavey's Landing, Salt Creek, Stimpson, and D'Olive Creek and three other sites in Baldwin County, Alabama; and possibly Bat Creek, Tennessee. Organic examples have come from: Cooper Farm and Thirteen Acre Field Mound, Alabama; Brown Bluff, Gibson Shelter, Indian Bluff, Indian Creek Shelter, and Whitney Shelter, Arkansas; Etowah and a mound near Augusta, Georgia; Mounds Plantation and Trudeau, Louisiana; Spiro, Oklahoma; Cliffty Creek Rockshelter, Tennessee.

ground of broken twill, as in a mat from Cliffty Creek Rockshelter in eastern Tennessee and fragments from Etowah (Drooker 1992:Figure 21; Robert S. Peabody Museum, Andover, MA, Catalog No. 61376). This is the same combination that appears to have been in use at Bottle Creek and nearby sites, but of course the small sizes of most impressed sherds make it impossible to be certain that this was the only way the structures were employed to make patterns there.

At least three eighteenth- and early-nineteenth-century examples of Cherokee cane baskets in complex patterns incorporating 4/1 broken twill "damask" together with straight twill have survived, collected from western South Carolina and southeastern Tennessee (Bushnell 1906:678–679,

Pl. XXXVI; Hill 1997:38, 100). It is quite possible that the prehistoric eastern tradition incorporated such patterns, or they might have developed later in the east than in the west.

Bottle Creek "saltpan" impressions contain much information about local traditions in basketry. The dominant 4/1 broken twill structure is congruent with Mississippian preferred basketry structures south of the Cumberland River. The few examples of two-structure matting are comparable to finely made mortuary goods at archaeological sites east of the Mississippi.

To find out what people were wearing, though, we will have to look elsewhere, probably at earlier sites such as Beckum Village, where a broad range of fabric types were impressed on "saltpan" sherds (Wimberly 1960). We may never have direct evidence of how elites or commoners dressed at the Bottle Creek ceremonial center, but perhaps eventually we will gain a better idea of garments worn by people at smaller special-purpose sites not far away.

11 / Water Travel and Mississippian Settlement at Bottle Creek

Christopher B. Rodning

INTRODUCTION

Water travel would have been a major component of the lifeways of native peoples in deltaic environments such as the wet landscape surrounding the Mississippian town at Bottle Creek. For this reason archaeologists have taken an interest in reports of an aboriginal canal at Bottle Creek. In this chapter I review ethnohistoric and archaeological evidence from the lower Southeast to consider what role water travel might have played in Mississippian settlement of Mound Island. I then describe the alleged canal at Bottle Creek (Figure 11.1). I draw here from my survey of the canal channel and its surroundings and aerial photos of Mound Island (Figure 11.2). These lines of evidence suggest that the presumed Mississippian canal is most likely a relict channel of the intermittent stream currently known as Dominic Creek.

This conclusion does *not* mean that the material culture of boats and native practices of water travel did not play a significant role in the lifeways of Mississippian people in southwestern Alabama. Archaeological models of subsistence and settlement patterns in this kind of environment in the Southeast certainly highlight the significance of horticulture and foraging in estuarine and riverine settings (Brose 1984; Brown 1984; Campbell 1959; Curren 1976; Knight 1977; Larson 1980; Lewis 1988). People may have lived at scattered farmsteads or even in villages similar to early-eighteenth-century native settlements along the bluffs of the Mobile-Tensaw Delta, but they probably also maintained seasonal foraging/fishing encampments in the delta and surrounding regions (Davis 1984b:224–229; Knight 1984:209–215). Given the watery environment present in and around the Mobile-Tensaw Delta, dugout canoes like those known from archaeological and ethnohistoric evidence would have offered an essential means of travel (Fuller 1992; McWilliams 1981:42–46, 1988:8–9; McGahey 1974; Stowe 1974).

11.1. Douglas E. Jones and Ian W. Brown crossing the presumed "canal" west of mounds C and D at Bottle Creek.

My goal in this chapter is to make the simple but significant point that water travel probably *did* shape Mississippian settlement of the swampy woodland environment of southwestern Alabama. I first review ethnohistoric and archaeological evidence about native watercraft in the American South. I then describe aboriginal canals in Florida and Alabama including the alleged canal beside the mounds at Bottle Creek. These mounds represent the most prominent Mississippian center in the Alabama and Mississippi portions of the northern Gulf Coast (Greenwell 1984:151; Knight 1984:206; Walthall 1980:269). This ancient town was built in the midst of a swampy river delta. Its placement alone speaks to the significance of water travel as a force in shaping Mississippian settlement and social dynamics in the area.

DUGOUT CANOES IN THE ANCIENT AMERICAN SOUTH

European colonists described native practices of making and paddling dugout canoes (Swanton 1911:66–67, 1946:589–598). Dugout canoes were quite common in both coastal and inland areas. There were broad similarities in the ways that native people in different parts of the South built them, even though there was variation from one region of the Southeast

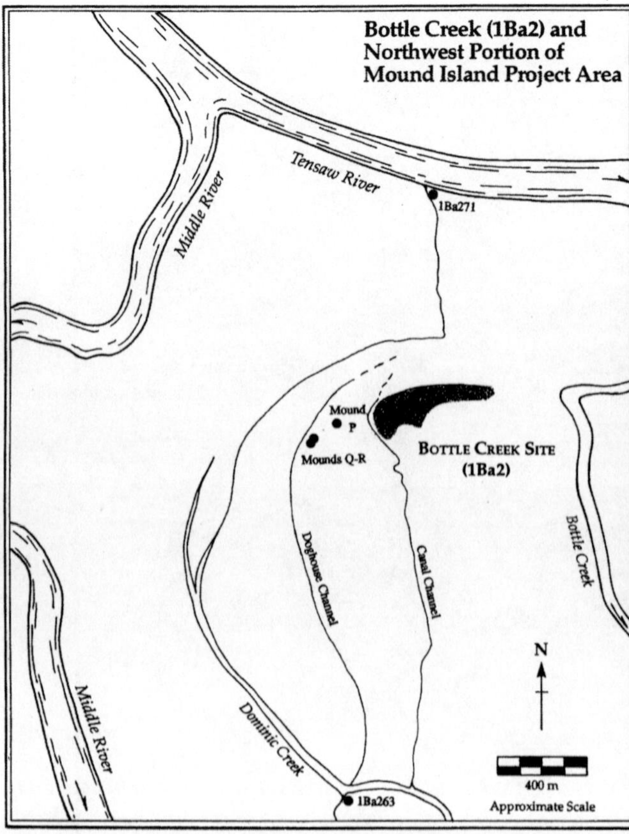

11.2. Location of the "canal channel" traced from an aerial photograph of Mound Island (from the *Mound Island Project*, by Fuller and Brown, copyright 1998 by the Alabama Museum of Natural History, used by permission).

to another in the kind of wood that was available and the kind of waterways there were to travel. Native boat-builders first felled selected trees by burning their trunks, perhaps doing some chopping but for the most part just letting the trees fall once the fires burned through them (Swanton 1946:Plate 74). Then they would burn the limbs from the treetops and place the log on frameworks of wooden posts designed to hold the canoe off the ground. Fires underneath the canoe would help remove bark from the outside. Shell scrapers and perhaps stone tools also would have helped in shaping the outer surfaces of canoes. In some cases, patches of bark may have been left on the ends of dugouts. Logs were hollowed out by setting fires inside them, and by scraping the insides of the logs with stone axes and shell tools. Placing mud at the ends and sides of the canoes would have helped in controlling these fires, and throughout the whole process native boat-builders were simply alternating between burning and scraping. Hollowing out the logs created room for people and gear, and several people could sit or stand inside a dugout canoe even while carrying a considerable amount of cargo with them (Swanton 1946:Plate 52). Dugouts were commonly made of bald cypress, but it is less clear what kind of wood might have been the preferred material for making paddles. Cypress and many other woods were of course widely available to native people in the northern Gulf Coast region, and residents of Mound Island almost certainly had access to raw materials for making stone axes and stone or shell scrapers.

Archaeologists have identified several dugout canoes from southern Alabama, southern Mississippi, and northwestern Florida (Fuller 1992; Newsom and Purdy 1990:165; Stowe 1974). Some dugouts have squared or rounded platforms at their ends, in some cases with mooring holes drilled through them to serve as attachments for bow and stern lines. The insides of many dugouts bear marks from scraping and gouging, and the charring present on several canoes reflects the role of fire in shaping these boats. Holes punched in the bald cypress dugout found at the Swan Lake site in Mississippi indicate that Mississippian canoes were sometimes repaired to prolong their use lives. Radiocarbon dates of bald cypress canoes from Alabama and Mississippi indicate that this form of watercraft was indeed made by late prehistoric native boat-builders (Fuller 1992).

Hundreds of prehistoric canoes found in peat bogs and other waterlogged sites in eastern and southern Florida and in lakes in coastal North Carolina attest the great antiquity of this form of watercraft in southeastern North America (Newsom and Purdy 1990:176; Phelps 1989; Ward and Davis 1999:201–202). The oldest canoes in the Southeast are more than three thousand years old, although most date to the past two thousand years (McGahey 1974:4–5; Newsom and Purdy 1990:168–170). Ethnohistoric sources indicate that native canoes in the Southeast served many purposes, including hunting and fishing as well as transporting food and raw materials (McWilliams 1981:42–46; Newsom and Purdy 1990:176–178). Ancient native people living in the marshy landscape of eastern North Carolina seem to have cached several bald cypress dugout canoes in Lake Phelps and in other lakes and ponds within this marshy environment (Phelps 1989). This practice would have enabled them to travel across water when such transport was desirable or necessary, perhaps during seasonal visits to areas where specific resources were available. Keeping bald cypress dugouts in the water would have helped to preserve them and would have served to hide the canoes. Some of the dugouts found in Alabama and Mississippi may have been stored in select watery spots for similar reasons (Fuller 1992).

Investigators have found neither dugout canoes nor boat-building tools at Bottle Creek. However, dugouts comparable to archaeologically and ethnohistorically known watercraft in the Southeast were almost certainly paddled to and from the Bottle Creek mound center. Perhaps further archaeological study of Bottle Creek will reveal clues about the material culture of Mississippian water travel in this region. Meanwhile, what has already attracted archaeological interest is the canal that was presumably built by late prehistoric residents of Mound Island. Aboriginal canals have been identified at other localities along the Gulf Coast, especially in Florida.

ABORIGINAL CANALS IN THE GULF COAST REGION

Archaeologists have described several prehistoric canals in the Calusa domain of southwestern Florida (Luer 1989, 1998; Marquardt 1986, 1992). The Calusa chiefdom dominated the social and geopolitical landscape of southern Florida during the late prehistoric and protohistoric periods, and Calusa villages relied primarily on fishing and gathering rather than on farming as a subsistence strategy. Southwestern Florida is a wet environment characterized by many streams and marshes on the mainland and on islands off the coast itself, and several canals in the region connect different waterways and in many cases would have offered shortcuts to prehistoric paddlers. Many of these native canals demonstrate considerable engineering expertise in planning and maintenance (Luer and Wheeler 1997). Several link mound centers to villages and outlying hamlets (Wheeler 1995, 1998a). These spatial relationships between canals and native settlements as well as ethnohistoric evidence all demonstrate that canals were critical to travel routes within this watery landscape. Calusa canoeists carried tribute and conducted exchange by traveling along these canals, and thus chiefs derived benefits from the travel networks in which canals were included. Calusa chiefs convened councils and war parties, and participants were probably often mobilized by water travel. Canals and watercraft meanwhile eased the movement of fishers and gatherers to areas where they could find desired resources. Unlike their Mississippian counterparts in provinces further north, the Calusa did not practice horticulture (Larson 1980:23–34). But like Mississippian chiefdoms, the Calusa could mobilize resources and people in ways that favored the maintenance of social stratification between chiefs and commoners (Lewis 1978:31–36; Marquardt 1986:63; Widmer 1988:279).

Archaeologists have described several categories of native canals found in mainland marshes and on islands off the coast of southwestern Florida (Luer 1989:125–126). Some of these canals are moats or ponds incorporated *within* sites. Others are much longer connections *between* sites or between different navigable waterways. For example, the Pine Island canal runs from the Pineland village on the western side of this island at the mouth of Charlotte Harbor to burial mounds on the eastern edge of the island. Both sites date to the late prehistoric period. The canal, which averages 9 m wide and 4 km long, would have enabled canoeists to paddle *across* rather than *around* Pine Island. Although its existence is unconfirmed, another mainland canal may have led from the coast to the Corbett mound. Even without the Pine Island canal, prehistoric paddlers could have traveled from the sound or Charlotte Harbor some 15–20 km south to the mouth of the Caloosahatchee River, and then 25 km upriver to Corbett. The possible mainland canal may have offered a more direct route that would have been as many as 20 km shorter than traveling along natural waterways, including the Caloosahatchee River, en route to Corbett. Further south was a canal that ran some 1.3 km from Naples Bay to the Gulf of Mexico and had embankments that ranged from 1.2 to 2.4 m in height (Luer 1998). Further inland was a network of some 5.9 km of canals connecting the Ortona mounds to Lake Okeechobee and the Caloosahatchee watershed (Wheeler 1995). Much further south in Florida are the Mud Lake and Snake Bight canals, which skirt the Bear Lake mound and connect Whitewater Bay to Florida Bay and the Gulf (Wheeler 1998a). Another canal in northwestern Florida was designed primarily for convenience and calm passage, connecting Choctawhatchee Bay to the Gulf (Wheeler 1998b).

These canals served as conduits for water travel that shaped regional settlement patterns and social dynamics within the ancient chiefdoms of southwestern Florida (Luer 1998:33–34). The canal at Naples Bay demonstrates a significant reliance on water travel. Its embankments are the result of a vast earthmoving project. The scale of this investment reflects not only the presence of a chief or group of chiefs but the capability of such leaders to mobilize the laborers needed to build and maintain the canal and the resources to support them. The Naples Bay and Pine Island canals both demonstrate an interest in making water travel routes shorter and safer and perhaps even controlling what and who traveled through them. Certainly, canals demanded significant investment in construction and maintenance. However, canals may have offered great benefits to societies reliant on water travel in estuarine and riverine environments, and to community leaders interested in the traffic of people and resources that moved across them.

Mississippian chiefs at Bottle Creek clearly possessed the kind of authority needed to build a canal. Elites at Bottle Creek were probably the most powerful Mississippian chiefs in southern Alabama and southern Mississippi and may have had close ties with paramount chiefs at Moundville (Knight 1984:206; Walthall 1980:269; Johnson, Chapter 8). The mounds at Bottle Creek are themselves material manifestations of the authority and status of its chiefs (Morgan, Chapter 3). Constructing these mounds may have taken place in communal events that built community ties while creating platforms for ritual practices and elite residences. Digging a canal probably would have been a relatively easy task in terms of engineering and mobilizing labor compared to building the major mounds themselves.

It is less clear why Bottle Creek residents would have needed or wanted to build a canal. One reason may have been that the mounds themselves are 1 km away from the Tensaw River and half that distance from the navigable waters of Bottle Creek, and canals would have facilitated travel between these earthworks and destinations in the delta and surrounding regions. Another related reason may have been that local residents relied on resources brought to Mound Island from other parts of the delta and from Mobile Bay, whether as tribute to Bottle Creek chiefs or as resources brought back from the seasonal farmsteads and foraging camps maintained by Bottle Creek households in outlying areas.

Archaeologists have recorded aboriginal canals along the northern Gulf Coast. One known as Walker's Canal has been identified at Four Mile Point near the southeastern corner of Choctawhatchee Bay in northwestern Florida (Wheeler 1998b:180). This canal was 1.19 km long and ranged from 3.0 to 3.7 m deep. It connected two dune lakes in an area characterized by shifting sand dunes and high water tables. Ceramics and other artifacts found along the course of the canal suggest that it was built during the late prehistoric period. Another canal has been recorded at the Ryan site near Strong's Bayou at the southeastern edge of Mobile Bay in southern Alabama (Trickey 1958:389). Shell middens and other archaeological evidence of settlement are present at both ends of this canal. Unfortunately, this and two other reported canals near the coast in southern Alabama are no longer visible on the landscape, and thus it is difficult to confirm whether they were aboriginal canals or not (Trickey 1958:389). However, the canal in northwestern Florida was indeed built during the late prehistoric period by a group of people who must have considered canoe travel significant enough to devote the energy needed to build and maintain a canal (Wheeler 1998b:179). The main point to make here is simply that late prehistoric native peoples of the northern Gulf Coast were entirely capable of the engineering and labor mobilization needed to build canals, and life in their watery environment may have favored the placement of canals in select localities. It follows that residents of places like Mound Island may have found canals to be helpful or desirable alterations to their landscape, and also that modifications to natural waterways may have served them well.

THE ARCHAEOLOGY OF THE PRESUMED CANAL AT BOTTLE CREEK

Mississippian townspeople at Bottle Creek were certainly capable of building great mounds, and building a canal from the mounds to navigable streams such as Dominic Creek or Bottle Creek may not have been a major challenge by comparison. Some of the fruits of foraging and farming in the surrounding deltaic and estuarine environment may have been brought to Bottle Creek in dugout canoes, and this mode of travel and transport would seem preferable to traveling overland through the wet and seasonally inundated swamps. Was water travel significant enough to the lifeways of the Mississippian community at Bottle Creek for them to have built a canal? And did such a canal link the Bottle Creek mounds themselves to navigable streams that led downriver to the bay and upriver toward Moundville and other destinations?

After visiting Bottle Creek, an antiquarian from Wesleyan College—A. Bigelow—described an ancient aboriginal canal (1853). He only mapped the section of the canal beside the known mounds (Figure 1.4). He reasoned that the canal wound its way through the swamp from the mounds to the navigable waters of the Tensaw River or Bottle Creek itself (I shared this impression when I began writing my college honors thesis on this topic), and that much of the material for building the mounds themselves may have come from the canal. Archaeological literature from the twentieth century describes this channel as a prehistoric canal, and in some cases maps place it at the edge of the Bottle Creek site (Holmes 1963; but see Fuller and Brown 1998:134). In recent years Waselkov (1997) redrew the map of the mounds and canal at Bottle Creek (Figure 1.3), while Fuller and Brown (1998) reviewed aerial photos and conducted intensive archaeological surveys of Mound Island.

I myself conducted a surface survey one day during the summer of 1993 to learn where this presumed aboriginal canal led once it left the vicinity of the mounds at Bottle Creek. I did this survey as a member of the 1993 GCS field crew at Bottle Creek. My companions in this bushwhacking adventure were Kai Rodning and Clay Gentry. The design of this brief survey was simple—basically, we just walked along the canal and tried to follow its course. I expected the canal to run north to the Tensaw River or northeast to Bottle Creek itself, but neither expectation was borne out. Close to the mounds the canal has clearly defined edges. It ranges between 3 and 4 m wide, and is as much as 2 m deep in some places. The channel runs about 200 m north to south, bending around mounds C and D and turning southeast from where it passes Mound P. Several channels extend outward from both ends of the canal, but they are all natural formations. Beaver dams and lodges are and have been present along the canal, and these modifications to the landscape probably have helped to keep the canal full of water. Not far north and south of the mounds themselves, the canal is not visible at all.

Aerial photos of Mound Island further help assess the Bottle Creek canal. Photos taken during the winter of 1986 show a relict channel of Dominic Creek running through the Bottle Creek mound site itself. This relict channel is not clearly visible on photos taken during the summer when vegetation is much thicker. The canal is part of this relict stream channel. This evidence confirms our findings on the ground in 1993 that the presumed canal does not create a water route linking the mounds with any currently navigable streams. A more recent map shows the "Canal Channel" running parallel to the "Doghouse Channel" west of the main mound group toward the south end of Mound Island (Figure 11.2; Fuller and Brown 1998:133–134). A protohistoric site (Dominic Creek, 1Ba263) is present at the point where these channels meet Dominic Creek (Fuller and Brown 1998:105–115).

The significance of these relict channels to the history of native settlement at Bottle Creek does deserve further consideration. Were the mounds built along an ancient course of Dominic Creek? Did native earthmoving activities at this locality affect drainage patterns on Mound Island? The mounds at Bottle Creek are an outcome of a series of earthmoving efforts, conducted at a grand scale. It is conceivable that Bottle Creek residents widened or otherwise altered the course of the stream running through their settlement, either intentionally or unintentionally. After all, the section of the canal running just west of mounds C and D is very easily identified. And unlike other streambeds and swales in the surrounding swamp, this canal is always full of water. Perhaps mound-building or other intentional earthmoving activities "carved out" this section of a natural streambed. Maybe the so-called canal is an outcome of both ancient aboriginal activities and natural agents, including geomorphological processes and modifications by beavers of the local landscape.

Surveying the canal has led to valuable clues about late prehistoric settlement at the Bottle Creek mounds if not to any direct evidence of native watercraft or canal building. After trying to follow the canal channel north, we eventually came to Dominic Creek and followed it to its northern end (see Walthall 1980:269). Potsherds and the remnant of a shell midden (Tensaw River, 1Ba271) are present near the bank of the Tensaw River (Fuller and Brown 1998:54–55). West of the canal channel, we noticed a low mound (P) that is now included on the Bottle Creek site map (Figure 1.3; Walthall 1980:266). Formal surface collection and mapping of this and other mounds west of the main mound group was done in 1994 as part of the GCS survey of Mound Island (Fuller and Brown 1998:100–105). Currently, there is little direct evidence of watercraft or the practice of water travel at the Bottle Creek site itself. However, there are some clues that reflect the likely significance of water travel to late prehistoric lifeways at Mound Island and surrounding areas.

WATER TRAVEL AND THE MISSISSIPPIAN SETTLEMENT OF MOUND ISLAND

Several sources of evidence offer clues about the role of water travel in native settlement at Bottle Creek during the late prehistoric period. First, written descriptions and visual depictions by early European visitors to the Southeast show native people making and paddling dugout canoes. Second, archaeological evidence of Mississippian canoes from southern Alabama and Mississippi and at waterlogged sites in other parts of the South demonstrates widespread reliance on watercraft and water travel. The third piece of evidence is the placement of the mound center itself within a vast river delta. It is likely that people relied on water routes as much as or even more than overland trails for traveling across a wet woodland landscape and for transporting cargo. At a regional scale, water travel may have been critical for people visiting seasonal foraging and fishing camps in coastal and estuarine settings south of Mound Island. At a broader interregional scale, water travel may have been the primary means of interaction between Mississippian chiefs at Bottle Creek and their counterparts at Moundville several hundred kilometers to the north. Meanwhile, the seasonal floods that cover much of Mound Island every year may have made it advisable for households to have dugout canoes or other watercraft on hand.

Other chapters in this book raise some interesting issues related to the study of Mississippian water travel in the greater Mobile Bay region. Quitmyer (Chapter 7) notes the presence of many marine and estuarine species in zooarchaeological assemblages at Bottle Creek. Arguably, these resources were transported at least part of the way from Mobile Bay to Bottle Creek by boat and most likely by dugouts. Furthermore, some species of barnacles found at Bottle Creek probably arrived there in boats that had traveled across Mobile Bay or the Gulf itself. Scarry (Chapter 5) argues that considerable amounts of maize were processed elsewhere before being brought to the mounds at Bottle Creek. Does this represent tribute brought to Bottle Creek chiefs? Was it brought to Bottle Creek by boat? Tribute or not, it is very likely that dugout canoes were an important means of getting foodstuffs and other resources to Bottle Creek from outlying areas. How else could they have gotten there, after all? Given the scale of the Bottle Creek earthworks, it certainly seems likely that many people in the region were drawn to this mound center for social and ritual reasons. And if there were several hundred people living at the Bottle Creek site, they probably needed to travel by water to places where they could farm and forage for the resources needed to sustain a major Mississippian town.

Continuing archaeological study of Mound Island and the surrounding landscape should yield more evidence about Mississippian watercraft and water travel. Further fieldwork may recover remnants of dugout canoes and boat-building tools. Regional settlement studies will shed light on patterns of movement and social interaction by different native communities in this watery landscape. Even though this chapter has challenged the identification of the canal at Bottle Creek as an intentional addition to the landscape of this major mound center, water travel almost certainly played a major role in Mississippian settlement and lifeways at this town and in its environs.

Acknowledgments. This chapter grew out of my senior honors thesis in anthropology at Harvard College. Thanks to Ian Brown for giving me the opportunity to participate in archaeology at Bottle Creek and for offering very valuable guidance. Thanks to Richard Fuller for sharing with me his knowledge of aboriginal dugout canoes and the archaeology of Mound Island and surrounding areas. Thanks to Stephen Williams, Robert Preucel, Carole Mandryk, Gordon Willey, William Marquardt, Eliot Pratt, Alan Grumet, Joshua Swidler, Kai Rodning, Soren Rodning, Clay Gentry, Melissa Chang, Beth Messmore, and Becky Frank for their contributions and guidance. Thanks to all of these people and to Greg Waselkov, Cameron Wesson, Vernon Knight, David Brose, Bram Tucker, Hunter Johnson, David Morgan, Tony Boudreaux, Jon Marcoux, and Margaret Scarry for helping me mold this paper into its current form. I appreciate the support I received as an undergraduate anthropology concentrator in the Department of Anthropology at Harvard University, and I am grateful for the support of the Ford Undergraduate Research program. I am grateful to my parents, Charles and Mary Rodning, for supporting and encouraging my participation in archaeology. This paper owes much to them and to generous encouragement and sound advice from Hope Spencer.

12 / Concluding Thoughts on Bottle Creek and Its Position in the Mississippian World

Ian W. Brown

INTRODUCTION

As is evident from the preceding chapters, much knowledge has been derived from the recent work at the Bottle Creek site and in the surrounding Mound Island region. Perhaps of most importance to posterity was the contribution that the Gulf Coast Survey made in elevating this site to National Historic Landmark status. Its importance has been recognized nationally and measures have been taken by the state of Alabama to preserve the site for posterity (Brown and Fuller 1999). Although the Gulf Coast Survey undertook three field seasons of archaeological survey and excavations at Bottle Creek, followed by another season of survey on Mound Island and along the surrounding waterways, it must be admitted that our research has really only just touched upon the potential of Bottle Creek for addressing and resolving many anthropological and historical issues in the Mobile-Tensaw Delta and adjacent regions. The site is so enormous and the deposits so deep and rich that one could spend a lifetime digging at Bottle Creek and never really understand what the site is all about.

SPECIFIC CONTRIBUTIONS OF THE BOTTLE CREEK PROJECT

One major contribution of our work over the years has been the refinement of a cultural chronology for the Bottle Creek site (Figure 2.14; Appendix B), as well as a regional culture chronology for late prehistoric times (Figure 1.5; Appendix A). As a result of Richard Fuller's work, we now have an excellent understanding of the material culture of the Bottle Creek I and II phases (A.D. 1250–1550), especially its pottery, and we can demonstrate changes in popularity of the numerous types and varieties through time. Whereas we merely hypothesized the Bottle Creek I and II phases prior to the Gulf Coast Survey work (Fuller and Brown 1993a), now we can demonstrate significant material changes in the stratigraphic record. Mound A has been particularly useful in this study, with supplemental information having come from Mound C. Controlling time is essential for understanding how other Pensacola culture sites in the Mobile Bay region and the Mobile-Tensaw Delta relate to each other and to the Bottle Creek site.

Through the analyses of Irvy Quitmyer and C. Margaret Scarry, we can see how valuable it has been to "look small." What a different vision of Bottle Creek subsistence we would come away with had the mesh size of our screens been larger. We would not have known, for example, just how common tiny schooling fishes were to the diet of the Bottle Creek inhabitants. Nor would we have realized that these same people basically ignored acorns and hickory nuts. We would have missed the presence at Bottle Creek of the gladiator elimia (*Elimia hydei*) snail, which came from the Black Warrior drainage, and we certainly would not have detected evidence for yaupon holly (*Ilex vomitoria*) berries on the small house mounds. Such finds are important because they force us to ask other questions. How, for example, did the gladiator elimia get to Bottle Creek? Quitmyer suggests it was attached to the hull of a dugout canoe that had come from north-central Alabama. Could it have come from Moundville, the great Mississippian center that we believe had strong connections with Bottle Creek? We will never know for sure, of course, but at least now we have hard evidence that direct contact did take place between the Black Warrior drainage and Bottle Creek.

The presence of yaupon seeds at Bottle Creek raises a host of questions. The black drink was one of the prime ritual beverages of Mississippian peoples in the Southeast, and yaupon is the evidence for its existence (Hudson 1979). At Bottle Creek we found the seeds on the house mounds surrounding the central area of the site. Scarry has argued that the seeds serve as evidence for the beverage, rather than its ingredients, as the seeds came from berries that were attached to branches. The branches, in turn, held the precious leaves that the Bottle Creek people brewed to make the black drink. Scarry believes that the residents of the site merely discarded the berries with the branches on the mounds where the brewing occurred. But what is significant here is that investigators did not find the yaupon seeds in the Mound A deposits, not necessarily because the black drink was not consumed there, but more important, because it was not prepared there.

The presence of yaupon perhaps tells us something about who produced certain foodstuffs and who then used them, but this is slim evidence, to be sure. Support comes from the pottery that inhabitants of the site employed in the preparation and serving of food. Hunter Johnson has shown us that there is a significant difference between the vessel shapes in the assemblages in Mound A. Before mound construction began in the Mound A unit (D100), the frequency of jars and pans was similar to that observed throughout the Mound C deposits (C100). These food preparation containers were much more common than bowls and bottles in these nonelite contexts. As soon as the D100 unit began to take on an elite status, however, what with the first mound construction stage of Mound A, bowls and bottles increased markedly. The implication is that the inhabitants of Mound A, presumably the principal nobility on the site, were served either by the occupants of Mound C or by the people who lived on the other house mounds that form a ring around the western and northern periphery of the elite center.

As a result of Scarry and Johnson's research, there is ample evidence to suggest that the people who lived on the house mounds were retainers for the nobility who resided in the central part of the site. This is not to say that food was never consumed on the house mounds or, conversely, that meals were never prepared on Mound A, as it is logical to presume these activities occurred in both areas. All that we can say for sure is that vessel shapes and plant remains form a well-defined pattern that requires an explanation. The principal pattern observed is that food preparation, relative to serving, was more common on at least one of the house mounds than on Mound A.

But were the residents of the house mounds so very different from the occupants of Mound A? I suspect not. Certainly their pottery did not differ much, as it is clear that they used the same types and varieties throughout the site. Moreover, there was no marked difference in the quality of the wares in the various contexts and everyone seems to have eaten the same food. Quitmyer has demonstrated that the majority of the people on the site ate shellfish and fish. Although the Mound A occupants tended to consume somewhat larger clams and had a preference for freshwater species, there really was not a great disparity in the kinds and quantities of food that the inhabitants of Bottle Creek ate, and this fact does not seem to have altered through time.

Corn (*Zea mays*) was found everywhere at Bottle Creek. Scarry believes it to have been the principal plant food consumed at the site, and what is most interesting is that the kernels were generally removed from the cobs at off-mound locations, perhaps even away from the site itself. What this may mean is that the corn that came to Bottle Creek was already in a prepared state, even that which came to the people who lived on the house mounds. Could this have been tribute? Does this imply that there were at least three social classes in the local expression of Pensacola culture, with the true commoners having lived off-site? I think so, but without having household data, much of this is speculation. Nevertheless, it is a strong working hypothesis that is based on some solid material evidence.

Excavations in Mound L in 1991 revealed that much more construction activity took place at Bottle Creek than was once thought to have been the case. We now know that Mound L itself sits upon an artificial platform, and it is possible that other mounds on the site are similarly placed. We also know that Mound L was built using temporary walls of vertical posts. As earth was piled on and the mound grew in size, these posts were removed and other lines were positioned at higher elevations. In this manner, the soil stayed in place long enough for the mound to attain the desired shape.

David Morgan has shown that the builders of Mound L used the same form of earthwork construction that was employed in the design of the Mound B terrace. First the builders erected a clay platform to set the form. Then they applied sequential walls of vertical posts as they piled on alternating, thin layers of silt and sand, thereby giving the mound bulk. To hold it all in place, they applied a clay cap to the Mound B terrace, as was also the case with Mound L. For both mounds, there was evidence for some form of temporary usage of the mound surfaces, perhaps reflective of feasting, as the workers applied the various soil layers. A series of stacked hearths marked such uses in Mound L, most of which had microliths in association. As Paul Jackson discusses, these tools are reflective of a very different function for Mound L in its early history. Why this should be so bears further investigation.

Once the builders had applied a clay cap to the surfaces of Mound L and the Mound B terrace, they built structures atop them. For the Mound B terrace, evidence exists for wall trench buildings that were built during or after the Bottle Creek II phase (A.D. 1400–1550). The multitude of post features that occurred on the top of Mound L reflects frequent and heavy usage of this mound. As Silvia has revealed, the inhabitants constructed several buildings on Mound L both during and after the Bottle Creek II phase. Who these people were who occupied the structures atop Mound L remains a mystery, but one thing is certain—they made a lot of buildings! Probable structural forms include circular single set post, rectangular single set post, and rectangular wall trenches arrangements.

At least one of the Mound L houses had daub walls. Penelope Drooker's study of fabric impressions in the daub has revealed that builders sometimes applied mats to the walls of the houses at Bottle Creek. She also has revealed that these mats were generally of a higher quality than the fabrics the inhabitants used to mold their pottery pans. It is apparent that through time the Bottle Creek people shifted from using pliable fabrics to using basketry in fashioning such vessels, but was this change due to cultural or functional factors? That we do not know.

BOTTLE CREEK IN THE MISSISSIPPIAN WORLD

In his discussant comments on the Bottle Creek symposium at the 1995 Southeastern Archaeological Conference, Vernon J. Knight asked us who the person was who lived on Mound L in the early eighteenth century, and why that individual was so poverty-stricken when it came to European materials? Surely this individual must have known of the existence of such objects, but for some reason very few historic items made their way into the ground at Mound L. This is certainly a strange situation for an eighteenth-century Indian component. Contemporary sites in the region had lots of glass beads, buttons, gunflints, and other European items, but not Mound L. Silvia reasoned that it may simply have been a hunting camp (see Chapter 4), and she may be right, but it still seems unusual that this person should have selected this specific spot to camp, especially as it is not near an active body of water. Then again, Bottle Creek is a most unusual place.

Just what kind of a place was Bottle Creek? This may seem like a strange question to ask at the end of a book. The volume started off with some advice to a field director as to how to get to the Bottle Creek site and the rest of the book shows what one will find once one gets there, but this still does not address what kind of a place it might have been to the Indians who lived there. Was the site's location selected for defense? Perhaps economy played a greater role. Or maybe religion was the primary motivating factor for people to occupy Bottle Creek. Perhaps all of these reasons fit into the formula, as well as others not yet defined.

A Place of Defense?

Considering the difficulties in getting to Bottle Creek, one might suppose that its inhabitants selected the site first and foremost for its defensive properties. From the perspective of the year 2003, Bottle Creek certainly is in an inaccessible location. But, as Christopher Rodning has shown, for a boat-oriented culture it is situated right "along the highway." Its actual positioning, therefore, does not seem all that attuned for defense, but as there is evidence from the mounds C and D tests for a palisade around at least a portion of the site, defense must be taken into consideration. A palisade by itself, of course, does not signify defense. For that we would wish to see some bastions. They may exist at Bottle Creek, but we have no evidence for them as yet. I should also stress that palisades with bastions do not automatically mean that defense was a priority. At Cahokia, for example, the log palisade with square bastions was built and rebuilt in the late Stirling and early Moorehead phases, but only around the central part of the site (Demel and Hall 1998:204–206; Emerson 1997:49–52; Iseminger et al. 1990; Pauketat 1994:91–92). Is that the only part of the site that the Cahokians cared about, or was it just another way of demarcating sacred space or perhaps of protecting the material accumulations of the elite (Pauketat 1994:92)?

Could Bottle Creek have been a place to which the local population fled in times of stress? Stout and Lewis (1998:171–172) seem to think as much for the Adams site, a Mississippian town in Kentucky. It, too, was constructed on an island of high ground in a seasonally flooded cypress swamp, in a position that they refer to as a naturally defensive siting. Perhaps this is true of Bottle Creek, but the evidence that we have at present is that the Pensacola culture settlement pattern was fairly dispersed in the Mobile-Tensaw Delta. Why would anyone head to a central spot under duress, rather than just flee further into the swamp? Having said this, I should note that the nineteenth-century Seminole Indians of Florida made good use of Withlacoochee Cove, a remote sanctuary in the swamp, as a staging ground for raids against the U.S. army (Weisman 1989:92–123), so it is possible that Bottle Creek may have served such a purpose.

A Newly Settled Site?

Mississippian towns, with their mound-and-plaza combination, were often built on what had been substantial Late Woodland villages. This is clearly seen for many Baytown and Coles Creek sites in the Lower Mississippi Valley (Kidder 1998; Williams and Brain 1983:363–378), as well as for sites in western Kentucky (Stout and Lewis 1998:178). At the Moundville site in Alabama there is some Late Woodland West Jefferson phase material scattered around the site, but it pales in comparison with what comes immediately thereafter in the Moundville I phase (Steponaitis 1983:151–152; Walthall and Wimberly 1978:122–123; Wesson 1998:101). Knight and Steponaitis (1998:11–12) believe that Moundville probably was not occupied prior to about A.D. 1050, but out in the Black Warrior Valley it was different. There, in the floodplain, the West Jefferson phase is far better represented than at Moundville (Hammerstedt 2000; Jackson 1996, 2000, 2001; Jenkins 2001; Walthall 1980:205–207). A similar situation exists at Bottle Creek. Certainly there is some evidence for Late Woodland occupation at the site, but it is minor compared to what was going on in nearby locations around Mound Island (Morgan 2001).

Neither Moundville nor Bottle Creek became important settlement locations until Mississippian usage. This situation is not unusual in the Mississippian world. There are many cases in which towns were established "from scratch," with no heaps of midden to suggest that others found these same locations attractive earlier (Lewis and Stout 1998b:233). I am not necessarily saying that Mississippian pioneers moved into a vacant frontier, as appears to be the case for the Roods phase in the Chattahoochee Red Hills (Blitz and Lorenz 1999; Jenkins 1978:83–84; Schnell et al. 1981:244–245), but the Bottle Creek site itself appears to have been a Mississippian idea and plan. Knight (1998) has argued that Moundville was planned right from the beginning, and I believe the same is true for Bottle Creek.

Was Bottle Creek an Economic Center?

> Assuming that Mississippian communities sought the most efficient routes to the largest population centers, those rivers that drained the most extensive territories had greater strategic advantages in expanding exchange networks than did those watercourses with smaller drainage basins. This may be another reason why Bottle Creek is located where it is—near the mouth of the largest river system between the Mississippi and the Apalachicola—while near the mouths of the lesser river systems only smaller Mississippian centers have been found. Perhaps Bottle Creek functioned as a "gateway community": a place uniquely situated to control the greatest volume of traffic within or across regions (Hirth 1978). Specifically, the Bottle Creek center and polity had the potential to control the major water route between coast and interior for a vast segment of the northern Gulf Coast.
>
> Blitz and Mann 2000:105

As suggested by Blitz and Mann, Bottle Creek could have been a gateway community. Hirth (1978:37) argued that gateway communities usually developed as a response to increased trade or to the settling of sparsely populated frontier areas. Such settlements are often located to one side of their hinterland, with the hinterlands radiating out from their respective gateways. Bottle Creek's position was at the neck of an hourglass-shaped area (a bottleneck, if you will) that ran from interior to coast, a perfect textbook gateway location. Considering that the easiest way to travel and transport goods between these areas was by water, the flow of trade would have had to go right by Bottle Creek. It is reasonable to conclude that the elite of Bottle Creek would have had a say in, if not the control of, this north-south trade.

It is also possible that Bottle Creek could have served as a rendezvous, a meeting point for the conduct of trade (Brown 1999; Jackson 1991). One thing to look for at rendezvous sites is a mixture in the stylistic patterning of ceramics, a situation similar to what Milner and O'Shea (1998:199) observed at Late Woodland enclosure sites in northern Lower Michigan. Middle Woodland mound sites in that region are believed to have served as seasonal foci for dispersed foragers, but that situation changed in Late Woodland times as those sites are thought to have become enclosures for trade rendezvous. It is important to note that rendezvous sites are generally thought of as neutral locations, claimed by both groups or neither group, and they tend to occur at junctions between territories to afford access by outsiders. This is not the case with Bottle Creek. Not only is it not located at the juncture of a territory, but it is hard to conceive of it as a neutral site. As for the mixing of ceramic styles, there is some evidence for it at Bottle Creek, but it is minimal and not well understood. Everywhere else on the site the Pensacola pottery types hold up nicely, but the pottery found deep within Mound L is truly a hodgepodge. When we were digging it in 1991, Fuller and I jokingly referred to the mound as "the hotel," because the pottery, more often than not, seemed to have as much connections with the Lower Mississippi Valley as it did with Pensacola. The pottery from these test units still has not been dealt with to my satisfaction. To sum up this section, I do not believe Bottle Creek ever served as a rendezvous. As the principal town of the Pensacola culture, however, I do believe it was a classic gateway community.

The Bottle Creek Town

Lewis et al. (1998:5) list the main architectural features of "Mississippian Culture" as "plazas, platform mounds and other earthworks, entryways, various means of segregating space and activities, defensive works, and natural terrain features." Moreover, they distinguish between a Mississippian town and a Mississippian mound center. The former is "a habitation center with a public area, such as a plaza or courtyard, that may be flanked by one or more mounds." Mound centers, on the other hand, "are planned sites with earthworks but little or no archaeological evidence of habitation." According to these definitions, Bottle Creek, with its intensive habitation debris, should be classified as a town. What is characteristic of all Mississippian towns and mound centers is the mound-plaza association (Stout and Lewis 1998:151).

In cultures around the world, plazas tend to be very special architectural features. They represent the space between visible architectural expressions. They also are the place of the people, the communal spaces where the populace comes together to share in rituals and events that unite them as a community:

> [Plazas] are capable of expressing religious, political, communal, and social sentiments, often at the same time. They provide a public space that is an intermediary between the sacred and profane, but they are

> also areas from which protests against the authority of both powers can be waged. Above all, plazas are public areas, where individuals interact and community consensus is built. (Lewis et al. 1998:15)

And in the Mississippian world,

> A central plaza surrounded by mounds was a common characteristic of many of the larger Mississippian sites in the Southeast. Plazas were part of the town plan in that they were designed to focus community activity. They became the locale of special-purpose ceremonies and structures around which communities grew. Plazas probably also held public events, feasts, markets, and games (e.g., chunky). (Demel and Hall 1998:206)

It is reasonable to suppose that the plaza at Bottle Creek, which is contained between mounds A, B, L, M, and N, served similar purposes. Future excavations may someday reveal a large, centrally located post (or posts) in the Bottle Creek plaza, as is typical of many Mississippian and Fort Ancient sites. Often associated with these posts are large storage pits (Mehrer and Collins 1995:37, 40, 45; Nass and Yerkes 1995:66). These posts would have served as places to tie and torture prisoners, to display war trophies, and to serve as goals in the ballgame. The storage pits would be associated with feasting that accompanied such events.

The plaza is arguably the most critical element in the planning and development of Mississippian towns. Therefore, it is logical to assume that the plaza came first in the creation of a town, followed by the construction of surrounding mounds (Lewis et al. 1998:11–16). Considerable planning must have gone into the erection of Mississippian mounds and, more often that not, mounds were built on top of an earlier structure that had significance to the people. For example, in their discussion of woodhenges at Cahokia, Demel and Hall (1998:217) mention that prominent posts were found beneath mounds. It is clear that these posts were standing prior to mound construction. In some cases the mounds were even constructed around the posts. Appropriate to this discussion is the large well-preserved post that we found at the base of the mound D excavation unit (C101). We had no idea at the time why it was there, but we did feel that its position was significant and we questioned why it had been preserved so well. (This post has been saved and kept continually in water, but it has not yet been studied.) Perhaps it was a marker post for the construction of this mound, but if so, this would suggest that Mound D was purposefully built. All evidence points to Mound D having been accretional, as with Mound C and the other mounds that flank the northern part of the site.

The mounds in the center of Bottle Creek are noticeably different from the house mounds. Mounds A, B, L, and M[1] clearly were built in stages. Instead of growing through the steady deposit of garbage, these four mounds rose above the plaza through intent. As Lewis et al. argue, the height of the mound is not necessarily the critical factor in its construction; rather, "What is important is that it placed one or more architectural features (and the individuals who controlled them) at odds with the rest of the community by creating a visible differential between it and the surrounding elements of the total community design. The differential may have served to elevate the status of an individual, a family, a lineage, a god, or some combination of these" (Lewis et al. 1998:17). One thing that seems quite clear is that the size and dimensions of most Mississippian mounds and plazas are in proportion. In a study of Mississippian towns in Kentucky, Stout and Lewis (1998) argue that because of this proportional relationship, it is improbable that the mounds and plazas evolved together. If mounds were to increase in size through time at a site, as many obviously did, instead of reorganizing the plaza to suit the mounds, there seems to have been more of a tendency among Mississippian peoples to add second plazas. In the Lower Mississippi Valley this can be seen best at the Lake George (Williams and Brain 1983:335–342) and Winterville (Brain 1989:104–106) sites.

> Our main point is that, viewed architecturally, principal mound–main plaza spatial relationships could not have evolved together. These relationships were fixed by design fairly early in the history of a town and they changed little over time. Barring the discovery of major Mississippian cut-and-fill sections in the towns, the principal mound–main plaza data suggest that big mound-and-plaza complexes started out big, small mound-and-plaza complexes started out small, and they all pretty much stayed that way. Where they did change, we may find evidence of major cut-and-fill type Mississippian engineering projects designed to redefine the spatial relationships of the mound-and-plaza complex. (Stout and Lewis 1998:161)

This raises an interesting question with regard to the central area of Bottle Creek. In general, the mound-and-plaza relationship seems to be in

1. Although Mound N contributes to forming the border for the central portion of the site, it is very different from the other four mounds. It is a tiny mound and, although it has not been excavated, there is strong evidence for food remains (especially rangia shells) constituting its make-up. Its proximity to Mound L suggests that it may be associated with the activities that took place there.

proportion, and yet we know from our tests that at least three of the four mounds (A, B, and L) that encircle the plaza underwent multiple stages of construction. How is it possible that the mounds could have increased in size and yet still "fit" the plaza? It is of course possible that the initial designers had expansion in mind when they designed the site. In other words, Bottle Creek may have started off with a massive plaza, but with small mounds that eventually would "grow into it." There is no evidence for a second plaza at the site, so that never seems to have been an option. Another possibility is that the Bottle Creek people applied the "cut-and-fill" method, as described above. But seeing that there was so little to cut into in this swamp environment, the more logical approach would have been to dig, pile up, and expand. The "canal" would have been an important source for this soil (Rodning, Chapter 11). There is certainly evidence for expansion on the site, especially in the vicinity of Mound L. Much of the lobe shown in Figure 1.3 seems to have been artificial. What I suspect (but cannot yet demonstrate archaeologically) is that this expansion of the plaza area to the south occurred after the initial construction of Mound A, when the site's planners realized that a larger plaza might be advantageous. If this did happen, it would be logical to assume that Mound L and possibly Mound M are younger than the first stages of mounds A and B.

Like plazas, borrow pits are often neglected in the study of Mississippian landscapes. They are the "holes in the donuts," the voids that are not particularly stimulating. The numerous bodies of water that occurred around the core of the Bottle Creek site must have been critical features of the landscape when the site was inhabited. In addition to the open canal, which still exists between mounds C and P, water-filled borrow pits had to have been quite common at Bottle Creek. Two of these pits are still quite visible today and fill up readily during wet spells, so one can imagine just how prominent they were at the peak of site use. Demel and Hall (1998:220–224) argue that these generally ignored features of the Mississippian landscape must have been critical in site planning and operation.

The people of Bottle Creek often removed soil to add to mounds, so an important question is, what did they do with the borrow pits afterward? A series of shovel tests run across the borrow pit north of Mound B was not too illuminating. We dug until we struck water, in most cases 1–1.5 m below ground surface. With visions of Key Marco in mind (Gilliland 1975; 1989), I expected to find a wooden figure or two, or at least masses of refuse, but nothing of the sort emerged—only muck. Were these pits simply breeding grounds for mosquitoes, as they are now? Or were they places for daily ritual bathing, or perhaps "aquatic medicinal gardens; as containers of esoteric healing knowledge," as suggested by Demel and Hall (1998:222). We do not know—we may never know—but it is logical to presume that at one time borrow pits were not only much larger features on the Bottle Creek landscape than they are now, but that they had an important function in the lives of the people.

THE BOTTLE CREEK CHIEFDOM

I think most people would agree that Bottle Creek was the principal town for the Pensacola culture and that it was a Mississippian chiefdom (Blitz 1993:5–30), but the nature of that chiefdom is ambiguous. Bense (1994: 234–238) describes Bottle Creek as a "complex chiefdom," but was it a paramount chiefdom (Pauketat 1994:31–39)? Did it have control of the smaller simple chiefdoms that centered on the bay systems of the coast (Bense 1989; Blitz and Mann 2000:48–62, 101–105; Knight 1984:215; Phillips 1989), or was it just another "normal" chiefdom, albeit with rather large mounds? A major characteristic of chiefdoms throughout the world is that there is an organized structure of socialized inequality. In short, one small part of the population, a hereditary elite, has access to power and economic resources unavailable to the rest of the populace (Anderson 1990; Barker and Pauketat 1992; Blitz 1993; Earle 1987, 1991; Emerson 1997; Fried 1967; Pauketat 1994; Peebles and Kus 1977; Sahlins 1972; Service 1962; Steponaitis 1991). The Bottle Creek site certainly fits this definition as a place where authority was manifested, but it is difficult to appreciate just what its chiefdom may have consisted of (two-tiered settlement hierarchy, three-tiered, or what?) when fieldwork has only been conducted at the center. It is worth remembering that an emphasis on elites at large mound sites, although important, only provides part of the story (Lafferty 1998:127).

> The early emphasis on the temple-town model was derived from a normative outlook on how past societies were organized and from a common perspective in archaeological interpretations that included an inclination to be concerned first with elite and ceremonial activities such as the construction and use of mounds and the burial of high-status individuals. Although this may be the most dramatic way to study chiefdoms, it is not necessarily the most profitable or logical. Unless households, as the basic units of economic activity and social and biological reproduction, are thoroughly investigated, studies focused on the higher levels of social integration must continue to rely on a variety of unexplored assumptions. (Rogers 1995:25)

This point is well taken. Although we are gaining an appreciation of the existence of "support sites" for the center (Scarry, Chapter 5), the farmsteads that were the sources for Bottle Creek's sustenance, we have very little data as to the makeup of their households, a point Knight (1977:148) made many years ago. And yet this information is absolutely critical for understanding the settlement hierarchy (Rogers 1995; Smith 1995). Outside of the Bottle Creek site itself, our understanding of Pensacola culture structures and diet in the region is minimal, although there are some important contributions (Gremillion 1996; Knight 1987; Morgan 2001; Silvia 2000). I am hopeful that it will someday be possible to do for Bottle Creek and its hinterlands what Mehrer and Collins (1995) were able to do for Cahokia; or J. Scarry (1995) for Apalachee homesteads; Nass and Yerkes (1995) for Fort Ancient societies; Sullivan (1995) and Schroedl (1998) for eastern Tennessee Mouse Creek and Dallas phase societies; Hatch (1995) for Lamar sites in the Oconee River Valley of Georgia; Mistovich (1995) and Welch (1998) for Mississippian occupations in the Black Warrior River Valley; Jackson and Scott (1995) for Mississippian sites in the Tombigbee River Valley of Mississippi and Alabama; Pertulla (1998) for the Powers phase in the Western Lowlands of Missouri; and Benn (1998) for Mississippian settlements in northeast Arkansas. But we have a long way to go. Until we obtain data on the household level, to learn what is "normal," we will not be able to tell whether there were specialized sites like civic nodes, civic-ceremonial nodes, priest-mortuary ceremonial nodes, temple nodes, and the like (Emerson 1997:81–192; Mehrer and Collins 1995:50; Smith 1995:244).

Were There Specialists at Bottle Creek?

The existence of specialists, or at least specialized craft production, has been addressed only lightly in this volume, and yet it is a critical issue in understanding the operation of chiefdoms (Muller 1984; Pauketat 1987b; Prentice 1983, 1985; Yerkes 1983, 1986, 1989, 1991). Hunter Johnson looked at the function of ceramics in comparing activities on Mound C and on and below Mound A. He did find differences, to be sure, but the differences relate more to food preparing versus food serving than to the existence of specialists. Thus far there is no evidence whatsoever for special pottery having been made or used at Bottle Creek. If there were indeed specific people whose job it was to produce such objects, they are not yet recognized in the archaeological record.

The existence of a microlithic industry, concentrated in the lower levels of Mound L, suggests that a group of artisans may have existed at Bottle Creek, but again, we would need to look at whether or not such activities occurred at households in the region to determine just how unusual these activities really were (Rogers 1995:29; Smith 1995:246–248). Even at the Bottle Creek site itself, excavations have been limited, so we cannot say with certainty just how restricted the microlithic industry really was. And without use-wear analysis of these objects, such as what Nass and Yerkes have done in their study of Mississippian and Fort Ancient sites (Nass and Yerkes 1995:75; Yerkes 1989, 1991), we can only speculate concerning to what the microliths were actually applied. Paul Jackson argues for shell and mica, which seems reasonable, but the evidence is slim for either.

The Importance of Place

Who were the people who continued to live at Mississippian towns after general site abandonment? This is a question that Stout and Lewis (1998:178) ask with regard to sites in the Ohio-Mississippi Confluence region, and it is just as applicable to Bottle Creek. I suspect that it has something to do with the importance of place:

> Whether houses, palaces, marketplaces, or ceremonial precincts, the spaces in which people live and interact are socially meaningful. This social space is not a homogenous cross-cultural entity, but represents the unique cultural milieu within which it is created and used, with both spaces and meanings open to alteration through continued social interaction and use. (Wesson 1998:95)

"Place" is a term one will rarely find in the index or table of contents of an anthropological text (Geertz 1996:259). Even the Oxford English Dictionary has difficulty coming to terms with the history and many meanings of the term, what with six three-column pages devoted to it (Frake 1996:234). And yet the concept of place is critical in anthropology.

> The banalities and distractions of the way we live now lead us, often enough, to lose sight of how much it matters just where we are and what it is like to be there. The ethnography of place is, if anything, more critical for those who are apt to imagine that all places are alike than for those who, listening to forests or experiencing stones, know better. (Geertz 1996:262)

WAS BOTTLE CREEK A SACRED PLACE?

If "place" is difficult to understand, consider how much more complex it is to comprehend the meaning of "sacred place." *The Atlas of Sacred Places* (Harpur 1994) divides its sites into five categories: 1) Monuments and landscapes that become sacred because of their association with saints or spiritual teachers; 2) important burial places; 3) eternal shrines that evoke a sense of a mythic past; 4) spaces adorned in great artwork to glorify God; and 5) the destination of pilgrimages. A total of 33 sacred sites are included in this atlas, only two of which are from the Americas—Cahokia and Téotihuacan. Considering that these are the two largest sites in North America and Mesoamerica, respectively, I have a feeling that a certain amount of politics affected their inclusion. Having said that, I do think it is probable that the site of Cahokia was sacred, if only for the activities that took place there (Williamson 1984:240–250). But there were many other places in the Eastern Woodlands that were sacred to the Indians (Cantor 1993). Most of these places probably fit within the second or third categories listed above. Some places are "naturals" for selection as sacred sites—large caves, for instance, or isolated rocks that seem to spring from the earth (DiBlasi 1996; Henson 1986:85–87; Watson 1986:115–116, 1996:161–163).

"Listening to forests or experiencing stones"—there is a lot of thick description in this phrase of Geertz's (1996:262). Twice in my life I have felt that I was standing on sacred ground. The first time was in 1982 when I visited the Castlerigg stone circle with my cousin Tom Clare, archaeologist for the county of Cumbria. This Late Neolithic–Early Bronze Age edifice is located just outside the town of Keswick in England's Lake District (Clare 1981:13–14). It was not so much the size of the circle that impressed me; rather, its geographical positioning made me feel as if I were at the center of the world. In each cardinal direction stretched a valley, with me standing in the middle of it all. The only other time I had such a feeling was in 2000 when I took a 15-mile hike to see the Shrine of the Stone Lions in the center of Bandelier National Monument (Hoard 1989:69, 81). In and of itself, the tiny stone circle that encloses the vaguely lion-like stones is a singularly unimpressive affair. Only when one looks around does one realize why its location was sacred, and why the Zuni and other Pueblo Indians still walk hundreds of miles in their pilgrimages to stuff feathers and other amulets into the crevices between the stones of the circle (Stuart 1989:39, 89, 91,104–106). Although I am drifting toward the metaphysical realm (and getting out of my comfort-zone) I do believe that the meaning ("feeling" is probably a better word) of locations like Castlerigg and the Shrine of the Stone Lions transcends cultural boundaries. Obviously I went to these spots because they were known landmarks, but once I stood on them I knew why they were regarded as such.

This is not true of Bottle Creek. There is nothing in the geography of the site to suggest at first glance that it is a significant spot. Only with a map is it possible to appreciate that Bottle Creek is located centrally in the Mobile-Tensaw Delta. The Indians must have recognized this fact to some extent, but the rivers and bayous are too winding to plot exact locations. Rather, I suspect that they recognized they were roughly in the middle and that was good enough. But good enough for what? A location along the river system was clearly important, but was it really necessary to establish a settlement out in the middle of a swamp and build up a land base? Why not just occupy the bluffs along the Mobile River, as did the historic Tomés, Naniabas, or Mobilians (Waselkov and Gums 2000:6–21). Surely this approach would have been more sensible—at least in economic terms. Even in political terms, it made very little difference whether a principal town was established along a high river bluff or in the middle of a flood-prone river valley. Moundville serves as a good example. The initial Mississippian inhabitants of Bottle Creek must have realized that their new settlement was going to be under water for a good portion of the year. One twelve-month stretch would have revealed that situation to them pretty quickly. Haywick's study of sediments in Mound A (see Chapter 2) have clearly shown that flooding was a regular part of life at Bottle Creek, and that site use must have been intermittent. So, in considering all the disadvantages of Bottle Creek's physical location, the question we keep coming back to is why was it chosen?

Although I cannot prove it, not by any maneuvering of quantitative data, I believe that Bottle Creek was situated on Mound Island because the location itself was sacred. But it was not sacred in the same sense as Castlerigg or the Shrine of the Stone Lions. Geographical analyses alone could predict the importance of their locations. With Bottle Creek I think we are looking at something more in line with the sacred ground of a Gettysburg, a Mt. Vernon, or a Bethlehem. I think Mound Island was chosen as a settlement not so much because it was an ideal place, but because it was a critical place in the early history of the Mobile-Tensaw Delta Mississippians. Over the centuries, through its continued use by the prime elite, the importance of the site, as a sacred place, must have taken on mythical proportions, so much so that even after the population declined it remained a focal point for local and regional inhabitants.

Location matters. That truth is something that Thunen (1998) stresses in his discussion of the geometric embankment at the Pinson Mounds site in Tennessee:

> This analysis suggests that the builders, rather than using a single, formal planning model, utilized architectural principles to create a cultural place from a unique geographic space at the Pinson Mounds site. This suggests that location was a critical factor in the creation of the Eastern Citadel. Once the location was selected, the builders used a variety of planning principles to design and build their cultural place. (Thunen 1998:67)

I do not mean to imply that Bottle Creek is an "enclosure" in the usual sense of the term, because there are no visible rings, squares, or octagons that encircle areas (Mainfort and Sullivan 1998b). But for anyone who has ever visited Bottle Creek, the sense of enclosure certainly exists. First you are totally encircled by rivers. If that is not enough, you are enclosed by swamp on all sides. We know from cores and test excavations at Mound L that a major portion of the southern part of the site was built up, presumably to provide a sense of relief. And if you approach the site from the north the house mounds themselves sit upon a bank. Whether the bank itself is totally natural or not is unknown, but the general sense is that the whole site rises up out of the swamp, and by doing so forms a symbolic enclosure. We know from the excavations in mounds C and D that a palisade encircled a portion of this raised area, which perhaps gave added definition to the site. Of course the issue then becomes, is this fact evidence for sacredness, defense, or both (Milner and O'Shea 1998:181)? Jon Gibson considered this same question for the Poverty Point site, a Late Archaic settlement in Louisiana:

> These correlations convince me that Poverty Point was a sacred place, a place of ritual and rite, a place of spirits and power, a place of mystery and magic. Historical analogs and archaeological matches are just too numerous for all to be coincidental. (Gibson 1998:30)

But it is important that Gibson emphasizes Poverty Point was also a secular place, and it is difficult to separate the two (Gibson 2000:270–271). The same could be said of Bottle Creek, where the sacred and profane probably went hand-in-hand. It is interesting that Poverty Point is the only enclosure site in Mainfort and Sullivan's (1998a) *Ancient Earthen Enclosures* volume that has an abundance of both domestic and ritual artifacts associated with the enclosure. But one should also note that Poverty Point is different from other sites with enclosures in that its rings served as bases for occupation. In a way this is analogous to Bottle Creek and its ring of house mounds that partially surround the central area. I do not mean to imply from all of this that Bottle Creek was a latter-day Poverty Point. They are the products of two completely different cultural traditions, after all. But it is the history of their usage that may be analogous. Poverty Point may have started off sacred, maybe not, but because of its age and history its sacredness probably increased over time. I believe that Bottle Creek became more sacred with age, too, as did Moundville.

A Prehistoric Necropolis?

It is probable that Bottle Creek's primary purpose changed over the years. I do think it was a sacred place right from the first time Mississippian people ventured on the site around A.D. 1100, but it continued to be the site of a mix of secular and sacred activities for much of its history. Between

A.D. 1250 and 1550, when most of the mound construction seems to have taken place, Bottle Creek probably was the political, economic, and spiritual center of Pensacola culture, but there is evidence to suggest that the site experienced some major changes in the sixteenth century. Richard Fuller noticed long ago that the mounds that constitute the eastern and western edges of the Bottle Creek site are very different from both the central mounds and the house mounds (O, P, Q, and R). These peripheral mounds are conical and built of a sandy soil, much like Bear Point phase burial mounds of the Ginhouse Island complex that dates between A.D. 1550–1700 (Fuller 1998:30–32; Fuller and Brown 1998:100; Fuller et al. 1984:134–160). Mound O probably contained the burial reported by Bigelow (1853:189), although Stowe was not able to confirm this point in his excavations (Fuller and Brown 1998:100; Stowe and Fuller 1993:19). We have not as yet excavated the other three mounds (P–R), but surface collections have revealed materials dating no earlier than the Bear Point phase (Fuller and Brown 1998:100–103).

If these mounds are indeed sixteenth- or seventeenth-century burial repositories, it raises an interesting question. They would have been erected just after the main part of the Bottle Creek site was depopulated, or at least had a significant population reduction. Having said this, I should immediately point out that we lack data that is normally used for population studies. We do not have the kind of archaeological information that exists at Moundville for estimating population (Powell 1991, 1998; Steponaitis 1998). In lieu of extensive block excavations that would reveal settlement data and mortuary remains, we must rely on middens and surface collections to address the degree of occupation, and this is a dangerous way to draw conclusions. All that we can really say at this point is that after the Bottle Creek II phase, at about A.D. 1550, refuse drops off dramatically on the site. Presumably this is a sign of a reduction in population.

I should stress that Bottle Creek continued to be occupied, even as late as the mid-eighteenth century, but mound use had diminished and mound construction was negligible. Despite the reduction in population, Bottle Creek seems to have become a repository for the dead, or rather a necropolis, during its final one to two centuries of use. The same development occurred at Moundville a couple of centuries earlier (Knight 1997:240–241; Knight and Steponaitis 1998:18–19). Note, however, that this interpretation for Bottle Creek is predicated on mounds O–R actually being burial mounds, and this assumption has not yet been proven.

Perhaps in a way analogous to Christians of medieval Europe, who wished to be buried *ad sanctos*, either in the church yard or preferably in the church itself (Ariès 1981:45–56), the late prehistoric/protohistoric Indian elite wished to be buried at or near the sacred site of their ancestors.

> In some cultures, a cemetery (or burial mound, or earthwork?) may be understood not as simply a place to deposit the dead but also as the place where the spirits of the dead are symbolically incarcerated, and where they can be placated, neutralized, or simply provided with a place of proper communion with the living. (Riordan 1998:75)

The Fort Ancient site, a hilltop enclosure in Ohio, is another example of a site whose function changed through time (Connolly 1998; Moorehead 1890; Squier and Davis 1998:18–21, Pl. VII [1848]). The very structured "architectural grammar" of this site broke down in its later history as it took on a mortuary function. Although this is a Hopewellian site, the point is still valid that over time a sacred site became increasingly associated with a mortuary role.

> Fort Ancient was a multipurpose site. Just as the Scioto sites cannot be called solely mortuary sites, Fort Ancient cannot be called solely a defensive site. The full range of activities reported at most earthwork centers are also recorded at Fort Ancient (Connolly 1996). This observation suggests that the significance of hilltop enclosures as a site type has more to do with physiographic location than actual function. Therefore, it will be useful to assess the site functions of Fort Ancient within the broader sphere of regional manifestations of the Hopewell culture. (Connolly 1998:112–113)

Again, what Connolly emphasizes is that location is important, which brings us back to what makes a location, a specific place, potentially sacred in the first place? I do not think that we can answer this question for Bottle Creek, but we can address why the function of this town changed through time as it took on more of the trappings of a necropolis. An analogous situation existed at Moundville. As noted by Knight and Steponaitis (1998:17–21), people started to abandon Moundville at around A.D. 1300, leaving only the elite and their retainers as permanent residents. One explanation offered is that this centrifugal effect was a purposeful effort of the elite to enhance the sanctity of Moundville—in other words, push the commoners out. A similar situation seems to have existed at Cahokia slightly earlier, during the Moorehead phase (A.D. 1200–1275) (Emerson 1997:52–53). Wesson, on the other hand, believes something else was involved at Moundville:

> Another interpretation of this pattern is that as elite control of sacred space increased, an increasing number of individuals opted out of the system and either established individual farmsteads or moved to other communities. With the imposition of greater elite control at Moundville,

> perhaps people grew dissatisfied with their increasing physical and existential distance from the hierophanous center and went out to create new sacred landscapes. As Eliade (1959:43) states, "the religious man sought to live as near as possible to the Center of the World," and it was the center of the world that Moundville's sacred landscape represented. By vacating Moundville, nonelites became more distant from the existential center, a counterintuitive movement if the local built environment continued to represent a potent, and necessary, sacred landscape. Perhaps continued elite manipulation of the plaza-periphery group and the alienation such actions imposed on nonelites led Moundville to become primarily a necropolis during the period from A.D. 1300 to 1450. (Wesson 1998:119–120)

It is interesting to me that Moundville and Bottle Creek seem to have experienced the same pattern of relatively abrupt planned settlement, succeeded by vibrant growth and habitation, followed by population dispersion and, finally, use as a necropolis. One important difference is that whereas Moundville experienced year-round usage, Bottle Creek was probably only seasonally occupied, even during the peak of its occupation between A.D. 1250–1550. Another major difference between Moundville and Bottle Creek relates to dates. Bottle Creek was coming into its own just as population was beginning to disperse from Moundville. Could Bottle Creek have been one of the new sacred landscapes created, as Wesson states above? Certainly the Moundville connections are there early in Bottle Creek's history. It was another 250 years before Bottle Creek went into the cycle of dispersion and mortuary emphasis. We do not know if the reason for this change was the same as at Moundville, but it is significant that the cycle itself was the same. Whether or not people were establishing other sacred landscapes elsewhere in the sixteenth century we do not know, because soon all was disrupted by the appearance of the Spaniards and the diseases that spread in their wake (Dobyns 1983; Ramenofsky 1987; Smith 1987).

FINAL THOUGHTS

While at Fort Louis on the Mobile River in March of 1702, Pierre le Moyne d'Iberville wrote in his journal:

> The 4th. I sent my brother [Bienville] to examine several abandoned Indian settlements on the islands in the vicinity. . . .
>
> My brother came back this evening. He had observed several sites formerly occupied by Indians, which war with the Conchaque [Choctaw] and the Alibamons had made them abandon. Most of these settle-

> ments become flooded to a depth of half a foot during high water. These settlements are on islands, this river being full of them for 13 leagues. He got an Indian to show him the place where their gods are, about which all the neighboring nations make such a fuss and to which the Mobilians used to come and offer sacrifices. The Indians claim that a person cannot touch them without dying on the spot and that they came down from the sky. A gun had to be given the Indian who showed where they were; he did not get closer to them than 10 steps away, and with his back turned. It took a search to locate them on a little hill among the canes, near an old village that is destroyed, on one of these islands. The gods were brought here. They are five images—a man, a woman, a child, a bear, and an owl—made of plaster in the likeness of Indians of this country. I personally think that some Spaniard in the time of Soto made the figures of these Indians in plaster. Apparently it was done a long time ago. We have them at the settlement. The Indians who see them here are amazed at our boldness and amazed that we do not die as a result. I am taking the images to France, though they are not particularly interesting. (d'Iberville in McWilliams 1981:168–169)

The site that Bienville visited three hundred years ago, "the place where their gods are," is undoubtedly Bottle Creek (Hamilton 1976:56; Higginbotham 1991:70–71; Stowe and Fuller 1993:10, 12; Waselkov and Gums 2000:8–9). Note that this is the location where "the Mobilians used to come and offer sacrifices." Apparently this site was significant to a number of other groups in the Southeast, too, as suggested by Charlevoix in a journal entry dated December 25, 1721, while he was among the Natchez Indians:

> The greatest part of the nations of Louisiana, had formerly their temples as well as the Natchez, and in all these temples a perpetual fire is kept up. It should even seem, that the *Maubilians* enjoyed a sort of primacy in religion, over all the other nations in this part of Florida; for when any of their fires happened to be extinguished through chance, or negligence, it was necessary to kindle them again at theirs. (Charlevoix in O'Neill 1977:154)

Could Bottle Creek have remained a religious center long after its demise as a sociopolitical center? We know that the site itself was in decline at least by A.D. 1550, but we must not lose sight of the fact that significant occupation did continue for the next two centuries. The nature of this occupation is a topic of considerable significance. Again we come back to the individual or individuals who lived on Mound L in the mid-eighteenth century. Despite the fact that European objects were plentiful in the region at this time, this particular inhabitant or inhabitants was starved for such items. But perhaps this was purposeful. Brent Weisman (1989:82–123) observed a similar situation with the nineteenth-century Seminole of Withlacoochee Cove in northern Florida. He was amazed to find so few European objects at the camps that he excavated in this cove. It was almost as if the Indians had deliberately removed European objects from their material trappings. Weisman feels that a form of nativism, in which the Seminoles purposefully tried to remove all that was not aboriginal from their lives, might explain this absence.

> It [Withlacoochee Cove] was for a time the hotbed of the Indian resistance, the place where only those militant few who were determined to remain in Florida migrated and the place where the Indian military forces achieved their highest level of tactical organization. Many of the Seminoles who eventually resided in the Cove had previous experience with the Creek nativistic movements in the first decades of the 1800s. The appeal made by a Withlacoochee prophet would not have been strange. (Weisman 1989:122)

Was there a prophet at Bottle Creek, or was the last inhabitant of Mound L just a poorly equipped hunter? We may never know, but there is now enough evidence to suggest that although Bottle Creek was very quiet in historic times, it was not forgotten. I believe that between A.D. 1550 and 1750 Bottle Creek continued to play the role of a principal sacred center for the region, and perhaps for a significant part of southern Alabama and Mississippi. I also believe that the individual who resided on Mound L in the eighteenth century is very important to this story. What he or she was doing at the site potentially may reveal much about cultural dynamics in the Mobile-Tensaw Delta and in surrounding regions in the transition from prehistory to history.

Appendix A

Archaeological Phases Represented at the Bottle Creek Site

Andrews Place Phase
Period: Early Mississippi
Time: A.D. 1100–1250
Culture (Variant): Moundville
Pottery Tradition: Middle Mississippian
Pottery Diagnostics: The complex is characterized by early Moundville types/varieties such as Moundville Incised, *var. Moundville*, in association with minor numbers of terminal Weeden Island (e.g., "Wakulla") and transitional Coles Creek pottery. Other markers include Mississippi Plain bowls and peaked loop handles on jars.
Chronological Relationships: Moundville I phase.
Bibliography: Fuller 1998:24–25

Bear Point Phase
Period: Protohistoric
Time: A.D. 1550–1700
Culture (Variant): Pensacola
Pottery Tradition: Middle Mississippian
Pottery Diagnostics: Markers are Pensacola Incised, *vars. Bear Point* and *Perdido Bay;* D'Olive Incised, *var. Arnica;* and Moundville Incised, *var. Douglas.* Pensacola Incised, *vars. Pensacola, Rutherford,* and *Matthews Landing* also are diagnostic but are less common. Diagnostic rim modes include "Arnica," "Bear Point," and "Douglas."
Chronological Relationships: Alabama River phase; Four Mile Point phase.
Bibliography: Fuller 1998:28–29.

This appendix is based on an unpublished document written by Fuller and Brown (1993b).

Bottle Creek I Phase
Period: Middle Mississippi
Time: A.D. 1250–1400
Culture (Variant): Pensacola
Horizon: Saltpan
Pottery Tradition: Middle Mississippian
Pottery Diagnostics: Pensacola Incised, *var. Jessamine*, D'Olive Incised, *var. Dominic*, and Mound Place Incised, *var. McMillan* are the principal markers. The "Jessamine" rim mode also is diagnostic. D'Olive Engraved and the "Dominic" rim mode occur in the Bottle Creek I and Andrews Place phases. Moundville Incised, *var. Bottle Creek*, D'Olive Incised, *vars. D'Olive* and *Mary Ann*, Salt Creek Cane Impressed, *var. Salt Creek*, and Mound Place Incised, *var. Waltons Camp* are present in the Bottle Creek I and Bottle Creek II phases. Bottle Creek I assemblages also may include secondary numbers of Moundville II pottery such as Moundville Incised, *vars. Carrollton*, *Moundville* (with short rays), and *Snows Bend*, Mound Place Incised, *var. Akron*, Moundville Engraved, and Kimmswick Fabric Impressed, *var. Langston*. Also diagnostic of the Bottle Creek I phase is a Plaquemine-related complex featuring shell-tempered versions of Anna Incised, Carter Engraved, and L'Eau Noire Incised.
Chronological Relationships: Moundville II phase; Anna phase.
Bibliography: Fuller 1998:27.

Bottle Creek II Phase
Period: Late Mississippi
Time: A.D. 1400–1550
Culture (Variant): Pensacola
Horizon: Southeastern Ceremonial Complex
Pottery Tradition: Middle Mississippian
Pottery Diagnostics: Principal markers are Pensacola Incised, *vars. Gasque* and *Holmes*, plus greater numbers of Moundville Incised, *var. Bottle Creek*. Other markers are the "D'Olive" and "Gasque" rim modes. Also common are Salt Creek Cane Impressed, *var. Salt Creek* and Mound Place Incised, *var. Waltons Camp*. Generally, incising increased and engraving decreased from the Bottle Creek I phase to the Bottle Creek II phase; therefore, Pensacola Incised and D'Olive Incised increased at the expense of Moundville Engraved and D'Olive Engraved.
Chronological Relationships: Moundville III phase.
Bibliography: Fuller 1998:27–28.

Coden Phase
Period: (Late) Late Woodland
Time: A.D. 750–1100

(The Coden phase is believed to last as late as A.D. 1100 in the Mobile Bay/Alabama coast region, but may have ended earlier in the Mobile-Tensaw Delta)
Culture (Variant): "Wakulla" (late Weeden Island)
Horizon: Terminal Gulf, Late Paddle Stamping
Pottery Tradition: Mixed Gulf and Southern Appalachian
Pottery Diagnostics: Significant increases in check stamped (Wakulla Check Stamped and Pontchartrain Check Stamped) and plain wares at the expense of the rectilinear and curvilinear incised and punctated (Gulf Tradition) decorations that dominate the earlier Tate's Hammock phase.
Chronological Relationships: Late Weeden Island ("Wakulla") phases to the east; Bayou Ramos and Morgan phases to the west; McLeod and Autauga phases to the north.
Bibliography: Fuller 1998:18–19.

Port Dauphin Phase
Period: Early Historic
Time: A.D. 1700–1750
Culture (Variant): Eastern Choctawan
Pottery Tradition: Gulf Historic
Pottery Diagnostics: Principal markers are well-made bowls tempered with very fine angular shell (Bell Plain, *var. Graveline*) or fine flaky shell (*var. Ft. Conde*). Decoration includes curvilinear, narrow parallel-line incisions (Port Dauphin Incised, which is stylistically related to Fatherland Incised), red filming (Chicot Red) or, rarely, zoned punctation (late, narrow-line version of Owens Punctated).
Other Characteristics: "Colono" attributes, such as ring bases and cup handles.
Other Artifacts: Early-eighteenth-century French artifacts typically occur in Port Dauphin components.
Chronological Relationships: Doctor Lake complex; Natchez phase.
Bibliography: Fuller 1998:35.

Tate's Hammock Phase
Period: (Early) Late Woodland
Time: A.D. 400–750
Culture (Variant): Weeden Island
Horizon: Gulf III
Pottery Tradition: Gulf
Pottery Diagnostics: Largely characterized by Weeden Island and Coles Creek types. Rectilinear neck decoration (e.g., Coles Creek Incised, Carrabelle Incised, Carrabelle Punctated, Mazique Incised, Evansville Punctated, and Tucker Ridge Pinched) and curvilinear zoning (Weeden Island

Punctated, Weeden Island Incised, and French Fork Incised) are common. Another marker, especially for the early part of the Tate's Hammock phase, is Weeden Island Red. Wakulla Check Stamped and Pontchartrain Check Stamped are present, but are not as common as in the later Coden phase.

Chronological Relationships: An indigenous development out of the Middle Woodland Porter phase. Tate's Hammock pottery shares numerous parallels with pottery of middle Coles Creek phases to the west and middle Weeden Island phases to the east.

Bibliography: Brose et al. 1983; Fuller 1998:16–18; Walthall 1980.

Appendix B

Radiocarbon Dates Secured at the Bottle Creek Site

	Beta No.*	GCS No.	Provenience	C14 Age (Date)	C13 Adjusted (Date)	Cal. C13 Adjusted Date	
						1 Sigma	2 Sigma**
Mound A	79684	3	D100M1	580+/–60 (1370) B.P.	560+/-60 (1390) B.P.	a.d. 1315–1345 and A.D. 1390–1425	A.D. 1295–1450
	79685	6	D100S2	670+/-60 (1280) B.P.	630+/-60 (1320) B.P.	A.D. 1295–1405	A.D. 1275–1425
	79686	9	D100X12	1070+/-80 (880) B.P.	1030+/-80 (920) B.P.	A.D. 970–1040	A.D. 875–1195
Mound C	71152	1	C100E	460+/-60 (1490) B.P.	410+/-60 (1540) B.P.	A.D. 1440–1510 and A.D. 1590–1620	A.D. 1420–1650
	71153	8	C100I	650+/-70 (1300) B.P.	580+/-60 (1370) B.P.	A.D. 1310–1360 and A.D. 1380–1420	A.D. 1290–1440
	71154	14	C100K	560+/-60 (1390) B.P.	490+/-60 (1460) B.P.	A.D. 1410–1450	A.D. 1320–1340 and A.D. 1390–1500
	71155	19	C100N	710+/-60 (1240) B.P.	650+/-60 (1300) B.P.	A.D. 1290–1400	A.D. 1270–1420
	71156	31	C100S1	630+/-60 (1320) B.P.	610+/-60 (1340) B.P.	A.D. 1300–1410	A.D. 1280–1430
Mound D	79682	31	C101J	660+/-50 (1290) B.P.	660+/-50 (1290) B.P.	A.D. 1290–1325 and A.D. 1340–1390	A.D. 1275–1410
	79683	11	C101X3F2	750+/-60 (1200) B.P.	720+/-60 (1230) B.P.	A.D. 1265–1300	A.D. 1220–1395
Mound L	79679	10	A100X102A	780+/-60 (1170) B.P.	730+/-60 (1220) B.P.		
	79680	7	A102X41	740+/-80 (1210) B.P.	740+/-80 (1210) B.P.	A.D. 1235–1300	A.D. 1170–1400
	79681	16	A102X136A	1120+/-70 (830) B.P.	1090+/-70 (860) B.P.	A.D. 885–1015	A.D. 790–1040

* All samples are charred material; analyzed by Beta Analytic Inc., 1994 and 1995.

** Recommended calibration age range for interpretation.

References Cited

Agresti, Alan, and Barbara F. Agresti

1979 *Statistical Methods for the Social Sciences.* Dellen Publishing Co., San Francisco.

Allan, Aljean W.

1983 An Analysis of Lithic Materials from the Lubbub Creek Archaeological Locality. In *Excavations in the Lubbub Creek Archaeological Locality*, edited by Christopher S. Peebles, pp. 138–193. Prehistoric Agricultural Communities in West Central Alabama, vol. 2. Museum of Anthropology, University of Michigan, Ann Arbor.

Anderson, David G.

1990 Stability and Change in Chiefdom-Level Societies: An Examination of Mississippian Political Evolution on the South Atlantic Slope. In *Lamar Archaeology: Mississippian Chiefdoms in the Deep South,* edited by Mark Williams and Gary Shapiro, pp. 187–213. University of Alabama Press, Tuscaloosa.

Ariès, Philippe

1981 *The Hour of Our Death.* Alfred A. Knopf, New York.

Arnold, W. S., D. C. Marelli, T. M. Bert, D. S. Jones, and I. R. Quitmyer

1991 Habitat-Specific Growth of Hard Clams Mercenaria mercenaria (L.) from the Indian River, Florida. *Journal of Experimental Marine Biology and Ecology* 147:245–265.

Asch, Nancy B., and David L. Asch

1985 Archeobotany. In *The Hill Creek Homestead and the Late Mississippian Settlement in the Lower Illinois Valley*, edited by M. Conner, pp. 115–170. KAC Research Series 1. Center for American Archaeology, Kampsville, IL.

Aten, Lawrence E.

1981 Determining Seasonality of *Rangia cuneata* from Gulf Coast Shell Middens. *Bulletin of the Texas Archeological Society* 52:179–200.

Barker, Alex W., and Timothy R. Pauketat (editors)

1992 *Lords of the Southeast: Social Inequality and the Native Elites of Southeastern North America.* Archeological Papers of the American Anthropological Association No. 3. American Anthropological Association, Washington, D.C.

Benn, David W.

1998 Moon: A Fortified Mississippian-Period Village in Poinsett County, Arkansas. In *Changing Perspectives on the Archaeology of the Central Mississippi River Valley*, edited by Michael J. O'Brien and Robert C. Dunnell, pp. 225–257. University of Alabama Press, Tuscaloosa.

Bense, Judith A.

1985 (editor) *Hawkshaw: Prehistory and History in an Urban Neighborhood in Pensacola, Florida.* University of West Florida, Office of Cultural and Archaeological Research, Reports of Investigation No. 7. Pensacola.

1989 *The Pensacola Archaeological Survey.* Vol. 1. Pensacola Archaeological Society Publication No. 2. University of West Florida, Pensacola, Florida.

1994 *Archaeology of the Southeastern United States: Paleoindian to World War I.* Academic Press, New York.

Bigelow, A.

1853 Observations on some Mounds on the Tensaw River. *The American Journal of Science and Arts* 15(43), Art. 21, pp. 186–192.

Bitgood, Mark J.

1989 *The Baytown Period in the Upper Tensas Basin.* Lower Mississippi Survey Bulletin No. 12. Peabody Museum, Harvard University, Cambridge.

Blitz, John H.

1983 The Summerville I Community. In *Excavations in the Lubbub Creek Archaeological Locality*, edited by Christopher S. Peebles, pp. 254–278. Prehistoric Agricultural Communities in West Central Alabama, vol. 1. Museum of Anthropology, University of Michigan, Ann Arbor.

1993 *Ancient Chiefdoms of the Tombigbee.* University of Alabama Press, Tuscaloosa.

Blitz, John H., and Karl G. Lorenz

1999 The Early Mississippian Frontier in the Lower Chattahoochee Valley. Paper presented at the Symposium "Frontiers, Peripheries, and Backwaters: Social Formations at the Edges of the Mississippian World," 56th Annual Meeting of the Southeastern Archaeological Conference, Pensacola.

Blitz, John H., and C. Baxter Mann

2000 *Fisherfolk, Farmers, and Frenchmen: Archaeological Explorations on the Mississippi Gulf Coast.* Archaeological Report No. 30. Mississippi Department of Archives and History, Jackson.

Brain, Jeffrey P.

1979 *Tunica Treasure.* Papers of the Peabody Museum of Archaeology and Ethnology 71. Harvard University, Cambridge.

1988 *Tunica Archaeology.* Papers of the Peabody Museum of Archaeology and Ethnology 78. Harvard University, Cambridge.

1989 *Winterville: Late Prehistoric Culture Contact in the Lower Mississippi Valley.* Archaeological Report No. 23. Mississippi Department of Archives and History, Jackson.

Brandon, Jamie C., and Robert C. Mainfort, Jr.

1995 Textile Impressed Ceramics from the Oliver Site, Obion County, Tennessee. *Tennessee Anthropologist* 20(1):58–73.

Brose, David S.

1983 Rethinking the French Presence in the Upper Great Lakes. In *Lulu Linear Punctated: Papers in Honor of George Irving Quimby*, edited by Robert C. Dunnell and Donald K. Grayson, pp. 209–252. Anthropological Papers 72. Museum of Anthropology, University of Michigan, Ann Arbor.

1984 Mississippian Period Cultures in Northwestern Florida. In *Perspectives on Gulf Coast Prehistory*, edited by David D. Davis, pp. 165–197. Ripley P. Bullen Monographs in Anthropology and History No. 5. University Press of Florida, Gainesville.

1985 "Willey-Nilly" or the Archaeology of Northwest Florida and Adjacent Borderlands Revisited. *Florida Anthropologist* 38(1–2):156–162.

1990 Apalachee Impostors? Paper presented at the 47th Annual Meeting of the Southeastern Archaeological Conference, Mobile, Alabama.

1991 *Yesterday's River: The Archaeology of 10,000 Years along the Tennessee-Tombigbee Waterway*. The Cleveland Museum of Natural History, Cleveland, and the U.S. Army Corps of Engineers, Mobile.

2001 Introduction to Eastern North America at the Dawn of European Colonization. In *Societies in Eclipse: Archaeology of the Eastern Woodland Indians, A.D. 1400–1700*, edited by David S. Brose, C. Wesley Cowan, and Robert C. Mainfort, Jr., pp. 1–7. Smithsonian Institution Press, Washington, D.C.

2002 Museum Paradigms and the History of Southeastern Archaeology. In *Histories of Southeastern Archaeology*, edited by Shannon Tushingham, Jane Hill, and Charles H. McNutt, pp. 13–25. University of Alabama Press, Tuscaloosa.

Brose, David S., Patricia Essenpreis, John Scarry, Helga Bluestone, Anne Forsythe and W. B. Clapham, III

1976 Contributions to the Archaeology of West Florida: The 1970–72 Field Seasons at the Cayson Site (8Ca3) and the Yon Site (8Li2). *Anthropology Department Reports in Archaeology* 2: 1–143. Case Western Reserve University, Cleveland.

Brose, David S., Ned J. Jenkins, and Russell Weisman

1983 *Cultural Resources Reconnaissance Study of the Black Warrior–Tombigbee System Corridor, Alabama, Volume 1, Archaeology*. Report Submitted to the U.S. Army Corps of Engineers, Mobile District. Department of Geology and Geography, University of South Alabama, Mobile.

Brose, David S., and George W. Percy

1978 Fort Walton Settlement Patterns. In *Mississippian Settlement Patterns*, edited by Bruce D. Smith, pp. 81–114. Academic Press, New York.

Brose, David S., and Nancy M. White

1999 Introduction: Clarence B. Moore's Work in Northwest Florida, 1901–1918. In *The Northwest Florida Expeditions of Clarence Bloomfield Moore*, edited by D. Brose and N. M. White, pp. 1–41. Classics in Southeastern Archaeology. University of Alabama Press, Tuscaloosa.

Brown, Ian W.

1979 *Early 18th Century French-Indian Culture Contact in the Yazoo Bluffs*

Region of the Lower Mississippi Valley. Ph.D. dissertation, Department of Anthropology, Brown University, Providence, Rhode Island.

1980 *Salt and the Eastern North American Indian: An Archaeological Study*. Lower Mississippi Survey Bulletin No. 6. Peabody Museum of Archaeology and Ethnology, Harvard University, Cambridge.

1982 *The Southeastern Check Stamped Pottery Tradition: A View from Louisiana*. Midcontinental Journal of Archaeology Special Paper No. 4. Kent State University Press, Kent, Ohio.

1984 Late Prehistory in Coastal Louisiana: The Coles Creek Period. In *Perspectives on Gulf Coast Prehistory*, edited by Dave D. Davis, pp. 94–124. Ripley P. Bullen Monographs in Anthropology and History No. 5. University Press of Florida, Gainesville.

1985 *Natchez Indian Archaeology: Culture Change and Stability in the Lower Mississippi Valley*. Archaeological Report No. 15. Mississippi Department of Archives and History, Jackson.

1988 Some Thoughts on the Shrimping Hypothesis and Coastal Ceramic Diversity in the Lake Pontchartrain Region. *Mississippi Archaeology* 23(1): 34–42.

1993 Recent Investigations at the Bottle Creek Site, Baldwin County, Alabama. Paper presented at the 1993 Alabama Archaeological Society Annual Winter Meeting, Decatur, Alabama.

1994 The Bottle Creek Project, 1993 Excavations: Interim Report to the National Endowment for the Humanities. Gulf Coast Survey, Alabama Museum of Natural History, University of Alabama, Tuscaloosa.

1995 The Bottle Creek Project, 1994 Excavations: Interim Report to the National Endowment for the Humanities (RO-22516–92). Gulf Coast Survey, Alabama Museum of Natural History, University of Alabama, Tuscaloosa.

1998 *Decorated Pottery of the Lower Mississippi Valley: A Sorting Manual*. Mississippi Archaeological Association and Mississippi Department of Archives and History, Jackson.

1999 Contact, Communication, and Exchange: Some Thoughts on the Rapid Movement of Ideas and Objects. In *Raw Materials and Exchange in the Mid-South*, edited by Evan Peacock and Samuel O. Brookes, pp. 132–141. Archaeological Report No. 29. Mississippi Department of Archives and History, Jackson.

2002 An Archaeological Survey in Clarke County, Alabama. Report Submitted to the Alabama Historical Commission, Montgomery. Gulf Coast Survey, Alabama Museum of Natural History, University of Alabama, Tuscaloosa.

n.d. Bottle Creek Reflections. Unpublished ms. Gulf Coast Survey, Alabama Museum of Natural History, University of Alabama, Tuscaloosa.

Brown, Ian W., and Richard S. Fuller

1991 Recent Archaeological Investigation at Bottle Creek (1Ba2), a Pensacola Mound Center in the Mobile-Tensaw Delta. Paper presented at the 48th Annual Meeting of the Southeastern Archaeological Conference, Jackson, Mississippi.

1993a (editors) *Bottle Creek Research: Working Papers on the Bottle Creek Site (1Ba2), Baldwin County, Alabama.* Journal of Alabama Archaeology 39(1–2).

1993b A Preliminary Report on Gulf Coast Survey Excavations at the Bottle Creek Site, 1991. In *Bottle Creek Research: Working Papers on the Bottle Creek Site (1Ba2), Baldwin County, Alabama,* edited by Ian W. Brown and Richard S. Fuller, pp. 151–169. Journal of Alabama Archaeology 39(1–2).

1999 Master Plan for Managing the Bottle Creek Site National Historic Landmark. Report to the Alabama Historical Commission (Grant #97–15–0022). Gulf Coast Survey, Alabama Museum of Natural History, University of Alabama, Tuscaloosa.

Brown, James A.

1976 *Spiro Studies,* vol. 4. University of Oklahoma, Norman.

Burch, J. B.

1989 *North American Freshwater Snails.* Malacological Publications, Hamburg, Michigan.

Bushnell, David I.

1906 The Sloane Collection in the British Museum. *American Anthropologist* 8:671–685.

Caldwell, Joseph R.

1958 *Trend and Tradition in the Prehistory of the Eastern United States.* American Anthropological Association, Memoir No. 88 and Illinois State Museum, Scientific Papers Vol. 10. Springfield, Illinois.

Campbell, T. N.

1959 Choctaw Subsistence: Ethnographic Notes from the Lincecum Manuscript. *Florida Anthropologist* 12(1):9–24.

Cantor, George

1993 *North American Indian Landmarks: A Traveler's Guide.* Visible Ink Press, Detroit.

Chapman, Jefferson, and Andrea B. Shea

1981 The Archaeobotanical Record: Early Archaic Period to Contact in the Lower Little Tennessee River Valley. *Tennessee Anthropologist* 6(1):61–84.

Chase, David W.

1998 Prehistoric Pottery of Central Alabama. *Journal of Alabama Archaeology* 44(1–2):52–98.

Clare, T[homas]

1981 *Archaeological Sites of the Lake District.* Frome Moorland Publishing, Asbourne, Derbyshire, England.

Connolly, Robert P.

1996 *Middle Woodland Period Hilltop Enclosures.* Ph.D. dissertation, University of Illinois at Urbana-Champaign.

1998 Architectural Grammar Rules at the Fort Ancient Hilltop Enclosure. In *Ancient Earthen Enclosures of the Eastern Woodlands,* edited by R. C. Mainfort, Jr., and L. P. Sullivan, pp. 85–113. University Press of Florida, Gainesville.

Curren, Cailup B., Jr.
1976 Prehistoric and Early Historic Occupation of the Mobile Bay and Mobile Delta Area of Alabama with an Emphasis on Subsistence. *Journal of Alabama Archaeology* 22(1):61–84.
1978 The Zooarchaeology of the D'Olive Creek Site (1Ba196). *Journal of Alabama Archaeology* 24(1):33–51.

Curren, Caleb
1992 *Archeology in the Mauvila Chiefdom: Native and Spanish Contacts during the Soto and Luna Expeditions.* The Mauvila Project of the Mobile Historic Development Commission, Mobile.

Dahlberg, M. E.
1975 *Guide to Coastal Fishes of Georgia and Nearby States.* University of Georgia Press, Athens.

Davis, Dave D.
1981 Ceramic Classification and Temporal Discrimination: A Consideration of Later Prehistoric Stylistic Change in the Mississippi River Delta. *Midcontinental Journal of Archaeology* 6(1):55–89.
1984a (editor) *Perspectives on Gulf Coast Prehistory.* Ripley P. Bullen Monographs in Anthropology and History No. 5. University Press of Florida, Gainesville.
1984b Protohistoric Cultural Interaction along the Northern Gulf Coast. In *Perspectives on Gulf Coast Prehistory*, edited by Dave D. Davis, pp. 216–231. Ripley P. Bullen Monographs in Anthropology and History No. 5. University Press of Florida, Gainesville.

DeJarnette, David L. (editor)
1976 *Highway Salvage Excavations at Two French Colonial Period Indian Sites on Mobile Bay, Alabama.* Report Submitted to the Alabama Highway Department, Montgomery. University of Alabama Museums, Tuscaloosa.

Delisle, Guillaume
1718 "Carte de la Louisiane et du Cours du Mississipi [*sic*]" with inset "Carte Particuliere des Embouchures de la Rivie. S. Louis et de la Mobile." Reproduced in *The Southeast in Early Maps*, 3rd ed., by William P. Cumming, pp. 212–214, Map 170. University of North Carolina, Chapel Hill, 1998.

Demel, Scott J., and Robert L. Hall
1998 The Mississippian Town Plan and Cultural Landscape of Cahokia, Illinois. In *Mississippian Towns and Sacred Spaces: Searching for an Architectural Grammar*, edited by R. B. Lewis and C. Stout, pp. 200–226. University of Alabama Press, Tuscaloosa.

DiBlasi, Philip J.
1996 Prehistoric Expressions from the Central Kentucky Karst. In *Of Caves and Shell Mounds*, edited by Kenneth C. Carstens and Patty Jo Watson, pp. 40–47. University of Alabama Press, Tuscaloosa.

Dobyns, Henry F.
1983 *Their Number Become Thinned: Native American Population Dynamics in Eastern North America.* University of Tennessee Press, Knoxville.

Dodd, J. Robert, and Robert J. Stanton, Jr.
1981 *Paleoecology, Concepts and Applications.* John Wiley and Sons, New York.

Drooker, Penelope B.
1991 Mississippian Lace: A Complex Textile Impressed on Pottery from the Stone Site, Tennessee. *Southeastern Archaeology* 10(2):79–97.
1992 *Mississippian Village Textiles at Wickliffe.* University of Alabama Press, Tuscaloosa.
1993 Matting and Fabric Impressions from Bottle Creek. In *Bottle Creek Research: Working Papers on the Bottle Creek Site (1Ba2), Baldwin County, Alabama,* edited by Ian W. Brown and Richard S. Fuller, pp. 115–132. Journal of Alabama Archaeology 39(1–2).
1995 Fabrics Impressed on Pottery at the Bottle Creek Site (1Ba2), Alabama. Report Submitted to Gulf Coast Survey, Alabama Museum of Natural History, University of Alabama, Tuscaloosa.

Duggan, Betty J., and Brett H. Riggs
1991 *Studies in Cherokee Basketry.* Occasional Paper No. 9. Frank H. McClung Museum, University of Tennessee, Knoxville.

du Ru, Paul
1934 *Journal of Paul du Ru (February 1 to May 8, 1700), Missionary/Priest of Louisiana,* translated by Ruth L. Butler. Caxton Club, Chicago.

Earle, Timothy K.
1987 Chiefdoms in Archaeological and Ethnohistorical Perspective. *Annual Review of Anthropology* 16:279–308.
1991 *Chiefdoms: Power, Economy, and Ideology.* Cambridge University Press, Cambridge.

Eliade, Mircea
1959 *The Sacred and the Profane.* Harcourt and Brace, New York.

Emerson, Thomas E.
1997 *Cahokia and the Archaeology of Power.* University of Alabama Press, Tuscaloosa.

Ensor, H. Blaine
1980 An Evaluation and Synthesis of Changing Lithic Technologies in the Central Tombigbee Valley. *Southeastern Archaeological Conference Bulletin* 22:83–90.
1981 *Gainesville Lake Area Lithics: Chronology, Technology and Use.* Archaeological Investigations in the Gainesville Lake Area of the Tennessee-Tombigbee Waterway, vol. 3. Report of Investigations No. 13. Office of Archaeological Research, University of Alabama, Tuscaloosa.
1991 The Lubbub Creek Microlith Industry. *Southeastern Archaeology* 10(1): 18–39.
1993 *Historic Resources Assessment, Tennessee-Tombigbee Waterway Wildlife Mitigation Project, Mobile and Tensaw River Deltas, Alabama.* Report Submitted to the U.S. Army Corps of Engineers, Mobile District, Contract No. DACW01–92–P-1563. Panamerican Consultants, Tuscaloosa, Alabama.

Ford, James A.
1951 *Greenhouse: A Troyville-Coles Creek Period Site in Avoyelles Parish,*

Louisiana. Anthropological Papers of the American Museum of Natural History, Vol. 44, Pt. 1. New York.

Ford, Richard I.

1973 The Moccasin Bluff Corn Holes. In *The Moccasin Bluff Site and the Late Woodland Cultures of Southwestern Michigan,* edited by R. Betteral and H. Smith, pp. 188–197. Museum of Anthropology, University of Michigan, Anthropological Papers No. 49. Ann Arbor.

Fowler, Melvin L. (editor)

1973 *Explorations into Cahokia Archaeology.* Revised edition. Bulletin 7, Illinois Archaeological Survey, Urbana. Originally published 1969.

Frake, Charles O.

1996 Pleasant Places, Past Times, and Sheltered Identity in Rural East Anglia. In *Senses of Place,* edited by Steven Field and Keith H. Basso, pp. 229–257. School of American Research Press, Santa Fe, New Mexico.

Fried, Morton H.

1967 *The Evolution of Political Society.* Random House, New York.

Fritz, Gayle J.

1987 The Trajectory of Knotweed Domestication in Prehistoric Eastern North America. Paper presented at the 10th Annual Meeting of the Society of Ethnobiology, Gainesville, Florida.

Fuller, Richard S.

1992 Mississippian Canoes in the Deep South: Examples from Mississippi and Alabama. Paper presented at the 49th Annual Meeting of the Southeastern Archaeological Conference, Little Rock, Arkansas.

1996 Mississippi through Early Historic Period Shell Tempered Pottery in the Pensacola Culture Area: How to Classify Types, Varieties, and Modes (Version 1.2). Unpublished ms. on file at Gulf Coast Survey, Alabama Museum of Natural History, University of Alabama, Tuscaloosa.

1998 Indian Pottery and Cultural Chronology of the Mobile-Tensaw Basin and Alabama Coast. *Journal of Alabama Archaeology* 44(1–2):1–51.

Fuller, Richard S., and Ian W. Brown

1992a Recent Archaeological Investigations at Bottle Creek (1Ba2), a Mississippian Mound Center in the Mobile-Tensaw Delta of Southwest Alabama. Paper presented at the 57th Annual Meeting of the Society for American Archaeology, Pittsburgh.

1992b Recent Research at the Bottle Creek Mounds, SW Alabama. *Lamar Briefs* No. 19, pp. 5–6. Watkinsville, Georgia.

1993a Analysis of Bottle Creek Pottery at the Alabama Museum of Natural History. In *Bottle Creek Research: Working Papers on the Bottle Creek Site (1Ba2), Baldwin County, Alabama,* edited by Ian W. Brown and Richard S. Fuller, pp. 36–114. Journal of Alabama Archaeology 39(1–2).

1993b Archaeological Phases and Complexes of the Mobile Basin and Alabama Gulf Coast from 1200 B.C. to the Historic Period. Unpublished ms. on file at Gulf Coast Survey, Alabama Museum of Natural History, University of Alabama, Tuscaloosa.

1994 Recent Excavations at Bottle Creek. Paper Presented at the Winter Meeting of the Alabama Archaeological Society, Troy.

1995a The Mystery of Mound Island. *Nature South* 5(1):4–10.

1995b Sites in the Hood: Archaeological Survey in the Vicinity of Bottle Creek. Paper Presented at the Winter Meeting of the Alabama Archaeological Society, Selma.

1996–99 The Indians of Mound Island: Archaeology in the Mobile-Tensaw Delta. An Exhibition at the Alabama Museum of Natural History, Tuscaloosa, Alabama (April 1996–November 1997) and Baldwin County Courthouse, Bay Minette, Alabama (November 1997–March 1999).

1998 *The Mound Island Project: An Archaeological Survey in the Mobile-Tensaw Delta.* Alabama Museum of Natural History Bulletin No. 19. Tuscaloosa.

Fuller, Richard S., and Diane Silvia Fuller

1987 *Excavations at Morgan, a Coles Creek Mound Complex in Coastal Louisiana.* Lower Mississippi Survey Bulletin No. 11. Peabody Museum, Harvard University, Cambridge.

Fuller, Richard S. and Diane E. Silvia

1984 Ceramic Rim Effigies in Southwest Alabama. *Journal of Alabama Archaeology* 30(1): 1–48.

Fuller, Richard S., Diane E. Silvia, and Noel R. Stowe

1984 *The Forks Project: An Investigation of the Late Prehistoric–Early Historic Transition in the Alabama-Tombigbee Confluence Basin (Phase I: Preliminary Survey).* Report Submitted to the Alabama Historical Commission. University of South Alabama, Archaeological Research Laboratory, Mobile.

Fuller, Richard S., and Noel R. Stowe

1982 A Proposed Typology for Late Shell Tempered Ceramics in the Mobile Bay/Mobile-Tensaw Delta Region. In *Archaeology in Southwest Alabama: A Collection of Papers,* edited by Cailup B. Curren, Jr., pp. 45–93. Alabama Tombigbee Regional Commission, Camden.

Fundabark, Emma L., and Mary D. F. Foreman

1957 *Sun Circles and Human Hands: The Southeastern Indians, Art, and Industries.* Emma Lila Fundabark, Luverne, Alabama.

Galloway, Patricia K.

1993 Ethnohistory. In *The Development of Southeastern Archaeology,* edited by Jay K. Johnson, pp. 78–108. University of Alabama Press, Tuscaloosa.

Geertz, Clifford

1996 Afterword. In *Senses of Place,* edited by Steven Field and Keith H. Basso, pp. 259–262. School of American Research Press, Santa Fe, New Mexico.

Giardino, Marco J.

1985 *Ceramic Attribute Analysis and Ethnic Group Composition: An Example from Southeastern Louisiana.* Ph.D. dissertation, Department of Anthropology, Tulane University, New Orleans.

Gibson, Jon L.

1998 Broken Circles, Owl Monsters, and Black Earth Midden: Separating Sacred and Secular at Poverty Point. In *Ancient Earthen Enclosures of the Eastern Woodlands,* edited by R. C. Mainfort, Jr., and L. P. Sullivan, pp. 17–30. University Press of Florida, Gainesville.

2000 *The Ancient Mounds of Poverty Point: Place of Rings.* University Press of Florida, Gainesville.

Gilliland, Marion S.

1975 *The Material Culture of Key Marco.* University Press of Florida, Gainesville.

1989 *Key Marco's Buried Treasure: Archaeology and Adventure in the Nineteenth Century.* Ripley P. Bullen Monographs in Anthropology and History No. 8. University of Florida Press and Florida Museum of Natural History, Gainesville.

Gingerich, P. D.

1989 *New Earliest Wasatchain Mammalian Fauna from the Eocene of Northwestern Wyoming: Composition and Diversity in a Rarely Sampled High-Floodplain Assemblage.* University of Michigan, Papers on Paleontology No. 28. Ann Arbor.

Goggin, John M.

1949 Cultural Traditions in Florida Prehistory. In *The Florida Indian and His Neighbors,* edited by John W. Griffin, pp. 13–44. Rollins College Inter-American Center, Winter Park, Florida.

Greenwell, Dale

1984 The Mississippi Gulf Coast. In *Perspectives on Gulf Coast Prehistory,* edited by David D. Davis, pp. 125–155. Ripley P. Bullen Monographs in Anthropology and History No. 5. University Press of Florida, Gainesville.

Gregory, Hiram F., and Clarence H. Webb

1975 Chitimacha Basketry. *Louisiana Archaeology* 2:23–38.

Gremillion, Kristen J.

1993 Prehistoric Maize from Bottle Creek. In *Bottle Creek Research: Working Papers on the Bottle Creek Site (1Ba2), Baldwin County, Alabama,* edited by Ian W. Brown and Richard S. Fuller, pp. 133–150. Journal of Alabama Archaeology 39(1–2).

1996 Archaeobotany at Old Mobile. Paper presented at the Symposium "French Colonial Mobile, 1702–1711: An Archaeological Perspective," 53rd Annual Meeting of the Southeastern Archaeological Conference, Birmingham, Alabama.

Grimm, William C.

1966 *How to Recognize Shrubs.* Castle Books, New York.

Hally, David J.

1983a Use Alteration of Pottery Vessel Surfaces: An Important Source of Evidence for the Identification of Vessel Function. *North American Archaeologist* 4:1–25.

1983b The Interpretive Potential of Pottery from Domestic Contexts. *Midcontinental Journal of Archaeology* 8:163–196.

1986 The Identification of Vessel Function: A Case Study from Northwest Georgia. *American Antiquity* 51(2):267–295.

Hamilton, Peter J.

1976 *Colonial Mobile,* edited by C. G. Summersell. Reprinted. University of Alabama Press, Tuscaloosa. Originally published 1910.

Hamilton, T. M.
1980 *Colonial Frontier Guns.* Fur Press, Chadron, Nebraska.

Hammerstedt, Scott W.
2000 *Characteristics of Late Woodland and Mississippian Settlements in the Black Warrior Valley, Alabama.* M.A. thesis, Department of Anthropology, University of Alabama, Tuscaloosa.

Harper, Roland
1944 *Preliminary Report on the Weeds of Alabama.* Geological Survey of Alabama Bulletin 53. Tuscaloosa.

Harpur, James
1994 *The Atlas of Sacred Places: Meeting Points of Heaven and Earth.* Henry Holt & Co., New York.

Harris, Donald A.
1971 A French Colonial Well: Its Construction, Excavation and Contents. *The Conference on Historic Site Archaeology Papers 1970,* Vol. 5, Pt. 1, pp. 51–80.

Hatch, James W.
1995 Lamar Period Upland Farmsteads of the Oconee River Valley, Georgia. In *Mississippian Communities and Households,* edited by J. D. Rogers and B. D. Smith, pp. 135–155. University of Alabama Press, Tuscaloosa.

Haywick, Douglas W.
1995 Grain Size Analysis of Sediment Samples Collected by the Alabama Museum of Natural History. Unpublished ms. on file at Gulf Coast Survey, Alabama Museum of Natural History, University of Alabama, Tuscaloosa.

Heldman, Donald P.
1973 *Archaeological Investigations of Fort Toulouse: 1972–73.* Report Submitted to the Alabama Historical Commission and the National Park Service (Grant No. 1–01–72–00021), Montgomery and Washington, D.C.

Henson, B. Bart
1986 Art in Mud and Stone: Mud Glyphs and Petroglyphs in the Southeast. In *The Prehistoric Native American Art of Mud Glyph Cave,* edited by Charles H. Faulkner, pp. 81–108. University of Tennessee Press, Knoxville.

Higginbotham, Jay
1991 *Old Mobile, Fort Louis de la Louisiane, 1702–1711.* Reprinted. University of Alabama Press, Tuscaloosa. Originally published 1977, University of Alabama Press, Tuscaloosa.

Hill, Sarah H.
1997 *Weaving New Worlds: Southeastern Cherokee Women and Their Basketry.* University of North Carolina Press, Chapel Hill.

Hirth, Kenneth G.
1978 Interregional Trade and the Formation of Prehistoric Gateway Communities. *American Antiquity* 43(1):35–45.

Hoard, Dorothy
1989 *A Guide to Bandelier National Monument,* 3rd ed. Los Alamos Historical Society, Los Alamos, New Mexico.

Holmes, Nicholas H., Jr.
1963 The Site on Bottle Creek. *Journal of Alabama Archaeology* 9(1):16–27.
Holmes, William H.
1896 Prehistoric Textile Art of the Eastern United States. *Thirteenth Annual Report of the Bureau of Ethnology to the Secretary of the Smithsonian Institution 1891–1892*, pp. 3–46. Government Printing Office, Washington, D.C.
1903 Aboriginal Pottery of the Eastern United States. In *Twentieth Annual Report of the Bureau of American Ethnology to the Secretary of the Smithsonian Institution 1898–99*, pp. 1–201. Government Printing Office, Washington, D.C.
Hudson, Charles (editor)
1979 *Black Drink: A Native American Tea.* University of Georgia Press, Athens.
Iseminger, William R., Timothy R. Pauketat, B. Koldehoff, L. S. Kelly, and Leonard Blake
1990 *The Archaeology of the Cahokia Palisade: The East Palisade Investigations.* Illinois Cultural Resources Study 14. Illinois Historic Preservation Agency, Springfield.
Jackson, H. Edwin
1991 The Trade Fair in Hunter-Gatherer Interaction: The Role of Intersocietal Trade in the Evolution of Poverty Point Culture. In *Between Bands and States,* edited by Susan A. Gregg, pp. 265–286. Occasional Paper 9. Center for Archaeological Investigations, Southern Illinois University, Carbondale.
Jackson, H. Edwin, and Susan L. Scott
1995 Mississippian Homestead and Village Subsistence Organization: Contrasts in Large-Mammal Remains from Two Sites. In *Mississippian Communities and Households,* edited by J. D. Rogers and B. D. Smith, pp. 181–200. University of Alabama Press, Tuscaloosa.
Jackson, Paul D.
1996 *An Examination of Late Woodland Features in the Tombigbee, Black Warrior, and Tennessee River Valleys.* M.A. thesis, Department of Anthropology, University of Alabama, Tuscaloosa.
2000 The Coeval Occupations of West Jefferson and Moundville I Phase Sites in West-Central Alabama. Paper presented at the 57th Annual Meeting of the Southeastern Archaeological Conference, Macon, Georgia.
2001 Late Woodland and Early Mississippian Transitions in the Black Warrior River Valley. Paper presented at the Symposium "Through a Glass Darkly: The Woodland-Mississippian Interface in Alabama Prehistory," 58th Annual Meeting of the Southeastern Archaeological Conference, Chattanooga, Tennessee.
Jenkins, Ned J.
1978 Prehistoric Chronology of the Lower Chattahoochee Valley: A Preliminary Statement. *Journal of Alabama Archaeology* 24(2):73–91.
2001 Terminal Woodland/Mississippian Development in the Warrior/Tombigbee Drainage. Paper presented at the Symposium "Through a Glass Darkly: The Woodland-Mississippian Interface in Alabama Prehistory,"

58th Annual Meeting of the Southeastern Archaeological Conference, Chattanooga, Tennessee.

Jenkins, Ned J., and H. Blaine Ensor

1981 *The Gainesville Lake Area Excavations.* Archaeological Investigations in the Gainesville Lake Area of the Tennessee-Tombigbee Waterway, vol. 1. Report of Investigations No. 11. Office of Archaeological Research, University of Alabama, Tuscaloosa.

Jenkins, Ned J., and Teresa Paglione

1982 Lower Alabama River Ceramic Chronology: A Tentative Assessment. In *Archaeology in Southwest Alabama: A Collection of Papers,* edited by Cailup B. Curren, Jr., pp. 5–18. Alabama Tombigbee Regional Commission, Camden.

Johannessen, Sissel

1993 Farmers of the Late Woodland. In *Foraging and Farming in the Eastern Woodlands,* edited by C. Margaret Scarry, pp. 57–77. University Press of Florida, Gainesville.

Jones, Walter B., and David L. DeJarnette

1933 *Sixth Annual Report to the Board of Regents of the Alabama Museum of Natural History.* Alabama Museum of Natural History, University of Alabama, Tuscaloosa.

Karklins, Karlis and Norman F. Barka

1989 The Beads of St. Eustatius, Netherlands Antilles. *Journal of the Society of Bead Research* 1:55–80.

Kidder, Tristram R.

1998 Mississippi Period Mound Groups and Communities in the Lower Mississippi Valley. In *Mississippian Towns and Sacred Spaces: Searching for an Architectural Grammar,* edited by R. B. Lewis and C. Stout, pp. 123–150. University of Alabama Press, Tuscaloosa.

King, Frances B.

1987 *Prehistoric Maize in Eastern North America: An Evolutionary Evaluation.* Ph.D. dissertation, Department of Anthropology, University of Illinois, Urbana-Champaign.

1994 Variability in Cob and Kernel Characteristics on North American Maize Cultivars. In *Corn and Culture in the Prehistoric New World,* edited by S. Johannessen and C. Hastorf, pp. 35–54. Westview Press, Boulder, Colorado.

Kniffen, Fred B.

1936 A Preliminary Report on the Indian Mounds and Middens of Plaquemines and St. Bernard Parishes. In *Lower Mississippi River Delta, Reports on the Geology of Plaquemines and St. Bernard Parishes,* pp. 407–422. Department of Conservation, Louisiana Geological Survey, Geological Bulletin 8.

Knight, Vernon J., Jr.

1976 Ethnohistorical Research. In *Highway Salvage Excavations at Two French Colonial Period Indian Sites on Mobile Bay, Alabama,* edited by David B. DeJarnette, pp. 142–152. University of Alabama Museums, Tuscaloosa.

1977 The Mobile Bay-Mobile River Delta Region: Archaeological Status Report—July 1976. *Journal of Alabama Archaeology* 23(2):137–154.

1980 Comments on Brose and Percy's "Fort Walton Settlement Patterns." *Florida Journal of Anthropology* 5(1):20–25.

1984 Late Prehistoric Adaptation in the Mobile Bay Region. In *Perspectives on Gulf Coast Prehistory*, edited by David D. Davis, pp. 198–215. Ripley P. Bullen Monographs in Anthropology and History No. 5. University Press of Florida, Gainesville.

1987 Mississippian *Rangia* Middens and Aboriginal Fishing on Mobile Bay. Unpublished paper on file, University of Alabama, Office of Archaeological Services, Moundville, Alabama. Also presented at the 44th Annual Meeting of the Southeastern Archaeological Conference, Charleston, South Carolina as "Mobile Bay—West Florida: Evidence for Shrimp Procurement."

1989 Symbolism of Mississippian Mounds. In *Powhatan's Mantle: Indians in the Colonial Southeast*, edited by Peter H. Wood, Gregory A. Waselkov, and M. Thomas Hatley, pp. 279–291. University of Nebraska Press, Lincoln.

1992 Preliminary Report on Excavations at Mound Q, Moundville. Paper Presented at the 49th Annual Meeting of the Southeastern Archaeological Conference, Little Rock, Arkansas.

1995 Chronology and Use of Public Architecture at the Moundville Site: Excavations in Mounds R, E, F, and G. Second interim report, National Science Foundation award No. 0220568.

1996 (editor) *The Moundville Expeditions of Clarence Bloomfield Moore*. University of Alabama Press, Tuscaloosa.

1997 Some Developmental Parallels between Cahokia and Moundville. In *Cahokia: Domination and Ideology in the Mississippian World*, edited by Timothy R. Pauketat and Thomas E. Emerson, pp. 229–247. University of Nebraska Press, Lincoln.

1998 Moundville as a Diagrammatic Ceremonial Center. In *Archaeology of the Moundville Chiefdom*, edited by Vernon J. Knight, Jr., and Vincas P. Steponaitis, pp. 44–62. Smithsonian Institution Press, Washington, D.C.

2001 Characterizing Elite Midden Deposits at Moundville. Paper presented at the 66th Annual Meeting of the Society for American Archaeology, New Orleans.

Knight, Vernon J., Jr., and Sherée L. Adams

1981 A Voyage to the Mobile and Tomeh in 1700, with Notes on the Interior of Alabama. *Journal of Alabama Archaeology* 27(1):32–56.

Knight, Vernon J., Jr., and Vincas P. Steponaitis

1998 A New History of Moundville. In *Archaeology of the Moundville Chiefdom*, edited by Vernon J. Knight, Jr., and Vincas P. Steponaitis, pp. 1–25. Smithsonian Institution Press, Washington, D.C.

Krause, Richard A.

1988 *The Snodgrass Small Mound and Middle Tennessee Valley Prehistory*. Tennessee Valley Authority Publications in Anthropology No. 52. Tennessee Valley Authority, Chattanooga.

Kuttruff, Jenna T., Sandra G. DeHart, and Michael J. O'Brien

1998 7500 Years of Prehistoric Footwear from Arnold Research Cave, Missouri. *Science* 28(5373):132–137.

Lafferty, Robert H., III

1998 Landscape Change and Settlement Location in the Cairo Lowland of Southeastern Missouri. In *Changing Perspectives on the Archaeology of the Central Mississippi River Valley*, edited by Michael J. O'Brien and Robert C. Dunnell, pp. 124–147. University of Alabama Press, Tuscaloosa.

Lankford, George, Michael Rushing, and Gregory Spies

1976 A Summary of the Situation at 1Ba2: The "Bottle Creek Site." Unpublished ms. on file at Gulf Coast Survey, Alabama Museum of Natural History, University of Alabama, Tuscaloosa.

Larson, Lewis H.

1971 Archaeological Implications of Social Stratification at the Etowah Site, Georgia. In *Approaches to Social Dimensions of Mortuary Practices*, edited by James A. Brown, pp. 58–67. Society for American Archaeology, Memoir No. 25.

1980 *Aboriginal Subsistence Technology on the Southeastern Coastal Plain during the Late Prehistoric Period.* Ripley P. Bullen Monographs in Anthropology and History No. 2. University Press of Florida, Gainesville.

Lazarus, Yulee W., and Carolyn B. Hawkins

1976 *Pottery of the Fort Walton Period.* Temple Mound Museum, Fort Walton Beach, Florida.

Lee, C. H., I. R. Quitmyer, C. T. Espenshade, and R. E. Johnson

1984 *Estuarine Adaptations during the Late Prehistoric Period: Archaeology of Two Shell Midden Sites on the St. Johns River.* University of West Florida, Office of Cultural and Archaeological Research, Reports of Investigations No. 5. Pensacola.

Le Page du Pratz, Antoine S.

1763 *The History of Louisiana . . .* T. Becket and P. A. De Hondt, London.

Lewis, Clifford M.

1978 The Calusa. In *Tacachale: Essays on the Indians of Florida and Southeastern Georgia during the Historic Period*, edited by Jerald T. Milanich and Samuel Proctor, pp. 19–49. Ripley P. Bullen Monographs in Anthropology and History No. 1. University Press of Florida, Gainesville.

Lewis, R. Barry

1988 Fires on the Bayou: Cultural Adaptations in the Mississippi Sound Region. *Southeastern Archaeology* 7(2):109–123.

Lewis, R. Barry, and Charles Stout (editors)

1998a *Mississippian Towns and Sacred Spaces: Searching for an Architectural Grammar.* University of Alabama Press, Tuscaloosa.

1998b The Town as Metaphor. In *Mississippian Towns and Sacred Spaces: Searching for an Architectural Grammar*, edited by R. B. Lewis and C. Stout, pp. 227–241. University of Alabama Press, Tuscaloosa.

Lewis, R. Barry, Charles Stout, and Cameron B. Wesson

1998 The Design of Mississippian Towns. In *Mississippian Towns and Sacred*

Spaces: Searching for an Architectural Grammar, edited by R. B. Lewis and C. Stout, pp. 1–21. University of Alabama Press, Tuscaloosa.

Lindsey, Mrs. E. M.
1964 Cooper Farm Salvage Project. *Journal of Alabama Archaeology* 10:22–29.

Lopinot, Neal H.
1984 *Archaeobotanical Formation Processes and Late Middle Archaic Human-Plant Interrelationships in the Midcontinental U.S.A.* Ph.D. dissertation, Department of Anthropology, Southern Illinois University, Carbondale.

Luer, George P.
1989 Calusa Canals in Southwestern Florida: Routes of Tribute and Exchange. *Florida Anthropologist* 42(2):89–130.
1998 The Naples Canal: A Deep Indian Canoe Trail in Southwestern Florida. *Florida Anthropologist* 51(1):25–36.

Luer, George P., and Ryan J. Wheeler
1997 How the Pine Island Canal Worked: Topography, Hydraulics, and Engineering. *Florida Anthropologist* 50(3):115–131.

Mainfort, Robert C., Jr., and Lynne P. Sullivan
1998a (editors) *Ancient Earthen Enclosures of the Eastern Woodlands.* University Press of Florida, Gainesville.
1998b Explaining Earthen Enclosures. In *Ancient Earthen Enclosures of the Eastern Woodlands,* edited by R. C. Mainfort, Jr., and L. P. Sullivan, pp. 1–16. University Press of Florida, Gainesville.

Marquardt, William H.
1986 The Development of Cultural Complexity in Southwest Florida: Elements of a Critique. *Southeastern Archaeology* 5(1):63–70.
1992 (editor) *Culture and Environment in the Domain of the Calusa.* University of Florida, Institute of Archaeology and Paleoenvironmental Studies, Monograph No. 1. Gainesville.

Marrinan, Rochelle A., and Nancy M. White
1998 Smoke and Mirrors in Modeling Fort Walton Culture, Northwest Florida. Paper presented at the 55th Annual Meeting of the Southeastern Archaeological Conference, Greenville, South Carolina.

Martin, Alexander C., and William D. Barkley
1961 *Seed Identification Manual.* University of California Press, Berkeley.

Mason, Ronald J., and Gregory Perino
1961 Microblades at Cahokia, Illinois. *American Antiquity* 26(4): 553–557.

May, Edwin B.
1976 Holocene Sediments of Mobile Bay, Alabama. *Alabama Marine Resources Bulletin* 11:1–25. The Alabama Marine Resources Laboratory, Dauphin Island.

McGahey, Samuel O.
1974 A Prehistoric Dugout Canoe. *Mississippi Archaeology* 9(8):4–5.

McIntire, William G.
1958 *Prehistoric Indian Settlements of the Changing Mississippi River Delta.* Louisiana State University Studies, Coastal Studies Series No. 1. Louisiana State University Press, Baton Rouge.

McWilliams, Richebourg G. (translator and editor)
1981 *Iberville's Gulf Journals.* University of Alabama Press, University.
1988 *Fleur de Lys and Calumet: Being the Pénicaut Narrative of French Adventure in Louisiana.* Reprinted. University of Alabama Press, Tuscaloosa. Originally published 1953.

Medford, Claude, Jr.
1977 Chitimacha Split Cane Basketry: Weaves and Designs. *American Indian Art* 3(1):56–61, 101.

Mehrer, Mark W., and James M. Collins
1995 Household Archaeology at Cahokia and in Its Hinterlands. In *Mississippian Communities and Households,* edited by J. D. Rogers and B. D. Smith, pp. 32–57. University of Alabama Press, Tuscaloosa.

Mikell, Gregory A.
1992 The Fort Walton Mississippian Variant on the Northwest Florida Gulf Coast. *Southeastern Archaeology* 11(1):51–65.

Milanich, Jerald T.
1994 *Archaeology of Precolumbian Florida.* University Press of Florida, Gainesville.

Milanich, J. T., J. Chapman, A. S. Cordell, S. Hale, and R. A. Marrinan
1984 Prehistoric Development of Calusa Society in Southwest Florida: Excavations on Useppa Island. In *Perspectives on Gulf Coast Prehistory,* edited by David D. Davis, pp. 258–314. Ripley P. Bullen Monographs in Anthropology and History No. 5. University Press of Florida, Gainesville.

Miller, Joan
1988 Experimental Replication of Early Woodland Vegetal Fiber Slippers. *Southeastern Archaeology* 7(2):132–137.

Miller, Naomi F.
1988 Ratios in Paleoethnobotanical Analysis. In *Current Paleoethnobotany,* edited by C. Hastorf and V. Popper, pp. 72–85. University of Chicago Press, Chicago.

Milner, Claire McHale, and John M. O'Shea
1998 The Socioeconomic Role of Late Woodland Enclosures in Northern Lower Michigan. In *Ancient Earthen Enclosures of the Eastern Woodlands,* edited by R. C. Mainfort, Jr., and L. P. Sullivan, pp. 181–201. University Press of Florida, Gainesville.

Miner, Horace
1936 The Importance of Textiles in the Archaeology of the Eastern United States. *American Antiquity* 1(3):181–192.

Mistovich, Tim S.
1995 Toward an Explanation of Variation in Moundville Phase Households in the Black Warrior Valley, Alabama. In *Mississippian Communities and Households,* edited by J. D. Rogers and B. D. Smith, pp. 156–180. University of Alabama Press, Tuscaloosa.

Moore, Clarence B.
1899 Certain Aboriginal Remains of the Alabama River. *Journal of the Academy of Natural Sciences of Philadelphia* 11:289–337.
1905a Certain Aboriginal Remains of the Black Warrior River. *Journal of the*

Academy of Natural Sciences of Philadelphia 13:125–244. In *The Moundville Expeditions of Clarence Bloomfield Moore,* edited by V. J. Knight, Jr., pp. 21–142. University of Alabama Press, Tuscaloosa (1996).
1905b Certain Aboriginal Remains of Mobile Bay and on Mississippi Sound. *Journal of the Academy of Natural Sciences of Philadelphia* 13:279–297.
1907 Moundville Revisited. *Journal of the Academy of Natural Sciences of Philadelphia* 13:337–405. Reprinted in *The Moundville Expeditions of Clarence B. Moore,* edited by V. J. Knight, Jr., pp. 143–224. University of Alabama Press, Tuscaloosa (1996).

Moorehead, Warren K.
1890 *Fort Ancient: The Great Prehistoric Earthwork of Warren County, Ohio.* Robert Clarke and Co., Cincinnati.
1932 *Etowah Papers.* Published for Phillips Academy by the Yale University Press, New Haven.

Morgan, David W.
2001 The Late Woodland/Early Mississippi Period Transition in Southwest Alabama: Colonization or *In Situ* Development? Paper presented at the Symposium "Through a Glass Darkly: The Woodland-Mississippian Interface in Alabama Prehistory," 58th Annual Meeting of the Southeastern Archaeological Conference, Chattanooga, Tennessee.

Morse, Dan F., and Louis Tesar
1974 A Microlithic Tool Assemblage from a North West Florida Site. *Florida Anthropologist* 27(2):89–106.

Muller, Jon
1984 Mississippian Specialization and Salt. *American Antiquity* 49(3):489–507.

Muniz, M.
1994 A Sclerochronological Assessment of Harvesting Pressure on *Rangia cuneata* from Bottle Creek, Alabama. Unpublished ms. on file at Environmental Archaeology Laboratory, Department of Anthropology, Florida Museum of Natural History, Gainesville.

Nass, John P., Jr., and Richard W. Yerkes
1995 Social Differentiation in Mississippian and Fort Ancient Societies. In *Mississippian Communities and Households,* edited by J. D. Rogers and B. D. Smith, pp. 58–80. University of Alabama Press, Tuscaloosa.

Neitzel, Robert S.
1965 *Archeology of the Fatherland Site: the Grand Village of the Natchez.* Anthropological Papers of the American Museum of Natural History, Vol. 51, Pt. 1. New York.

Neuman, Robert W.
1990 *An Introduction to Louisiana Archaeology.* Reprinted. Louisiana State University Press, Baton Rouge. Originally published 1984.

Newsom, Lee A., and Barbara A. Purdy
1990 Florida Canoes: A Maritime Heritage from the Past. *Florida Anthropologist* 43(3):164–180.

Nickerson, Norton H.
1953 Variation in Cob Morphology among Certain Archaeological and Ethno-

logical Races of Maize. *Annals of the Missouri Botanical Gardens* 40: 79–111.

O'Neill, Charles E. (editor)

1977 *Charlevoix's Louisiana: Selections from the History and the Journal,* by Pierre F. X. de Charlevoix. Louisiana State University Press, Baton Rouge.

Pauketat, Timothy R.

1987a A Functional Consideration of a Mississippian Domestic Vessel Assemblage. *Southeastern Archaeology* 6:1–15.

1987b Mississippian Domestic Economy and Formation Processes: A Response to Prentice. *Midcontinental Journal of Archaeology* 12(1):77–88.

1994 *The Ascent of Chiefs.* University of Alabama Press, Tuscaloosa.

Peebles, Christopher S.

1978 Determinants of Settlement Size and Location in the Moundville Phase. In *Mississippian Settlement Patterns,* edited by Bruce D. Smith, pp. 369–416. Academic Press, New York.

Peebles, Christopher S., and Susan M. Kus

1977 Some Archaeological Correlates of Ranked Societies. *American Antiquity* 42(3):421–448.

Pertulla, Timothy K.

1998 Powers Fort: A Middle Mississippian–Period Fortified Community in the Western Lowlands of Missouri. In *Changing Perspectives on the Archaeology of the Central Mississippi River Valley,* edited by Michael J. O'Brien and Robert C. Dunnell, pp. 169–199. University of Alabama Press, Tuscaloosa.

Peters, Robert H.

1983 *The Ecological Implications of Body Size.* Cambridge University Press, Cambridge.

Phelps, David S.

1989 *Ancient Pots and Dugout Canoes: Indian Life as Revealed by Archaeology at Lake Phelps.* Pettigrew State Park, Creswell, North Carolina.

Phillips, John C.

1989 *Archaeological Testing of the Hickory Ridge Site (8Es1280): A Mississippian Stage Cemetery in Escambia County, Florida.* Reports of Investigation No. 26, Institute of West Florida Archaeology, University of West Florida, Pensacola.

Phillips, Philip

1970 *Archaeological Survey in the Lower Yazoo Basin, Mississippi, 1949–1955,* 2 vols. Papers of the Peabody Museum of Archaeology and Ethnology 60. Harvard University, Cambridge.

Pope, Melody K.

1986 Microdrills from the Moundville Region: Technology, Function and Context. Paper presented at the 43rd Annual Meeting of the Southeastern Archaeological Conference, Nashville.

1989 *Microtools from the Black Warrior Valley: Technology, Use, and Context.* M.A. thesis, Department of Anthropology, State University of New York, Binghamton.

Powell, Mary L.
1991 Ranked Status and Health in the Mississippian Chiefdom at Moundville. In *What Mean These Bones? Studies in Southeastern Bioarchaeology*, edited by Mary L. Powell, Patricia S. Bridges, and Ann M. W. Mires, pp. 22–51. University of Alabama Press, Tuscaloosa.
1998 Of Time and the River: Perspectives on Health during the Moundville Chiefdom. In *Archaeology of the Moundville Chiefdom*, edited by Vernon J. Knight, Jr., and Vincas P. Steponaitis, pp. 102–119. Smithsonian Institution Press, Washington, D.C.

Prentice, Guy
1983 Cottage Industries: Concepts and Implications. *Midcontinental Journal of Archaeology* 8(1):17–48.
1985 Economic Differentiation among Mississippian Farmsteads. *Midcontinental Journal of Archaeology* 10(1):77–122.

Pyle-Spring, Devon
1989 Analysis of the Collection—1Ba2. Unpublished senior project in Archaeological Studies, Oberlin College, Oberlin, Ohio.

Quitmyer, Irvy R.
1985 Zooarchaeological Methods for the Analysis of Shell Middens at Kings Bay. In *Aboriginal Subsistence and Settlement Archaeology of the Kings Bay Locality, Vol. 2: Zooarchaeology*, edited by William H. Adams, pp. 33–48. Reports of Investigations No. 2. Department of Anthropology, University of Florida, Gainesville.

Quitmyer, Irvy R., H. Stephen Hale, and Douglas S. Jones
1985 Paleoseasonality Determination Based on Incremental Shell Growth in the Hard Clam, *Mercenaria mercenaria*, and Its Implications for the Analysis of Three Southeast Georgia Coastal Shell Middens. *Southeastern Archaeology* 4(1):27–40.

Quitmyer, Irvy R., and Douglas S. Jones
1992 Calendars of the Coast: Seasonal Growth Increment Patterns in Shells of Modern and Archaeological Southern Quahogs, *Mercenaria campechiensis*, from Charlotte Harbor, Florida. In *Culture and the Environment in the Domain of the Calusa*, edited by William H. Marquardt, pp. 247–264. University of Florida, Institute of Archaeology and Paleoenvironmental Studies, Monograph 1. Gainesville.
2000 The Over Exploitation of Hard Clams (*Mercenaria* spp.) from Five Archaeological Sites in the Southeastern United States. *Florida Anthropologist* 3(2–3):158–168.

Ramenofsky, Ann F.
1987 *Vectors of Death: The Archaeology of European Contact*. University of New Mexico Press, Albuquerque.

Reitz, Elizabeth J.
1982 Availability and Use of Fish along Coastal Georgia and Florida. *Southeastern Archaeology* 1(1):65–88.

Reitz, Elizabeth J., and Dan Cordier
1983 Use of Allometry in Zooarchaeological Analysis. In *Animals and Archae-*

ology: Shell Middens, Fishes, and Birds, edited by J. Clutton-Brock and C. Grigson, pp. 237–252. BAR International Series No. 183, London.

Reitz, Elizabeth J., and Irvy R. Quitmyer

1988 Faunal Remains from Two Coastal Georgia Swift Creek Sites. *Southeastern Archaeology* 7(2):95–108.

Reitz, Elizabeth J., Irvy R. Quitmyer, H. Stephen Hale, Sylvia J. Scudder, and Elizabeth S. Wing

1987 Application of Allometry to Zooarchaeology. *American Antiquity* 52(2): 304–317.

Reitz, Elizabeth J., and Elizabeth S. Wing

1999 *Zooarchaeology.* Cambridge University Press, Cambridge.

Riordan, Robert V.

1998 Boundaries, Resistance, and Control: Enclosing the Hilltops in Middle Woodland Ohio. In *Ancient Earthen Enclosures of the Eastern Woodlands,* edited by R. C. Mainfort, Jr., and L. P. Sullivan, pp. 68–84. University Press of Florida, Gainesville.

Rodning, Christopher B.

1994 *The Role of Waterways in Mississippian Occupation of the Mobile Basin, Southwestern Alabama.* Honors thesis, Department of Anthropology, Harvard University, Cambridge.

Rogers, J. Daniel

1995 The Archaeological Analysis of Domestic Organization. In *Mississippian Communities and Households,* edited by J. D. Rogers and B. D. Smith, pp. 7–31. University of Alabama Press, Tuscaloosa.

Rogers, J. Daniel, and Bruce D. Smith (editors)

1995 *Mississippian Communities and Households.* University of Alabama Press, Tuscaloosa.

Rushing, Michael T.

1976 Description of the Bottle Creek Site. Paper Presented at the French Regime Symposium, Mobile, Alabama.

Russo, M., Ann S. Cordell, Lee Newsom, and S. Scudder

1991 *Faunal Report on Horr's Island: The Archaeology of the Archaic and Glades Settlement and Subsistence Patterns.* Key Marco Developments, Marco Island, Florida.

Sahlins, Marshall

1972 *Stone Age Economics.* Aldine, Chicago.

Scarry, C. Margaret

1986 *Change in Plant Procurement and Production during the Emergence of the Moundville Chiefdom.* Ph.D. dissertation, Department of Anthropology, University of Michigan, Ann Arbor.

1993a Plant Remains from the Big Sandy Farms Site (1Tu552), Tuscaloosa County, Alabama. In *Big Sandy Farms: A Prehistoric Agricultural Community Near Moundville, Black Warrior River Floodplain, Tuscaloosa County, Alabama,* by H. B. Ensor, pp. 205–233. Report of Investigations No. 68. Alabama Museum of Natural History, Division of Archaeology, Tuscaloosa.

1993b Variability in Mississippian Crop Production Strategies. In *Foraging and*

Farming in the Eastern Woodlands, edited by C. Margaret Scarry, pp. 78–90. University Press of Florida, Gainesville.

1994 Variability in Late Prehistoric Corn from the Lower Southeast. In *Corn and Culture in the Prehistoric New World*, edited by S. Johannessen and C. Hastorf, pp. 347–367. Westview Press, Boulder, Colorado.

1995 *Excavations on the Northwest Riverbank at Moundville: Investigations of a Moundville I Residential Area.* Report of Investigations 72. Alabama Museum of Natural History, Division of Archaeology, Tuscaloosa.

Scarry, C. Margaret, and Vincas P. Steponaitis

1997 Between Farmstead and Center: The Natural and Social Landscape of Moundville. In *People, Plants, and Landscapes: Studies in Paleoethnobotany*, edited by K. J. Gremillion, pp. 107–122. University of Alabama Press, Tuscaloosa.

1998 Domestic Life on the Northwest Riverbank at Moundville. In *Archaeology of the Moundville Chiefdom*, edited by Vernon J. Knight, Jr., and Vincas P. Steponaitis, pp. 63–101. Smithsonian Institution Press, Washington, D.C.

Scarry, John F.

1984 *Fort Walton Development: Mississippian Chiefdoms in the Lower Southeast.* Ph.D. dissertation, Department of Anthropology. Case Western Reserve University, Cleveland.

1995 Apalachee Homesteads: The Basal Social and Economic Units of a Mississippian Chiefdom. In *Mississippian Communities and Households*, edited by J. D. Rogers and B. D. Smith, pp. 201–223. University of Alabama Press, Tuscaloosa.

Schmidt-Nielsen, Knut

1984 *Scaling: Why is Animal Size So Important?* Cambridge University Press, Cambridge.

Schnell, Frank T., Vernon J. Knight, Jr., and Gail S. Schnell

1981 *Cemochechobee: Archaeology of a Mississippian Ceremonial Center on the Chattahoochee River.* Ripley P. Bullen Monographs in Anthropology and History No. 3. University Press of Florida, Gainesville.

Schoeninger, Margaret J., and Mark R. Schurr

1998 Human Subsistence at Moundville: The Stable-Isotope Data. In *Archaeology of the Moundville Chiefdom*, edited by Vernon J. Knight, Jr., and Vincas P. Steponaitis, pp. 120–132. Smithsonian Institution Press, Washington, D.C.

Scholtz, Sandra C.

1975 *Prehistoric Plies: A Structural and Comparative Analysis of Cordage, Netting, Basketry, and Fabric from Ozark Bluff Shelters.* Research Series No. 9. Arkansas Archeological Survey, Fayetteville.

Schroedl, Gerald F.

1975 *Archaeological Investigations at the Harrison Branch and Bat Creek Sites in the Tellico Reservoir.* University of Tennessee, Department of Anthropology, Report of Investigations No. 10. Knoxville.

1998 Mississippian Towns in the Eastern Tennessee Valley. In *Mississippian Towns and Sacred Spaces: Searching for an Architectural Grammar*, edited by R. B. Lewis and C. Stout, pp. 64–92. University of Alabama Press, Tuscaloosa.

Sears, William H.

1954 The Sociopolitical Organization of Pre-Columbian Cultures on the Gulf Coastal Plain. *American Anthropologist* 56 (3):339–346.

1977 Prehistoric Culture Areas and Culture Change on the Gulf Coastal Plain. In *For the Director: Research Essays in Honor of James B. Griffin,* edited by Charles E. Cleland, pp. 152–185. Museum of Anthropology, University of Michigan, Anthropological Papers No. 61. Ann Arbor.

Service, Elman R.

1962 *Primitive Social Organization: An Evolutionary Perspective.* Random House, New York.

Shannon, Claude E., and W. Weaver

1949 *The Mathematical Theory of Communication.* University of Illinois Press, Urbana.

Shapiro, Gary, and Bonnie G. McEwan

1992 *Archaeology at San Luis: The Apalachee Council House.* Florida Bureau of Archaeological Research, Florida Archaeology No. 6, Pt. 1. Tallahassee.

Sheldon, Craig T., Jr., and John W. Cottier

1983 *Origins of Mobile: Archaeological Excavations at the Courthouse Site, Mobile, Alabama.* Auburn University Archaeological Monograph No. 5. Auburn, Alabama.

Silvia, Diane

2000 *Indian and French Interaction in Colonial Louisiana during the Early Eighteenth Century.* Ph.D. dissertation, Department of Anthropology, Tulane University, New Orleans.

Silvia, Diane E., and Gregory A. Waselkov

1993a *Archaeological Monitoring of Bent 15 (North Bound) for the New Dog River Bridge.* Report Submitted to the Alabama Department of Transportation. Center for Archaeological Studies, University of South Alabama, Mobile.

1993b *Roads to the Past: Phase II Archaeological Research and Testing Prior to Interstate-10 Revisions in Mobile, Alabama.* Center for Archaeological Studies, University of South Alabama, Mobile.

Smith, Bruce D.

1979 Measuring the Selective Utilization of Animal Species by Prehistoric Human Populations. *American Antiquity* 44(1):155–160.

1985a The Role of *Chenopodium* as a Domesticate in Pre-Maize Garden Systems of the Eastern United States. *Southeastern Archaeology* 4(1):51–72.

1985b *Chenopodium berlandieri* ssp. *jonesianum:* Evidence for a Hopewellian Domesticate from Ash Cave, Ohio. *Southeastern Archaeology* 4(2):107–133.

1995 The Analysis of Single-Household Mississippian Settlements. In *Mississippian Communities and Households,* edited by J. D. Rogers and B. D. Smith, pp. 224–249. University of Alabama Press, Tuscaloosa.

Smith, Marvin T.

1987 *Archaeology of Aboriginal Culture Change in the Interior Southeast: De-*

population during the Early Historic Period. University of Florida Press and the Florida State Museum, Gainesville.

Squier, Ephraim G., and Edwin H. Davis

1998 [1848] *Ancient Monuments of the Mississippi Valley.* Smithsonian Institution Press, Washington, D.C.

Steponaitis, Vincas P.

1983 *Ceramics, Chronology, and Community Patterns: An Archaeological Study at Moundville.* Academic Press, New York.

1991 Contrasting Patterns of Mississippian Development. In *Chiefdoms: Power, Economy, and Ideology,* edited by Timothy K. Earle, pp. 193–227. Cambridge University Press, Cambridge.

1998 Population Trends at Moundville. In *Archaeology of the Moundville Chiefdom,* edited by Vernon J. Knight, Jr., and Vincas P. Steponaitis, pp. 26–43. Smithsonian Institution Press, Washington, D.C.

Stout, Charles, and R. Barry Lewis

1998 Mississippian Towns in Kentucky. In *Mississippian Towns and Sacred Spaces: Searching for an Architectural Grammar,* edited by R. B. Lewis and C. Stout, pp. 151–178. University of Alabama Press, Tuscaloosa.

Stowe, Noel R.

1974 A Preliminary Report on Four Dugout Canoes from the Gulf Coast. *Journal of Alabama Archaeology* 20(2):194–203.

1985 Pensacola Variant and the Bottle Creek Phase. *Florida Anthropologist* 38(2):144–149.

1989 The Pensacola Variant and the Southeastern Ceremonial Complex. In *The Southeastern Ceremonial Complex: Artifacts and Analysis,* edited by P. Galloway, pp. 125–132. University of Nebraska Press, Lincoln.

n.d. Archaeological Excavations at Port Dauphin. Unpublished Report on file at the University of South Alabama Archaeological Laboratory, Mobile.

Stowe, Noel R., and Richard S. Fuller

1993 The Bottle Creek Mounds—History of Archaeological Research Prior to 1990. In *Bottle Creek Research: Working Papers on the Bottle Creek Site (1Ba2), Baldwin County, Alabama,* edited by Ian W. Brown and Richard S. Fuller, pp. 10–29. Journal of Alabama Archaeology 39(1–2).

Stowe, Noel R., Richard S. Fuller, Amy Snow, and Jennie Trimble

1981 *A Preliminary Report on the Pine Log Creek Site 1Ba462.* Unpublished ms. on file at the University of South Alabama, Archaeological Research Laboratory, Mobile, Alabama.

Stuart, David E.

1989 *The Magic of Bandelier.* Ancient City Press, Santa Fe, New Mexico.

Stuiver, Minze, and P. J. Reimer

1986 A Computer Program for Radiocarbon Age Calibration. *Radiocarbon* 28:1022–1030.

Sullivan, Lynne P.

1995 Mississippian Household and Community Organization in Eastern Tennessee. In *Mississippian Communities and Households,* edited by J. D. Rogers and B. D. Smith, pp. 99–123. University of Alabama Press, Tuscaloosa.

Swanton, John R.
1911 *Indian Tribes of the Lower Mississippi Valley and Adjacent Coast of the Gulf of Mexico.* Smithsonian Institution, Bureau of American Ethnology Bulletin No. 43. Government Printing Office, Washington, D.C.
1946 *The Indians of the Southeastern United States.* Smithsonian Institution, Bureau of American Ethnology Bulletin No. 137. U.S. Government Printing Office, Washington, D.C.

Swingle, H. A., and D. G. Bland
1974 Distribution of the Estuarine Clam *Rangia cuneata* Gray in Coastal Waters of Alabama. *Alabama Marine Resources Bulletin* No. 10, pp. 9–16.

Tanner, Helen H.
1989 The Land and Water Communication Systems of the Southeastern Indians. In *Powhatan's Mantle: Indians in the Colonial Southeast,* edited by Peter H. Wood, Gregory A. Waselkov, and M. Thomas Hatley, pp. 6–20. University of Nebraska Press, Lincoln.

Thunen, Robert L.
1998 Defining Space: An Overview of the Pinson Mounds Enclosure. In *Ancient Earthen Enclosures of the Eastern Woodlands,* edited by R. C. Mainfort, Jr., and L. P. Sullivan, pp. 31–56. University Press of Florida, Gainesville.

Trickey, E. Bruce
1958 A Chronological Framework for the Mobile Bay Region. *American Antiquity* 23(4):388–396.

Trickey, E. Bruce, and Nicholas H. Holmes, Jr.
1971 A Chronological Framework for the Mobile Bay Region, Revised, 1970. *Journal of Alabama Archaeology* 17(2):115–128.

Tukey, John. W.
1977 *Exploratory Data Analysis.* Addison-Wesley, Cambridge.

Velleman, Paul F., and David C. Hoaglin
1981 *Applications, Basics and Computing of Exploratory Data Analysis.* Duxbury Press, Boston.

Wagner, Gail E.
1994 Corn in Eastern Woodlands Late Prehistory. In *Corn and Culture in the Prehistoric New World,* edited by S. Johannessen and C. Hastorf, pp. 335–346. Westview Press, Boulder, Colorado.

Walker, Karen J.
1992 The Zooarchaeology of Charlotte Harbor's Prehistoric Maritime Adaptation: Spatial and Temporal Perspectives. In *Culture and the Environment in the Domain of the Calusa,* edited by William H. Marquardt, pp. 265–366. University of Florida, Institute of Archaeology and Paleoenvironmental Studies, Monograph No. 1. Gainesville.

Walker, R. L.
1985 Growth and Optimum Seeding Time for the Hard Clam *Mercenaria mercenaria* (L.), in Coastal Georgia. *The Nautilus* 99(4):127–133.

Walker, R. L., and K. R. Tenore
1984 The Distribution of the Hard Clam, *Mercenaria mercenaria,* in Wassaw Sound, Georgia. *Estuaries* 7(1):19–27.

Walthall, John A.
1980 *Prehistoric Indians of the Southeast: Archaeology of Alabama and the Middle South.* University of Alabama Press, Tuscaloosa.

Walthall, John A., and Thomas E. Emerson (editors)
1992 *Calumet and Fleur de Lys: Archaeology of Indian and French Contact in the Midcontinent.* Smithsonian Institution Press, Washington, D.C.

Walthall, John A., and Ned J. Jenkins
1976 The Gulf Formational Stage in Southeastern Prehistory. *Southeastern Archaeological Conference Bulletin* 19:43–49.

Walthall, John A., and Steve B. Wimberly
1978 Mississippian Chronology in the Black Warrior Valley: Radiocarbon Dates from Bessemer and Moundville. *Journal of Alabama Archaeology* 24(2):118–124.

Ward, H. Trawick, and R. P. Stephen Davis, Jr.
1999 *Time before History: The Archaeology of North Carolina.* University of North Carolina Press, Chapel Hill.

Waselkov, Gregory A.
1991 *Archaeology at the French Colonial Site of Old Mobile (Phase I: 1989–1991).* University of South Alabama, Anthropological Monograph No. 1. Mobile.
1993 A Contour Map of the Bottle Creek Site. In *Bottle Creek Research: Working Papers on the Bottle Creek Site (1Ba2), Baldwin County, Alabama,* edited by Ian W. Brown and Richard S. Fuller, pp. 30–35. Journal of Alabama Archaeology 39(1–2).
1997 Mapping at the Bottle Creek Archaeological Site. Final Report Submitted to the Alabama Historical Commission. Department of Sociology and Anthropology, University of South Alabama, Mobile.
1999 *Old Mobile Archaeology.* University of South Alabama Archaeology Booklet 1. Center for Archaeological Studies, Mobile.

Waselkov, Gregory A., and Bonnie L. Gums
2000 *Plantation Archaeology at Rivière aux Chiens, ca. 1725–1848.* University of South Alabama Monograph 7. Center for Archaeological Studies, Mobile.

Waselkov, Gregory A., and Diane E. Silvia Mueller
1991 Two Major Mississippian Sites in Southwest Alabama. Paper presented at the 48th Annual Meeting of the Southeastern Archaeological Conference, Jackson, Mississippi.

Watson, Patty Jo
1986 Prehistoric Cavers of the Eastern Woodlands. In *The Prehistoric Native American Art of Mud Glyph Cave,* edited by Charles H. Faulkner, pp. 109–116. University of Tennessee Press, Knoxville.
1996 Of Caves and Shell Mounds in West-Central Kentucky. In *Of Caves and Shell Mounds,* edited by Kenneth C. Carstens and Patty Jo Watson, pp. 159–164. University of Alabama Press, Tuscaloosa.

Webb, Clarence H., and Ralph R. McKinney
1975 Mounds Plantation (16CD12), Caddo Parish, Louisiana. *Louisiana Archaeology* 2:39–127.

Weisman, Brent R.

1989 *Like Beads on a String: A Culture History of the Seminole Indians in North Peninsular Florida.* University of Alabama Press, Tuscaloosa.

Welch, Paul D.

1991 *Moundville's Economy.* University of Alabama Press, Tuscaloosa.

1998 Outlying Sites within the Moundville Chiefdom. In *Archaeology of the Moundville Chiefdom,* edited by Vernon J. Knight, Jr., and Vincas P. Steponaitis, pp. 133–166. Smithsonian Institution Press, Washington, D.C.

Wenhold, Lucy L.

1936 A 17th Century Letter of Gabriel Díaz Vara Calderón, Bishop of Cuba, Describing the Indians and Indian Missions of Florida. *Smithsonian Miscellaneous Collections* 95(16):1–14.

Wesson, Cameron B.

1998 Mississippian Sacred Landscapes: The View from Alabama. In *Mississippian Towns and Sacred Spaces: Searching for an Architectural Grammar,* edited by R. B. Lewis and C. Stout, pp. 93–122. University of Alabama Press, Tuscaloosa.

Wheeler, Ryan J.

1995 The Ortona Canals: Aboriginal Canal Hydraulics and Engineering. *Florida Anthropologist* 48(4):265–281.

1998a Aboriginal Canoe Canals of Cape Sable. *Florida Anthropologist* 51(1): 15–24.

1998b Walker's Canal: An Aboriginal Canal in the Florida Panhandle. *Southeastern Archaeology* 17(2):174–181.

White, Nancy M.

1982 *The Curlee Site (8Ja7) and Fort Walton Development in the Apalachicola-Lower Chattahoochee Valley, Northwest Florida.* Ph.D. dissertation, Department of Anthropology, Case Western Reserve University, Cleveland.

Widmer, Randolph J.

1988 *The Evolution of the Calusa: a Nonagricultural Chiefdom on the Southwest Florida Coast.* University of Alabama Press, Tuscaloosa.

Wilkinson, Leland

1990 *SYGRAPH: the System for Graphics.* SYSTAT, Evanston, Illinois.

Willey, Gordon R.

1949 *Archeology of the Florida Gulf Coast.* Smithsonian Miscellaneous Collections 113. Smithsonian Institution, Washington, D.C.

Willey, Gordon R., and Philip Phillips

1958 *Method and Theory in American Archaeology.* University of Chicago Press, Chicago.

Willey, Gordon R., and Richard B. Woodbury

1942 A Chronological Outline for the Northwest Florida Coast. *American Antiquity* 7(3):232–254.

Williams, Samuel C.

1930 *Adair's History of the American Indians.* Watauga Press, Johnson City, Tennessee.

Williams, Stephen, and Jeffrey P. Brain

1983 *Excavations at the Lake George Site, Yazoo County, Mississippi, 1958–*

1960. Papers of the Peabody Museum of Archaeology and Ethnology 74. Harvard University, Cambridge.

Williamson, Ray A.

1984 *Living the Sky: The Cosmos of the American Indian.* Houghton Mifflin, Boston.

Wimberly, Steve B.

1960 *Indian Pottery from Clarke County and Mobile County, Southern Alabama.* Alabama Museum of Natural History Museum Paper No. 36. Geological Survey of Alabama, University of Alabama, Tuscaloosa.

Wing, E. S., and A. B. Brown

1979 *Paleonutrition: Method and Theory in Prehistoric Foodways.* Academic Press, New York.

Wing, Elizabeth S., and Irvy R. Quitmyer

1985 Screen Size for Optimal Data Recovery: A Case Study. In *Aboriginal Subsistence and Settlement Archaeology of the Kings Bay Locality, Vol. 2: Zooarchaeology,* edited by William H. Adams, pp. 49–58. Reports of Investigations No. 2. Department of Anthropology, University of Florida, Gainesville.

Wolf, D. A., and E. N. Petteway

1968 Growth of *Rangia cuneata* Gray. *Chesapeake Science* 9(2):99–102.

Yerkes, Richard W.

1983 Microwear, Microdrills, and Mississippian Craft Specialization. *American Antiquity* 48(3):499–518.

1986 Licks, Pans, and Chiefs: A Comment on "Mississippian Specialization and Salt." *American Antiquity* 51(2):402–404.

1989 Mississippian Craft Specialization on the American Bottom. *Southeastern Archaeology* 8(2):93–106.

1991 Specialization in Shell Artifact Production at Cahokia. In *New Perspectives on Cahokia: Views from the Periphery,* edited by James B. Stoltman, pp. 49–64. Monographs in World Archaeology No. 2. Prehistory Press, Madison, Wisconsin.

Ziegler, A. C.

1973 *Inference from Prehistoric Faunal Remains.* Addison-Wesley Module in Anthropology No. 43. Reading, Massachusetts.

Zschomler, Kristen, and Ian W. Brown

1996 *Alabama Archeology, Now and Forever?* Alabama Historical Commission, Montgomery.

Contributors

David S. Brose is Director of the Schiele Museum in Gastonia, North Carolina. He has been Professor of Anthropology at Case Western Reserve, Cleveland State, and the University of Toronto. As Chief Curator of the Cleveland Museum of Natural History, he directed nearly twenty years of archaeological survey and excavation in northwest Florida and adjacent states. In addition to his work in the Southeast, Brose has conducted major archaeological projects in the Great Lakes and Ohio Valley regions. He earned his doctorate at the University of Michigan.

Ian W. Brown is Professor of Anthropology at the University of Alabama. He directs the Gulf Coast Survey at the Alabama Museum of Natural History, where he is also Curator of Gulf Coast Archaeology. Brown received his doctorate from Brown University. In addition to his work in the Mobile-Tensaw Delta of Alabama, he has conducted major archaeological projects in western Mississippi and along the coast of Louisiana. Most recently he has excavated the Laboratory on Avery Island, the birthplace of Tabasco brand pepper sauce.

Penelope B. Drooker is Associate Scientist (Archaeology) and Curator of Anthropology at the New York State Museum. Her research on archaeological and ethnographic eastern North American fabrics and basketry makes good use of her long-time experience as a handweaver. Drooker is the editor of two recent volumes, *Beyond Cloth and Cordage: Archaeological Textile Research in the Americas* (2000, with Laurie Webster) and *Fleeting Identities: Perishable Material Culture in Archaeological Research* (2001).

Richard S. Fuller is an archaeologist who specializes in the prehistory and history of the southeastern United States. He was educated at the University of South Alabama and worked for many years as an Archaeological

Research Assistant with the Gulf Coast Survey of the Alabama Museum of Natural History. He is the co-author (with Ian W. Brown) of *Bottle Creek Research: Working Papers on the Bottle Creek Site (1Ba2), Baldwin County, Alabama* (1993) and *The Mound Island Project: An Archaeological Survey in the Mobile-Tensaw Delta* (1998), and the author of "Indian Pottery and Cultural Chronology of the Mobile-Tensaw Basin and Alabama Coast" (1998).

Paul D. Jackson is an Archaeologist and a partner of Panamerican Consultants Inc., one of the largest archaeological firms in the Southeast. He directs all Alabama and Georgia archaeological and architectural projects and runs the Tuscaloosa office operations. Jackson received his Master's degree from the University of Alabama. In addition to his experience supervising and managing numerous field projects, he specializes in Late Woodland/transitional Mississippian societies in the Southeast.

Hunter B. Johnson is an Instructor at Jacksonville State University, where he teaches courses related to cultural resource management archaeology. He also assists in the oversight and coordinating of both research and CRM projects. He has participated in or directed a number of research and CRM projects in Alabama, Mississippi, and Georgia. Johnson's research has focused primarily on Mississippian culture ceramics and settlement patterns in the southeastern United States. His previous experiences include work at several large mound centers, notably the Bottle Creek and Moundville sites in Alabama and the Anna site in Mississippi. He is the co-author (with Edmond A. Boudreaux) of "Test Excavations at the Florence Mound: A Middle Woodland Platform Mound in Northwest Alabama" (2000).

David W. Morgan is a Faculty/Research Associate at Northwestern State University, Louisiana, where he also is the Assistant Director of the Cultural Resource Office. Morgan received his master's degree from the University of Alabama in 1994, and currently is completing his doctoral dissertation at Tulane University. Morgan's principal area of research is the central Gulf Coast. He has conducted archaeological research at sites in Louisiana, Mississippi, and Alabama.

Irvy R. Quitmyer is a research assistant in Environmental Archaeology at the Florida Museum of Natural History. His work has focused on subsistence behavior and environment of maritime people of the southeastern United States and Caribbean Basin. Quitmyer is the author or co-author of over fifty articles on topics of method and theory in zooarchaeology, the seasonal procurement of animal resources, and the effects of human beings on their environment.

James Reid is an artist who lives in Seattle. As a student at the University of Alabama in the early 1990s, he was commissioned to do a series of sketches of the Bottle Creek excavations. Reid received his Master's degree in sculpture at the University of Washington and has displayed his work at the Henry Art Gallery and the Bellevue Art Museum in Seattle.

Christopher B. Rodning is a Ph.D. candidate in anthropology at the University of North Carolina at Chapel Hill. His dissertation is a study of the social history of a protohistoric Cherokee town in the southern Appalachians. He is also currently involved in an ongoing archaeological study of Mississippian settlement in the upper Catawba River Valley in western North Carolina. Rodning is co-editor (with Jane M. Eastman) of *Archaeological Studies of Gender in the Southeastern United States* (2001).

C. Margaret Scarry is Associate Professor in the Department of Anthropology at the University of North Carolina at Chapel Hill. She received her doctorate from the University of Michigan. Through her work as an archaeological and paleoethnobotanical consultant, she has dealt with archaeobotanical materials from virtually all the Southeast and all time periods. She has been involved in research in Alabama for over twenty years, where her research has focused on the intersection of foodways and social relations within the context of the emergence of the late prehistoric Mississippian chiefdoms, including Moundville and Bottle Creek. She is the editor of *Foraging and Farming in the Eastern Woodlands* (1993) and author of "Domestic Life on the Northwest Riverbank at Moundville" (1998).

Diane E. Silvia is the Historic Preservation Planner for the City of Key West, Florida. She received her doctorate from Tulane University. Silvia has worked throughout the Southeast, most extensively in southwest Alabama. She moved to the Florida Keys in 1995 where she has expanded her research to underwater archaeology. She is the co-author (with Gregory Waselkov) of *Archaeology at the Krebs House (Old Spanish Fort), Pascagoula, Mississippi* (1995).

Index